International Corporate Governance

A Case Study Approach

International Corporate Governance

A Case Study Approach

Edited by

Christine A. Mallin

Professor, Corporate Governance and Finance
Director, Centre for Corporate Governance Research,
University of Birmingham, UK
Editor, Corporate Governance: An International Review

Edward Elgar
Cheltenham, UK • Northampton, MA, USA

Published by
Edward Elgar Publishing Limited
Glensanda House
Montpellier Parade
Cheltenham
Glos GL50 1UA
UK

Edward Elgar Publishing, Inc.
136 West Street
Suite 202
Northampton
Massachusetts 01060
USA

A catalogue record for this book
is available from the British Library

Library of Congress Cataloguing in Publication Data
International corporate governance : a case study approach / edited by Christine
A. Mallin.
     p. cm.
   Includes index.
   1. Corporate governance—Case studies. 2. Comparative management—Case
studies. 3. Corporate governance—Europe—Case studies. 4. Corporate
governance—Asia, Southeastern—Case studies. 5. Corporate governance—
South Africa—Case studies. 6. Corporate governance—Turkey—Case studies.
I. Mallin, Chris A.

HD2741.I588 2006
352.2'66—dc22
                                                                    2005049722

ISBN-13: 978 1 84542 035 5
ISBN-10: 1 84542 035 7

Printed and bound in Great Britain by MPG Books Ltd, Bodmin, Cornwall

Contents

List of figures   vii
List of tables   ix
List of contributors   xi

International corporate governance: introduction and overview   1
Christine A. Mallin

PART 1   CORPORATE GOVERNANCE IN EUROPE

1   Royal Dutch Shell: the overbooking of reserves   7
    Bernard Taylor
2   Standard Life: a study of one of the UK's oldest
    institutional investors   47
    Christine A. Mallin
3   Strong blockholders and corporate governance structures
    that improve minority shareholders' protection: the case of
    Telecom Italia   57
    Andrea Melis
4   Indra: the history of a successful privatization   82
    Silvia Gómez Ansón and Jaime Bonet Madurga
5   Managerial reasoning in takeover battles: the case of
    Sanofi-Synthélabo and Aventis   104
    Axel v. Werder and Till Talaulicar

PART 2   CORPORATE GOVERNANCE IN CENTRAL
         AND EASTERN EUROPEAN COUNTRIES

6   The Northern Russia Electric Company case: to whom is
    the Director-General accountable: the company, the board
    of directors or the controlling shareholder?   145
    James Gillies
7   Polish supervisory boards in practice – a few snapshots   160
    Izabela Koładkiewicz

PART 3 CORPORATE GOVERNANCE IN SOUTH EAST ASIA

 8 Corporate governance in Singapore: a case study   187
    Martin J. Conyon
 9 The rise and fall of China's corporate dragon: Kelon and
    its old and new owners   218
    Guy S. Liu and Pei Sun
10 Will the Japanese corporate governance system survive?
    Challenges of Toyota and Sony   246
    Megumi Suto and Motomi Hashimoto

PART 4 CORPORATE GOVERNANCE: ADDITIONAL DIMENSIONS

11 v-NET: a case of family owned conglomerates   269
    Melsa Ararat, Burcu Sener and Esin Taboglu
12 The structure and governance of Eskom – a case study   284
    Reuel J. Khoza and Mohamed Adam

Index   309

Figures

1.1	The Royal Dutch Shell Group structure	18
1.2	One company: Royal Dutch Shell plc	38
3.1	Telecom Italia's ownership structure (ordinary shares)	63
3.2	Telecom Italia's control structure (updated at 31 October 2004)	64
3.3	The Italian typical accountability and monitoring system	65
4.1	Evolution of profitability	88
4.2	Evolution of efficiency	89
4.3	Adjusted stock market returns	90
4.4	Evolution of employment	90
4.5	Evolution of leverage	91
4.6	Evolution of dividends	92
4.7	Indra Sistemas SA ownership structure	94
4.8	IPO's share allocation	95
4.9	Indra Sistemas SA board of directors' composition	96
6.1	Governance and senior management structure of Northern Russia Electric Company	147
6.2	Ownership structure of Northern Russia Electric Company	148
8.1	Stock price performance at ST Engineering	197
8.2	Substantial ownership structure in ST Engineering	208
9.1	The production volume of refrigerators at Kelon (1985–96, thousands)	221
9.2	The shareholding structure of Kelon (1992–96)	222
9.3	The shareholding structure of Kelon after stock flotation (year-end 1999)	223
9.4	Expenses to sales ratios at Kelon and its competitors (1996–2000)	227
9.5	Sales and operating profits at Kelon (1996–2000, RMB million)	229
9.6	Profitability at Kelon (1996–2000)	230
9.7	The amount of 'other receivables' at Kelon (1996–2003, RMB thousands)	232
9.8	Gu Chujun's business conglomerate as of year-end 2004	235

9.9	Sales and operating profits at Kelon (1999–2003, RMB million)	237
9.10	Profitability at Kelon (1999–2003)	238
9.11	Expenses to sales ratios in Kelon and its competitors (1999–2003)	238
10.1	Internal governance system of Toyota	253
10.2	Internal governance system of Sony (July 2004)	258
12.1	World industrial electricity prices and sales by category	288
12.2	Eskom group structure	296
12.3	Governance structure of Eskom Holdings Ltd	302

Tables

1.1	Royal Dutch/Shell Group board committees	19
2.1	Standard Life group funds under management £bn	51
2.2	Board and board committee membership	53
3.1	Telecom Italia's core shareholders in 1997, just after privatization	59
3.2	Summary of the major events (period 1997–2004)	62
3.3	Telecom Italia equity	62
3.4	Board of directors and board committees	67
3.5	Composition of the internal control committee: Telecom Italia vs Parmalat	70
5.1	Key figures about Sanofi-Synthélabo and Aventis (as of 31 December 2003)	110
5.2	Major events in the takeover battle	112
5.3	Argumentation by Sanofi-Synthélabo, based on the information notice about its offer for Aventis's shares from 26 January 2004	121
5.4	Argumentation by Aventis, based on the press release from 5 March 2004 about its rejection of the offer	129
6.1	Director representation of shareholders of Northern Russia Electric Company	149
8.1	Fifteen Singapore mainboard companies by market capitalization	190
8.2	Board composition and committee membership at ST Engineering	199
8.3	Directors' remuneration at ST Engineering in 2003	203
8.4	Shareholder distribution in ST Engineering	206
8.5	Major shareholders in ST Engineering (Top 20)	207
8.6	Descriptive statistics	211
8.7	Regression results	211
9.1	Kelon's top ten shareholders after Hong Kong and Shenzhen quotation	225
9.2	Major fund diversion between Kelon and Guangdong Kelon (Rongsheng) Group (1997–2001)	231

9.3	Key financial and accounting data at Greencool Technology Holdings Co. Ltd (1998–2003, RMB thousands)	236
10.1	Sales of Toyota by sections and by region (consolidated base)	250
10.2	Ownership structure of Toyota	251
10.3	Sales of Sony by sections and by region (consolidated base)	256
10.4	Ownership structure of Sony	257
10.5	Performance of Toyota and Sony for 1985–2003	261
11.1	v-NET ownership structure	272
11.2	Shareholding structure of v-NET after Sorytel transfer	274
12.1	International comparisons by capacity and sales – major electricity utilities in the world rated by sales	287
12.2	Major electricity utilities in the world – rated by generation capacity	289
12.3	Eskom high-level performance	290

Contributors

Mohamed Adam Corporate Counsel/Company Secretary, Eskom, South Africa, email: mohamed.adam@eskom.co.za

Melsa Ararat Director, Corporate Governance Forum of Turkey, Sabanci University, Turkey, email: melsaararat@sabanciuniv.edu

Jaime Bonet Madurga Associate Professor of Systems Engineering and Automatic Control, University of Oviedo, Spain, email: Jaime@uniovi.es

Martin J. Conyon Professor of Management, The Wharton School, University of Pennsylvania, USA, email: conyon@wharton.upenn.edu

James Gillies Dean Emeritus of the Schulich School of Business, Canada, email: jgillies@schulich.yorku.ca

Silvia Gómez Ansón Associate Professor of Finance and Accounting, University of Oviedo, Spain, email: sgomez@uniovi.es

Motomi Hashimoto Senior Manager, Corporate Planning Department, Nomura Asset Management Co., Ltd, Japan, email: hashimoto-1p69@jp.nomura.com

Reuel J. Khoza Chairman, AKA Capital (Pty) Ltd, Bryanston, South Africa, email: rjk@akacapital.co.za

Izabela Koładkiewicz Assistant Professor, Leon Koźmiński Academy of Entrepreneurship and Management, Warsaw, Poland, email: Izabela@wspiz.edu.pl

Guy S. Liu Lecturer in Economics, Brunel University, UK and Visiting Professor, Sichuan University Business School, China, email: Guy.Liu@Brunel.ac.uk

Christine A. Mallin Professor of Corporate Governance and Finance, Director of the Centre for Corporate Governance Research, University of Birmingham, UK, and Editor, *Corporate Governance: An International Review*, email: c.a.mallin@bham.ac.uk

Andrea Melis Associate Professor of Accounting and Business Administration, University of Cagliari, Italy, email: melisa@unica.it

Burcu Sener Senior Associate, Taboglu and Ates, Attorneys at Law, Istanbul, Turkey, email: burcu.sener@taboglu.av.tr

Pei Sun Lecturer in Industrial/Managerial Economics, Nottingham University Business School, UK, email: Pei.Sun@nottingham.ac.uk

Megumi Suto Professor, Graduate School of Finance, Accounting and Law, Waseda University, Japan, email: megumi.suto@waseda.jp

Esin Taboglu Partner, Taboglu and Ates, Attorneys at Law, Istanbul, Turkey, email: esin.taboglu@taboglu.av.tr

Till Talaulicar Research Associate, Technical University of Berlin, Germany, email: t.talaulicar@ww.tu-berlin.de

Bernard Taylor Emeritus Professor of Strategic Management, Director, Centre for Board Effectiveness, Henley Management College, UK, email: jillfo@henleymc.ac.uk

Axel v. Werder Professor of Organization and General Management, Technical University of Berlin, Germany, email: a.werder@ww.tu-berlin.de

International corporate governance: introduction and overview

Christine A. Mallin

Corporate governance has become a global phenomenon. The financial scandals and collapses which have hit almost every country without exception have ensured that interest continues to grow unabated. Countries around the globe are either developing corporate governance codes or guidelines, or revamping those that they already have in existence. Global governance principles such as the OECD principles, originally issued in 1999, have been amended to take into account developments in the corporate governance arena and the revised OECD principles introduced in 2004.

Debate continues around such issues as whether boards should be accountable to wider stakeholder groups and, if so, who these groups are; the remuneration of directors; the role of institutional investors; the relationship between the company and its auditors, and many other areas. However certain common core themes have begun to emerge and these include the important role that can be played by independent non-executive directors; the appropriateness of key board sub-committees, including the audit committee and the remuneration committee. There is also a growing awareness that companies cannot operate in isolation from the wider society in which they are located, and that they need to consider the interests of groups other than shareholders if their longer term sustainability is to be maintained.

The purpose of this volume is to highlight, through various case studies, how corporate governance has evolved in a number of countries around the world and to illustrate its application in specific case study companies. The volume has four parts which focus on different regions and encompass different legal structures (civil law versus common law); different ownership structures; and differing governance structures.

CORPORATE GOVERNANCE IN EUROPE

Part 1 focuses on corporate governance in various European countries. Within Europe there exists both the unitary board system of governance and the dual board system. The UK, for example, has a unitary board whereby executive and non-executive directors serve on one board; on the other hand, many European countries have a dual board system where there is a supervisory board and a management board. The supervisory board may have employee members (and indeed in countries such as Germany, employee membership of the supervisory board is mandated by the co-determination rules).

In Chapter 1, Bernard Taylor details the problems that led to the Royal Dutch/Shell Group overstating its proven reserves of oil and gas, and the subsequent strategies to rebuild its reputation and restore trust in it. In Chapter 2, Chris Mallin charts the development of corporate governance in the UK and the role of institutional investors in UK corporate governance. She illustrates her chapter with the case of Standard Life, one of the UK's oldest institutional investors. Standard Life is proactive in corporate governance matters and hence in its approach to governance matters in its investee companies. It is also going through a fascinating time in its history as it moves towards demutualization.

Andrea Melis provides an insightful study of Telecom Italia and how it has introduced reforms which help to improve protection of minority shareholders' interests. Silvia Gómez and Jaime Bonet provide a detailed analysis of the successful privatization of Indra, the leading information technology and defence systems company in Spain. After privatization Indra introduced significant corporate governance changes, including board restructuring and new remuneration schemes. Subsequently the company has achieved significant increases in efficiency, profitability and growth.

Finally in this part, Axel v. Werder and Till Talaulicar detail the corporate decisions made by Sanofi-Synthélabo and Aventis' top management in a takeover battle. They have chosen this case as they state that good corporate governance requires that corporate decisions are made on a sound base and are transparent to the shareholders and other stakeholders of the company. Their case illustrates the decision processes involved within a corporate governance context.

CORPORATE GOVERNANCE IN CENTRAL AND EASTERN EUROPEAN COUNTRIES

Russia and Poland are the two countries featured in this part of the book. James Gillies gives an intriguing account of the relationships between the company, the board and the controlling shareholder in a utilities company in Russia. Meanwhile in a Polish context, Izabela Koładkiewicz analyses Polish supervisory boards in a selection of mini case studies in Poland.

Corporate governance is still very much an emergent political issue in both Russia and Poland and therefore in both cases the authors of the two chapters have either used fictitious companies but drawn heavily on real life data or changed the companies' names, both for their own protection and for that of the companies.

CORPORATE GOVERNANCE IN SOUTH EAST ASIA

In this section, the range of corporate governance practices in South East Asia is clearly identified. The financial crisis of 1997 affected many of the so-called 'tiger economies', including Singapore (although it was not hit as badly as some of its neighbours), whilst Japan has experienced the bursting of its own economic bubble in recent years, at the same time as China's economy has been marching towards a socialist market economy.

Martin Conyon's chapter focuses on Singapore and the case of Singapore Technologies Engineering (ST Engineering), a company which has very high levels of transparency and disclosure. Singapore utilizes a unitary board structure, although it has significant state ownership of firms as well as the presence of other large blockholders. Effective ownership operates through a pyramid structure.

The next chapter in this part is by Guy Liu and Pei Sun and uses the example of Kelon to illustrate the evolution of ownership structure and governance process in China.

In the context of Japan, Megumi Suto and Motomi Hashimoto discuss corporate governance developments in Japan, highlighting the changes that have affected Japanese companies in the 1990s. They compare and contrast two 'giants' in Japan, Toyota and Sony, and show the contrasts in their governance styles.

CORPORATE GOVERNANCE: ADDITIONAL DIMENSIONS

The final part contains case studies from two countries: Turkey and South Africa. Melsa Ararat, Burcu Sener and Esin Taboglu have written an interesting case based on the fictional company v-Net (again political constraints warrant the use of a fictional case which draws on the personal knowledge of the authors). They show the types of problems that might arise in the case of a family-owned conglomerate in Turkey.

The final case by Reuel J. Khoza and Mohamed Adam details the evolution of governance in state-owned enterprises in South Africa, using the case of ESKOM to illustrate this. South Africa's corporate governance code is one of the most comprehensive, if not the most comprehensive, in the world. It embraces an inclusive approach taking account of various stakeholders' needs. This final case clearly shows how the adoption of the code impacts on the development of corporate governance in South African companies.

CONCLUSIONS

This volume contains case studies from many different regions around the globe, reflecting various ownership structures, legal systems, political and cultural aspirations. The development of corporate governance is at different stages in different countries, although all seem to value the core concepts of corporate governance including transparency and disclosure, and the benefits that good corporate governance can bring to both individual companies and to countries as a whole.

I would like to thank the authors for their time in writing the case studies. The authors, like the countries represented in the book, constitute a range of nationalities, and are from various professional backgrounds including academics, lawyers and company directors. What they have in common is an enthusiastic interest in corporate governance and how that is shaping the companies and the countries they have written about. I trust that readers of this volume will enjoy the various chapters and that new generations of students will in turn be enthused with the concept of corporate governance and become aware of the many benefits it can bring.

PART 1

Corporate governance in Europe

PART I

Corporate Governance in Europe

1. Royal Dutch Shell: the overbooking of reserves

Bernard Taylor

SHELL SHOCK. CASE A: WHY DO GOOD COMPANIES DO BAD THINGS?*

INTRODUCTION

On 9 January 2004 the Royal Dutch/Shell Group became involved in Britain's biggest business scandal since the Guinness Affair of 1986, after it emerged that the company had overstated its proven reserves of oil and gas. This concerns 'a reduction of 4.47 billion barrels (23%) from the previously reported end-2002 figures of 19.5 billion barrels' (Malcolm Brinded, Managing Director of Shell Transport, *Annual Report and Accounts 2003*, p. 3).

'Proved Reserves'

Royal Dutch/Shell define proved reserves as follows:

> Proved reserves are the estimated quantities of oil and gas which geological and engineering data demonstrate with reasonable certainty to be recoverable in future years from known reservoirs under existing economic and operating conditions … Oil and gas reserves cannot be measured exactly since estimation of reserves involves subjective judgment and arbitrary determinations. All estimates are subject to revision. (The Shell Report 2002, p. 26)

During January 2004, relative to the *FTSE World Oil & Gas Index*, shares in Shell Transport & Trading fell by 17 per cent and shares in Royal Dutch Petroleum fell by 10 per cent (Thomson Datastream, cited in *Financial Times* 2004, p. 21).

---

* This case was compiled from published sources, and public information. It is intended to be used as the basis for class discussion rather than to illustrate either effective or ineffective handling of a management situation.

BRITAIN'S MOST ADMIRED COMPANY

Shell 2001: Britain's Most Admired Company

Shell is one of Europe's most admired companies. Each year *Management Today* asks the chief executives of Britain's ten largest companies in 24 sectors to rate each company in their sector on a scale of one to ten against nine criteria. In December 2001 these 240 chief executives rated Shell Transport & Trading Britain's 'most admired' company with a score of 73.72 out of 100. The citation said: 'Chairman Philip Watts exemplifies the good sense that made Shell this year's winning company.' One of the academic researchers, Dr Michael Brown of Nottingham Business School explained the choice as a reaction to 11 September, and the economic recession: 'When it's raining and the landscape is flooding, people cluster around the strongest mountains – they go where they feel safest' (Blackhurst 2001, p. 46).

> Pragmatic Shell headed by the anonymous Philip Watts since Sir Mark Moody Stuart retired in the summer, was seen as a secure haven. Shell's marketing success is often overlooked. It is one of the few companies in the world (Mercedes and Nike are others) and possibly the only one in the UK that can advertise its products merely by showing its logo minus a name. In uncertain times, such reassurance, built up over the years with campaigns like 'You can be sure of Shell' supplies a warm comfort blanket.
>
> Shell's drive to the summit may have been helped by the sector's advanced knowledge of a smart deal in the offing. Soon after the deadline for voting passed, Shell disclosed that it had become the largest US petrol retailer after concluding a deal worth £2.5bn with a Saudi partner to take over Texaco service stations. That left Shell with 22,000 retail sites in the US. (Blackhurst 2001, p. 46)

The reviewer added, 'Even so, if analysts and fund managers had been voting, Shell would not have topped the rankings'.

In the summer Shell was heavily criticised by analysts accusing the management of offering the market inconsistencies, vagueness and contradictions. The outcry was sparked by a presentation to analysts by the company's exploration and production division, in which Shell admitted it was downgrading its annual growth target from 5 per cent to 3 per cent.

In the *Fortune* Global Hundred published in July 2001, Royal Dutch/Shell Group was ranked sixth among 'the world's largest corporations' and second to Daimler Chrysler in 'Europe's Top 25'. As the editors pointed out 'higher crude-oil prices meant that oil producers were able to turn black gold into black ink' and 'on average petroleum refiners' revenues grew 39% and their profits increased 124%, an earnings jump bigger than in any other industry' (Kahn 2001, p. 96). According to *Fortune* in the fiscal year 2000/1 Shell reported revenues of US$149 billion – up 42 per cent on 1999/2000 – and profits were US$13 billion, an increase of 48 per cent over the previous year. At this time Shell had 90 000 employees.

CORPORATE SOCIAL RESPONSIBILITY

In the Shell Annual Report for 2001 Philip Watts wrote a personal message as Chairman of the Committee of Managing Directors:

> In a troubled and unsettled world, we delivered our second best ever earnings in 2001. Our returns were among the best in the industry and we have met the challenging promises we made to our shareholders three years ago. We continue to focus on delivering robust profitability, while leveraging our competitive edge to grow value … At the same time we are striving to fulfil our commitments to society based on our strong Business Principles. This included using the principles of sustainable development in all our operations – taking account of their social and environmental consequences as well as the economic dimension. We believe long-term competitive success depends on being trusted to meet society's expectations. (The Shell Report 2001, p. 1)

The Shell Report 2001 provided a comprehensive analysis of Shell's economic, social and environmental performance, and many of the results were independently verified.

Alois Flatz, Head of Research at Sustainable Asset Management, an independent consultant to companies on social and environmental reporting, was favourably impressed by The Shell Report. He wrote: 'Shell's commitment to sustainability has increasingly gained credibility as key strategic decisions have been made to back up their high profile communication on this subject. Moreover, the clear links between business principles and performance indicators establishes Shell's reporting on sustainability as being best in the class' (The Shell Report 2001, p. 9).

'Our Business Principles'

Shell's 'Business Principles' are communicated to management, employees and all stakeholders. They can also be found in Shell's Annual Report to Shareholders. They recognize the company's responsibilities to its shareholders, customers, business partners and the societies in which they operate. Shell wishes to make a contribution to social and economic development, to safeguard the environment and to mitigate the risks to their investments.

They also stress the need for Shell's people 'to compete fairly and ethically', to maintain safe and healthy operations and 'to provide full relevant information about their activities to legitimately interested parties subject to any overriding consideration of business confidentiality and costs'.

Business integrity is a core value. 'Shell companies insist on honesty, integrity and fairness in all aspects of their business and expect the same in their relationships with all those with whom they do business.' Also 'all business transactions on behalf of a Shell company must be reflected accurately and fairly in the accounts of the company in accordance with established procedures and be subject to audit' (The Shell Report 2001, p. 25).

Implementing Business Principles

The Shell Report had a special feature on 'Doing Business with Integrity'. This was in two parts: on Bribery and Whistleblowing.

Bribery

On the subject of bribery the company reported that:

> Shell companies seek to compete fairly and ethically – no bribes, no political payments and fair competition. In 2001, 13 cases were reported in which bribes were offered to Shell staff or they were detected soliciting and/or accepting bribes directly or indirectly. In nine of these cases, employees refused the bribes and the cases were reported. In three cases employees were dismissed. The remaining case is under investigation. We report only the number of proven cases, but investigate many more suspected incidents; even when not proven thorough investigations make it clear that we mean what we say with 'no bribes'. (The Shell Report 2001, p. 9)

The Report includes a table indicating the number of bribes offered and the dollar values involved for the years 1998–2001.

Whistleblowing

The Report also included a Whistleblowing Case Study: 'Increasingly Shell companies are providing means for employees to raise concerns in confidence and without risk of reprisal, using mechanisms such as hotline numbers or whistleblowing schemes.'

> In the USA a 24-hour, seven-days-a-week Ethics and Compliance Helpline is open to Shell people who have a query on legal and ethical conduct or who want to report concerns or violations … The US helpline is part of a programme to ensure that all employees are aware of the Group's Business Principles and Code of Conduct in the USA which includes key policies unique to the USA. A Corporate Ethics and Compliance Officer supports this effort. (The Shell Report 2001, p. 8)

In 2000, Shell companies in Nigeria also introduced a policy encouraging staff to report unethical behaviour (anonymously if necessary) and as a result of this policy nine employees were dismissed and eight contractors were removed from Shell's suppliers' list.

THE EMERGING OIL CRISIS

The Oil Crisis

On Friday 30 July 2004 oil prices surged to a 21-year high reaching US$43.80 a barrel on the New York Mercantile Exchange. In London Brent crude climbed to US$41.74, a 15-year high (*The Sunday Times* 2004). On the other hand, despite high oil prices the largest oil companies have in recent years replaced only three-quarters of their production. The result of growing demand and companies' unwillingness to plough more resources into finding oil is a tight supply situation. Add to this the continuous threat to oil supplies in Iraq and Saudi Arabia and the likelihood of government restrictions on oil supplies in Russia.

So what is the future prospect? Experts are forecasting that the demand will rise by more that 50 per cent in the next 20 years. Yet there is little prospect of a significant increase in supplies. According to the International Energy Agency demand will grow at 'a breakneck pace', but investment is unlikely to follow suit. This means higher prices for the foreseeable future (Stelzer 2004).

The high prices are having a magical effect on the profits of the international oil companies. In the last week of July 2004 Exxon Mobil reported that the company had earned almost US$6 billion in the second quarter of the year, an all-time record for any US company in a three-month period.

> But the major oil companies are not responding to higher prices and earnings by increasing their search for oil. Exclude Russia and BP's output is declining. So are Shell's and Chevron Texaco's. Production at Exxon Mobil is more or less flat. Only Total with its commitment to Africa and Asia seems to be stepping up production. (Stelzer 2004)

THE NEW CHAIRMAN/CHIEF EXECUTIVE

Philip Watts was appointed Chairman and Managing Director of Shell Transport and Trading plc in August 2001 at the age of 56. He had had an outstanding career with Shell spanning 30 years, which had taken him to South East Asia, Africa, the Middle East and Continental Europe. He had worked his way up the organization in Exploration and Production – from seismologist and geophysicist to Exploration Manager – before being appointed Chief Executive of Exploration and Production in 1997.

During the 1990s he moved into general management, first as Managing Director: Nigeria, next as Coordinator of Regulatory Affairs: Europe and then as Director for Planning, the Environment and External Affairs in London. His abilities were also recognized outside Shell. He was elected to the Executive Committee of the World Business Council for Sustainable Development and at around the same time he became Chairman of the UK's governing body of the International Chamber of Commerce (ICC).

THE OVERBOOKING OF RESERVES

Philip Watts was no doubt chosen to be Chairman and Chief Executive of Shell because of his successful track record in Exploration and Production.

From 1991 to 1994 he was Managing Director of the Shell Petroleum Development Corporation in Nigeria. Shell has extracted an estimated US$30 billion worth of oil from Nigeria, but at a huge environmental cost, particularly in the region of Ogoni. When Ken Saro-Wiwa started a popular protest movement that threatened to disrupt oil production, the Nigerian government (which receives a substantial income from oil revenues) reacted quickly by sending troops into the protesters' villages.

Shell formed a crisis group to rebuild its reputation with environmentalists and the task force was led by Philip Watts. Another factor which clinched his promotion was his unflinching determination to deliver results for the company. Unfortunately the record shows that he may have been too optimistic in forecasting the performance which might be achieved from the Nigerian and other fields which he knew well.

An independent report by Davis Polk, a US law firm, states that by early 2000 it was clear to Shell's exploration and production unit, of which Philip Watts was then Group Managing Director, that the Nigerian reserves 'could not be produced as originally projected or within its current licence periods' (Durman and Kemeny 2004, pp. 3.8, 3.9).

Leaked company memos also show that production from the Yibal field in Oman began to decline in 1997, but Watts believed that a new technology called 'horizontal drilling' might enable the company to 'extract more from such mature fields' and that year the proven oil reserves figures for Oman were mistakenly increased as a result.

In Australia too, Shell had celebrated the discovery of half a billion barrels of oil equivalent in the Gorgon gas field. But it was going to be very hard to exploit these reserves. Although Shell had a small exploration base there, the company would need to build a large gas liquefaction plant on Barrow Island, which was a Class A protected nature reserve. So the gas plant would be subject to environmental impact studies and the Australian government would be under intense pressure to protect the unique wild life. Shell's partners in the Gorgon project, Exxon Mobil and Chevron, have not included the Gorgon field in their lists of proven reserves (Datar 2004).

On the other hand in 2003 Sir Philip Watts and Walter van de Vijver working together scored a major success. By a spate of shuttle diplomacy involving many flights to Russia, they convinced President Putin to allow Shell to have access to 'the world's next big oil province' (Kemeny 2004a, p. 5).

ENRON, WORLDCOM AND SARBANES-OXLEY

Enron

Philip Watts became Chairman and Chief Executive of Shell Transport and Trading in the summer of 2001 and in the autumn of the same year the world business community was rocked by the Enron Affair, the first of a series of high-profile corporate scandals and failures which led to a radical reform of company law and regulation in the USA.

In mid-October 2001, Enron, the Houston oil and gas company, reported a third-quarter loss of US$638 million and disclosed a US$1.2 billion reduction in shareholder equity partly related to off-balance sheet partnerships which had falsified the company's results. This was the largest corporate bankruptcy in American history and the consequences were appalling. Their auditors, Arthur Andersen, one of the world's leading accountancy firms, were convicted of obstruction, fined US$500 000 and the Andersen partnership was dissolved. The Chairman/CEO Kenneth Lay and the Chief Financial Officer (CFO) Andrew Fastow resigned and they were prosecuted for fraud. Investors lost billions of dollars on their shares and Enron's employees also lost their pensions and thousands of them lost their jobs (Lacay and Ripley 2002).

WorldCom

After the Enron debacle, President Bush was asked to tighten up the regulation of corporations and auditors. He refused, saying that he did not want to punish the majority of company executives who were acting properly because of what seemed to be the bad behaviour of 'a few bad apples'. Then came the WorldCom scandal. On 25 June 2002 the board of WorldCom, America's second largest mobile phone operator, revealed that their top executives had inflated the company's profits by US$3.8 billion. (This number has since grown to US$9 billion.) During 2002 alone, WorldCom's shareholders lost US$3 billion, many thousands of employees lost their jobs and the company was put up for sale. WorldCom's auditors were Arthur Andersen and as at Enron they had turned a blind eye to the fraud in which the company's accountants had categorized billions of dollars of annual operating costs as capital expenditures, so that the expenses could be stretched out over a number of years. In the financial year 2001 this allowed the company to turn an annual operating loss of US$662 million into a US$2.4 billion profit (Lacay and Ripley 2002).

After this revelation the FBI and the Securities and Exchange Commission (SEC) indicted WorldCom's top executives, and the US's largest state pension fund, CalPERS, launched a suit to regain some of the US$580 million which the fund had lost on its WorldCom shares.

Other Re-statements

In the summer of 2002 Xerox Corporation also revealed that their accounts for 2001 had overstated their operating earning by US$1.4 billion. In fact, during 2002, 240 companies notified the SEC that they wished to re-state their accounts. This was four times the number of re-statements which were recorded only five years earlier in 1997 (Byrne 2002, p. 73).

The Sarbanes-Oxley Act

After Enron, WorldCom, Xerox and a spate of other accounting scandals, the US Congress and business leaders urged the President to take action to reassure investors, to restore confidence in the integrity of US corporations and financial markets and to discourage fraudulent corporate behaviour (Cameron *et al.* 2002; Lavelle and McNamee 2002).

On 30 July 2002 President Bush signed the Sarbanes-Oxley Act, which established a new, much tougher regime of regulations to control the actions of Boards of Directors, corporate executives, accountants and auditors. The Act included the following arrangements:

- Tougher penalties for corporate fraud
  The legislation creates penalties for corporate fraud of up to 20 years for destroying or altering documents sought in federal investigations. Also chief executives who certify false financial reports will face prison terms of 10–20 years and fines of US$1 million to US$5 million.

- An independent accounting oversight board
  The new law creates a new (independent) five-member private sector board to oversee the accounting industry – with subpoena authority and disciplinary powers.
- Restrictions on auditors' consulting
  The law would restrict consulting and other non-auditing services that accounting firms could provide to clients.
- Curbs on financial analysts
  The SEC is empowered to impose new rules on financial analysts to prevent conflicts of interest.
- Facilitation of investors' lawsuits
  The Act also extends the period of time in which defrauded investors might bring lawsuits against companies.
- Form 6k filing
  The requirements on Form 6k filing came into force on 29 August 2002 – a more detailed and onerous reporting system.
- Empowering the audit committee
  The audit committee of the board, consisting of independent directors, should have the authority to propose external auditors to the shareholders.
- Loans to top executives
  The Act placed a ban on subsidized personal loans to top executives and required prompt disclosure of share dealings to repay company loans.
- Vouching for financial statements
  Separately, 700 companies with annual revenues of more that US$1.2 billion must meet an SEC deadline to confirm that their chief executives and chief financial officers will vouch for the veracity of their companies' accounts.
- Dual listings
  Shortly afterwards the SEC made it clear that European and Asian companies with US listings would be covered by the Sarbanes-Oxley Act, but the application of certain provisions would be negotiable.

In the summer of 2002 the impact of the Sarbanes-Oxley Act was re-enforced by the new listing requirements issued by the New York Stock Exchange and Nasdaq which require firms

1. to get shareholder approval for all stock-option plans;
2. to have a majority of independent directors on their boards;

3. to have only independent directors on the audit committee and
    the committees that select chief executives and deal with executive
    compensation. (*The Economist* 2002)

CORPORATE GOVERNANCE IN THE UK

The corporate scandals in the USA and the Sarbanes-Oxley Act prompted
a review of regulation across the European Union and particularly in the
UK. In Britain there was a traditional bias in favour of self-regulation – for
Codes of Practice rather than new laws, and reliance on professions to set
standards and discipline their own members.

Ever since the bankruptcy of Enron, British accountants had been quietly
congratulating themselves that 'it couldn't happen here'. But, particularly
after the Sarbanes-Oxley Act, the regulation of British auditors and
accountants seemed inadequate. In the last five years the US SEC has
required 1200 companies to correct their audited accounts. By comparison,
Britain's Financial Reporting Review Panel – with only one full-time
accountant, acted as a kind of ombudsman. The Panel only investigated
if there was a complaint. In 12 years the Panel had made only 67 inquiries
and had requested 15 re-statements and in most cases the companies had
been let off with a caution (*The Economist* 2003).

However, behind the scenes the British government was planning to
establish an independent regulator along the lines of the US Accounting
Oversight Board and early in 2004 they announced the establishment of
the Financial Reporting Council, which will incorporate the Financial
Reporting Review Panel and is also responsible for regulating the accounting
profession and the inspection of audits (Kemeny 2004b).

After the publication of the Cadbury Report in 1992, Britain became a
pioneer in Corporate Governance and the Cadbury Code became a model
for the self-regulation of quoted company boards in other countries. The
past decade saw over a dozen inquiries advocating:

1. an expanded role for non-executive directors;
2. tighter control of executive remuneration;
3. fuller disclosure and transparent financial reporting;
4. the active engagement of institutional shareholders; and
5. independent regulation of accountants and auditors.

These recommendations were brought together in a New Combined Code
which took effect in July 2003 and was intended to make boards more

independent and more effective in controlling chief executives and their management teams.

At the same time the Netherlands and other continental countries were reviewing their company laws and developing their own corporate governance codes. Particularly relevant to Shell was the Tabaksblat Committee Code, which was also published in 2003. So Philip Watts' watch from July 2001 to March 2004 coincided with a period of intense activity which led to the reform of laws, regulations and codes of practice aimed at imposing tighter controls on executive teams, their accountants and auditors.

CORPORATE GOVERNANCE AT SHELL

Shell was founded in 1907 through a merger between a Dutch oil company, which was partly owned by the Dutch royal family, and Shell, which was an international trading company. However, instead of forming one company with one set of shareholders they established the Royal Dutch/Shell Group as a joint venture between two companies and two groups of shareholders. The Royal Dutch Petroleum Company, which is based in The Hague and listed on the Dutch stock exchange, has a 60 per cent interest in the Group. Shell Transport and Trading plc has its headquarters in London, is listed on the London stock exchange and owns a 40 per cent interest in the Group. For this reason Shell has two boards of directors. Under Dutch law, Royal Dutch has a two-tier structure with a supervisory board and a management board and Shell Transport operates under the British system with a unitary board.

These two 'parent company' boards are responsible for appointing the directors to the two 'holding companies': Shell Petroleum NV and the Shell Petroleum Company Ltd. The Group Managing Directors of these companies form the Committee of Managing Directors – the top management team running the Royal Dutch Shell Group, which consists of Service Companies, Operating Companies and Regions (see Figure 1.1). One or two of these Group Managing Directors also sit on the parent company boards, i.e. on the management board in the Netherlands and on the unitary board in Britain.

In practice, the Royal Dutch supervisory board and the Shell Transport board do a great deal of work together. For example, their three main committees – Group Audit, Social Responsibility and Remuneration and Succession – have members from both boards, but Shell Transport has a separate Nomination Committee (see Table 1.1).

From 2001 to 2003 Sir Philip Watts was both Chairman of the Board and Managing Director of Shell Transport. He was also Chairman of the

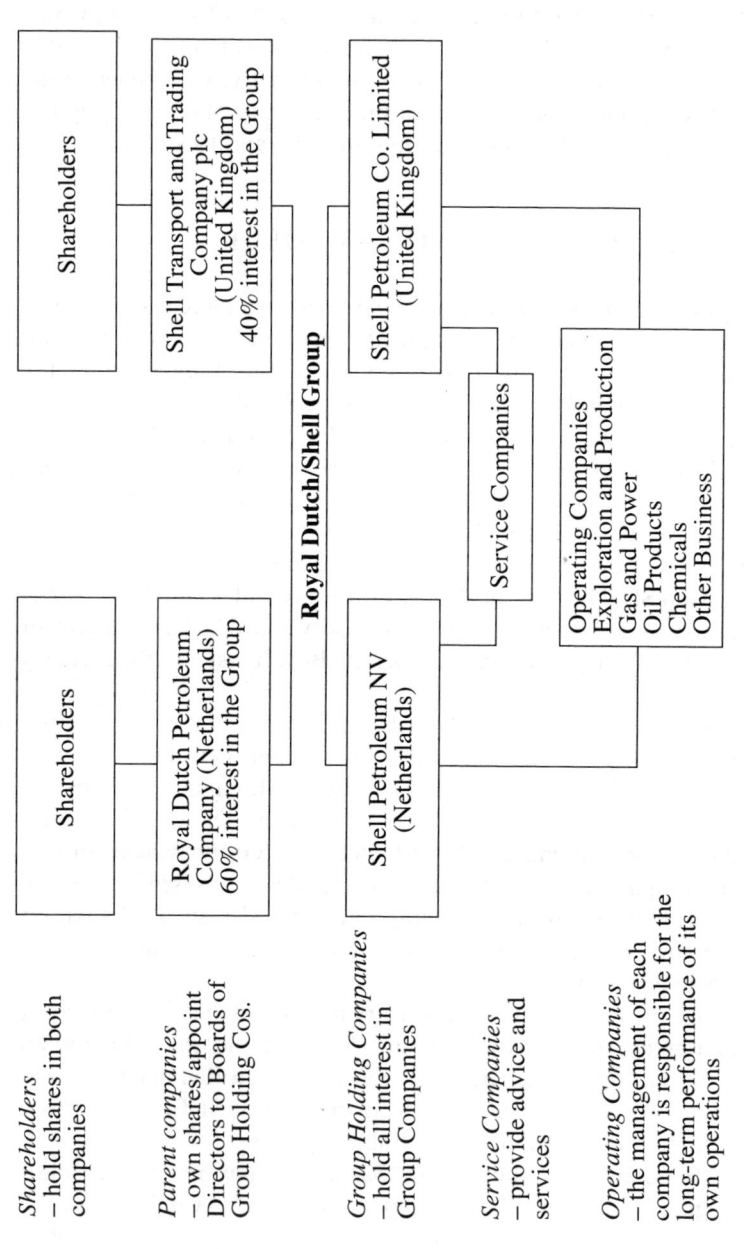

Shareholders
– hold shares in both companies

Parent companies
– own shares/appoint Directors to Boards of Group Holding Cos.

Group Holding Companies
– hold all interest in Group Companies

Service Companies
– provide advice and services

Operating Companies
– the management of each company is responsible for the long-term performance of its own operations

Royal Dutch/Shell Group

Shareholders

Shell Transport and Trading Company plc (United Kingdom) 40% interest in the Group

Shell Petroleum Co. Limited (United Kingdom)

Shareholders

Royal Dutch Petroleum Company (Netherlands) 60% interest in the Group

Shell Petroleum NV (Netherlands)

Service Companies

Operating Companies
Exploration and Production
Gas and Power
Oil Products
Chemicals
Other Business

Source: Annual Report and Accounts (2003, p. 6).

Figure 1.1 The Royal Dutch Shell Group structure

18

Table 1.1   Royal Dutch/Shell Group board committees

	Royal Dutch	Shell Transport
Group audit	Aad Jacobs	Sir Peter Burt
	Lawrence Ricciardi	Luis Giusti
	Henny de Ruiter	Nina Henderson
Social responsibility	Jonkheer Aarnout Loudon	Lord Oxburgh
	Maarten van den Bergh	Teymour Alireza
	Wim Kolc	Dr Eileen Buttle
Remuneration & succession	Jonkheer Aarnout Loudon	Sir Peter Job
	Lawrence Ricciardi	Nina Henderson
	Henny de Ruiter	Sir John Kerr
	Prof. Hubert Markl	
Shell Transport nomination	Lord Oxburgh	
	Sir Peter Burt	
	Sir Peter Job	
	Sir John Kerr	

Source: Annual Report and Accounts (2003, p. 9).

Committee of Managing Directors (CMD) and the other members of the CMD were the other Group Managing Directors Jeroen van den Veer, Chief Executive of Chemicals and Walter van de Vijver, Chief Executive of Exploration and Production.

Under Sir Philip Watts' chairmanship, the board of Shell Transport included a number of eminent and experienced non-executive directors:

- Sir Mark Moody-Stuart KCMG (UK), Managing Director and Chairman of Shell Transport from 1997 to 2001;
- Lord Oxburgh KBE, FRS (UK), former Chief Scientific Adviser to the Ministry of Defence;
- Nina Henderson (USA), previously Corporate Vice President of Bestfoods, a major US foods company;
- Luis Giusti (Venezuela), formerly Chairman/CEO of Petroleos de Venezuela;
- Sir Peter Job KBE (UK), previously Chief Executive of Reuters;
- Sir John Kerr GCMG (UK), previously Head of the Diplomatic Service and Principal Private Secretary to the Chancellor of the Exchequer;
- Teymour Alireza (Saudi Arabia), Chairman of the National Pipe Company, Saudi Arabia;

- Sir Peter Burt FRSE (UK), Executive Deputy Chairman of HBOS plc and former Governor of the Bank of Scotland; and
- Dr Eileen Buttle (UK), former government scientist, Trustee of environmental non-governmental organizations.

During 2003 there were a total of 17 board meetings and they were well attended. Judith Boynton, the Group Chief Financial Officer, was appointed a Group Managing Director and Executive Director of Shell Transport in July 2003, and she regularly attended the board meetings until she resigned on 18 April 2004.

The Group Audit Committee

The Royal Dutch Petroleum Company also had an impressive supervisory board and some of the directors were members of the Group Audit Committee (GAC).

- Aad Jacobs (Netherlands), Chairman of the Committee, a former Chairman of the Board of Management of ING Group, a major Dutch financial services company;
- Lawrence Ricciardi (USA), previously President of RJR Nabisco Inc.; and
- Henny de Ruiter, Managing Director of Royal Dutch from 1983 to 1994.

The other committee members were: Sir Stephen Burt, Luis Giusti and Nina Henderson – all directors on the Shell Transport Board.

During 2003 there were a total of six meetings of the GAC and the members attended virtually all the meetings.

In its 2003 Annual Report and Accounts, Shell Transport & Trading Company plc reviewed its corporate governance arrangements against the requirements of the New Combined Code. The key points from this review are listed below:

- Independent directors
  Of the nine non-executive directors on the Shell Transport Board, seven are wholly independent of any personal business connection with the companies of the Royal Dutch/Shell Group. Accordingly, the structure of the board during the year observed the New Combined Code provision that it should have a majority of 'independent non-executive directors'.

- The Chairman
  Sir Philip Watts was Chairman of the Board and Group Managing
  Director of Shell Transport throughout 2003.
- The Chairman's other commitments
  Sir Philip Watts' other commitments during the year included
  membership of the World Business Council for Sustainable
  Development and Chairman of the International Chamber of
  Commerce's UK governing body (Annual Report and Accounts 2003,
  p. 121).
- Performance evaluation
  During 2003 the Shell Transport Board carried out a series of
  evaluations of
  - the board as a whole;
  - individual members;
  - the Chairman; and
  - board committees.
  The Chairman evaluated the directors individually. For the collective
  appraisal they used a questionnaire. The Chairman was evaluated by
  the Senior Independent Director, Lord Oxburgh and the non-executive
  directors (Annual Report and Accounts 2003, p. 121).
- Dialogue with shareholders
  The dialogue with institutional shareholders was maintained through
  an investor relations programme agreed by the board. In 2002 the
  board nominated Lord Oxburgh as Senior Independent Director and
  arranged for him and other directors to attend Quarterly Institutional
  Investors Presentations when appropriate.
- Auditor's remuneration
  Audit fees for Shell Transport amounted to £129 000 in 2003 – up
  from £31 000 in 2002. The fees payable to PriceWaterhouseCoopers
  LLP for non-audit services in the UK were £31 600 in 2003.

'UNBOOKING' THE RESERVES

9 January 2004: a Shell public relations executive told journalists and
investors that the company had carried out a review of its 'proved' oil and
gas reserves. As a consequence the figures would be reduced by 20 per cent.
This revision would cut the value of the reserves by 3.9 billion barrels of
oil equivalent (boe) from 19.5 to 15.6 billion.

Shell shareholders were shocked by this surprise announcement and in
a few days they saw the price of their shares fall by over 10 per cent. The
institutional investors also complained about the way they had been treated

– that this important announcement had been made by a middle manager
– and not by Sir Philip Watts himself.

5 February: four weeks later Sir Philip Watts apologized on television for
his absence from the presentation of the revised figures. However, he was
being overtaken by events.

19 February: the US SEC launched an investigation into the downgrading
of the reserves.

3 March: Sir Philip Watts, the Chairman/Chief Executive and Walter van
de Vijver, the Chief Executive of Exploration were forced to resign.

17 March: the US Department of Justice opened a criminal investigation
into Shell's unbooking of reserves.

18 March: the company reduced its estimate of reserves for a second time by
a further 250 million barrels and postponed the publication of the Annual
Report and Accounts, and the Annual Meeting with the shareholders.

22 March: there was a meeting between Shell's directors and their institutional
shareholders.

19 April: the company announced a third cut in oil reserves and Judy
Boynton the Chief Financial Officer resigned.

24 May: Shell's proved oil reserves were reduced for a fourth time to 14.35
billion barrels of oil equivalent (boe). This represented a reduction of 26
per cent on the initial figure (19.5bn boe). Shell's Annual Report was finally
published and the two Annual General Meetings were scheduled for 28
June (Harris 2004).

Estimating Reserves

These revelations about the company's reserves have left many former
executives puzzled. Shell's internal processes for checking the state of its
reserves were thought to be as safe as Fort Knox. Each year in The Hague
around 30 of the company's most senior staff, including Philip Watts, would
hear evidence from the exploration and production people in the field.
The annual 'programme discussions' could take three hours – starting with
technicalities and moving on to detailed explanations by staff about their
estimates of reserves (Kemeny 2004a, 3–5).

The process started in the field. Teams of technical staff would regularly review the data coming in from the wells. If they found any indications that underground reserves were greater or lower than expected, the new information had to be reported immediately to the head office of Shell's Dutch business in The Hague. If the adjustment was significant – more than 5 per cent – a team would arrive from head office. But at some stage in the past three years something had started to go wrong. As early as 2002 Shell's management realized that the company was not finding enough oil to replace production – a key measure of an oil company's future profitability. Years of opportunistic investments had left Shell with a legacy of small fields which did not match the company's production requirements. To remedy this, it would require a major new initiative – an acquisition or an entry into a new field.

It is alleged that a decision was made to relax the rules by which the company accounted for proven reserves – a measure used by the SEC to determine whether oil and gas can be produced with 'reasonable certainty' using current technology. Shell's decentralized management – which is often cited as a strength – became in this case, a weakness. Some units were run as small kingdoms, with different practices adopted in different subsidiaries and divisions.

The dam broke in January 2004 when Shell admitted the 20 per cent overstatement of reserves. The reclassification was blamed largely on the overbooking of developments in Nigeria and at Ormen Lange, a gasfield off the Norwegian coast.

The issue now is 'who knew what and when?' Company documents from late in 2003 which were leaked to the *New York Times* said that Shell's top manangement had concluded that 1.5 billion barrels, 60 per cent of its Nigerian reserves, did not meet the SEC's accounting standards for proven reserves. However, the management were reluctant to change the figures for fear of damaging the relationship with the Nigerian government.

Philip Watts and Walter van de Vijver may have been forced to take the blame for the overbooking of the reserves. But it seemed unlikely that they, and Judy Boynton, Shell's CFO, were the only senior executives who knew about the 'cover up'. In early April Walter van de Vijver issued a public statement making this clear:

> From the inception of my tenure as head of Exploration and Production I worked diligently to diagnose and improve the health of the business. I regularly communicated to the Committee of Managing Directors the nature and quantity of the potentially non-compliant reserves and our efforts to assess the magnitude of the problem, prevent recurrence and implement off-setting measures.

Analysts and investors hoped that the company would not merely blame the three senior managers but would offer some broader proposals to improve corporate governance and internal control in the Shell Group. Eric Knight, who represents CalPERS, the largest US public-sector pension fund said: 'The question is who is running the group and who is responsible when there is a problem. The truth of the matter is that it is everybody and nobody' (Kemeny 2004a, 5).

WHAT WENT WRONG?

Press reports show that Shell was not the only oil company which had to re-calculate and re-state its estimates of proved reserves. On 29 June 2004, Norsk Hydro had cut its global reserve figure by 6.6 per cent. Also differing interpretations of the SEC rules have led to different companies booking different estimates for the same field. For example, for the Ormen Lange gas field in the North Sea the companies booked the following proved reserves: BP: 80 per cent, Norsk Hydro: 49 per cent, Exxon Mobil: 35 per cent, Statoil: 25 per cent, Shell: 20 per cent.

On 29 June 2004 BP also re-stated its proved reserves to bring them in line with the SEC's definition. BP raised its proved reserves by 23 million barrels to 18.36 billion. This was because in deciding whether a project is a sound investment, BP uses its own planning price of US$20 per barrel to determine its reserve levels and the SEC used the end of year price which was US$30.10. As BP explained 'An investment is made for 20–25 years, therefore we wouldn't make an investment decision based on one day's price' (Boxell 2004, p. 29; George 2004, p. 29).

How Shell's management came to overestimate their reserves of oil and gas is unclear. A number of possibilities have been advanced:

1. Over-optimistic forecasting
   In their forward planning, senior executives of oil and gas companies must rely on the estimates which they receive from geophysicists and exploration managers. The estimation of reserves is not an exact science. Both technologists and executives need to make assumptions about the volume and quality of the reserves, their accessibility and the rate at which they can be extracted and so on. Shell's managers might well have believed that there were more reserves in the ground or that a higher proportion of the oil could be extracted using modern technologies.
2. Decentralization
   Shell's organization is highly decentralized. National organizations were semi-autonomous and their executives might have overestimated their production, e.g. in Australia and Nigeria.

3. The executive bonus

   In the late 1990s Shell's management had been encouraged to aim for 'stretch targets' and these numbers were linked to an incentive bonus. This too could have motivated them to inflate their estimates of reserves.

4. Philip Watts' drive for success

   Philip Watts was highly motivated and willing to take risks. He had worked his way up the levels of the organization finding and producing oil in Indonesia, Sierra Leone, Malaysia and Brunei. In Nigeria he had continued to produce the oil despite the opposition of local protesters and international pressure groups. Clearly he thought he could do it again.

5. The Securities and Exchange Commission (SEC)

   It is conceivable that the regulators in London and The Hague would not have investigated Shell's estimates of their oil and gas reserves. In the event it was the US SEC which queried the figures; the British and Dutch authorities took action only after the SEC had started their formal investigation.

THE INTERNAL INVESTIGATION

In early February 2004 the Group Audit Committee (GAC) commissioned an internal investigation into how the overbooking had occurred. The investigation was carried out by the US law firm Davis Polk & Wordwell and they were given access to the internal memos and the minutes of the Committee of Managing Directors (CMD). When their report was published on 19 April, Lord Oxburgh, the non-executive director who took over Sir Philip Watts' role as Chairman said the company sought to limit the blame for what went wrong at Shell to 'the human failings' of a few individuals.

Jeroen Van der Veer, the new Chief Executive of Shell and Chairman of the CMD promised 'behavioural and cultural change' at the company to ensure its reserving policy was accurate and to create a clear line of command at the top of the company. He stated: 'We want to foster a culture where bad news can be passed up the line without fear of reprisal'. Malcolm Brinded, who had taken over as head of exploration and production at Shell, attempted to reassure the financial markets that there would be no more bad news. He said the company had carried out a 'painstaking and thorough' review which would 'draw a line' under Shell's difficulties (Griffiths 2004, p. 19).

The Davis Polk Report published the in-company emails which passed between Walter van de Vijver and Sir Philip Watts from the time when Mr van de Vijver had taken over from Sir Philip Watts in August 2001. From the start Mr van de Vijver felt they were 'caught in a box' 'due to aggressive booking of reserves in 1997–2000' (Durman and Kemeny 2004, pp. 9–10).

As early as 11 February 2002, van de Vijver told the CMD that the company might have overstated its reserves by 2.3 billion barrels because they were ignoring SEC guidelines (Warner 2004). He wrote, 'Recently the SEC issued clarifications that make it apparent that the Group guidelines for booking reserves are no longer fully aligned with the SEC Rules' because of 'potential environmental and commercial showstoppers' (Datar 2004).

Under the SEC definition reserves are called 'proven' if thay can be extracted economically and sold for profit. If reserves are not 'proven' in this way oil companies are required to admit that and say that the reserves are only 'probable' (Datar 2004). In van de Vijver's opinion the 'showstoppers', i.e. factors which were preventing Shell from getting these reserves to market, were being ignored. He pointed to overbookings in Australia, Norway, the Middle East and most of all Nigeria, where there was political unrest and environmental damage.

28 May 2002: Philip Watts wrote to van de Vijver emphasizing that it was vital not to unbook the unproven reserves until new reserves had been found to replace them. He should consider 'the whole spectrum of possibilities … leaving no stone unturned'.

2 September 2002: Van de Vijver sent a note to the CMD with a copy to Judith Boynton, Shell's finance director, emphasizing the difficulty Shell would have in achieving 100 per cent Reserves Replacement Ratio (RRR) for 2002 – the target which had been set. 'Unfortunately we are struggling on all key criteria … RRR remains below 100% due to aggressive overbooking in 1997–2000' (Reece 2004, p. 4). (Shell is replacing only between 50 per cent and 60 per cent of the oil it produces. BP and other big rivals manage 100 per cent to 150 per cent).

The Whistleblower

Eventually it was through Walter van de Vijver that the issue was made public. In the autumn of 2003 he asked Frank Coopman, the Chief Financial Officer of the Exploration and Production unit to make an assessment of Shell's proved reserves. Coopman made his analysis and reported that the figures for 'proved reserves in Shell's 2002 financial statement were materially wrong' (*CFO Europe* 2004, p. 46). He wrote that to hide this fact would 'constitute a violation of US Securities law and the multiple listing requirements'.

Walter van de Vijver replied in no uncertain terms: 'This is absolute dynamite, not at all what I expected and needs to be destroyed.' Walter van de Vijver said he wanted a report with some positive suggestions which he could present to the CMD. However, Frank Coopman, like some other whistleblowers, lost his job and has since left the company. Judith Boynton, Shell's Chief Financial Officer complained that she had not been consulted about the report on the reserves position which had been prepared by Frank Coopman. She had somehow been cut out of the loop and she also left Shell in April 2004.

In the autumn of 2003 van de Vijver could see the writing on the wall. On 9 November he wrote to Sir Philip Watts in some desperation: 'I am becoming sick and tired about lying about the extent of our reserves and the downward revisions which need to be done because of far too aggressive/ optimistic bookings.' Then in December he wrote to a colleague: 'We are heading towards a watershed reputational disaster ... The problem was created in the 90s and foremost in 1997–00. I will not accept cover-up stories that it was OK then but not OK with the better understanding of SEC rules now, and it took us two and a half years to come to the right answer' (Reece 2004, p. 4).

On 8 December van de Vijver submitted a 42 page report to the CMD. A comprehensive audit of reserves had just been completed and this showed the reserves had been overstated by 3.6 billion barrels. With the SEC investigation in progress the CMD had no alternative but to inform shareholders and the public about the real situation and the announcement was planned for 9 January. Shortly afterwards a Dutch acquaintance of van de Vijver told a journalist:

> It's because he respected the company so much that he didn't want to blow the whistle but instead ordered an investigation and tried to remedy the problem through the company. He is a man who has invested his whole life in Shell and believed its ethos of looking after its employees fairly and for life. He was the archetypal company man who was on course to take over the company. (Durman and Kemeny 2004)

THE FINES AND THE COURT CASES

On 15 July 2004 the BBC *Money Programme* interviewed investors, regulators and lawyers to discover what their reactions had been to the 'Shell affair'. A US oil analyst Fadel Gheit said: 'Most investors and analysts had almost blind faith in the company and its management. Unfortunately all this came to a screeching halt after this disclosure'. Peter Montagnon of the Association of British Insurers said: 'Most people will have a stake in this, if they have a pension, Shell is such a large company that, if you have a pension pot, some of it is in Shell. So when you have an announcement like this the value of your pension pot is reduced accordingly'.

Within a few days of the Shell announcement, the price of Shell Transport shares fell by 8 per cent and the market value of the company fell by 8 per cent. The video reporter concluded 'Millions and millions of people had investments either directly in Shell or through their pension plans. They may not have known they were investors in Shell, but now they know that Shell lied to them and cost them money'.

Stanley Bernstein, a New York lawyer, also contributed to the programme. He is leading a class action against Shell on behalf of a group of shareholders, based on the false declaration which Shell's CMD signed and submitted to the SEC in March 2003. This booked 19.3 billion barrels of oil reserves, whereas the corrected figure agreed on 24 May 2004 was only 14.35 billion barrels. He said:

> Shell had lied intentionally and had deceived the public about how much oil it had in the ground and how certain it was that the oil could be brought to market. Once the truth came out the stock price dropped precipitously to reflect the fact that the company was not as valuable as its competitors were.

He also spoke of the reactions of the regulators,

> When you have a fraud perpetrated over a long period of time. When you have a fraud perpetrated by the very heads of the company with specific responsibility for this core issue, the regulators are going to get their teeth into this and make sure there is appropriate punishment for the individuals involved.

Executive Payoffs and Bonuses

Shareholders were concerned that the executives who were responsible for exaggerating the estimates of Shell's proved reserves were given large grants of salaries and pensions. For example, Sir Philip Watts received a final payoff of £1 million and an annual pension of over £580 000 (Datar 2004). Newspaper reports suggested that both Walter van de Vijver and Judith Boynton also received payoffs of around £1 million each (Griffiths 2004).

Shareholders also suggested that the executive bonus system might have encouraged managers to overbook the reserves. However, a Shell spokesperson replied that this measure of operational performance accounted for only 6 per cent of annual bonus payments (Harrison 2004).

The Fines

On Friday 30 July 2004 Shell paid £83 million (US$151 million) in fines to draw a line under its disputes with the US SEC and UK's Financial Services Authority (FSA). The SEC had accused the company of having breached fraud, internal control and reporting requirements. The FSA said the Group had committed 'market abuse' (Hoyos *et al.* 2004). Press reports stated that there was still a strong chance that Shell will face a criminal prosecution before the US Department of Justice. There was also a possibility that individuals might face civil and criminal cases.

HOW DID SHELL RESPOND?

Jeroen van der Veer, who as Chairman of the Committee of Managing Directors (CMD) replaced Sir Philip Watts when he resigned in March 2004, was working with the new non-executive Chairman of Shell Transport & Trading, Lord Oxburgh, to clarify Shell's complex governance structure and to install a stronger and more independent system of financial reporting and control. All the time, Shell management was under intense scrutiny from shareholders and the media. Jeroen van der Veer said: 'It is by far the most difficult part of my career. There is huge pressure all the time and you are living absolutely in a glass house with magnifying glasses on top wherever you go' (Hargreaves 2004).

In the Annual Report and Accounts for 2003 Shell described the measures which had been taken to strengthen their corporate governance and financial control systems:

1. An independent chairman
    After the departure of Sir Philip Watts, who was both Chairman and Chief Executive of Shell Transport, the two roles have been separated and Lord Oxburgh, a non-executive director, has been appointed to the job of non-executive Chairman.
2. The internal inquiry
    The Group Audit Committee (GAC) commissioned an independent review by US lawyers Davis Polk of the overbooking of the reserves. They also sanctioned the publication of a summary of the report and accepted its recommendations.
3. Booking of reserves
    In future, the CMD and the GAC will take a formal role in reviewing the booking of reserves and there will be a 'systematic use of external reserves' expertise to provide challenge and assurance at critical points in the reserves booking and reporting process (Malcolm Brinded, Annual Report and Accounts 2003, p. 3).
4. Corporate governance codes
    The Annual Report and Accounts and the Board's processes had been adapted to ensure that they conformed to the UK Combined Code, the

Sarbanes-Oxley Act and the rules of the New York Stock Exchange. In the Netherlands the company would take account of the Tabaksblat Committee's Code.

5. The overbooking of reserves and compliance with regulations
    The investigation and report to the GAC by Davis Polk & Wordwell listed the deficiencies which had led to the overbooking of reserves:
    (a) the Group's guidelines for booking proved reserves were inadequate;
    (b) the Group's CMD and the Parent Company Boards were not provided with appropriate information to form disclosure judgements;
    (c) the Chief Financial Officers of the businesses did not have direct reporting responsibility to the Group Chief Financial Officer;
    (d) there was a lack of understanding of the meaning and importance of the SEC rules; and
    (e) there was a control environment that did not emphasize the paramount importance of the compliance element of proved reserves decisions (Annual Report and Accounts 2003, pp. 40–1).

    All these issues had been addressed to strengthen and clarify reporting procedures. Also to emphasize the importance of compliance with the requirements of regulators, in future the company's lawyers would be involved at every stage and the Group Legal Director would attend meetings of the CMD and the parent company boards (Annual Report and Accounts 2003, pp. 41–2).

6. Unifying the two boards and a possible merger?
    In response to further pressure from institutional investors, Shell formed a steering committee of Shell board members to look at alternatives to the present dual board structure and commissioned Citigroup and NM Rothchild to act as financial advisers to the steering committee on corporate restructuring. On 11 August 2004 the company announced that it had reached a 'preliminary agreement' to unify its two boards and had asked its financial advisers to assess the feasibility of merging its Dutch and British holding companies.

WHAT FURTHER ACTION IS REQUIRED?

So what went wrong and what should be done to prevent it happening again?

1. 'A few individuals?'
    The Davis Polk report and Lord Oxburgh, the Chairman of Shell, suggested that the overbooking was the fault of 'a few individuals'.

Hopefully, these individuals could be asked to resign, the control systems would be improved and it would be possible to draw a line under the whole sequence of events. But Walter van de Vijver made it clear in his opinion that he had told everybody who counted at Shell, certainly the CMD and the Board of Directors, about his concerns over the state of the company's reserves (Kemeny 2004a).

2. A simpler organization structure?

   Some of Shell's institutional investors thought the problems could be much broader. The company was a joint venture between two companies which were subject to different laws and different governance codes. There were two sets of boards and a 'Conference' where the Dutch supervisory board and the British unitary board met to discuss strategy. At the executive level the Group was coordinated by three Group Managing Directors meeting in a Committee of Managing Directors. It was not surprising that some investors called the present structure 'Byzantine'.

3. Big-hitting non-executive directors?

   Other investors were asking for 'the injection of some senior big-hitting independent directors who would take an unjaundiced view of Shell's predicament'.

4. Tighter controls?

   Certainly the SEC would demand a reorganization of Shell's internal processes for checking the state of its reserves and its accounts generally – including the internal audit and the relationship with the external auditors – where were the external auditors?

5. Finding new reserves?

   A gulf still separated Shell from BP and Exxon-Mobil. In 2004, Shell replaced its oil and gas at 63 per cent of the production rate. So at the current rate of production Shell had 10.2 years of oil left in the ground. BP and Exxon had between 13.5 and 14 years, so Shell was starting from a base 30 per cent lower than its rivals.

   As Sir Philip Watts insisted, the first objective must be to raise the replacement rate from 63 per cent to 100 per cent – so that the reserves in the ground would be maintained. This would involve routine development work to rebook the downgraded barrels by bringing them up to SEC criteria. According to Clay Smith of Commerzbank, Shell expected that of the 4.7 billion downgraded reserves, 85 per cent will be re-classified as 'proven reserves' over the next ten years (Morgan 2004, p. 5).

6. Increased investment or acquisitions?

   To get access to new fields, for example in Iraq, Iran, Libya or China, Shell will probably have to spend more money and take more risks. Shell is planning to increase its capital expenditure from an average of

US$13 billion a year to US$14.5 billion for future years – the majority of which will be spent on exploration and development.

BP had spent US$14 billion a year over the past two years – including some fairly risky deals in Russia. In addition, BP had acquired reserves through acquisitions and mergers with Amoco, Atlantic Richfield and Burmah Castrol. To quote one analyst 'You have to ask whether Shell can do it by itself, or whether it is going to do it like BP – by acquisition (Morgan 2004, p. 5). This also raised the question whether Shell could manage a merger or acquisition with a corporate structure in two countries.

7. Loss of trust?

Finally, Shell's leadership faced a deeper problem. Shell, once regarded by many as a paragon of honesty and fair dealing, had had its reputation spoiled by the actions of its top management team. Thousands of Shell's employees around the world would feel that they too had lost something valuable – the pride of working for a company which has an unblemished reputation for integrity and ethical behaviour.

It took Shell many decades to build this reputation. How can this reputation be rebuilt? And how is it possible to prevent Shell executives, at the top level, from risking the company's reputation in the future?

SHELL SHOCK. CASE B: REBUILDING REPUTATION AND RESTORING TRUST*

INTRODUCTION

This case has been written to be used with *Shell shock. Case A: Why do good companies do bad things?* Case A describes the crisis which occurred in January 2004 over the re-booking of Shell's proven oil and gas reserves. Case B covers the period from October 2004 to February 2005 and outlines the measures which the new Shell management took in an effort to rebuild the company's reputation and to win back the confidence of the regulators, investors, employees, customers and the public.

During this period Shell's top management were dealing with four major problems:

1. Re-stating Shell's proven reserves: This involved a detailed investigation of the state of the company's wells and oilfields, using independent

---

* This case was compiled from published sources and public information. It is intended to be used as the basis for class discussion rather than to illustrate either effective or ineffective handling of a management situation.

auditors approved by the SEC and prolonged discussions to ensure that their 'proven reserves' complied with the SEC's arcane rules.
2. Finding new reserves: The management were then faced with the problem of how to find or acquire new reserves.
3. Changing the dual structure: Major shareholders insisted that the management should simplify their dual organization with two companies, two boards and two headquarters.
4. Re-building morale and changing behaviour: The management needed to restore employee morale and establish a more ethical and compliant corporate culture.

RESTATING SHELL'S PROVEN RESERVES

Estimating proven oil reserves is not an exact science. Rather, for Shell and other major Western oil companies with interests in the USA, it has become a subject for protracted negotiation with the SEC. The SEC believes 'proven reserves' should include only oil and gas which can be profitably extracted from the ground. To establish this figure Shell has employed specialist independent auditors to examine its estimates from around the world. When he announced the company's financial results for 2004 on 3 February 2005 Jeroen van der Veer, Shell's chief executive said: 'We looked at 1,500 fields and analysed 12,000 wells' (Boxell and Bickerton 2005). This involved 'a detailed review of 100% of the Group's asset base'. More than 3000 staff were trained on SEC-compliant reserves procedures (Newswire-FirstCall 2005, p. 4). External consultants made 30 internal audits and the reported figures were agreed by the Exploration and Production Reserves Committee, the Group Executive Committee and the two parent boards.

One reason for a further downgrade of reserves was the SEC's 'technical' definition of reserves which forbids the inclusion of 600 million barrels of petroleum reserves held in Athabasca oil sands in Canada because the oil has to be extracted by open pit mining. Shell is producing 80 000 barrels of oil a day from Athabasca, but is unable to book the reserves. For similar reasons Shell was forced to exclude bitumen production from its Canadian Peace River site.

The SEC has also been criticized for insisting that oil companies should use the year-end oil price when calculating oil reserves. A growing proportion of reserves is held in joint ventures where companies are paid in 'barrels of oil'. A higher oil price suggests that companies own fewer barrels of oil. So the 2004 year end price of US$40 (for West Texas intermediate crude) has led to most companies cutting reserves. Companies such as Exxon Mobil and BP believe it is more sensible to use their long-term price assumptions of US$20 – the figure they use when investing. Under UK rules which allow for the use of the US$20 price, BP replaced 110 per cent of the oil and gas it extracted in 2004. But under SEC rules this was reduced to 89 per cent.

As Lord Browne explained at the BP shareholders' meeting on 9 February 2005, reserves are a matter of interpretation. 'It's a bit like saying how would I like to read Shakespeare, in English or in French? Naturally because I am English I would prefer the UK rules.' The major oil companies have commissioned Cambridge Energy Research Associates to make recommendations on how to end the confusion.

2004: A Year of Extremes

On 3 February 2005 Jeroen van der Veer presented Shell's financial results for 2004. He said '2004 was a year of extremes'. Shell posted profits of US$18.5 billion (£7.8 billion) – record annual earnings for a European company, on the back of record crude oil prices. However, after a further review of proven reserves with the SEC, the management had been obliged to cut the total reported by a further 10 per cent, by 1.4 billion from 14.35 billion to 12.95 billion barrels of oil equivalent.

The Royal Dutch/Shell Group had now been forced to cut its proved oil reserves by a third in 12 months. The group admitted that in 2004 it could book only enough proved reserves to cover between 15 per cent and 25 per cent of the 2004 production. This suggested that Shell had a major problem in finding new reserves and despite the record profits, promises of generous dividends and a buy-back of shares, the company's shares in London fell 1.7 per cent to 471.8p (Newswire-FirstCall 2005).

FINDING NEW RESERVES

Shell is not the only firm which is having problems finding oil. All major oil companies face difficulties because of:

- rapidly declining reserves;
- soaring costs; and
- lack of access to cheap new reserves.

Declining Reserves

The last wave of growth for big Western firms came in the 1970s when they were expelled from the giant fields in the Persian Gulf. Then, out of desperation, Exxon, BP and others invested billions to explore for oil outside the Middle East – in the Gulf of Mexico, the North Sea and Alaska. Today these fields are ageing and their reserves are declining.

The International Energy Agency forecasts a growing gap between supply and demand. They believe US$3 trillion will have to be invested between 2005 and 2030 to generate new supplies to meet the anticipated demand (*The Economist* 2004, p. 81).

Increasing Costs

The exploration cost per barrel declined from US$20 to around US$6 during the 1980s through the introduction of new technologies like 3D seismic imaging. During the 1990s costs remained low. But over the past three years they have risen sharply because there are fewer breakthrough technologies and the oil companies are not adopting the new technologies quickly enough.

Lack of Opportunity

As the major firms are excluded from the best oil assets in the Middle East and the production of the newer fields is declining, Exploration and Production is being pushed into more remote and difficult areas like the Siberian tundra and the deeper waters off Madagascar and Brazil. However, senior executives in leading companies like BP and Exxon Mobil claim that there is no shortage of investment opportunities for oil and especially for gas. There are indications that the oil companies are now putting more energy and resources into exploration and production – but perhaps too late (*The Economist* 2004, p. 81).

In the next five years Shell expects to bring a large proportion of the downgraded reserves into the 'proven' category. The Russian experience shows what can be done to increase recovery rates, for example, by the adoption of new technologies like horizontal wells and computerized reservoir management systems. In 2004 Lukoil, Russia's No. 1 producer, increased its proven reserves by 4.7 per cent and Yukos, the No. 2 producer, raised its proven reserves by 13.2 per cent. These estimates are confirmed by the American Society of Petroleum Engineers (SPE) according to SEC standards (Bush 2004).

Shell's Difficulties

Malcolm Brinded, head of Exploration and Production, said that he was 'reasonably confident' that the company would replace 100 per cent of the oil it would extract, on average, over the next five years but most of the recovery would come at the end of the five-year period. However some commentators have serious doubts about this forecast. One former exploration executive told the *Financial Times'* correspondent: 'There is no way Shell can "find" its way out of trouble' (Boxell and Bickerton 2005, p. 21).

The *Financial Times* reported that 'the company also has a hard task in restoring damaged morale within the core exploration and production unit and recruiting the 1,000 engineers it needs to get itself back on track' (Boxell and Bickerton 2005, p. 21).

Shell depends on Nigeria for 9 per cent of its oil and it is estimated that local militias and gangsters are stealing US$1 billion worth of oil a year from the pipelines and wells. In December 2004 Shell announced that local protests would disrupt the flow of 10 per cent of its Nigerian crude until the end of February (Purefoy and Koenig 2005).

For some investment analysts, the revelation that Shell had replaced only 15–25 per cent of the depletion in its reserves in 2004 was truly alarming. According to Sanford Bernstein, oil companies need a 137 per cent reserve replacement ratio just to ensure a yearly production increase of 3 per cent. An ING report on Pan European oils for 2006 forecasted that all European oil companies except Shell would replace between 150 per cent and 200 per cent of their reserves. Total, the French oil company, would replace over 200 per cent.

CHANGING THE DUAL STRUCTURE

From the time in January 2004 when the company reported it had overestimated its proved reserves by 20 per cent, activist shareholders began asking: 'How can this have happened in a well-managed company?' Part of the answer seemed to lie in the dual company structure, which meant that responsibility and authority were divided and unclear.

There were:

1. Two companies with two sets of shareholders:
   (a) Royal Dutch Petroleum was registered in the Netherlands and held 60 per cent of the share capital;
   (b) Shell Transport & Trading was listed on the London Stock Exchange and held 40 per cent of the share capital.
2. Two boards of directors with two company chairmen:
   (a) Royal Dutch Shell Petroleum had a Dutch two-tier board with a non-executive supervisory board and an executive board of management;
   (b) Shell Transport & Trading had a unitary board with a non-executive chairman and a board with a majority of non-executives and a minority of executives.

3. Two headquarters, one in The Hague and one in London:
    (a) Senior managers moved between these two headquarters and the top executive team consisted of a committee of three managing directors.
    (b) The Chief Executive of the Shell Group was the chairman of this Committee of Managing Directors.

The Timetable

In January 2004, after the re-booking of the reserves, the Shell share price plummeted and the shareholders demanded action. Sir Philip Watts, the Chief Executive and Walter van der Vijver, the Managing Director of Exploration and Production, both resigned and Judy Boynton, Shell's Chief Financial Officer lost her job but stayed with the company.

In February 2004 the US Securities and Exchange Commission (SEC) launched a major investigation into the downgrading of reserves, estimates of which were cut on a further two occasions.

In March 2004 the Shell Group management said they would consider the shareholders' views on the company's governance and organization structure.

The Shareholder Revolt

Initially, Shell executives said the reserves problem was a rare event caused by the actions of a few individuals and they rejected shareholders' claims that Shell's structure was antiquated and required reform. But Shell's large investors demanded further action. In particular, the Association of British Insurers (ABI), Britain's leading group of institutional shareholders, threatened to vote against some key motions at the company's Annual General Meeting and, in response, the management promised to review the company's structure.

Eric Knight, Managing Director of Knight Vinke Asset Management, a New York fund manager, suggested that the Royal Dutch/Shell Group should be managed by:

1. a unified board;
2. with strong independent directors; and
3. a more powerful and accountable CEO.

At present, he said, Royal Dutch Petroleum, which dominates the Group is a 'closed shop'. The members of its supervisory and management boards control nominations to both those boards.

In July 2004 Jeroen van der Veer, the new Chief Executive, said that the Group had accepted the need to unify its dual boards.

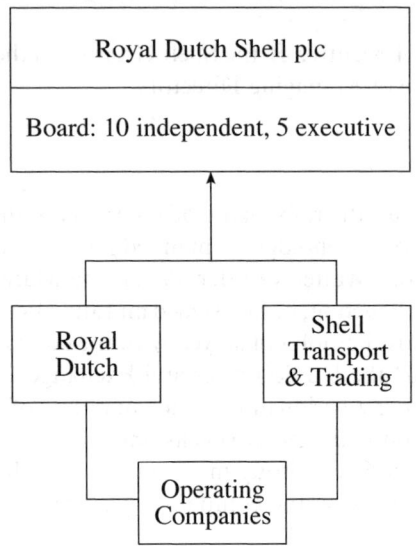

Source: Boxell and Bickerton (2004).

Figure 1.2   One company: Royal Dutch Shell plc

Finally on 28 October 2004 the top management of Royal Dutch/Shell presented the new structure for merging the two companies and unifying the dual boards (Smith 2004) (see Figure 1.2). Lord Oxburgh, the Chairman of Shell Transport & Trading, the UK holding company, described the occasion as 'a great day' and 'a historic moment'. He added 'We will be able to move on from a very complex corporate structure that everybody found difficult to understand' (Boxell and Bickerton 2004).

In retrospect, commentators asked why it had taken Shell management so long to simplify their organization and why it had required strong pressure from their institutional investors to convince them that a major restructuring was necessary.

The New Company

Jeroen van der Veer, the Chief Executive of the combined group, said that the new company structure was the result of negotiations with investors, governments, employee representatives and various interest groups.

- *Investors* were pleased that the lines of authority were now clear – from management through the board to the shareholders. Also the new deal enables Dutch and British shareholders to receive their own domestic dividends.
- *Governments* – Both governments could expect to receive the same levels of corporation tax as they had in the past.
- *Top management* – Aad Jacobs, who was formerly Chairman of Royal Dutch Petroleum, would be the chairman of the new group until 2006. So both the new Chairman and the new Chief Executive would be Dutch.
- *Headquarters* – The company would have one headquarters, which would be located in The Hague. This would involve the transfer of 200 jobs from London to the Netherlands. Also, for tax purposes, the company would be resident in the Netherlands.
- *The British corporate structure* – However, to quote *NRC*, the Dutch national evening newspaper: 'Inside the walls it is indeed British' (Boxell and Bickerton 2004). The new company would be registered in the UK and listed on the London Stock Exchange. This would ensure that the company would have a single board with executive and non-executive directors sitting together.

The new board will have five executives and ten non-executives. Lord Oxburgh said that 'new blood' on the board was a priority and current non-executives would leave within the next two years.

The Takeover

In the former structure Royal Dutch controlled 60 per cent of the combined group, with Shell Transport & Trading controlling the remaining 40 per cent. Under the new structure, Royal Dutch will take over Shell Transport and the new company will be listed on the London market. However, before the merger could occur the proposal must be approved at the Royal Dutch Petroleum's Annual General Meeting of shareholders at The Hague in April 2005.

Easier Acquisitions

A further advantage of the new unified structure is that it will make it easier for the company to use Shell shares to acquire companies with valuable reserves. This had been difficult to arrange with the dual share structure.

Faster Decision-making

Mr van der Veer also stressed the advantages of having one management structure instead of two headquarters and a committee of managing directors. 'If you have a more simple structure, where you spend less time in lots of meetings and with fewer executives, you make faster decisions.'

A Welcome from Fund Managers

Representatives of major institutional investors welcomed the prospect of the merger, the restructuring and the listing on the London Stock Exchange. They said: 'This is more revolutionary than expected', and 'Mr van der Veer has now delivered on all his promises'. He had promised the shareholders that the unified group would be more performance-driven, more accountable and less complex.

Also 'the UK listing will see increased buying by index funds' and the single listing would give Shell greater flexibility for mergers and acquisitions as shares from a unified company would be more attractive to a target company than shares issued from two separate companies. A Dutch fund manager said shareholders were pleased that the company would seek an independent chairman after 2006 (Morrison and Bickerton 2004).

A Credit Rating Downgrade?

In October 2004, in the same week the company unveiled plans to dismantle the 97-year-old dual structure to create a single board, the credit rating agency Standard & Poor's said it had put the oil group's long-term debt in 'credit watch' and hinted that the company could lose its AA* credit rating (Hosking 2004). The trigger for the threat was Malcolm Brinded's warning at the meeting that (in addition to the 20 per cent cut in proven reserves which was announced in January 2004) in a detailed scrutiny of just over half the reserves, investigators had found a further 900 million of the remaining 14.35 billion barrels must now be downgraded. This was not the end of the story; the investigation was continuing and more reserves would probably be downgraded in the next few months.

The disappointment of shareholders was also reflected in the share price. Although the price of oil was buoyant, Shell's share price was slow to recover from the impact of the crisis. From a high of 420p in January, the price plummeted to 350p after the announcement of the misbooking of reserves and it returned to 420p only in September/October when the company profits surged as a result of divestments and record oil prices (Thomson Datastream, quoted in Stafford and Flood 2004).

CHANGING BEHAVIOUR AND REBUILDING MORALE

Shell Management's Myopia

Outsiders struggle to understand the Shell culture. After the announcement of the merger and new organization, a *Sunday Times* columnist wrote:

> There were signs that Shell's maddening myopia when it comes to the bleeding obvious is still not completely cured. Lord Oxburgh and his fellow directors hailed the changes as 'a great day' – conveniently skipping over the fact that the day would never have arrived if they had not been goaded into action by six months of crisis and relentless shareholder pressure. It is this culture, the automatic assumption that everything Shell does must be right just because it is Shell, that will be Jeroen van der Veer's biggest challenge in his new role as chief executive of the merged Royal Dutch Shell. (Durman 2004)

About the same time, Jane Fuller wrote in the *Financial Times*:

> When Royal Dutch/Shell descended into crisis early this year it blamed 'human failings'. On that narrow interpretation it could chuck overboard the failing human beings ... and sail on with its structure and culture intact. By opting for the most radical structural solution it has admitted that the malaise ran deeper. Changing shape is one thing, changing behaviour is another ... Details of a big internal training exercise on compliance and the seriousness of the review of oil reserves gave some reassurance. For too long Shell has relied on its 'culture', which it assumed was morally superior, to ensure good behaviour. The test of its reforms – both internally and in its dealings with the outside – will be whether its new systems pick up human failings before they infect the whole company. (Fuller 2004)

Rebuilding Employee Morale

On 3 February 2005 Jeroen van der Veer, the chief executive of Royal Dutch/Shell, was due to present the company's financial results for 2004 (Newswire-FirstCall 2005). The previous day he made public the results of their bi-annual People Survey – a study of Shell employees' attitudes. In all, this included the answers to 81 questions, many of which could be compared with the results of the previous study, made in 2002, the year before the reserves crisis.

Mr van der Veer was naturally interested in the employees' views on the quality of his management team. In particular, how far had they succeeded in restoring employees' confidence and re-building morale, a year after the crisis?

The crucial question was: 'Do you think the company is well led?' In 2002, 67 per cent of the respondents said they felt the company was well led.

However, when employees were asked the same question at the end of 2004, only 47 per cent said the company was well led. Responding to the survey findings in a recent e-mail to staff, Mr van der Veer said 'I am not proud of these results. The strongest message is that you think Shell leadership at all levels can work harder to ensure that "enterprise first" [a change programme designed to build teamwork] is a reality'. He told staff that Shell's senior management would work hard 'to win back your confidence'. These comments followed other remarks he had made in December 2004, when he said that Shell's middle managers had lost faith in their senior executives, and his head and that of Malcolm Brinded, the chief of the Exploration and Production division, were 'on the block'. Morale problems in the Exploration and Production division seem to be particularly acute.

Ian Bickerton, writing in the *Financial Times*, quoted two individuals 'close to the company'. A Shell employee wrote, 'I am worried that far too little has visibly changed or happened. Those in charge of change are themselves tied to the old culture.' Another person who was involved with the company said 'employee turnover is a key issue, many Shell staff are unhappy and some of their best people are leaving' (Bickerton 2005).

POSTSCRIPT

On the 9th November 2005, the British Financial Services Authority (FSA) issued a statement which said that after an 18-month investigation they had decided not to take any further action against Sir Philip Watts and Walter van de Vijver over the mis-statement of Shell's hydrocarbon reserves. However, the FSA would not be liable to pay the executives' legal costs, which had so far been met by Shell. Commentators concluded that the FSA had not been able to substantiate the charge that Sir Philip Watts had knowingly misled the stock market. Sir Philip Watts' lawyers stated 'this vindicates the position Sir Philip has maintained throughout: that he acted properly and in good faith at all times' (Harrison, 2005).

REFERENCES

Annual Report and Accounts (2003), The 'Shell' Transport & Trading Company plc.
Bickerton, Ian (2005), 'Shell staff unhappy with leaders', *Financial Times*, 2 February.
Blackhurst, Chris (2001), '2001: Britain's most admired companies', *Management Today*, December.

Boxell, James (2004), 'BP surprises with upward adjustment', *Financial Times*, 30 June.

Boxell, James and Ian Bickerton (2004), 'Companies Royal Dutch/Shell restructure', *Financial Times*, 29 October.

Boxell, James and Ian Bickerton (2005), 'Shell needs something in reserve', *Financial Times*, 4 February.

Bush, Jason (2004), 'Oil: what's Russia really sitting on?', *Business Week*, 22 November.

Byrne, John A. (2002), 'Let's really clean up those numbers – now', *Business Week*, 15 July.

Cameron, Doug, Andrew Hill and Tally Goldstein (2002), 'New set of controls on corporate America', *Financial Times*, 12 August.

CFO Europe (2004), 'Blowing the whistle', May.

Datar, Rajan (2004), *Shell Shock*, BBC2 programme, 15 July.

Durman, Paul (2004), 'Reserves woes are still not over at united Shell', *Sunday Times*, 31 October.

Durman, Paul and Lucinda Kemeny (2004), 'Another brutal week for Shell as report makes Watts the fall guy', *The Sunday Times*, 25 April.

Financial Times (2004), 'Shell accounts get signed off at last', 25 May.

Fuller, Jane (2004), 'A triumph of form, now for the content', *Financial Times*, 29 October.

George, Nicholas (2004), 'Norsk Hydro restates reserves', *Financial Times*, June 30.

Griffiths, Katherine (2004), 'Shell looks to draw a line under reserves fiasco with shake-up of board structure', *The Independent*, 25 April.

Hargreaves, Deborah (2004), 'Shell fighter begins the big clean-up', *Financial Times*, 30 July.

Harris, Clay (2004), 'Shell accounts get signed off at last', *Financial Times*, 25 May.

Harrison, Michael (2004), *The Independent*, 16 July.

Harrison, Michael (2005), 'City watchdog drops action against ex-Shell Chairman', *The Independent*, 10 November.

Hosking, Patrick (2004), 'Shell threatened with AA rating downgrade', *The Independent*, 30 October.

Hoyos, Carola *et al.* (2004), 'Shell pays $15m in fines to watchdogs', *The Financial Times*, 30 July.

Kahn, Jeremy (2001), 'The world's largest corporations', *Fortune*, 23 July.

Kemeny, Lucinda (2004a), 'Ready to blow', *The Sunday Times*, 18 April.

Kemeny Lucinda (2004b), 'Watchdog with real bite for number crunchers', *Sunday Times*, 28 March.

Lacay, Richard and Amanda Ripley (2002), 'Persons of the year: the whistleblowers', *Time*, 30 December, pp. 18–43.

Lavelle, Louis and Mike McNamee (2002), 'Will overseas boards play by American rules', *Business Week*, 16 December, p. 38.

Morgan, Oliver (2004), 'Shell's ground zero', *The Observer*, 30 May.

Morrison, Kevin and Ian Bickerton (2004), 'Revolutionary move draws plaudits from investors', *Financial Times*, 29 October.

Newswire-FirstCall (2005), 'Royal Dutch/Shell Group of Companies: 2004 results', 3 February 2005, London: Newswire-FirstCall.

Purefoy, Christian and Peter Koenig (2005), 'Nigeria looms as wild card in Shell recovery', *Sunday Times*, 6 February.

Reece, Damian (2004), 'Revealed: bitter power battle that put Shell in the firing line', *The Independent*, 20 April.

Smith, Gordon (2004), 'Record oil prices help income', *Financial Times*, 29 October.

Stafford, Philip and Chris Flood (2004), 'Shell streamlining', *Financial Times*, 29 October.

Stelzer, Irwin (2004), 'Soaring oil price lubricates the advance of Kerry', *The Sunday Times*, 1 August.

The Economist (2002), 'Reforming corporate governance: in search of honesty', 17 August.

The Economist (2003), 'Accounting: holier than thou', 8 February, p. 85.

The Economist (2004), 'Oil company profits: not exactly what they seemed to be', 30 October.

The Shell Report (2001), 'Message from the Chairman', *People, Planet and Profits*.

The Shell Report (2002), *Meeting the Energy Challenge*, 5 March 2003.

The Sunday Times (2004), 'Oil prices keep gushing upwards', 1 August.

Warner, Jeremy (2004), 'Shell's convoluted whodunit script is worthy of fiction', *The Independent*, 20 April.

APPENDIX: THE SHELL SHOCK CASE TEACHING NOTE*

This classic corporate governance case describes a tragedy of Shakespearean proportions, which shows how the actions of the Shell chief executive undermined the reputation of Royal Dutch/Shell, one of Europe's leading and long-established companies. To quote Warren Buffett: 'It takes 20 years to build a reputation, and five minutes to ruin it. If you think about that, you'll do things differently'.

Teaching Objective

This case is designed to provide a launch pad for a wide-ranging class discussion about corporate governance:

- What is it?
- Why is it crucial to an organization's success?

---

* This case was written by Professor Bernard Taylor, Executive Director, Centre for Board Effectiveness, Henley Management College. It is intended to be used as the basis for class discussion rather than to illustrate either effective or ineffective handling of a business situation. The case was compiled from published sources. © 2004 Professor Bernard Taylor, Henley Management College, UK.

- What can go wrong? and
- How can it be made right?

Because of its general nature the case fits well at the start of a course – to introduce the topic, or near the end of a course – to examine what the group has learned.

Contents

The case is in two parts:
Shell Shock Case A: Why do good companies do bad things?
Shell Shock Case B: Rebuilding reputation and restoring trust.

Topics for Discussion

Shell Shock Case A: Why do good companies do bad things?
This case describes how the over-booking crisis occurred and what the impact was on Shell, its shareholders, employees and the public.

The class discussion falls naturally into three sections:

1. What were the origins of the problem?
   (a) Oil reserves.
       Short term and long term?
   (b) Corporate governance.
       Short term and long term?
2. What was the impact of the crisis?
   (a) On the company and its management?
   (b) On the shareholders and other stakeholders?
3. What action is required to remedy the situation?
   (a) To increase oil and gas reserves? and
   (b) To reform corporate governance?

In reviewing Shell's corporate governance it is helpful to provide participants with a model of the main elements in a corporate governance system, internal and external.

Shell shock case B: Rebuilding reputation and restoring trust
This case describes the measures which the new Shell management took in an attempt to rebuild the company's reputation and restore the trust of the shareholders and the other stakeholders.

The participants might review management's actions under the four headings in the case:

1. Restating Shell's proven reserves
2. Finding new reserves
3. Changing the dual structure
4. Rebuilding morale and changing behaviour.

For each issue they might be asked to:

1. Define the problem.
2. Explain what the management did.
3. Assess the impact and suggest what further action is required.

As a final discussion point the group could be asked to reflect on what they have learned about 'Rebuilding reputation and restoring trust'. Has Shell solved the problem? If not, what further actions are required? How long will it take and in the end what will the scandal have cost?

Timetable

This case can be used as the basis for:

1. One session: discussion of Case A only. For this purpose Case B should be distributed *after* the case discussion.
2. Two sessions: discussion of Case A, followed by a discussion of Case B.

© Professor Bernard Taylor
February 2005

2. Standard Life: a study of one of the UK's oldest institutional investors

Christine A. Mallin

INTRODUCTION

The wave of financial scandals and collapses around the world has highlighted the need for better corporate governance. In the UK, it was after the failures of Coloroll and Polly Peck that the Committee on the Financial Aspects of Corporate Governance was established in May 1991. The Committee published its report in 1992, and it became widely known as the Cadbury Report, after its Chair, Sir Adrian Cadbury. The Report is widely recognized as having set the foundations for a 'best practice' system of corporate governance, both in the UK and subsequently in many countries across the world which incorporated some or all of its recommendations into their own corporate governance codes.

At its core, the Cadbury Report (1992) recommended that companies should appoint three independent non-executive directors, separate the roles of Chair and CEO, and have an audit committee and a remuneration committee. A nomination committee was identified as one possible way to ensure a transparent appointments process. There have been numerous reports elaborating on aspects of the Cadbury Report over the last decade or so, including Greenbury (1995), Hampel (1998), the Combined Code (1998), Turnbull (1999), Higgs (2003), Smith (2003), and most recently the revised Combined Code (2003). The various codes generally view institutional investors as having a responsibility to exercise their power and influence appropriately in the companies in which they invest.

The Combined Code (2003) has two main parts: one on companies and one on institutional shareholders. The part on companies contains sections on directors, remuneration, accountability and audit, and relations with shareholders. In relation to directors, the Combined Code states that there should be an effective board, which is collectively responsible for the success of the company and a clear division of responsibilities at the head of the company (separation of the roles of Chair and CEO).

The inclusion of a balance of executive and non-executive directors (and in particular independent non-executive directors) on the board will help prevent an individual becoming too dominant, and a formal, rigorous and transparent procedure for the appointment of new directors to the board should help ensure that the most appropriate people are appointed as directors. Information should be provided to the board in a timely manner to enable it to make informed decisions, and all directors should regularly update their skills and knowledge. A formal and rigorous evaluation should be carried out annually of the board's performance and that of the committees and individual directors. Finally all directors should be put forward at regular intervals for re-election (as long as their performance remains satisfactory).

In relation to remuneration, the Combined Code advises that executive directors' remuneration should also be largely linked to company and individual director performance, and should be set through a formal and transparent procedure. It is recommended that a remuneration committee comprised of independent non-executive directors should be established.

Regarding accountability and audit, the board should give a balanced and comprehensible assessment of the company's position, and should maintain a sound system of internal controls. The board should establish an audit committee of independent non-executive directors.

Appertaining to relations with shareholders, there should be 'a dialogue based on the mutual understanding of objectives'. Whilst there should be ongoing dialogue between the companys' directors and its major shareholders, the annual general meeting is seen as a means of communicating with investors generally and encouraging their participation.

The part of the Combined Code (2003) relating to institutional investors recommends that institutional investors should have a dialogue with companies based, as previously mentioned, on the 'mutual understanding of objectives'. When evaluating governance arrangements in their investee companies, institutional investors should give appropriate emphasis to all relevant factors. As with earlier UK corporate governance codes, institutional investors are exhorted to make considered use of their votes.

Institutional investors are seen as having a particular role to play in the corporate governance of their investee companies and so they are increasingly encouraged to be more active in their approach and to try to ensure that 'hidden value' is released where possible.

Corporate governance can help ensure that future financial scandals and collapses are minimized as it is concerned with controls, both financial and otherwise, within the company which ensure that the company is efficiently and effectively run, and that assets are safeguarded. At the core of good corporate governance are the pillars of transparency, disclosure and accountability. Without these pillars, investors would not know what was going on in the company, so they are core both to attracting investment and to maintaining confidence in the company and hence the stock market. In their turn institutional investors should recognize their responsibilities and exercise their power in a considered and informed way.

INSTITUTIONAL OWNERSHIP IN THE UK

In the UK the institutional investors are very powerful because of the level of their share ownership – the Office of National Statistics (2005) showed that institutional investors own the majority of UK equity, with insurance companies, such as Standard Life, owning 17 per cent of UK equity at the end of 2004.

Institutional investors are seen as having a particularly important role to play in helping to ensure that corporate governance best practice is followed. This is because, in the UK, there has been a sea change in the level of share ownership by individuals and institutional investors. Whilst share ownership by individuals has decreased over the last 40 years, ownership by institutional investors has increased.

The Office of National Statistics (2005) showed that in 1963 individual investors owned 54 per cent of shares in the UK. The proportion of shares owned by this group fell steadily until it had dropped to just under 21 per cent by 1989, and by the end of 2004, the share ownership by individuals had dropped to just over 14 per cent.

In contrast to the individual investors' level of share ownership, the ownership of shares by the institutional investors (largely insurance companies and pension funds) has increased dramatically over the same period. Ownership by insurance companies has increased from 10 per cent in 1963 to 17 per cent in 2004, whilst that of pension funds has seen an increase to 16 per cent. There has also been a notable increase in the overseas level of ownership from 7 per cent in 1963 to 32 per cent in 2004. Many of the overseas shareholders are US investors who have traditionally tended to be more proactive in their approach to governance issues. In the US, the Employee Retirement Income Security Act (1974) mandates private pension funds to vote their shares. Given this emphasis on voting by private pension funds, public pension funds also tend to vote their shares.

With the growth in investment by US investors into UK equities, together with the increased interest both in corporate governance and the role of institutional investors as activist owners, there has been increasing pressure on institutional investors to vote their shares. Various groups have examined the problems of voting shares in the UK to try to ensure that these problems can be appropriately identified and resolved so that in the future voting levels will increase. These groups have included the National Association of Pension Funds (1999) Inquiry into UK Vote Execution, chaired by Yve Newbold, and the Shareholder Voting Working Group (SVWG). The NAPF Inquiry identified the cumbersome paper-based voting system as being problematic, together with a 'lack of auditability or adequate confirmatory procedure in the voting system' and communication problems between the pension funds, fund managers, custodians, registrars and companies. Subsequent to the NAPF report, the SVWG was established and highlighted many of the same problems continuing over the next few years. Paul Myners was invited to become the chair of the SVWG and two reports have been issued, in 2004 and another in 2005. Whilst good progress has been made with the introduction of an electronic voting system in the UK, the take-up by institutional investors was initially rather slow, although this has increased dramatically.

The increasing focus on the role of institutional investors was evidenced by the Institutional Shareholders' Committee (ISC) (2002) statement of the responsibilities of institutional investors. The ISC recommend that institutional shareholders clearly state their policy on activism including voting; that they should monitor performance of their investee companies, intervene as appropriate, and evaluate and report on their activism.

Another important area that has gained more emphasis in recent years is that of socially responsible investment (SRI). An important development in the UK was that, from 3 July 2000, pension fund trustees have had to take account of SRI in their Statement of Investment Principles. This change means that pension fund trustees must state 'the extent (if at all) to which social, environmental or ethical considerations are taken into account in the selection, retention, and realisation of investments' (amendment to Pensions Act 1995).

Recognition of the growing importance of SRI was also evidenced by the Association of British Insurers (ABI) (2003) with the publication of its disclosure guidelines on SRI. The ABI is an influential voice in institutional investors' involvement in corporate governance issues. The main focus of the guidelines is the identification and management of risks arising from social, environmental and ethical issues that may affect either short-term or long-term business value. Logically, appropriate management of these risks may mean opportunities to enhance value.

STANDARD LIFE

Standard Life has been established for 180 years. Originally called the Life Insurance Company of Scotland, it was founded on 23 March 1825 with a staff of three. It became Standard Life in 1832, changing its name by Act of Parliament. It established a sister company, Colonial Life Assurance Co. in 1845, with which it subsequently merged in 1866. Within the first 25 years of its life, the company had established agencies in Canada, India, Ireland, the West Indies, South America, China and the Far East. Although it continued to establish agencies overseas, including in Egypt, South Africa, Europe and Scandinavia, as it moved into the twentieth century it was decided to concentrate more on home business. Based in Edinburgh, it has grown to a vast organization accounting for 8 per cent of the total market share of insurance business in the UK, and with £108 billion assets under management. Table 2.1 charts the growth in group funds under management between 2000 and 2004. Standard Life is the largest mutual life assurance company in Europe. The business operates in six key areas: UK life and pensions, bank, healthcare, investments, Canada and International. This case study will concentrate on the UK life and pensions area.

Table 2.1   Standard Life group funds under management £bn

Year	Group funds under management £bn
2000	86
2001	83
2002	83
2003	96
2004	108

Note: 2000–2003 figures as at 15 November.
2004 figures as at 31 December.

Source: Standard Life Annual Report and Accounts 2004.

Standard Life takes a proactive stance both on corporate governance and on corporate social responsibility. In its 2004 annual report, the Chairman's Statement makes this point 'with over £100 billion of funds under management, it is important that Standard Life takes a strong stance on issues of corporate social responsibility'. This is discussed in more detail below.

Standard Life has been a long-term advocate of corporate governance activism. In fact, in the mid-1990s it took an active stance and voted against a plan by Farnell Electronics to buy an American distributor, Premier International. Standard Life was concerned at the size of the deal and the price that Farnell Electronics was proposing to pay for Premier International, as Farnell was proposing to more than double its share capital to buy a business nearly twice its size. Ultimately the vote at the extraordinary general meeting went in favour of Farnell Electronics' plan, its directors having made many presentations to institutional investors to convince them to vote in favour of the plan in the lead up to the extraordinary general meeting. However, Standard Life's stance was vindicated, given the issuance of profit warnings by the merged Premier Farnell and subsequent poor share price performance.

STANDARD LIFE CORPORATE GOVERNANCE STRUCTURE

Standard Life complies with the provisions of the Combined Code (2003), which have been discussed in detail earlier in the chapter.

In its 2004 annual report, Standard Life details its board structure and this is shown in Table 2.2. As can be seen from Table 2.2, Standard Life's board has a majority of non-executive directors. It has five board committees: audit committee (five members); demutualization committee (six members); investment committee (six members); nomination committee (six members); and remuneration committee (three members). The audit committee, remuneration committee and investment committee are comprised solely of non-executive directors (all of whom are deemed to be independent by the board of directors). Hugh Stevenson is the Senior Independent Director on the board.

The roles of Chair and Chief Executive Officer are split and their responsibilities are documented in the approved board charter. Similarly the roles and responsibilities of the board are detailed in the board charter.

The performance of the board as a whole, and of individual directors, is evaluated annually by a formal annual review process which utilizes questionnaires and interviews with all board members. The outcome of the evaluation can then inform future plans; in addition there is an ongoing programme of professional development.

Corporate social responsibility is also given a high profile at Standard Life and, as stated in the 2004 annual report, covers five areas: 'managing and developing our people, investing in our local communities, protecting our environment, being active and responsible investors, and engaging with our external stakeholders' (Standard Life 2004, p. 31). Looking in more detail at one of these areas, in relation to protecting the environment, Standard Life have aimed to reduce their consumption of energy, and the resulting emissions. In fact they have managed to reduce their electricity consumption by over 30 per cent in the period 1996–2004.

Table 2.2   Board and board committee membership

Position	Member of committees[a]
Chairman	
Sir Brian Stewart	NC, DC
Executive directors	
Sandy Crombie	NC, DC
John Hylands	DC
Claude Garcia	–
Trevor Matthews[b]	–
Non-executive directors	
Lord Blackwell	AC, RC, DC
Gerry Grimstone	RC, IC, DC
David Lewis[c]	AC, NC, IC
The Hon. Roy MacLaren[d]	IC
Alison Mitchell	IC
Sir Nicholas Monck	AC, IC
David Newlands	AC, NC, DC
Jocelyn Proteau	AC, NC
Hugh Stevenson	RC, NC, IC

Notes:
[a]   Committees: AC = audit committee; DC = demutualization committee; IC = investment committee; NC = nomination committee; RC = remuneration committee.
[b]   Trevor Matthews was appointed July 2004.
[c]   David Lewis resigned June 2004.
[d]   The Hon. Roy MacLaren retired November 2004.

Source: Standard Life Annual Report and Accounts 2004.

STANDARD LIFE – THE DEMUTUALIZATION QUESTION

In his authoritative work on Standard Life, Moss (2000) provides a fascinating history of the development of Standard Life, including key milestones along the way. The company was originally formed as a partnership, although it was converted into a limited company in 1910 and listed on the Stock Exchange. In 1925 Standard Life became a mutual company when it exchanged the 50 000 shares in issue at that time for perpetual loan stock (the latter being redeemed in 1991). As a mutual company, Standard Life is controlled by its members who can attend the annual general meeting and have voting rights (each member has one vote). Members can share in the profits and losses of the company by means of policy payouts.

However, in recent years, a strategic review has examined various possibilities for the future direction of the company, one of which is demutualization. In its 2004 annual report, Standard Life's board stated that given the changes in recent years and the environment in which it is operating, demutualization offers the best alternative. Standard Life had traditionally invested in the stock market and when prices fell there were inevitably implications, and together with low interest rates, this meant falling long-term investment returns and reduced capital bases. In addition new solvency rules being introduced by the Financial Services Authority mean that companies such as Standard Life have to keep more capital in reserve. Standard Life reviewed its options, and decided that demutualization was an appropriate strategy. By becoming a public limited company, it would unlock value for its members and it would also open up new opportunities for raising capital as there would be access to a wide range of potential investors. The company is currently progressing with its plans to demutualize in 2006.

CONCLUDING COMMENTS

In this chapter, various facets of Standard Life have been discussed. First the context for the development of corporate governance in the UK was set, this being the chief environment in which Standard Life developed and operates. We looked in some detail at the way in which corporate governance has developed with regard to institutional investors and noted the growing awareness of the influence and power of institutional investors and the consequent coverage by various codes and guidelines of the responsibilities of institutional investors. The importance of voting was noted together with some of the impediments that institutional investors may face when they try to vote their shares.

The corporate governance structure of Standard Life was examined along with their policies towards their investee companies. Finally there was a discussion of the strategy of Standard Life to move towards demutualization.

KEY LEARNING POINTS

The key learning points arising from this case are the development of corporate governance in the UK, particularly as it affects institutional investors and their investee companies, and as illustrated by the example of one the largest and oldest UK institutional investors, Standard Life.

Corporate governance codes developed because of a number of drivers: financial scandals and collapses, concentration of share ownership into the hands of institutional investors, growth of cross-border investment, and vast improvements in technology which made it easier for institutional investors to communicate, both nationally and internationally.

Standard Life's corporate governance structure is examined and we can see, for example, points of good practice such as the splitting of the roles of Chair and CEO, and the board being comprised of a majority of non-executive directors. In addition, Standard Life has the main board sub-committees such as audit, remuneration and nomination committee. It also has an investment committee, and as it moves towards a major change in its history, a demutualization committee.

An example of activism from its past, the Premier Farnell case, is discussed as a particularly interesting example of early activism on the UK corporate governance scene.

DISCUSSION QUESTIONS

1. To what extent should an institutional investor undertake an activist role in the companies in which it invests?
2. Do you feel that corporate governance best practice codes/guidelines give institutional investors in the UK enough guidance? Or too little, or too much?
3. Do you think that institutional investors should be legally obliged to vote their shares?
4. Critically evaluate Standard Life's corporate governance structure.
5. Critically evaluate the policies of large institutional investors, such as Standard Life, towards their investee companies.
6. What governance considerations might arise in moving from a mutual company to a demutualized company?

REFERENCES

Association of British Insurers (2003), *Disclosure Guidelines on Socially Responsible Investment*, London: ABI.

Cadbury, Sir Adrian (1992), *Report of the Committee on the Financial Aspects of Corporate Governance*, London: Gee & Co. Ltd.

Combined Code (1998), *Combined Code, Principles of Corporate Governance*, London: Gee & Co. Ltd.

Combined Code (2003), *The Combined Code on Corporate Governance*, London: The Financial Reporting Council.

Employee Retirement Income Security Act (1974), US Department of Labor, Washington DC, USA.

Greenbury, Sir R. (1995), *Directors' Remuneration*, London: Gee & Co. Ltd.

Hampel, Sir R. (1998), *Committee on Corporate Governance: Final Report*, London: Gee & Co. Ltd.

Higgs, D. (2003), *Review of the Role and Effectiveness of Non-Executive Directors*, London: Department of Trade and Industry.

Institutional Shareholders' Committee (2002), *The Responsibilities of Institutional Shareholders and Agents – Statement of Principles*, London: ISC.

Moss, M. (2000), *Standard Life 1825–2000, the Building of Europe's Largest Mutual Life Company*, Edinburgh: Mainstream Publishing.

National Association of Pension Funds (1999), *Report of the Committee of Inquiry into UK Vote Executive*, London: NAPF.

Office of National Statistics (2005), *Share Ownership: A Report on Ownership of Shares as at 31 December 2004*, Norwich: HMSO.

Smith, R. (2003), *Audit Committees Combined Code Guidance*, London: Financial Reporting Council.

Standard Life (2004), *Annual Report and Accounts 2004*, Edinburgh: Standard Life.

Turnbull, N. (1999), *Internal Control: Guidance for Directors on the Combined Code*, London: Institute of Chartered Accountants in England and Wales.

3. Strong blockholders and corporate governance structures that improve minority shareholders' protection: the case of Telecom Italia

Andrea Melis

INTRODUCTION

In international taxonomies of corporate governance systems, the Italian corporate governance system has been classified within the so-called insider-dominated systems (Franks and Mayer 1995; La Porta *et al.* 1999). However, because of its own unique features, it does not entirely fit into the international standard models (Melis 1999). Corporate governance regulation in Italy includes the so-called Draghi Reform (1998), the Preda Code (1999, updated in 2002), and the company law enforced in January 2004.

The Draghi Reform (1998), which is legally binding for all listed companies, regulates the Italian financial markets and corporate governance in listed companies, aiming to 'strengthen investors' protection and minority shareholders', by regulating listed corporations on issues such as shareholders' agreements, minority shareholders' rights, internal controls, public bids, external auditors' engagement, and the role of the board of statutory auditors as a monitor. It does not regulate the structure of the board of directors.

The Preda Code (1999, 2002), a Cadbury-like voluntary code of best practice, focuses on the role of the board of directors, with a particular emphasis on its composition and method of appointment, as well as providing some recommendations on the role of the board of statutory auditors.

The 2004 Company Act, *inter alia*, allows Italian listed companies to choose between a British-like unitary board structure (with an audit committee, entirely composed of independent directors, appointed by the board of directors, within the board), a two-tier board structure (with a management committee and a supervisory council, without mandatory labour representation), and the Italian traditional board structure with a board of directors and a board of statutory auditors.

The prevailing Italian corporate governance system is characterized by a relatively poor capital market orientation (Pagano *et al.* 1998), a limited role played by the market for corporate control and a rather concentrated control structure. In contrast to other main European corporate governance systems, neither banks (as in Germany) nor institutional investors (as in the UK) have a direct influence on the corporate governance system (Melis 1999). Banks usually exercise a direct influence in corporate governance only when a company gets into financial trouble, in order to safeguard their own interests. Institutional investors have usually played a marginal role because of their limited share ownership (Bianchi *et al.* 2001); however, their role might be changing over time (Bianchi and Enriques 2001).

The prevailing Italian corporate ownership and control structure is characterized by the presence of a blockholder, who is an active investor, willing and able to monitor the senior management effectively (e.g. Molteni 1997; Melis 1999; Bianchi *et al.* 2001). Whilst such a structure reduces the 'classic' agency problem between senior management and shareholders (senior managers who pursue their own self-interest at the expense of shareholders are likely to be displaced by the controlling shareholder), the agency problem is not eliminated, but shifted towards the relationship between different types of shareholders: the controlling shareholder and minority shareholders.

In Italy, the real concern of corporate governance is the potential abuse of power of the blockholder against minority shareholders (Melis 1999, 2000; La Porta *et al.* 2000). Paraphrasing Roe (1994), 'weak managers, strong blockholders and unprotected minority shareholders' sum up the key corporate governance issue in Italian listed companies (Melis 2000, p. 351).

The Parmalat case, although to some extent it is only an Italian case (Melis 2005), provides an excellent example of what may happen when an unaccountable strong blockholder is willing and able to wield its power at the expense of unprotected minority shareholders.

This chapter provides a case study which describes corporate governance structures and mechanisms at Telecom Italia S.p.A. Telecom Italia is one of the largest Italian companies. It is listed both on the Italian Stock Exchange, where it is a 'blue-chip' company belonging to the MIB30,[1] and on the New York Stock Exchange (NYSE), so that it is subject to US securities laws and, in particular, to the Sarbanes-Oxley Act.

Telecom Italia's corporate governance currently may be considered an example of Italian best practice, thanks to the company's efforts to strengthen minority shareholders' protection in order to be more competitive in capital markets.

COMPANY PROFILE AND BACKGROUND

Telecom Italia S.p.A. was created through the merger of five telecoms companies that were operators in the areas of domestic, long-distance, international, maritime and satellite services. In 1997 the five companies were merged into their holding company STET S.p.A., which then changed its name to Telecom Italia.

In 1997, the Italian government privatized Telecom Italia, selling its shares through an Italian public offering, and separate international and US public offerings. The government retained a 3.5 per cent stake as well as the 'golden share', which gave the government a set of veto powers, allowing it to block any investor acquisition that resulted in more than a 3 per cent ownership of the company. Approximately 1.5 million private investors also bought shares in the company. After its privatization, Telecom Italia was characterized by a rather widespread ownership and control structure that was uncommon according to Italian standards.

The government struggled to create a group of core shareholders, which eventually included some Italian banks and insurance companies, as well as the Agnelli family (Table 3.1).

Table 3.1   Telecom Italia's core shareholders in 1997, just after privatization

Assicurazioni Generali	1.0%
Credito Italiano	1.0%
IMI	0.8%
Banca Commerciale Italiana	0.5%
Monte dei Paschi di Siena	0.5%
Compagnia S. Paolo	0.6%
INA	0.5%
IFIL	0.6%
Fondazione Cariplo	0.5%
CSFB	0.7%
Total	*6.6%*

In November 1997, Mr Guido Rossi, the company's Chairman, resigned after a dispute with the Chief Executive Officer (CEO) over board involvement in company operations. In January 1998, a new Chairman was in place, backed by the Agnelli family via their family holding IFIL S.p.A. The Agnelli family had become the leading shareholder of the core shareholders (and of the whole company) with only 0.6 per cent of the share capital (Amatori and Colli 2000). A month later the new Chairman fired the CEO and withdrew the corporate strategic plan. In July, he resigned after serious irregularities were uncovered in Telecom Italia's financial statements.

As the management experienced intense turmoil, Telecom Italia became known as one of the worst managed companies in Italy. In November 1998, the share price was approximately 20 per cent below the privatization price. Mr Bernabé, former CEO at ENI S.p.A. (an Italian oil company) where he had managed a successful turnaround, was appointed CEO at Telecom Italia. The share price rose.

In February 1999, Olivetti S.p.A. launched a hostile takeover bid in competition with a German incumbent (Deutsche Telekom) which had already begun preliminary merger talks with the Italian company. In June 1999, Olivetti's leveraged buy-out[2] succeeded. All the core shareholders sold their shares, and Telecom Italia was under the control of Olivetti.

Colaninno[3] and his allies maintained the control of the entire group through a complex pyramidal structure.[4] In fact, the Olivetti group was a pyramidal group which had many levels, so that Colaninno and his partners were able to maintain control of the entire group with a relatively low direct investment of personal resources.

At the top of the pyramid there were Colaninno and his family, who owned 15 per cent of Fingruppo S.p.A., which itself owned 39 per cent of Bell SA (based in Luxembourg), which in turn owned 15 per cent of Olivetti, which controlled Tecnost S.p.A. with a 70 per cent ownership. The latter owned 51.02 per cent of Telecom Italia's ordinary shares. Telecom Italia controlled Telecom Italia Mobile (TIM) S.p.A., the high cash-flow making company which operated in the mobile industry, and other companies.

The financial structure that Colaninno and his allies carefully constructed for the takeover created many problems. In order to attempt to handle the huge debt that resulted from the takeover, senior management presented several plans which faced strong opposition from Telecom Italia's minority shareholders, since the plans were clearly against their interests. In this regard, the *Financial Times* commented: 'If Mr Colaninno does not have the resources to run TI without abusing minorities, he should sell it to someone who does' (24 May 2000).

In April and May 2001, two Telecom Italia board members resigned after alleging that Colaninno had misled the board of directors by failing to disclose his interests in a relevant transaction, as required by the company's corporate governance procedures.

In July 2001, Colaninno and his allies sold their controlling stake in Olivetti (and, by extension, Telecom Italia and its controlled companies) to Pirelli and the Benetton family for a price that represented an 80 per cent control premium over market price. A large control premium is believed to be correlated with 'private benefits of control', i.e. benefits that may be enjoyed only by controlling shareholders (Zingales 1994), thus it may be an indicator that the corporate governance system does not safeguard minority shareholders' interests (Melis 2002). Olivetti's minority shareholders were not given the opportunity to participate in the offer, since Pirelli and its allies did not reach the 30 per cent threshold.[5]

Mr Tronchetti Provera (via Camfin S.p.A) the Benetton family (via their family holding Edizione Holding S.p.A.), together with a financial company (Hopa S.p.A.) became the ultimate controlling shareholders of Telecom Italia, via a complex control structure. In December 2002, the Ministry of the Treasury sold its remaining stake in Telecom Italia ordinary and savings share capital.

Under market pressure from institutional investors, the control chain was reduced by merging Telecom Italia with Olivetti in August 2003. The company resulting from the merger adopted the name of Telecom Italia.

After the merger, the powers of the 'golden share' changed. While the Italian government maintained the power of approval (or veto) of the acquisition of major shareholdings in the company's voting capital, the powers of approving major shareholders' agreements and of appointment of one director and one member of the board of statutory auditors were given up.

Table 3.2 sums up the major events at Telecom Italia since its privatization.

OWNERSHIP AND CONTROL AT TELECOM ITALIA

Telecom Italia share capital is composed of voting and non-voting shares,[6] with the latter representing approximately one third of the total share capital (Table 3.3).

Analysis of the ownership and control structure shows a complex group of companies controlled by a strong blockholder through a pyramidal device and some shareholders' agreements. Olimpia S.p.A. (17.03 per cent), Hopa S.p.A. (3.37 per cent), the US institutional investor Brandes investment partners L.L.P. (3.62 per cent), Assicurazioni Generali S.p.A. (2.01 per cent) and Bank of Italy (2.25 per cent) are the major shareholders of Telecom Italia ordinary shares (Figure 3.1).

As disclosed in Telecom Italia's Form 20-F (see Telecom Italia 2004a), Olimpia, which *de facto* controls Telecom Italia, is controlled via agreements among its five shareholders: Edizione Holding, Pirelli, Hopa and two Italian banks: Unicredito S.p.A. and Banca Intesa S.p.A.

Table 3.2   Summary of the major events (period 1997–2004)

Date	Events
October 1997	The Italian Government privatizes TI. A group of 'core shareholders' is set up.
November 1997	Chairman resigns after disputes with CEO over corporate governance issues.
February 1998	Chairman resigns after serious irregularities were uncovered in financial statements.
November 1998	Bernabè, former ENI CEO, is appointed as Chairman.
February 1999	Olivetti launches a hostile takeover.
June 1999	The leverage buy-out succeeds. Colaninno and his allies control TI via a pyramidal device.
April–May 2001	Two TI directors resign after alleging that Colaninno had misled the board by failing to disclose his interests in a relevant transaction.
July 2001	Colaninno and his allies sell their controlling block of shares. The selling price includes an 80% control premium. Pirelli and the Benetton family control TI via a pyramidal device.
August 2003	Olivetti merges with TI to reduce the control chain.
December 2004	Telecom Italia launches a plan to merge with Telecom Italia Mobile, its largest listed subsidiary.

Table 3.3   Telecom Italia equity

Ordinary voting shares	10 315 317 624
Saving (non-voting) shares	5 795 921 069
Total	16 111 238 693
Nominal value	€0.55

Source: CONSOB database, updated at 2 December 2004.

The parties to the shareholders' agreements, *inter alia*, have agreed 'to use their best efforts' to appoint the board of directors of Telecom Italia according to the following criteria:

1. the appointment of one-fifth of the directors by Edizione Holding, without taking into account the directors whose designation is reserved, by law or corporate by-laws, to the market or other parties;
2. the appointment of one director by Banca Intesa;

3. the appointment of one director by Unicredito;
4. the appointment of the vice-president of the board from among the directors nominated by Edizione Holding;
5. in the event of the establishment of an executive committee, the election of one member from among the directors nominated by Edizione Holding.

Furthermore, Hopa is given the right to appoint one Olimpia director. Pirelli, Edizione Holding, Unicredito and Banca Intesa are to use their best efforts in order to foster the appointment of a director designated by Hopa to the Telecom Italia's board of directors.

Figure 3.2 shows a simplified control structure, identifying only the links that are more relevant to understanding the case study.

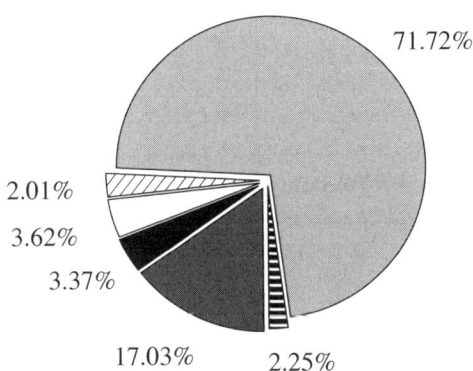

Source: Elaborated with data based on CONSOB database updated at 5 October 2004. (1) Free float includes all shareholdings with less than 2 per cent of the voting capital.

Figure 3.1   Telecom Italia's ownership structure (ordinary shares)

THE STRUCTURE OF THE BOARDS

Telecom Italia is characterized by the typical Italian board structure (see, for example, Telecom Italia S.p.A. 2004b), composed of a board of directors

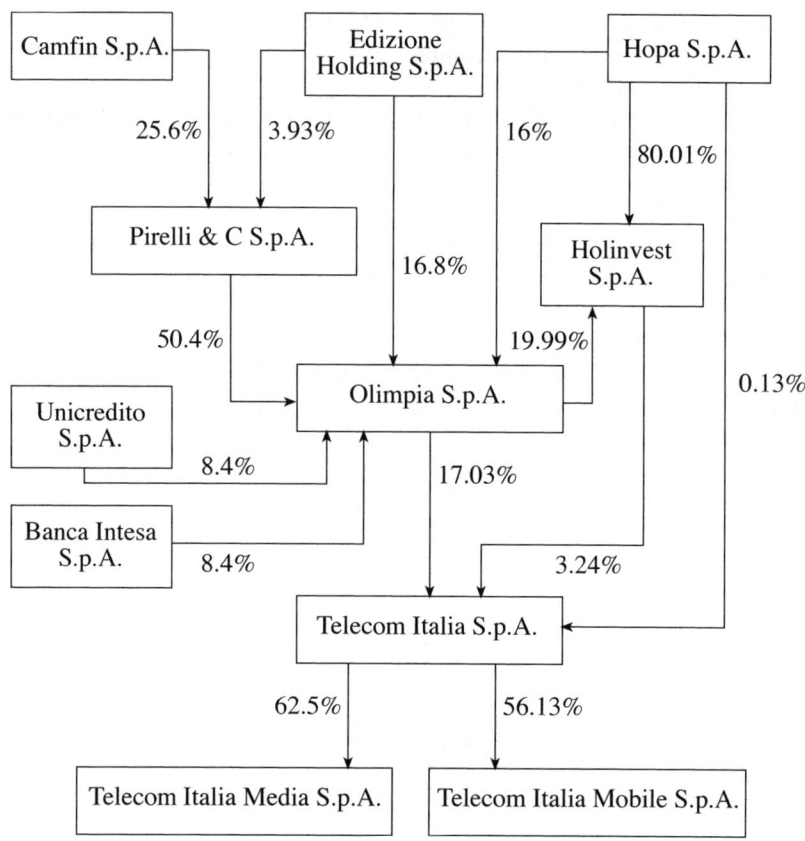

Figure 3.2   Telecom Italia's control structure (updated at 31 October 2004)

and a board of statutory auditors (named *Collegio sindacale* or *Collegio dei sindaci*). Both boards are appointed through the shareholders' general meeting.

Figure 3.3 shows the accountability and monitoring system that characterizes the Italian listed companies that, like Telecom Italia, choose the traditional structure of the boards.

THE BOARD OF DIRECTORS: ITS ROLE, APPOINTMENT AND COMPOSITION

The board of directors has the power (as well as the duty) to lead the company by pursuing the primary objective of creating value for its shareholders.

————— Appointment
············· Monitoring

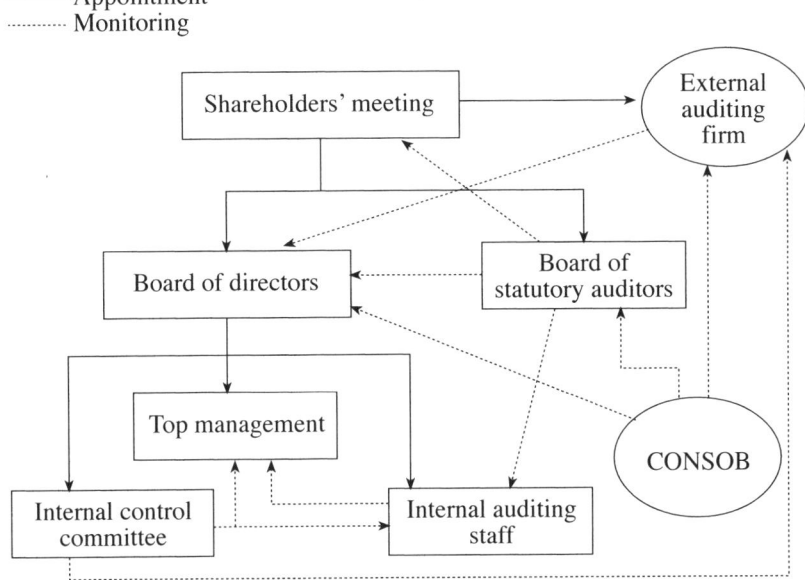

Source: Melis (2004, p. 77).

Figure 3.3 The Italian typical accountability and monitoring system

The following tasks are reserved for the exclusive competence of the board (see Telecom Italia S.p.A. 2001, 2002, 2003a, 2004b):

1. examining and approving the strategic, business and financial plans of the company and the group;
2. evaluating and approving the annual budget of the company and the group;
3. examining and approving transactions with a substantial impact on the corporate activity;
4. verifying the adequacy of the general organizational and administrative structure of the company and the group;
5. preparing and adopting corporate governance rules and the group's governance guidelines;
6. nominating the chairperson and managing director in strategic subsidiaries (excluding subsidiaries of listed subsidiaries);
7. evaluating and approving the periodic reports required by the applicable legislation.

In order to exercise its role, the board of directors is required by the company self-regulatory code (see Telecom Italia S.p.A. 2003b) to meet at least quarterly.

In 2003 the board of directors met 11 times. Board meetings were always well attended, with on average 81 per cent of the directors being present. In particular, independent directors had an overall attendance rate of 76 per cent (Telecom Italia S.p.A. 2004b).

Method of Appointment and Composition of the Board of Directors

According to corporate by-laws (see Telecom Italia S.p.A. 2004c), the members of the board of directors are elected by means of 'slates'. Such a system is designed in order to ensure an adequate representation on the board of directors drawn from lists presented by minority shareholders. Slates may be presented by shareholders who, individually or together with others, hold at least 1 per cent of the voting share capital.

Four-fifths of the directors are to be chosen from the slate that obtains the majority of the votes, one-fifth from the slates voted for by minority shareholders, that is 15 members are appointed by the controlling shareholders and four by the minority shareholders.

Telecom Italia's board of directors is composed of 19 members, with only three executive directors. Independent directors comprise the majority of the board's members: among the 16 non-executive directors (NEDs), ten are claimed to be independent[7] (see Telecom Italia S.p.A. 2004b).

Although the Preda Code (1999, 2002, para. 3) acknowledges that when a company like Telecom Italia is controlled by a group of shareholders the need for some directors to be independent from the controlling shareholders is essential, it only recommends that an adequate number of non-executive directors should be independent, in order to ensure the protection of the minority shareholders. However, Telecom Italia has chosen a higher benchmark and voluntarily complies with NYSE listing rules applicable to US companies, which require that independent directors comprise a majority of the board of directors.

Empirical evidence shows that having a board composed of a majority of independent directors is rather uncommon among Italian listed companies (Cavallari *et al.* 2003) (Table 3.4).

The Role of the Chairperson

The Chairperson and CEO positions are separated; however, the former is an executive director and some important management powers are delegated to her/him. This clearly does not comply with the recommendations of

Table 3.4 Board of directors and board committees

Position	Name	Board of directors			Internal control committee	Remuneration committee
		Executive	Non-executive	Independent		
Chairman	M. Tronchetti Provera	X				
Deputy chairman	G. Benetton		X			
Managing director	C. Buora	X				
Managing director and General manager	R. Ruggiero	X				
Director	P. Baratta		X	X		X
Director	J.R. Sotheby Boas		X	X		
Director	G. Consorte		X	X		
Director	D. De Sole		X	X	X	
Director	F. Denozza (1)		X	X	X	
Director	L. Fausti		X	X		X
Director	G. Ferrarini (1)		X	X	X	
Director	J.P. Fitoussi (1)		X			
Director	G. Mion		X			
Director	M. Moratti		X	X		
Director	M. Onado		X		X	
Director	R. Pagliaro		X	X		X
Director	P. Pistorio (1)		X			
Director	C.A. Puri Negri		X	X		
Director	L. Roth		X	X		

Source: Elaborated from company data – updated at May 2004. (1) Elected from the slate presented by minority shareholders jointly holding more than 1 per cent of the voting shares.

most international codes of best practice (for example Cadbury Report 1992), which recommend the separation of the two roles not only to avoid concentration of powers, but also because, as argued by Sir Adrian Cadbury (1999), chairing a board may require a set of qualities different from those needed to run a company.

However, regarding the separation between the Chairperson and the CEO, the Preda Code (1999, 2002, para. 4) only recommends that when the board of directors has delegated powers to the Chairperson, the company should disclose adequate information in its annual report on the powers delegated.

Telecom Italia complies with such recommendation. In fact, in its 2004 corporate governance report (see Telecom Italia S.p.A. 2004b) it is stated that:

> the Chairman is entrusted the powers needed to carry out every transaction relating to the company's activity, except for acquisitions and disposals of shareholdings involving control or affiliation, and of businesses or business segments where the value of the transaction exceeds €250 million. Moreover, the Chairman must sign jointly with a Managing director for the issue of guarantees in the interest of Telecom Italia or its subsidiaries where the amount exceeds €250 million and in the interest of third parties where the amount exceeds €100 million. The Chairman is authorized to act as a matter of urgency in the matters for which the Board of Directors is competent and is entrusted with the tasks of overseeing the management of confidential information and ensuring the effectiveness and adequacy of the internal control system.

Thus, the Chairperson (Mr Tronchetti Provera), who is also one of the most important shareholders, is delegated many powers to run the company. This makes the division of roles between the Chairperson, who is supposed to run the board, and the CEO, who is supposed to run the company, not adequately clear (Melis 2000).

BOARD OF DIRECTORS' COMMITTEES

In accordance with the corporate by-laws and the Preda Code (1999, 2002, paras 8.1 and 10.2), the board of directors established two committees from among its members:

1. the internal control and corporate governance committee; and
2. the remuneration committee.

Both of them are charged with making proposals and giving advice to the board of directors as a whole.

With regard to the nomination process, the Preda Code (1999, 2002, para. 7.2) recommends companies set up a nomination committee to propose candidates for election only when the board of directors believes that it is difficult for shareholders to make proposals, that is when the corporate control structure is dispersed. Telecom Italia has chosen not to set up a nomination committee because shareholders have never faced difficulties in proposing candidates for elections.

Role and Composition of the Internal Control and Corporate Governance Committee

The board of directors is required by the company self-regulatory code (see Telecom Italia S.p.A. 2003b, para. 12) to establish an internal control and corporate governance committee to provide advice and make proposals on the following issues:

1. assisting the board of directors in establishing guidelines for the internal control system and checking its proper functioning with reference to the management of the company's exposure to risks;
2. assessing the work programme prepared by the persons responsible for internal control and receive their periodic reports;
3. assessing, together with the managers responsible for administration and the external auditors, the appropriateness of the accounting standards adopted as well as their uniformity for the preparation of the consolidated accounts;
4. assessing the proposals put forward by auditing firms to obtain the audit engagement, the work programme for carrying out the audit as well as the results thereof, as set out in the external auditors' report and their letter of suggestions;
5. report to the board of directors on its activity and the adequacy of the internal control system at least every six months, when the annual and semi-annual accounts are approved.

Last but not least, the internal control and corporate governance committee is given the duty to supervise the compliance of the company's governance structure with the recommended corporate governance best practices, as well as its periodic update, in accordance with the improvements to the state of the art.

The Chairperson of the board of statutory auditors (or another member nominated by the Chairperson of the board of statutory auditors) is to take part in the work of the committee. The board of statutory auditors and the internal control and corporate governance committee may meet jointly when considered useful, in accordance with the topics on the agenda.

According to the company self-regulatory code (see Telecom Italia S.p.A. 2003b), the internal control and corporate governance committee is to be composed of independent non-executive directors, of whom at least one is to be chosen from the directors elected by minority shareholders in accordance with the slate system set forth by the corporate by-laws. Such composition should encourage the committee to carry out its functions autonomously and independently.

The committee is composed of four directors, all of whom are claimed to be non-executive and independent (see Table 3.4). Half of its members are directors who were elected by minority shareholders. This should foster the committee's independence from executive directors and the controlling shareholders.

As emerged in the Parmalat case (see Melis 2005), the independence (or the lack of it) of the internal control committee from the controlling shareholder(s) is a key aspect in assuring its effectiveness. Table 3.5 shows a brief comparison between the composition of this committee in Telecom Italia (example of good practice) and in Parmalat[8] (example of bad practice).

Table 3.5   *Composition of the internal control committee: Telecom Italia vs Parmalat*

	Telecom Italia	Parmalat
Number of members	4	3
Non-executive directors (%)	100	33
Independent directors (%)	100	0
Appointed by minority shareholders (%)	50	0

Source: Company sources. Data concerning Parmalat are based on Melis (2005).

At Telecom Italia the committee is currently composed of two professors of law (commercial law and financial markets law, respectively), a professor of economics who is also a former CONSOB officer, and a former CEO of Gucci group who also sits on the audit committees of Procter & Gamble and Bausch & Lomb.

Role and Composition of the Remuneration Committee

According to the company self-regulatory code (see Telecom Italia S.p.A. 2003b, para. 10), a remuneration committee is to be set up by the board of directors. The key role of such a committee is to submit proposals to the board of directors regarding the remuneration of the managing directors as well as of the directors (including the Chairperson) who are delegated some executive powers. It is up to the board of directors to determine the remuneration of the chairperson and the managing directors, taking into account the proposals of the remuneration committee, after consulting the board of statutory auditors.

The remuneration committee should provide that a part of their total remuneration is related to the corporate performance as well as to the achievement of specific objectives established in advance. It also has the duty to submit proposals for establishing the criteria for the remuneration of the top management (including stock-option plans or plans for the assignment of corporate shares).

As for the internal control and corporate governance committee, the remuneration committee should be composed of non-executive directors, of whom at least one is to be chosen from the directors elected by the minority shareholders.

The remuneration committee is composed of three members, all of whom are claimed to be independent non-executive directors (see Table 3.4). One of its members is a director elected by minority shareholders.

BOARD OF STATUTORY AUDITORS

The board of statutory auditors plays a key role in the corporate governance system. It has been identified as Telecom Italia's audit committee for the purposes of the applicable US legislation (see Telecom Italia S.p.A. 2004a).

According to the Draghi Reform (1998, art. 149), its main tasks and responsibilities include:

1. to check the compliance of acts and decisions of the board of directors with the law and the corporate by-laws and the observance of the so-called 'principles of correct administration' by the executive directors and the board of directors;
2. to review the adequacy of the corporate organizational structure for matters such as the internal control system, the administrative and accounting system as well as the reliability of the latter in correctly representing any company's transactions;
3. to ensure that the instructions given by the company to its subsidiaries concerning the provision on all the information necessary to comply with the information requirements established by the law are adequate.

Statutory auditors are appointed for three years and may be dismissed only with cause, that is in case of serious irregularities in the performance of their duties, such as failing to attend two consequent meetings, divulging 'confidential' information to the public or to specific shareholders, or failing to report corporate directors' misbehaviour to courts.

Despite the fact that the statutory auditors are appointed by the shareholders' general meeting, shareholders' freedom of choice is limited by the Draghi Reform (1998, art. 148), which requires corporate by-laws to provide the number of auditors (not less than three) as well as to ensure that one statutory auditor (or two, when the board is composed of more than three auditors) is appointed by the minority shareholders. Only in a board of statutory auditors that is composed of more than three members can minority shareholders appoint two auditors.

Telecom Italia's board of statutory auditors is composed of five members. Having a five-member board of statutory auditors is rather uncommon among Italian listed companies. CONSOB (2002) reports that only approximately 8 per cent of the listed companies (mainly financial companies) set up such a large board. Besides, Telecom Italia's corporate by-laws set up a threshold of 1 per cent of company voting shares for minority shareholders to appoint a statutory auditor. Such a low threshold makes appointing a statutory auditor easier for minority shareholders (Parmalat, for example, had set up a 3 per cent threshold).

As pointed out in Melis (2004), the size of the board of statutory auditors has a positive influence over the level of protection of minority shareholders.[9] In fact, the following powers may be exercised only by at least two statutory auditors jointly:

(a)   to seek the cooperation of the company's employees in performing their tasks; and
(b)   to convene a shareholders' meeting because of a directors' decision.

With regard to the financial literacy of statutory auditors, the Draghi Reform (1998, art. 148) requires that candidates are to be chosen out of a pool of chartered public accountants who have exercised audit activities for at least three years (a minimum of one of the auditors shall comply with this condition), experienced managers and academics in company-related subjects and sectors specified by corporate by-laws.[10] Telecom Italia's board of statutory directors is composed of two professors of accounting (including the Chairman) and three chartered public accountants.

THE EXTERNAL AUDITING FIRM: MANDATORY AUDITOR ROTATION AND THE GROUP PROCEDURE OF APPOINTMENT

In Italy the external auditing firm is appointed by the shareholders' meeting, taking into consideration the positive opinion of the board of statutory auditors. Its appointment lasts three years, and may be renewed twice. Italy is the only large economy to have made auditor rotation compulsory. After three appointments, that is nine years, the law (Draghi Reform 1998, art. 159) requires the company to rotate its lead audit firm.

In addition to the law, Telecom Italia has set up a specific procedure for the appointment of external auditors (see Telecom Italia S.p.A. 2003c) which provides that the auditor of Telecom Italia is the principal auditor of the entire group. Therefore, such an external auditor is to be preferred in conferral of appointments by subsidiaries for mandatory auditing. Recourse to other auditors must be authorized by the directors of Telecom Italia provided with delegated powers for internal controls. Such authorization will be issued on the basis of a positive opinion from the board of statutory auditors of Telecom Italia. As a result, in 2004 Ernst & Young has been selected as the audit firm for all of the companies of the Telecom Italia group.

With regard to the issues of auditor's independence, it has been argued (see, among others, Frankel *et al.* 2002) that fees paid to external auditors for non-audit services may increase the financial reliance of the auditor on the client, thus jeopardizing its independence of judgement. In order to foster external auditors' independence, non-audit services which are forbidden for the auditor of Telecom Italia (and all its subsidiaries) include:

1. bookkeeping;
2. the organization and implementation of information systems for financial accounting;
3. appraisal or valuation services, fairness opinions or contribution-in-kind reports;
4. actuarial services;
5. internal audit outsourcing services;
6. management functions;
7. investment, banking and insurance services;
8. legal and consultancy services unrelated to the audit.

PROCEDURES REGARDING RELATED PARTIES' TRANSACTIONS, HANDLING OF CONFIDENTIAL INFORMATION, INSIDER DEALING AND RELATIONS WITH INSTITUTIONAL INVESTORS AND OTHER SHAREHOLDERS

Telecom Italia has adopted special procedures in order to deal with issues of transaction with related parties, disclosure and handling of confidential information, insider dealing as well as relations with institutional investors and other shareholders.

Transactions with Related Parties

The Preda Code (1999, 2002, para. 11) recommends that transactions with related parties[11] should be treated according to criteria of 'substantial' and 'procedural' fairness. Companies are recommended to set up a procedure to deal with these transactions.

In its corporate governance report, Telecom Italia claims to have adopted a series of guidelines (see Telecom Italia S.p.A. 2003d) on how transactions with related parties are to be carried out in order to ensure both procedural and substantial fairness as well as transparency. Such transactions, including intra-group transactions (apart from those of a customary nature to be concluded at 'arm's length conditions'), need to be approved in advance by the board of directors. Provision is made for the board of directors to be adequately informed of all the relevant aspects, such as the nature of the relationship, the manner and conditions of carrying out the transaction, the evaluation procedures used, the rationale for the transaction and the company's interest in its implementation as well as its associated risks. Furthermore, if the related party is a director or a third party that is related via a director, the director may only provide clarification and must leave the meeting when the motion is examined and put to a vote.

According to the characteristics of the related-party transaction, the board of directors may require the assistance of experts, engaged to give an opinion on its economic clauses and/or legitimacy and/or technical aspects, in order to prevent such a transaction being concluded in inappropriate conditions. Experts are required to have adequate professional experience and qualifications in the field in question as well as independence and absence of conflicts of interests.

Disclosure and Handling of Confidential Information

The Preda Code (1999, 2002, para. 6) recommends companies adopt procedures for the internal handling and disclosure of price-sensitive information as well as information concerning transactions that involve financial instruments carried out by persons who have access to relevant information.

Telecom Italia complies with such recommendation: confidential information is managed by the director appointed for the purpose (currently the Chairperson) on the basis of procedures for the internal handling and disclosure to third parties of documents and information concerning the company, with special reference to price-sensitive information.

A procedure establishes the ways in which price-sensitive information is to be communicated to the market, identifies the corporate units involved and sets up guidelines for the action to be taken in the presence of rumours and in response to requests for information from CONSOB and the Italian Stock Exchange. Guidelines for meetings with the financial community and the press are provided, in order to ensure that information is not disclosed selectively.

A disclosure committee has also been established to provide assistance to the board of directors and senior management concerning the processing and handling of data and news necessary for the correct provision of information. In particular, the main tasks of the committee are:

1. to assist the board of directors in the preparation of corporate communications, the top management in the certification of the annual report in accordance with the Sarbanes-Oxley Act, and the director appointed to handle price-sensitive information;
2. to ensure that corporate communications are prepared correctly with a view to their approval by the competent body;
3. to monitor the application of the procedures and controls for the collection, analysis and retention of data and information for publication and filing, verify their adequacy and effectiveness and, if necessary, propose corrective measures;
4. to verify the correct application and need for updating of the 'Procedure for communicating price-sensitive information' and suggest improvements where appropriate;
5. to supervise the structure and updating of the company's website as regards its institutional contents.

The disclosure committee comprises the Chairperson and the General Counsel of the board of directors, the finance administration and control officers, the corporate and legal affairs officers and the corporate development and investor relations officers.

Code of Conduct for Insider Dealing

Telecom Italia has established a code of conduct for insider dealing which provides guidelines for the disclosure requirements and rules applicable to transactions involving financial instruments carried out by persons who, as a consequence of their position in the company, have access to information able to produce significant changes in the outlook for the profitability, financial position and/or balance sheet of the company (and the group) and likely, if made public, to have a significant effect on the share price.

In the event of non-compliance, when the offender is a member of the board of directors or a statutory auditor, the board of directors may propose the revocation of his/her appointment to the next shareholders' meeting.

Relations with Institutional Investors and Other Shareholders

The Preda Code (1999, 2002, para. 12) recommends companies designate a person or create a corporate structure to be responsible for relations with institutional investors and other shareholders. At Telecom Italia a corporate unit, headed by a managing director, is responsible for handling relations with the financial community in Italy and abroad. For private (retail) investors a toll-free number is provided. In addition, all corporate governance documents and other financial information are posted on the company website (section on investor relations), available in Italian and English language.

CONCLUSIONS

Corporate governance in Italy often concerns issues related to 'weak' managers, 'strong' blockholders and unprotected minority shareholders, with the latter in the role of potential victims of abuse of power of the controlling shareholder(s).

Telecom Italia, one of the largest Italian companies, listed on both the Italian Stock Exchange and the NYSE, has offered some examples of how minority shareholders may face difficulties in having their interest safeguarded. After a short period during which its ownership structure was widespread, its control structure has been characterized by a complex pyramidal group of companies controlled by a strong blockholder via some shareholders' agreements.

Since 2003, in order to be more competitive in capital markets, the controlling shareholders decided to reduce the chain of holding companies that control Telecom Italia by merging Olivetti with Telecom Italia. In

2005, the control chain is likely to be reduced further, as Telecom Italia has launched a plan to merge with Telecom Italia Mobile, its largest listed subsidiary. In addition, Telecom Italia's corporate governance structure has been modified in order to show the controlling shareholders' effort to foster minority shareholders' representation and protection.

Telecom Italia's corporate governance structure comprises a board of directors, a board of statutory auditors, three committees (internal control and corporate governance, remuneration, and disclosure) and an external auditor.

Within the board of directors, independent directors comprise the majority of the board's members. Furthermore, a 'slates' system allows minority shareholders to appoint one-fifth of the members of the board of directors.

The Chairperson and CEO positions are separated. However, the Chairperson, who is also one of the most important shareholders, is an executive director. This fact does not foster the division of roles between the Chairperson, who is supposed to run the board, and the CEO, who is supposed to run the company, but it is not against the recommendation of the Preda Code, since the powers delegated to the Chairperson are adequately disclosed in the corporate governance report.

While the disclosure committee is composed entirely of corporate insiders, both the internal control and corporate governance committee and the remuneration committee are composed of independent non-executive directors, with a good representation of directors appointed by minority shareholders.

The board of statutory auditors is composed of five financially literate members. Such a large size is rather uncommon among Italian listed companies and has a positive influence over the level of protection of minority shareholders, as only in a five-member board can minority shareholders appoint two statutory auditors.

In Italy external auditor rotation is mandatory. In addition to the law, Telecom Italia has set up a specific procedure for the appointment of external auditors which provides that the auditor of Telecom Italia is the principal auditor of the entire group. In order to foster auditors' independence, most non-audit services are generally forbidden for the auditor.

KEY LEARNING POINTS

The case study presented is of particular relevance with regard to how corporate governance issues are handled in a major Italian listed company which aims to be considered as an example of corporate governance best practice by capital markets. In particular, the case study points out that:

1. corporate governance in Italy is often characterized by issues related to strong controlling shareholders (also known as blockholders) and unprotected minority shareholders;
2. after its privatization in 1997, Telecom Italia offered some examples of how minority shareholders may face difficulties in the safeguarding of their interests, since its corporate governance structure allowed controlling shareholders to pursue their own interests at the expense of those of the minority shareholders.

The case study describes how since 2003 Telecom Italia's controlling shareholders have implemented the corporate governance structure and have simplified and reduced the long control chain to allow them to effectively control Telecom Italia and its subsidiaries with a limited amount of resources.

The case highlights that the main purpose of the above-mentioned actions was to build a strong corporate reputation with regard to minority shareholders' representation and protection in order to be more competitive in capital markets.

Taking into account the prevailing Italian corporate governance framework, the case provides an opportunity for an in-depth discussion about the key elements of Telecom Italia's corporate governance structure, which should reduce the agency problem between controlling and minority shareholders.

QUESTIONS

The following questions are worth discussing regarding Telecom Italia's attempt to be considered an example of Italian best practice in corporate governance issues:

1. To what extent is Telecom Italia's corporate governance structure adequate to foster minority shareholders' representation and protection?
2. Which are the main pros (and cons) of having institutional investors, with a relatively small amount of shares in the company, appoint their representatives to corporate boards?
3. To what extent may a corporate governance structure that improves minority shareholders' representation on boards reduce the agency problem between controlling and minority shareholders?

4. How does Telecom Italia's corporate governance structure differ from the prevailing Anglo-American corporate governance structures? Why?

NOTES

1. MIB30 is the Italian equity share market segment that includes companies with a capitalization above €800 million.
2. Leveraged buy-outs are takeovers in which the buyer borrows money and uses the target company's own cash flow to pay it back. See Jensen (1989).
3. Mr Roberto Colaninno was Olivetti's and Telecom Italia's CEO, as well as one of the controlling shareholders of Olivetti.
4. Pyramidal groups have been defined as 'organisations where legally independent firms are controlled by the same entrepreneur (the head of the group) through a chain of ownership relations' (Bianco and Casavola 1999, p. 1059). In these groups the holding company controls (directly or indirectly) the majority of voting rights of the companies which belong to the group and its ultimate control is either by a single entrepreneur, or a family or a coalition. This device is generally used to maximize the ratio between the amount of the resources controlled and the own capital invested to maintain the control. Their underlying concept is that company A owns a controlling stake in company B, which in turn owns a controlling stake in company C. Company A is still able to maintain control of C even though its direct stake in C is small.
5. Under Italy's takeover law an investor acquiring less than 30 per cent of the equity of a company is not legally obliged to make a full offer for all the company's shares.
6. The principle of 'one share one vote' is not adopted by Italian law. The only limitation to the issue of non-voting shares is that their total par value cannot be higher than the total par value of voting shares. By issuing non-voting shares listed companies may pursue two objectives at the same time. First, they have an alternative source for corporate funding, second, this source is risk-free for the management and control of the company, since it has no voting right, i.e. it is also effective to concentrate control in the hands of the blockholder.
7. The Preda Code (2002, para. 3) defines as independent a director who meets the following criteria: (a) s/he does not entertain, directly, indirectly or on behalf of third parties, nor has s/he recently entertained, with the company, its subsidiaries, the executive directors or the shareholder or group of shareholders who control the company, business relationships of a significance able to influence their autonomous judgement; (b) s/he does not own, directly or indirectly, or on behalf of third parties, a quantity of shares enabling them to control or notably influence the company or participate in shareholders' agreements to control the company; (c) s/he is not close family of executive directors of the company or person who is in the situations referred to in the above paragraphs.
8. When referring to Parmalat, the company taken into consideration is Parmalat Finanziaria S.p.A., Parmalat group's listed company.
9. Although the Preda Code (2002, para. 14) recommends that statutory auditors should be independent, act exclusively to pursue the interests of the company, rather than as stewards of the blockholder (or that specific group of shareholders that appointed them), statutory auditors might in fact have an incentive to maintain a link with the specific shareholders that enable their appointment, in order to be re-appointed (Melis 2004).
10. Telecom Italia's by-laws include the following subjects: telecommunications, information technology, online systems, electronics and multimedia technology, and subjects related to private and administrative law, economics and business administration.
11. See IAS 24 (IASB 2003) for a definition of 'transaction with related parties'.

REFERENCES

Amatori, F. and A. Colli (2000), 'Corporate governance: the Italian story', Bocconi University working paper, December.

Bianchi, M. and L. Enriques (2001), 'Corporate governance in Italy after the 1998 reform: what role for institutional investors', *CONSOB Quaderni di Finanza*, **43**, available at http://www.consob.it.

Bianchi, M., M. Bianco and L. Enriques (2001), 'Pyramidal groups and the separation between ownership and control in Italy', in F. Barca and M. Becht (eds), *The Control of Corporate Europe*, Oxford, UK: Oxford University Press, pp. 154–87.

Bianco, M. and P. Casavola (1999), 'Italian corporate governance: effects on financial structure and firm performance', *European Economic Review*, **43**(4), 1057–69.

Cadbury, A. (1999), 'What are the trends in corporate governance? How will they impact your company?', *Long Range Planning*, **32**(1), 12–19.

Cadbury Report (1992), *The Financial Aspects of Corporate Governance*, London, UK: Gee.

Cavallari, A., E. Goos, F. Laorenti and M. Sivori (2003), 'Corporate governance in the Italian listed companies', Milan, Italy: Borsa Italiana, available at http://www.borsaitalia.it.

CONSOB (2002), *Relazione Annuale 2001*, Rome, Italy: CONSOB.

Draghi Reform (1998), 'Testo unico delle disposizioni in materia di intermediazione finanziaria', Legislative decree N. 58/1998.

Financial Times (2000), 'Telecom Italia', 24 May.

Frankel, R., M. Johnson and K. Nelson (2002), 'The relation between auditor's fees for non-audit services and earnings management', *The Accounting Review*, **77**(Supplement), 71–105.

Franks, J. and C. Mayer (1995), 'Ownership and control', in H. Siebert (ed.), *Trends in Business Organization: Do Participation and Cooperation Improve Competitiveness?*, Tubingen, Germany: Mohr.

IASB (2003), *International Financial Reporting Standards – IAS 24 Related Parties Disclosures*, London, UK: IASCF.

Jensen, M. (1989), 'The eclipse of the public corporation', *Harvard Business Review*, **67**(5), 61–74.

La Porta, R., F. Lopez-de-Silanes and A. Shleifer (1999), 'Corporate ownership around the world', *Journal of Finance*, **54**(2), 471–517.

La Porta, R., F. Lopez-de-Sinales, A. Shleifer and R. Vishny (2000), 'Investor protection and corporate governance', *Journal of Financial Economics*, **58**(1), 3–27.

Melis, A. (1999), *Corporate governance. Un'analisi empirica della realtà italiana in un'ottica europea*, Turin, Italy: Giappichelli.

Melis, A. (2000), 'Corporate governance in Italy', *Corporate Governance – An International Review*, **8**(4), 347–55.

Melis, A. (2002), *Creazione di valore e meccanismi di corporate governance*, Milan, Italy: Giuffré.

Melis, A. (2004), 'On the role of the board of statutory auditors in Italian listed companies', *Corporate Governance – An International Review*, **12**(1), 74–84.

Melis, A. (2005), 'Corporate governance failures: to what extent is Parmalat a particularly Italian case?', *Corporate Governance – An International Review*, **13**(4), 478–88.

Molteni, M. (ed.) (1997), *I sistemi di corporate governance nelle grandi imprese italiane*, Milan, Italy: EGEA.

Pagano, M., F. Panetta and L. Zingales (1998), 'Why do companies go public? An empirical analysis', *Journal of Finance*, **53**(1), 27–64.

Preda Code (1999, 2002), *Code of Conduct*, Milan, Italy: Borsa Italiana.

Roe, M. (1994), *Strong Managers, Weak Owners. The Political Roots of American Corporate Finance*, Princeton, US: Princeton University Press.

Telecom Italia S.p.A. (2001) 'Informativa sul sistema di Corporate Governance ai sensi della sezione IA.2.12 delle istruzioni al Regolamento di Borsa Italiana S.p.A.' (Report on Corporate governance).

Telecom Italia S.p.A. (2002), 'Informativa sul sistema di Corporate Governance ai sensi della sezione IA.2.12 delle istruzioni al Regolamento di Borsa Italiana S.p.A.' (Report on Corporate governance).

Telecom Italia S.p.A. (2003a), 'Informativa sul sistema di Corporate Governance ai sensi della sezione IA.2.12 delle istruzioni al Regolamento di Borsa Italiana S.p.A.' (Report on Corporate governance).

Telecom Italia S.p.A. (2003b), 'Self regulatory code', October.

Telecom Italia S.p.A. (2003c), 'Group procedure for the appointment of auditors', October.

Telecom Italia S.p.A. (2003d), 'Rules of conduct for effecting transactions with related parties', October.

Telecom Italia S.p.A. (2004a), 'Form 20-F', available at http://www.sec.gov.

Telecom Italia S.p.A. (2004b), 'Informativa sul sistema di Corporate Governance ai sensi della sezione IA.2.12 delle istruzioni al Regolamento di Borsa Italiana S.p.A.' (Report on Corporate governance).

Telecom Italia S.p.A. (2004c), 'Corporate by-laws', July.

Zingales, L. (1994), 'The value of the voting right: a study of the Milan Stock Exchange experience', *The Review of Financial Studies*, **7**(1), 125–48.

USEFUL WEBSITES (WITH AN ENGLISH VERSION)

La Borsa Italiana – Italian Stock Exchange, http://www.borsaitalia.it
CONSOB – Italian Stock Exchange Commission, http://www.consob.it
Telecom Italia S.p.A., http://www.telecomitalia.it

4. Indra: the history of a successful privatization

Silvia Gómez Ansón and Jaime Bonet Madurga

INTRODUCTION

Indra Sistemas, SA is the leading Spanish information technologies and defence systems company, with revenues in 2003 of 987 million euros and a market value of 1859 million euros in December 2004. It is one of the 35 largest quoted Spanish companies. Its shares are quoted on the four Spanish Stock Exchanges: Madrid, Barcelona, Bilbao and Valencia, and its ordinary shares have been quoted on the Spanish Electronic or Continuous Market since March 1999. The company has also been included in the selective Ibex-35 Index since 1999 and is a member of the 'New Market' segment of the Spanish Stock Market. Among the international indices the company is included in the FTSE e-TX Index and the Dow Jones Global Index.

The company is one of the firms with a higher corporate reputation in Spain. In 2004 the company received the 'First Award for the Ibex-35 company with the best Corporate Governance and Information Transparency Practices', granted by the Foundation of Financial Studies ('Fundación de Estudios Financieros'), a foundation of the Spanish Institute of Financial Analysts, and the Recoletos Communication Group. Indra also ranks among the top three Ibex-35 companies with superior website-base shareholder information, according to a report from the IESE Business School Minority Shareholders' Forum, and it has been granted the 'Award for Innovation for Human Resources' by Expansion y Empleo for its HR management process re-engineering project. The company also obtained the Award 'Best IR by a company listed on one of the Eurozone's growth company markets' granted by the *Investor Relations* magazine in 2003 and was highly commended in 2004. In 2003 it was also highly commended by the same awards for the use of the Internet for investor relations.

Indra represents not only an example of a well-governed company in a civil law country context, but also of a successful privatization,[1] as it was one of the companies that was privatized in Spain during the last two decades of the twentieth century. These two characteristics determined the election of this company for a case study of corporate governance in Spain. Since its full privatization in 1999, the company started implementing proper corporate governance practices and publishing an annual Corporate Governance Report, in compliance with the recommendations of the Spanish Codes of Best Practices. The company's corporate governance is regulated by its by-laws, the General Shareholders' Meeting Regulations, the Board of Directors Regulations and the Internal Code of Conduct for Matters Relating to Security Markets. The board of the company represents, to a large degree, its ownership structure, which is a consequence of its privatization. In addition, the company has established three specialized committees and the board has started evaluating annually the quality and efficiency of its activities and those of the committees. Indra has also shown during recent years a strong commitment to transparency of information, a commitment that has been recognized by different organizations. Its commitment to proper corporate governance may help explain the post-privatization increases in profitability and efficiency that Indra has experienced.

SPAIN'S INSTITUTIONAL SETTING

Spain is a French civil-law country, with an average GNP among Western economies and a considerable number of medium-size companies quoted on the Stock Exchange. Studies by La Porta *et al.* (1997, 1998, 1999) suggest that firms in countries of French civil-law origin offer less protection to shareholders and creditors. Higher ownership concentration would be expected in these countries, and this is indeed the case for listed companies in Spain. According to La Porta *et al.* (1999), whilst the three largest shareholders hold 50 per cent of firms' shares in Spain, this figure stands at just 20 per cent in the USA, the UK and Japan. The proportion of firms with no controlling shareholder (i.e. a shareholder whose voting rights exceed 20 per cent) is 35 per cent for large listed companies and zero for medium-size listed companies in Spain, whereas levels for the USA stand at 80 per cent and 90 per cent respectively. The results of the studies by Crespí-Cladera and García-Cestona (2001) and Faccio and Lang (2002) reinforce these figures. For instance, the latter authors document that, for the whole sample of companies listed on the Spanish Stock Market, widely held companies amount to only 10 per cent when a 10 per cent of ownership is used as the threshold. According to Sacristan and Gómez Ansón (2004), in non-widely held companies, the main largest shareholder is a family group, followed by non-financial companies. Moreover, pyramids are quite frequent, as families tend to use indirect ownership and pyramids to channel their investments.

Actually, pyramids are present in quite a large proportion of the quoted firms, around 30 per cent, and there exists a significant deviation between cash flow rights and voting rights (38.88 per cent of the cash flow rights generated by the firms, versus 41.96 of the firms' voting rights). For instance, La Porta *et al.* (1999) calculate that pyramids exist in 38 per cent of Spanish firms, which contrasts starkly with the equivalent percentage in the USA, which stands at zero.

Although theoretical arguments would suggest that the issuance of dual class shares could be expected to be quite common in Spain, their use has, in fact, been limited (Faccio and Lang 2002; Corona 2002), even though they have been allowed under Spanish law since 1990. Cross-shareholdings which constitute another source of deviation from the 'one share, one vote' principle are also not as frequent in Spain, failing to reach the 10 per cent mark (Sacristan and Gómez Ansón 2004).

In Spain the first Code of Best Practice, the Olivencia Report, was issued in 1998 and was written by a mandate of the Ministry of Economy. It sets 23 recommendations that refer mainly to the structure of boards of directors: the board should be formed by a majority of non-executive directors; specialized committees, for example, auditing, remuneration or appointment committees, which should be made up of non-executive directors, should be set up; directors' pay details need to be disclosed; the board's size should be between 5 and 15 directors and a retirement age for directors should be established. The Olivencia Code also recommended that quoted companies should publish annually a voluntary Corporate Governance Report, following the Cadbury Code's philosophy of 'comply or explain'. The success of the Olivencia Report was limited. According to the results of questionnaires by the Spanish Supervisory Agency, in 2000 the mean compliance rate with the Code recommendations was 81 per cent among the 61 firms that answered the questionnaire, and 77 per cent in 2001 for the 67 firms that answered the questionnaire. Only two firms complied with all recommendations in 2000, and five in 2001. The questionnaires also revealed a relatively low degree of compliance with the 'comply or explain' rule, as a large number of quoted companies did not publish a Corporate Governance Report.

Following the recent corporate scandals and the Winter Report, the Ministry of Economy established in 2002 another committee that was to issue a second Code of Best Practice. The Aldama Report was published in January 2003. Its recommendations were similar to those of the Olivencia Report, but it emphasized the need to regulate the information provided by the companies to the market, in particular, the need to regulate the corporate governance information that should be released by quoted companies, both in the annual Corporate Governance Report and on the companies' web pages.

The Aldama Report coincided with a period of legislative reforms in Spain. At the end of 2002, the Law of Reform of the Financial System (Law 44/2002) established the obligation for quoted companies to set up an audit committee composed by a majority of non-executive directors. In July 2003, following the conclusions and recommendations of the Aldama Report, a law named the Transparency Law (Law 26/2003) reformed the Company Law and established the obligation to publish and file at the Spanish Supervisory Board an Internal Code of Conduct, a Rule of the Board of Directors and a Rule of the Shareholders' Meetings. The law also established the need to publish from 2004 onwards a compulsory annual Corporate Governance Report and to disclose corporate governance information in the company's web page. This law was further developed by a Rule of the Ministry of Economy (Orden ECO/3722/2003) and by a Directive of the Spanish Supervisory Agency (Circular 1/2004). This directive established the corporate governance information that companies should disclose both in the Annual Corporate Governance Report and on the web page. As a consequence of these legislative reforms, a significant number of quoted companies reformed their by-laws in 2003 and 2004, and transparency of information by quoted companies increased significantly.

THE SPANISH PRIVATIZATION PROCESS

Until the active privatization programme undertaken during the latter part of the twentieth century, the State in Spain had played an active role in the economy, whereas nowadays State ownership is almost negligible. Actually, State participation in the Spanish Stock Market decreased to 0.43 per cent in 2002. According to the OECD (2003), the privatization programme in Spain raised US$38 401 million between 1990 and 2001, thereby ranking Spain fourth, after the UK, France and Italy, among the 15 long-standing EU countries in terms of revenues from privatizations. The State's participation as a shareholder in the Spanish Stock Market consequently declined significantly. At the beginning of the 1990s the State held 16.64 per cent of Spanish stock market shares; in 1996 this figure fell to 10.87 per cent, then to 5.56 per cent in 1997, reaching just 0.58 per cent in 1998, after which it has remained almost constant (CCP 2003). The privatization of State-owned enterprises (SOEs) in Spain has been part of the process of economic restructuring founded upon liberalization and deregulation in the financial sector and key product markets. The privatization of SOEs started in the 1980s as a response to the economic crisis of the late 1970s and early 1980s, when there were high levels of inflation, interest rates and unemployment. There was a need to adjust the Spanish industry to the new economic environment being ushered in by Spain joining the European Community in 1986 and as a reaction to the opening-up of international markets (Cabeza and Gómez 2004). The process, which has been pushed along by Socialist and Conservative governments alike, between 1985–1996 and 1996–2003, respectively, has still not ended.

Between 1985, the starting point of the privatization process, and 2003, 131 State-owned companies were privatized in Spain. However, not all these State-owned companies were totally privatized; with the State retaining a percentage of the firms' capital some firms were only partially sold, and others were privatized in stages, as was the case of Indra Sistemas, SA. The methods of privatization used were mainly direct sales and public offerings, although in some cases auctioning was used (Cabeza and Gómez 2004). Overall, between 1985 and 2003, 14 firms were privatized through public offerings (18.12 per cent of the privatization processes). These public offerings, which were made with an underpricing of 11.70 per cent (Alvarez Otero 2000),[2] created a 'popular capitalism' in the stock market, increasing considerably the shareholdings held by individuals and families, from 24.44 per cent in 1992 to 28.31 per cent in 2002. The privatization process also helped enlarge the Spanish stock market. The Madrid stock exchange capitalization was 49 679.61 million euros in 1990. In 1995 it rose to 99 689.59 million euros and in the first semester of 2004 to 311 550.85 million euros. By June 2004, the market capitalization of companies privatized by public offerings during the last decade was 168 347.085 million euros, 56 per cent of the market capitalization of the firms that made up the Ibex-35 Index, and 54 per cent of the market capitalization of the Madrid Stock Exchange General Index.

Although the finance and economics literature suggests that privatization may increase firms' efficiency and different empirical studies, at the international level, support this prediction (Barberis *et al.* 1996; La Porta *et al.* 1997; D'Souza and Megginson 1999), the empirical evidence for the case of Spain is not conclusive. As reported by Cabeza and Gómez (2004), longitudinal studies for the Spanish market do not uncover significant evidence supporting an increase in the performance of privatized firms; nor do results of case studies point to the enhanced efficiency of privatized firms compared to their competitors.

HISTORY OF THE COMPANY

Indra's origins date back to the first quarter of the twentieth century, to the year 1921, when the first of the companies that would eventually form what is now Indra started its operation. Between 1986 and 1992 the company underwent a process of business restructuring and concentration that culminated in December 1992 with the merger of CESEL, SA and INISEL. By that time the company was a State-owned company. In 1995, the first privatization of the company took place. It was a partial privatization, as only 24.9 per cent of the company was sold to a foreign company, Thomson CSF. In 1998, the Spanish State Holding (SEPI) and Thomson CSF reached an agreement by which Thomson CSF reduced its participation in Indra from 24.99 per cent to 10.5 per cent, allowing the entrance of Spanish institutional investors. At the same time Thomson CSF was recognized as an industrial 'partner' and a collaboration agreement that aimed to optimize the cooperation between both companies was signed. In February 1999, the Spanish savings bank Caja Madrid and the Spanish bank Banco Zaragozano bought, respectively, 10.5 per cent and 3.9 per cent of Indra, consequently reducing Thomson CSF's stake to 10.5 per cent. Afterwards, in March 1999, the company underwent the major and definite privatization of a 66.09 per cent stake owned by the Spanish State through the State Holding SEPI. This second and final privatization of the company was made by means of a public offering.

Indra Sistemas, SA was one of 131 State-owned companies that were privatized in Spain between 1985 and 2003. As with many other SOEs it was privatized in different stages or phases, and the method of privatization combined the direct sale to a specialized firm (a partial sale of 24.9 per cent of the company to Thomson CSF in the first phase in 1995) and a public offering (in 1999). Prior to the first privatization, the company underwent a process of mergers that culminated in December 1992 with the merger between the two major companies, and business restructuring and reordering, implementing internal adjustments from 1986 up to 1995. With the know-how of its new stockholder, Thomson CSF, Indra focused on driving its process of consolidation and growth, strengthening its position in the Spanish market and opening other markets. In 1999, as with many of the other 'crown jewels' of the Spanish State, Indra was completely sold by a public offering and began quoting in the Stock Market. As happened with six more SOEs that were privatized through public offerings, the State retained at the time of privatization a 'golden share'.[3] Nowadays, Indra represents one of the privatized SOEs that helped enlarge the Spanish Stock Market, forming part of the selective Ibex-35 Index.

Indra Sistemas, SA represents an example of a successful privatization, with significant increases in profitability and efficiency. Figure 4.1 shows the evolution of the firm's profitability, measured by the ratio return on assets, over the pre- and post-privatization period, 1991–2002. The raw ROA ratio begins to be positive in the year before the first privatization (1994), coinciding with the end of the period of business restructuring, reordering of the businesses and implementation of internal adjustments. The evolution of profitability continued to be positive from that year onwards, reaching a peak the year before the second stage of the privatization, 1998. Nevertheless, we must note that just looking at the evolution of the raw ROA ratio could be misleading. Most of the Spanish State 'crown-jewels' were privatized at periods of economic growth, and that was also the case for Indra. Figure 4.1 also shows the evolution of the industry-adjusted ROA ratio. Again we observe a post-privatization positive evolution of this ratio, but for the year 1997. The positive figures reach the highest mark the year after the first privatization, 1996, while the second highest figure is shown by the year of the second privatization, 1999. Overall, while over the three years prior to the first privatization, from 1991 to 1994, the mean industry adjusted ROA was negative (–0.08), both over the three years after the first stage of the privatization, from 1996 to 1998, and over the three years after the second stage of the privatization, from 2000 to 2002, the mean industry-adjusted ROA ratios were positive, 0.02 and 0.01 respectively.

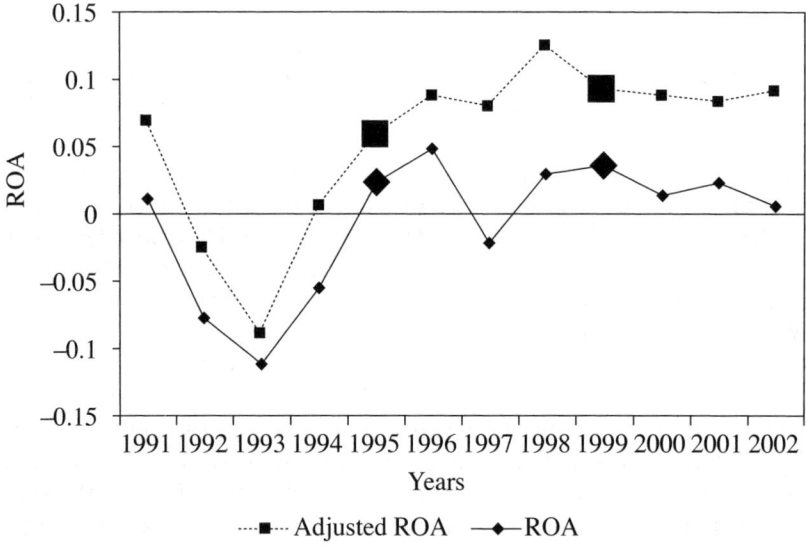

Figure 4.1   Evolution of profitability

Figure 4.2 shows the evolution of Indra's efficiency, in terms of sales efficiency, real sales per employee over the period 1990–2003. The firm's efficiency started increasing from the period of business restructuring before the stage of privatization and has not stopped increasing since then. Actually, while the mean sales over employees ratio amounted over the three years before the first stage of the privatization process to 0.05, it doubled in the three years following the first stage of the privatization (1996–1998) to 0.11, and it more than doubled over the three years after the second stage of the privatization process, 2000–2002, to 0.13. Although not shown, investment also increased significantly over the post-privatization years, with a mean ratio of increase of 11 per cent over the years 1996–2003. The post-privatization increases in profitability and efficiency have resulted in significant positive adjusted stock market returns (Figure 4.3).

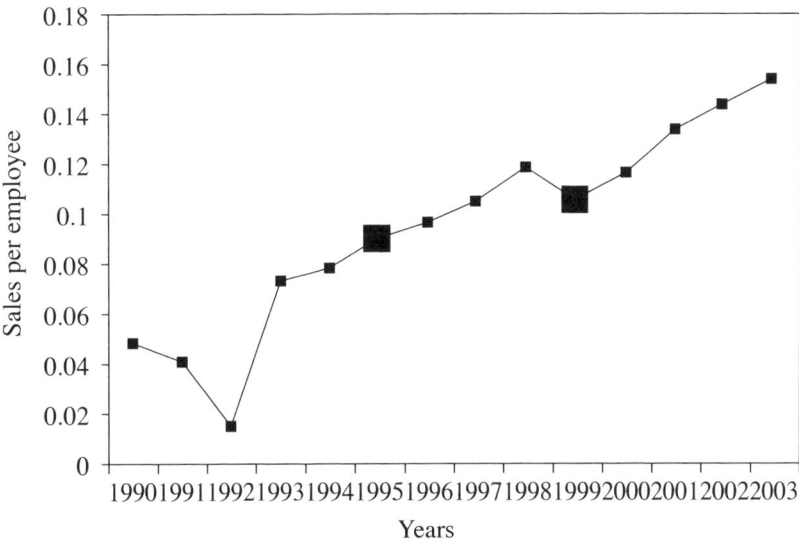

Figure 4.2   Evolution of efficiency

Although privatization does not automatically mean employment reductions in divested firms (Megginson and Netter 2001), different empirical studies report a decrease in employment after privatization processes, for example in the former Mexican SOEs (La Porta *et al.* 1999), in the privatization of the Argentine national freight and passenger railway system (Ramamurti 1997), or at the international level (Boubakri *et al.* 2001). Contrariwise, for Indra, the increase in efficiency and profitability was accompanied by a significant increase in employment, as shown in Figure 4.4. The increase in employment took place in the years before the first stage of the privatization process, and specially the years before and after the second stage of the privatization process. This increase in employment was possible because of the sharp and fast increase in sales

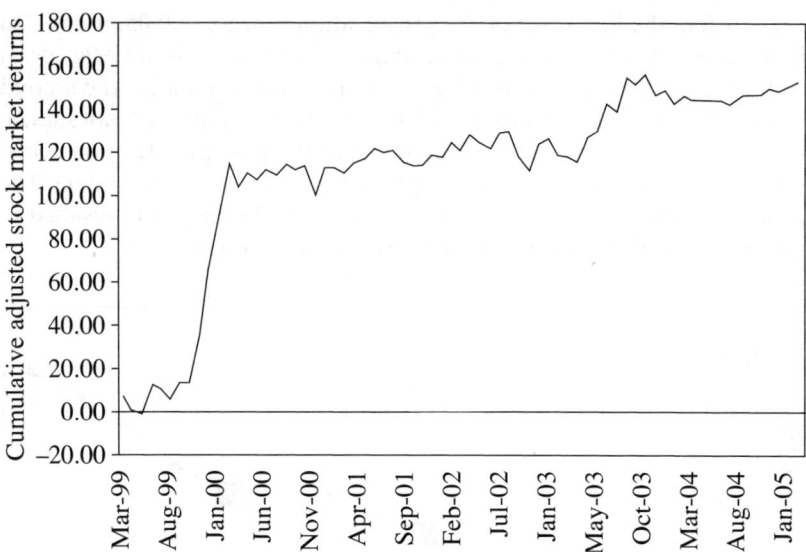

Figure 4.3   Adjusted stock market returns

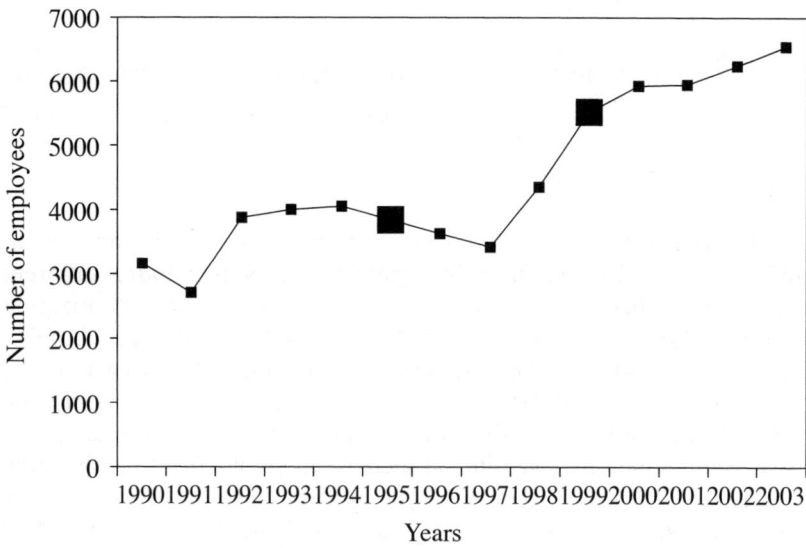

Figure 4.4   Evolution of employment

that the firm experienced after divestiture and was a consequence of the investment policy of the company.

Firms that move from public to private ownership are also expected to decrease their leverage because with the removal of government debt guarantees, the firms' borrowing costs will increase, and because newly privatized firms should have enhanced their access to public equity markets (Megginson *et al.* 1994). Indra's privatization process fits with this prediction, as the divestment of the firm was accompanied by a significant decrease in leverage. The sharp decline in debt was especially significant for the year of the first stage of the privatization process, 1995, and for the years after. Actually, compared to the leverage ratio over the three years prior to the first privatization, 1992–1994, a mean value of 96.37 per cent, in 2003, the ratio debt over assets amounted to 70.4 per cent, showing a decline of more that 25 per cent (see Figure 4.5).

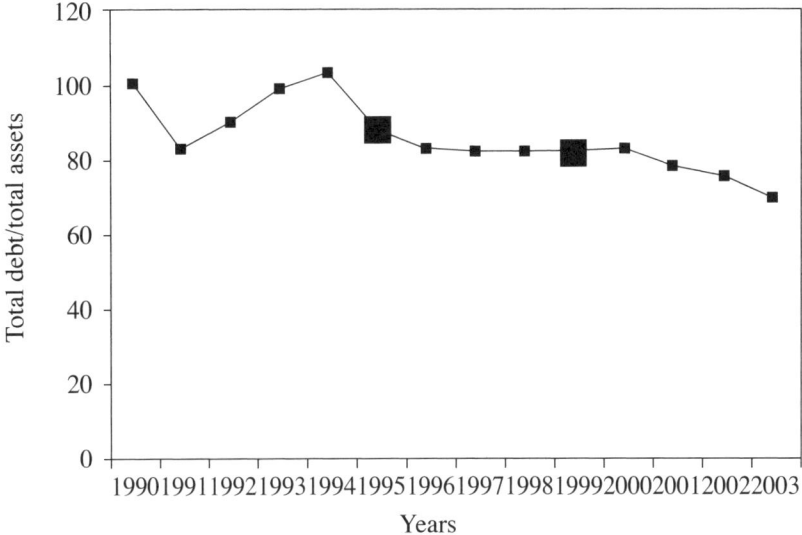

Figure 4.5   Evolution of leverage

The new economic situation of the firm after privatization allowed it to start paying dividends in 1996, the year after the first privatization took place. Since then, as shown in Figure 4.6, gross dividends have increased steadily, except in 1999, the year of the public offering. During the last years the increases in dividends have surpassed 25 per cent.

The case of Indra supports the finance and economics literature that suggests that privatization may increase firms' efficiency, and is in accordance

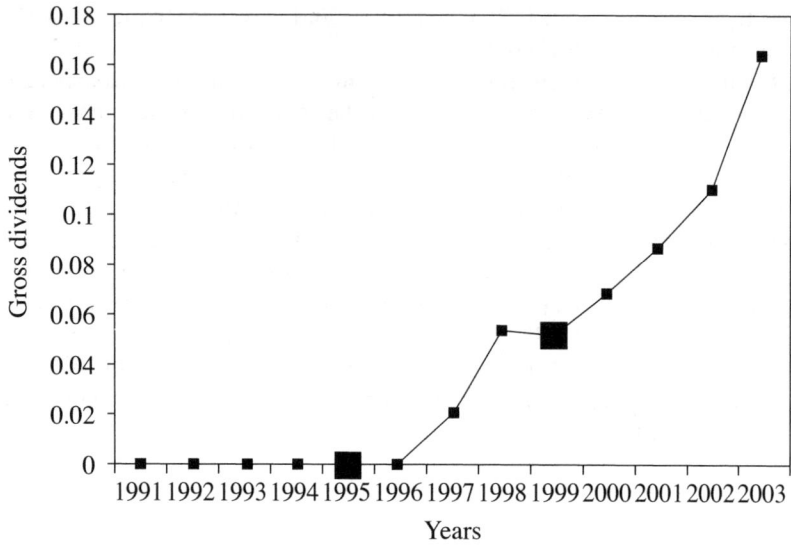

Figure 4.6   Evolution of dividends

with the empirical evidence reported by some international studies (Barberis *et al.* 1996; La Porta *et al.* 1997; D'Souza and Megginson 1999). Nevertheless, there are also studies, for example, those of Domberger (1993) and Martin and Parker (1995) for the UK, or Melle (1999) and Cabeza and Gómez (2004) for Spain, that do not find evidence of significant increases in firms' profitability and efficiency after divestment. For instance, for the Spanish case, Melle (1999) studied a sample of State-owned companies that were totally or partially sold by public offerings during the 1990s in Spain and reports no significant increase in the firms' performance after privatization. Cabeza and Gómez (2004) also fail to corroborate any post-privatization increase in efficiency or profitability for a large sample of firms privatized in Spain, once the firm's industry's performance is taken account of.

Consequently, Indra Sistemas, SA can be considered an example of a successful privatization within the Spanish context. The underlying reasons for its performance improvements may derive, as in privatization processes in general, from the pressure of financial markets on managers and the monitoring and discipline of profit-oriented investors, the possible use of performance-based compensation programmes, the redefinition of the firms' objectives, the managers' incentives and the new entrepreneurial opportunities opened to privatized firms (D'Souza *et al.* 2001). According to Shleifer and Vishny (1997), corporate governance is a crucial issue in privatization processes as it can explain the success or failure of a privatization programme. In support of this argument, Megginson *et al.* (1994) report important changes in the size and composition of the board of directors of privatized firms for a sample of privatized firms in 18 developing and industrialized countries. Boubakri *et al.* (2001) find that corporate governance mechanisms, in particular, controlling relinquishment by government, and foreign investors' involvement in the ownership structure of newly privatized firms, are the key determinants of profitability increases of privatized firms. Thus, we next analyse the corporate governance characteristics and structural changes of Indra after divestment and try to infer how these characteristics and changes may explain its success.

INDRA'S CORPORATE GOVERNANCE STRUCTURE

Indra's share capital amounts to 3 087 919 080 euros, represented by 154 395 954 shares with a face value of 0.20 euros. Of the total number of shares, 147 901 044 are ordinary shares (class A shares) and 6 494 910 are redeemable shares (class B, C and D shares). The redeemable shares were issued to provide coverage for option plans and all shares have the same rights. The company's largest blockholders are now: a Spanish savings bank, Caja Madrid, with a 10.03 per cent stake; Chase Nominees Ltd, which holds its 10.08 per cent stake on behalf of third parties; and Fidelity International Ltd, with 1.85 per cent. The treasury stock of the company amounted to 2.13 per cent by the beginning of 2005. Thus, the free-float amounted in January 2005 to 75.91 per cent (see Figure 4.7). Given this ownership structure the company presents, compared to the rest of the companies included in the selective Ibex-35 Index, a lower ownership concentration[4] and a higher degree of free-float. At present, there are no pacts or agreements among the company's shareholders involving an arrangement of their interests.

In Indra, internal ownership, that is, shareholdings held by the totality of directors, amount to 0.15 per cent, and that of executive directors to 0.08 per cent. These low figures are close to the percentage of shares held by directors in general, and specifically by executive directors, as a median, for the whole sample of Ibex-35 firms, 0.15 per cent and 0.02 per cent respectively.[5]

The company's ownership structure has evolved substantially since its first privatization. When the first stage of privatization took place, the company increased capital and incorporated a foreign company that also operated in the electronic defence sector, Thomson CSF, as a source for the foreign know-how.[6] By the time of the public offering in March 1999, which constituted the second stage of privatization, the State held 66.09 per cent of the company's shares, Thomson CSF had reduced its stake to 10.5 per cent, the savings bank Caja Madrid had a stake of 10.5 per cent and Banco

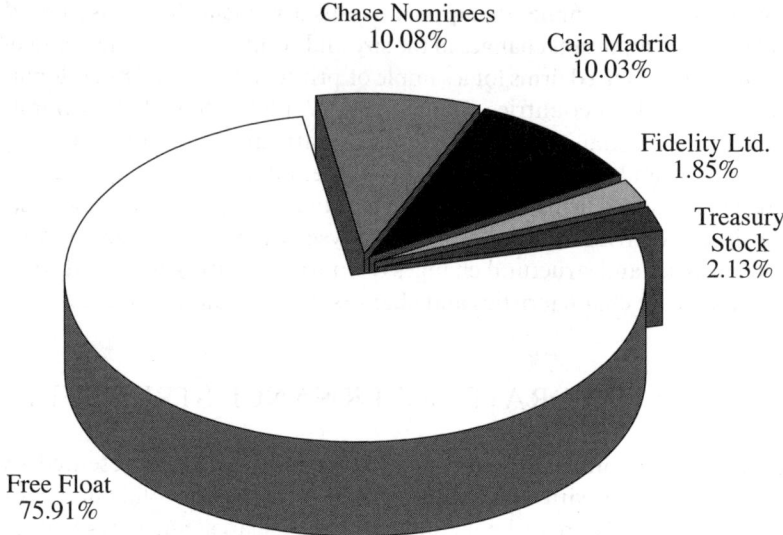

Figure 4.7   Indra Sistemas SA ownership structure

Zaragozano had a stake of 3.99 per cent. These last three private investors subscribed before the public offering to an agreement to form a stable group of shareholders for a period of at least three years after the public divestment of the firm. The agreement sought to give stability to the firm's ownership structure and a consensus that would allow stable management of the firm. The blockholders also agreed to nominate the directors and the management team, and included pacts over the general strategy of the company, its business plans and relevant transactions.

The share allocation of the public offering included four different fractions (see Figure 4.8): the small domestic investors' fraction (36.12 per cent of the offer), the employees' fraction (3.52 per cent of the offer), the Spanish institutional investors' fraction (20.98 per cent of the offer) and the international institutional investors' fraction (29.38 per cent of the offer), plus the 'green shoe'[7] (10 per cent). The design of this share issue privatization differed to some extent to the mean and median share issue privatizations worldwide, especially relative to the fraction of shares assigned to employees. According to the study of Jones *et al.* (1999), for a sample of 630 share issue privatizations executed by 59 national governments during the period 1977–1997, the percentage of the offer allocated to foreigners was, as a mean, 28.4 per cent (median value 11.5 per cent), while the percentage of the offer allocated to employees amounted to a mean value of 8.5, median value of 7.0.[8]

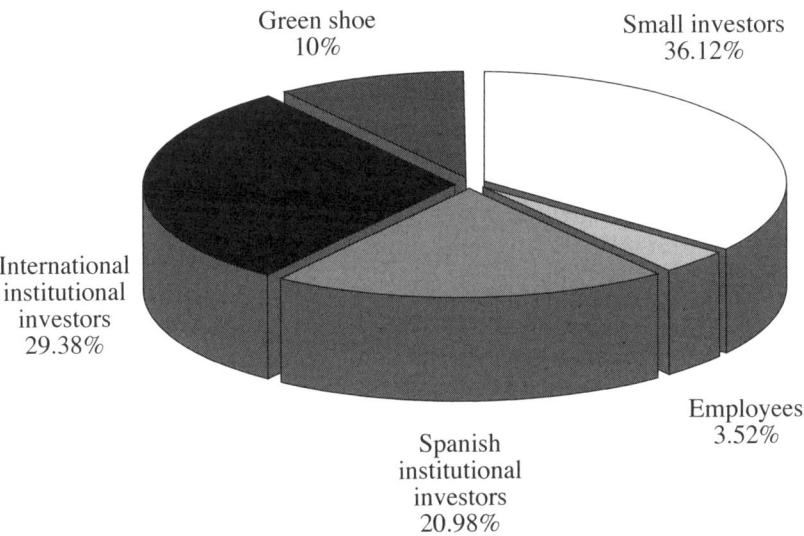

Green shoe
10%

Small investors
36.12%

International
institutional
investors
29.38%

Employees
3.52%

Spanish
institutional
investors
20.98%

Figure 4.8   IPO's share allocation

The form of the privatization process of the company regarding its ownership structure may also help explain its performance evolution. As different studies have reported, the presence of foreign investors, as in the first stage of the privatization process, may affect post-privatization performance positively (Smith *et al.* 1997). For the second stage of the privatization process, the public offering, the relinquishment of control by the State may help explain the efficiency gains. Actually, Boycko *et al.* (1996) predict efficiency gains from privatization only if control rights pass from the government to private investors. This was the case for Indra by the time of the public offering, except for the 'golden share' that the State retained until 2004 for the defence business of the company.[9]

Prior to the public offering of the company, its board of directors underwent a major restructuring. From a board formed by 17 directors and a Secretary and a Vice Secretary, the number of directors was reduced to 14, following the recommendations of the Olivencia Code that established the ideal board size between five and 15 directors. From the previous board, only two directors remained, the President of the company that had occupied the post of executive chair of the company since 1990, and the director named by the foreign blockholder, Thomson CSF. The new board of directors aimed to represent the new ownership structure of the company and was formed by two executive directors, five directors representing the major blockholders, two representing Caja Madrid, two Thomson CSF and one

Banco Zaragozano, and seven independent directors (see Figure 4.9). This restructuring of the board may help explain the increases in efficiency and profitability that the firm has experienced during the last few years. In this context, Barberis *et al.* (1996) cite new human capital as an important factor in increasing the probability of value-maximizing restructuring and D'Souza *et al.* (2001) report significant increases in efficiency for privatized firms with greater than 50 per cent changes or turnover in the board of directors, as was the case of Indra at the time of the public offering.

Recently, the structure of the board of directors of the company has not varied significantly, except the number of directors has decreased to 12 directors after the resignation of the directors that represented Banco Zaragozano, which divested in 2001, and Thales (formerly Thomson CSF), which divested in 2003. After privatization, one additional executive director was added to the board. The board size of 12 directors is slightly lower than the one shown by the mean Ibex-35 firm (FEF 2004), and close to the size reported, for example, by Barnhart *et al.* (1994) and Yermack (1996) for the US market. In January 2005 the board was formed by three executive directors and nine non-executive directors, seven of them being independent directors (see Figure 4.9). Consequently, the composition of the board of directors reflects to a large degree the firm's ownership structure. Although only a large shareholder is represented in the board, this is normal given that the other two major blockholders are depositors and institutional investors

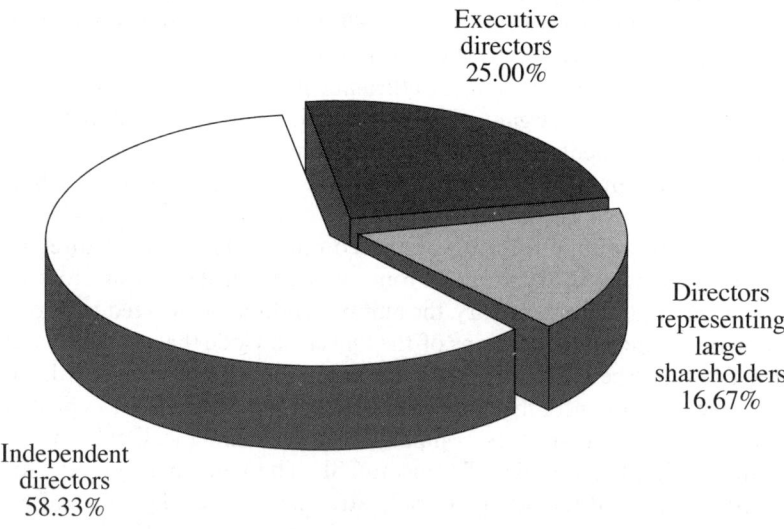

Figure 4.9 Indra Sistemas SA board of directors' composition

who usually do not participate in the board. Another positive aspect of the composition of the board is its lack of grey directors. Nevertheless, the percentage of executive directors is slightly higher than the percentage of this type of directors for the mean Ibex-35 firm (18 per cent).

Coinciding with the public offering and following the recommendations set up in the Olivencia Code in 1999, Indra approved a document containing the regulations of the board of directors and created three specialized committees within the board of directors: the executive committee, the audit and compliance committee[10] and the appointments and remuneration committee. The company presently maintains these same committees. The executive committee reasonably reflects the board's composition and is formed by two executive directors and five independent directors.[11] The appointments and remuneration committee are formed by three independent directors and one director representing the large blockholder Caja Madrid. The audit and compliance committee and the appointments and remuneration committee are chaired by an independent director and the audit and compliance committee publishes an activity report. The existence of these committees and their composition follows the recommendations of the Spanish Codes of Best Practice and can be considered a positive aspect of the firm's corporate governance structure since different authors and Codes of Best Practice suggest the positive influence of the existence of specialized committees within the board (Klein 1998; Kose and Lemma 1998).

Another aspect that the Codes of Best Practice frequently recommend is the separation of the posts of top executive of the company (CEO) and Chairman of the Board. In Spain, according to FEF (2004), a large number of the companies included in the Ibex-35 index have no separation (77 per cent). Similar figures are documented, also for Spain, by Faccio and Lang (2002). Indra is no exception in this sense: the Chairman of the Board is also the top executive of the company, but the firm has established a system by which the board, chaired by the Vice Chairman appointed from among the independent directors, annually evaluates the Chairman, without the latter being present.[12] It is also remarkable that the person that occupies the posts of top executive of the company and Chairman of the Board has not changed after the State's divestment and that the six managers that form the senior management of the company were already part of this body by the end of 1995. Five of them were also part of the senior management of the company before the first privatization took place in 1994. This evidence contradicts the theoretical arguments in favour of the change of the divested firm's upper management in order to maximize efficiency gains from privatization.[13] The company presents a high stability of its senior management team over more than a decade.

The remuneration of a firm's managerial team may also significantly influence its performance (Mehran 1995). Indra's company by-laws establish that the remuneration of the board should consist of a fixed amount, whose maximum amount is determined annually by the General Shareholders' Meeting and a stake in the company's profits. The General Meeting may also deliver shares or grant options on directors. The fixed amount in the company directors' remuneration scheme resembles that of its Ibex-35 peers, as 68.57 per cent of them also use fixed payments. Nevertheless, only a relatively small fraction of the Ibex-35 companies remunerate their directors using option plans (9 per cent; FEF 2004).

The remuneration of the senior executives is determined for each individual by the board of directors and consists of: a fixed remuneration in cash; a variable remuneration, likewise in cash, based on the degree of fulfilment of annual objectives; and remuneration in kind. The board, following the report of the appointments and remuneration committee, also establishes periodically some medium-term variable incentive programmes. In 2002 the board established the following medium-term incentives for Senior Executives:

(a) a variable remuneration after three years, conditional upon their remaining in the company, which accrues in 2005 on the basis of the fulfilment of the objectives established for the three previous years, which may on one sole occasion reach a maximum overall amount of 1.5 times the fixed annual remuneration; and

(b) options with an average duration of three and a half years exercisable from April 2005 to March 2007. Thus, the company has used options plans as an incentive for directors and managers. These options plans were established after the share issue privatization of 1999. The first option plan dates back to that year and it encompassed 104 executives of the company. In 2000, the company established another option plan for the employees who had not been beneficiaries of the 1999 plan (about 5000 employees) and in 2001 a remuneration option plan was set in place for directors.

Another key aspect of corporate governance is shareholders' rights. In civil law countries, shareholders' rights are less protected (La Porta *et al.* 1998). Key aspects of shareholders' rights relate to the shareholder attendance, representation and voting rights in general meetings and to the existence of anti-takeover defences. All shares issued by the company have the same voting rights and the company has published a set of rules for the General Shareholders' Meeting. The company recognizes the use of electronic and remote communication regarding shareholder attendance, representation and voting rights in general meetings in its by-laws. Since the termination in 2004 of the golden share that gave the Spanish State a hold over the company, no anti-takeover amendments are in place, i.e. provisions that limit shareholders' rights or establish a quorum superior to that required by the law for the Shareholders' Meeting or a majority above those required by law in order to approve either regular or special issues at the General Shareholders' Meeting.

Another important issue in corporate governance, especially after the Enron scandal, relates to the relationship between auditing and consulting services provided by auditors. The company's external auditors are appointed annually by the General Shareholders' Meeting at the proposal of the board of directors, following the report of the audit and compliance committee. In the last few years, the remuneration paid to the auditors corresponded entirely to its auditing services, with the auditing firm not rendering any other type of service to the company. Thus, it seems that no conflict of interest exists for auditors.

Transparency of information is also very important for corporate governance. At present, Spanish legislation makes it obligatory to publish an Annual Corporate Governance Report and substantial information regarding quoted firms' corporate governance issues on its web page. Indra was one of the pioneer companies in Spain in this sense. Since its full privatization in 1999, the company has published an Annual Corporate Governance Report following the 'comply or explain' rule.

Indra has also distinguished itself by the information published in its web page. It publishes not only the information now required by law, but other information recommended by the Spanish Codes of Best Practice, such as the reports from analysts, investment banks or rating agencies that regularly follow the movement of its shares. Actually, the company is one of the top-three Ibex-35 companies in providing information through its web page according to a report from the IESE Business School Minority Shareholders' Forum, and it was highly commended by the *Investor Relations* magazine in 2003 for its use of the Internet for investor relations.

Finally, during the last few years the company has furthered its commitment to stakeholders, establishing as a core value of its corporate responsibility the concept of innovation, given the importance of talent and knowledge for the company's business. Since 2003 the company has published an Annual Corporate Responsibility Report applying the practices recommended by the Global Reporting Initiative (GRI). The company has also established a Corporate Responsibility Management Plan as a framework for collaboration and dialogue with its main stakeholders: shareholders, employees, customers, suppliers, the environment, society and local communities. This plan started its operation in 2004 and will be implemented in three main phases. It includes the evaluation of the responsibility-related measures taken by the company, the launching of new initiatives and finally, the assurance of the coherence of the company's current and future responsibility policies, programmes and actions by implementing indicators that facilitate accountability. In December 2004 Indra signed the Global Compact principles.

KEY LEARNING POINTS

This chapter has analysed the characteristics and evolution of the corporate governance practices of a successfully privatized firm. After the full privatization of the company the board was almost completely restructured, specialized committees were created, and new remuneration schemes and incentives were put in place for directors, the management team and employees. In addition, the company made an effort to comply with the Codes of Best Practices recommendations, to be transparent by providing information both in its annual reports and on its web page, and to increase its commitment to stakeholders. This behaviour may help to explain the success the privatized company has achieved in the last few years with significant increases in efficiency, profitability, growth and market returns.

DISCUSSION QUESTIONS

1. What are the specific agency problems of State-owned enterprises?
2. Does privatization always solve those problems?
3. What factors may enhance efficiency improvements after privatization?
4. Why should corporate governance matter?
5. How do you explain that, without changing the management team after privatization, Indra's privatization process was successful?
6. What reasons are behind the importance of allowing the use of electronic means in General Shareholders Meetings?
7. Do you think a firm's commitment to corporate social responsibility is valued positively by investors?
8. When ownership concentration is high, do you think that the important issue is to have a board with a large majority of independent directors?

NOTES

1. It is also worth mentioning that there have been no major corporate governance scandals in quoted companies in Spain during the last decade. The closest scandal dates back to the Banesto crisis of 1993.
2. This underpricing is for the period 1985–97.
3. The Spanish State retained a 'golden share' in seven companies privatized by public offering (Argentaria, ENDESA, Iberia, Indra Sistemas, Repsol, Tabacalera and Telefónica). However, in 2002 the European Court questioned the use of golden shares by member states (Cases C-367/98, C-483/99 and C-503/99). The Court's decision obliged member states to modify their legislation. Law 5/1995, passed in Spain, which opened the door for the creation of golden sHares, was called into question in 2000 by Brussels. In May 2003, the European Court declared golden shares retained by the Spanish State in Repsol, ENDESA, Argentaria, Telefónica, Indra Sistemas and Tabacalera to be illegal, arguing that they impeded capital flows. As a result of this ruling, the Spanish State will not be able to exercise its golden share rights in the four companies where they still exist: Repsol, ENDESA, Telefónica and Iberia (Cabeza and Gómez 2004).
4. The mean value of free-float for the companies that formed the Ibex-35 Index amounted in 2003 to 56 per cent (FEF 2003).
5. Managerial ownership may also influence a firm's performance (Jensen and Meckling 1976), although, for high levels of managerial ownership, an entrenchment effect may predominate (Morck *et al.* 1988; Hermalin and Weisbach 1991; Fernández Alvarez *et al.* 1998; Himmelberg *et al*, 1999).
6. Note that the presence of foreign investors may affect the degree of post-privatization performance improvements. Some studies do document a significant positive relationship between profitability and foreign ownership (Smith *et al.* 1997).
7. A provision in an underwriting agreement which allows members of the underwriting syndicate to purchase additional shares at the original offering price. This is a useful provision for underwriters in the event of exceptional public demand. The name comes from the fact that Green Shoe Company was the first to grant such an option to underwriters, also called overallotment provision.
8. The level of employee share ownership may also influence the firm's post-privatization performance. Boycko *et al.* (1996) predict that employees are unlikely to support value-maximizing restructuring efforts.
9. It is also worth noting that no pyramidal structures are present in Indra. As reported by La Porta *et al.* (1999), pyramids are characteristic of civil law countries' firms. Agency problems, managerial entrenchment, tunnelling and consequently the expropriation of wealth from minority shareholders by large shareholders may be even more serious when there are pyramids, as the separation of cash flow and control rights may enhance managerial entrenchment and agency problems and give an incentive to the large blockholder to transfer wealth from the firms through the pyramidal structure. In 2003, 20 per cent of the firms included in the Ibex-35 presented a large shareholder owning the stakes through pyramids (FEF 2004).
10. Spanish Law currently requires that all quoted companies have an audit committee. In 2003, for 71 per cent of the companies the chairman of the audit committee was an independent director (FEF 2004).
11. Less than two-thirds of the Ibex-35 companies, 65.71 per cent, present an executive committee. Within these committees, the percentage of executive directors is higher than within the board: 34 per cent versus 17.89 per cent (FEF 2004).
12. The board, in accordance with the contents of the Regulations of the Board of Directors, also performs an annual evaluation of its own operation and the quality of its tasks, as well as those of the committees.
13. Accordingly, Megginson *et al.* (1994) and López de Silanes (1997) report higher performance gains for firms with changes in top management.

REFERENCES

Alvarez Otero, S. (2000), 'Las privatizaciones españolas mediante oferta pública inicial', *Actualidad Financiera*, April, 17–31.

Barberis, N., M. Boycko, A. Shleifer and N. Tsukanova (1996), 'How does privatisation work? Evidence from the Russian shops', *Journal of Political Economics*, **104**, 764–90.

Barnhart, S.W., M.W. Marr and S. Rosenstein (1994), 'Firm performance and board composition: some new evidence', *Managerial and Decision Economics*, **15**, 329–40.

Boubakri, N., J. Cosset and O. Guedhami (2001), 'Liberalization, corporate governance and the performance of newly privatized firms', Paper presented at the 3rd Annual Financial Market Development in Emerging and Transition Economies Conference.

Boycko, M., A. Sheilfer and R. Visnhy (1996), 'A theory of privatization', *Economic Journal*, **106**(1), 327–77.

Cabeza, L. and S. Gómez (2004), 'The Spanish privatization process: implications on the profitability and efficiency of divested firms', Working Paper, University of Oviedo, Spain.

CCP (2003), *Informe de actividades*, Madrid, Spain: Consejo Consultivo de Privatizaciones.

Corona, J. (2002), 'Reformas legales en el ámbito de la empresa familiar: situación actual y perspectivas', *Boletín de Estudios Económicos*, **177**, 501–16.

Crespí-Cladera, R. and M.A. García-Cestona (2001), 'Ownership and control of Spanish listed firms', in F. Barca and M. Becht (eds), *The Control of Corporate Europe*, Oxford: Oxford University Press, pp. 207–27.

D'Souza, J. and W. Megginson (1999), 'The financial and operating performance of privatised firms during the 1990s', *The Journal of Finance*, **54**(4), 1397–437.

D'Souza, J., W. Megginson and R. Nash (2001), 'Determinants of performance improvements in privatized firms: the role of restructuring and corporate governance', Paper presented at the AFA 2001 New Orleans Meetings.

Domberger, S. (1993), 'Privatization: what does the British experience reveal?', *Economic Papers*, **12**(2), 58–68.

Faccio, M. and L. Lang (2002), 'The ultimate ownership of Western European corporations', *Journal of Financial Economics*, **65**, 365–95.

FEF (2004), 'Observatorio de gobierno corporativo de las grandes sociedades cotizadas en el mercado de valores español (Ibex-35), 2003', Fundación de Estudios Financieros.

Fernández Alvarez, A.I., S. Gómez Ansón. and C. Fernández Méndez (1998), 'The effect of board size and composition on corporate performance', in M. Balling, E. Hennesy and R. O'Brien (eds), *Corporate Governance, Financial Markets and Global Convergence*, The Netherlands: Kluwer Academic Publishers, pp. 1–14.

Hermalin, B.E. and M.S. Weisbach (1991), 'The effects of board composition and direct incentives on firm performance', *Financial Management*, **20**, 101–12.

Himmelberg, C., R.G. Hubbard and D. Palia (1999), 'Understanding the determinants of managerial ownership and the link between ownership and performance', *Journal of Finance*, **54**, 435–69.

Jensen, M.C. and W.H. Meckling (1976), 'Theory of the firm; managerial behaviour, agency costs and ownership structure', *Journal of Financial Economics*, **3**, 305–60.

Jones, S., W. Megginson, R. Nash and J. Netter (1999), 'Share issue privatization as financial means to political and economic ends', *Journal of Financial Economics*, **53**, 217–53.

Klein, A. (1998), 'Firm performance and board committee structure', *Journal of Law and Economics*, **45**, 275–303.

Kose, J. and W.S. Lemma (1998), 'Corporate governance and board effectiveness', *Journal of Banking and Finance*, **22**, 371–403.

La Porta, R. and F. Lopez de Silanes (1999), 'Benefits of privatization – evidence from Mexico', *Quarterly Journal of Economics*, **114**, 1193–242.

La Porta, R., F. Lopez de Silanes and R. Vishny (1997), 'Legal determinants of external finance', *The Journal of Finance*, **52**, 1131–50.

La Porta, R., F. Lopez de Silanes and A. Shleifer (1999), 'Corporate ownership around the world', *Journal of Finance*, **54**, 471–517.

La Porta, R., F. Lopez de Silanes, A. Shleifer and R. Vishny (1998), 'Law and finance', *Journal of Political Economy*, **106**, 1113–55.

López de Silanes, F. (1997), 'Determinants of privatization prices', *Quarterly Journal of Economics*, **112**, 965–1025.

Martin, S. and D. Parker (1995), 'Privatization and economic performance throughout the UK business cycle', *Managerial and Decision Economics*, **16**, 225–37.

Megginson, W. and J. Netter (2001), 'From State to market: a survey of empirical studies on privatisation', *Journal of Economic Literature*, **39**, 321–89.

Megginson, W., R. Nash and M. Van Randerborgh (1994), 'The financial and operating performance of newly privatized firms: an international analysis', *The Journal of Finance*, **49**, 403–52.

Mehran, H. (1995), 'Executive compensation structure, ownership, and firm performance', *Journal of Financial Economics*, **38**, 163–84.

Melle, M. (1999), 'Algunos resultados efectivos de las privatizaciones en España: una primera aproximación', *Economía Industrial*, **330**, 141–58.

Morck, R., A. Shleifer and R.W. Vishny (1988), 'Management ownership and market valuation: an empirical analysis', *Journal of Financial Economics*, **20**, 293–315.

OECD (2003), *Privatising State-owned Enterprises. An Overview of Policies and Practices in OECD Countries*, Paris: OECD.

Ramamurti, R. (1997), 'Testing the limits of privatization: Argentine railroads', *World Development*, **25**, 1973–93.

Sacristan, M. and S. Gómez Ansón (2004), 'Family ownership, pyramids and firm performance', Working paper, Universidad Rey Juan Carlos, Madrid, Spain.

Shleifer, A. and R.W. Vishny (1997), 'A survey of corporate governance', *Journal of Finance*, **52**, 737–83.

Smith, S., C. Beon-Cheol and M. Vodopivec (1997), 'Privatization incidence, ownership forms and firm performance: evidence from Slovenia', *Journal of Competitive Economics*, **25**, 158–79.

Yermack, D. (1996), 'Higher market valuation of companies with a small board of directors', *Journal of Financial Economics*, **40**, 185–211.

5. Managerial reasoning in takeover battles: the case of Sanofi-Synthélabo and Aventis

Axel v. Werder and Till Talaulicar

INTRODUCTION

On 26 January 2004 the pharmaceutical company Sanofi-Synthélabo announced an unsolicited tender offer to acquire all of the shares of its competitor Aventis. Based on sales Aventis was twice as large as the bidder. Although both the management board and the supervisory board of Aventis rejected this offer immediately, Sanofi-Synthélabo maintained its attempt to gather control over its competitor. A takeover battle began. It followed an intensive and expensive corporate campaign to gain shareholders' support for each company's respective and conflicting strategy. In particular the two companies intended to convince their shareholders and the general public of their respective position. In other words, they were putting forward arguments that gave reasons why their recommendation was preferable and the opposing strategy should be refuted. Eventually Aventis's top management dismissed its defence. After Sanofi-Synthélabo had filed an improved offer, both the management board and the supervisory board of Aventis agreed to cooperate and recommended their shareholders to accept the new offer. By August 2004 Sanofi-Synthélabo had taken control of more than 95 per cent of Aventis's shares and voting rights. Thus the offer succeeded.

Mergers and acquisitions (M&As) are not an uncommon phenomenon studied from, *inter alia*, economic (Ghemawat and Ghadar 2000), capital market (Jensen and Ruback 1983), strategic management (Lubatkin and Lane 1996) or organizational behaviour (Jemison and Sitkin 1986) perspectives. Regarding corporate governance, M&As and particularly hostile takeover bids are the most important mechanisms of market control (Manne 1965). Corporate governance can be defined as 'the system by which companies are directed and controlled' (Cadbury 2002, p. 1). Corporate governance deals with the alignment of managerial decision-making with the interests of (other) corporate stakeholders and shareowners in particular. Since the interests of top management and shareholders can diverge, corporate governance mechanisms for controlling managers are necessary.

While it is still debatable which control arrangements are most effective, there is no doubt that some form of control is indispensable (Macey 1998, p. 913). Control mechanisms can either be internal because large shareowners or a supervisory board actively monitor management or external via the market for corporate control (Walsh and Seward 1990). According to the external governance perspective, the market disciplines management to pursue shareholder interests that are assumed to be aligned with high share prices. If top management neglects these interests, the market value of the company decreases and makes it a suitable target for a hostile takeover bid. If the bidder is successful he will dismiss the inefficient management after gaining control to do so. As a consequence top management has the incentive to pursue shareholder interests and to increase the value of the company in order to protect its own job.

However, this disciplining function of M&As is not the focus of our study. It is no secret that the selected case is inappropriate for exemplifying the free forces of the market because the course of the merger negotiations was very much influenced by the French government. Instead we intend to study this case in order to examine how the two companies involved in the battle substantiated their respective positions. That is, we will analyse the arguments put forward for reasoning or rejecting the proposed merger.

Good corporate governance requires that corporate decisions are made on a sound base and are transparent to the shareholders and other stakeholder groups of the company. The importance of the principle of transparency can hardly be exaggerated (see Fox 1998). Many rules and codes of corporate governance do not demand compliance but disclosure, which leads to transparency about how the companies have applied governance provisions and why they have done so (Gregory and Simmelkjaer 2002), that is, why the implemented governance modalities are viewed as appropriate under the specific circumstances of the company. Disclosing information about the chosen governance arrangements and the reasons for their appropriateness are deemed necessary in order to build and strengthen the confidence of the company's stakeholders. Disclosure and transparency can only be achieved by means of communication. Hence communication is a key tool for corporations to gain the confidence of their stakeholders and therefore a central issue of corporate governance.

Whereas communicating a proposed governance or management solution (like, for instance, a recommended merger) is important, these communications are, at the same time, difficult and complex management tasks. Communication about the proposed governance or management solutions is particularly crucial in the case of controversial measures, whose effectiveness is not straightforward. Accordingly company's constituencies may, initially, view other courses of action as preferable and deny approval. Managers, therefore, back their decisions by arguments because they want to convince – or must convince – their addressees of the soundness of that decision. Backing decisions with arguments informs addressees of the decisive points scrutinized in the problem-solving process. Thus managerial arguments reflect the thoroughness of the decision preparation or, in other words, its argumentation rationality (v. Werder 1999). Obviously the rationality of the argumentation, or the thoroughness of the decision preparation, can vary. Management decisions (for instance, about a governance structure or a merger) can be supported by more or less complex and convincing lines of reasoning, that is, decisions can be more or less sound.

In order to assess the thoroughness of managerial reasonings, a measurement instrument has been developed (v. Werder 1994, 1999) that has already been employed for evaluating the argumentation rationality of merger recommendations and other change actions in different countries (v. Werder *et al.* 2000). This instrument can generally be used for rating the thoroughness of the disclosed decision preparation about why a specific governance or management solution should be recommendable. None the less the questions remain whether successful decisions are prepared more thoroughly and whether more thorough arguments are perceived as more convincing. Whereas theoretically both the problem solutions and their accompanying communications will be more successful with more thorough supporting arguments, these effects can be less straightforward in practice. Studying the argumentation rationality of management decisions and communications is therefore important and will add to our knowledge about how to accomplish appropriate disclosure and transparency.

Using the case of a takeover battle as an example for analysing managerial reasonings seems to be particularly promising for several reasons. First, communicating the arguments for (and against) a proposed strategy is especially important in the case of takeover battles because the competing companies must necessarily seek to gain approval by their constituencies. Second, and related to the first issue, these arguments have to be put forward and publicly accessible in order to exert their intended convincing power. Therefore the arguments which reflect the thoroughness of the decision preparation are readily available. Finally it can be expected that the arguments put forward by the bidder and the target, respectively, will differ because the bidder in a takeover battle naturally emphasizes the advantages of the proposed merger strategy, whereas the target company stresses the downsides of a combined company. As a consequence analysing the arguments put forward by both the bidder and the target allows a more comprehensive assessment of the recommended course of action and gives a better impression of the 'whole picture'.

Regarding the case of Sanofi-Synthélabo and Aventis, we will scrutinize whether and how the reasonings put forward by the two companies differ. From an external governance perspective, managers must communicate convincingly in order to maintain or gain corporate control. If the shareholders do not trust managers to pursue a promising course of action they will engage in corporate governance and try to dismiss unsuccessful managers. In general the addressed shareholders must view the reasoning of the 'winner' of a takeover battle as superior because otherwise they would not have decided to tender their shares in the exchange offer. Yet more detailed reflections are necessary in order to find out how and to what extent the reasonings differ. We will introduce the basics of our measurement concept and subsequently apply the instrument to the reasonings put forward by Sanofi-Synthélabo and Aventis, respectively. More precisely we will analyse the content and the cognitive quality of the arguments in Sanofi-Synthélabo's initial offer for Aventis's shares as well as in the information notice about the rejection of this offer by Aventis.

Measuring the thoroughness of these arguments highlights their convincing power and gives hints to weak points which should have deserved additional attention in preparing the respective strategies and communications. Therefore these analyses are important for both managers and shareholders. Whereas the former can learn which additional aspects should be evaluated and communicated in order to present a thorough decision preparation, the latter can use the measurement instrument in order to assess whether the presented reasoning seems to be sufficiently sound or further arguments should be requested before the stockholders agree to tender their shares. Since in the present case Aventis's representatives eventually dismissed their rejection and recommended the merger, we finally scrutinize whether and to what extent the arguments against the merger stated in Aventis's rejection of the initial offer are indeed overruled by the revised offer. At the beginning we will start our study by presenting some basic background information about the pharmaceutical industry in general as well as the two studied companies and the takeover battle in particular.

BACKGROUND INFORMATION

In the pharmaceutical industry M&As are to be observed frequently because companies need a critical mass and have to be large enough to bear the efforts incurred by developing new products (Ben-Asher 2000). As a result, horizontal mergers have often been rationalized by claims of economies of scale and scope in R&D and sales (Danzon *et al.* 2004). On average, the R&D of a new medicine costs more than EUR 500 million and takes around 10–12 years between laboratory tests and market launch (for more details, see Ben-Asher 2000; Danzon 2000; Hara 2003). New product development is crucial because patent protection of existing inventions is limited in its duration. Many mergers and strong dependence on corporate innovativeness have changed the local distribution of the major players in the branch. Whereas German companies (like Bayer and Hoechst) dominated the market until the 1980s (Grant *et al.* 1988, p. 6), today the biggest companies are incorporated predominantly in the USA. The US market is not only the biggest but is also a very profitable one because US drug regulation allows higher prices for pharmaceuticals than does the price regulation in many other countries (Productivity Commission 2001). Hence a strong presence in the US market can be viewed as an important success factor for amortizing the high costs associated with product development.

Sanofi-Synthélabo and Aventis have in common that they are both the outcome of previous mergers which were both completed in 1999. Sanofi-Synthélabo was created by combining the pharmaceutical businesses of the energy company Total and the cosmetics company L'Oréal. The two companies have remained the largest shareholders of the new company (Table 5.1). In the same year, Rhône-Poulenc and Hoechst merged their pharmaceutical and agricultural businesses to form Aventis. Based on pharmaceutical sales, Sanofi-Synthélabo is ranked fifteenth and Aventis seventh among pharmaceutical companies worldwide. Basic data about Sanofi-Synthélabo and Aventis are reported in Table 5.1.

It is noteworthy that the governance structures of the two companies differ fundamentally, although both companies are incorporated pursuant to the French Commercial Code. This difference can be traced back to the fact that the French law allows stock corporations to opt for either a one-tiered structure with a unitary board of directors or a two-tiered structure which separates a management board for directing the company and a supervisory board for overseeing management (Monks and Minow 2004, p. 335). The possibility to opt between two different governance structures is particularly interesting because it is also offered in the Statute for a Societas Europaea (SE). According to article 38 of the Statute, the SE can comprise either an administrative organ (one-tier system) or a supervisory organ and a management organ (two-tier system) depending on the form adopted in the statutes (Council Regulation (EC) No. 2157/2001 of 8 October 2001 on the Statute for a European company (SE)). In French listed corporations a unitary board of directors is the most common form of organization (Association Française des Entreprises Privées and Mouvement des

Entreprises de France 2003, p. 4). However, Aventis applied a two-tier structure because one of the merging partners, Hoechst AG, was organized as a German stock corporation and therefore stipulated a supervisory board and a management board because in German law the two-tier structure is mandatory (see, for instance, Grundei and Talaulicar 2002, p. 4). As a consequence the combined company was intended to reflect this heritage.

Rumours about a merger between Sanofi-Synthélabo and Aventis were prevalent because both companies were vulnerable to hostile takeover bids and their combination could create a major player. Since this new group would be incorporated in France, the French government was known to favour a potential combination of the two companies. Although the government did not hold shares in either of the two companies, it had immense influence on pharmaceutical companies due to its authority for licensing and pricing drugs in the French market (see Productivity Commission 2001, pp. B.10–B.14). Concerning a potential combination, Sanofi-Synthélabo was under pressure, in particular, because the agreement of its two major owners to hold their shares was scheduled to expire at 2 December 2004. Accordingly it was reasonable to expect the share price to decrease if Total and L'Oréal made use of their right to sell their shares. As a consequence the value of Sanofi-Synthélabo would decrease and the company could become an easier target for hostile takeover bids.

Indeed, on 26 January 2004 Sanofi-Synthélabo announced an unsolicited offer for Aventis's shares. The offer consisted of a 'standard entitlement' of five Sanofi-Synthélabo shares and EUR 69 in cash for six Aventis shares as well as the two options of an 'all stock election' (that is, 35 Sanofi-Synthélabo shares for 34 Aventis shares) and an 'all cash election' (that is, EUR 60.43 for each Aventis share). Aventis shareholders were offered to select any combination of the elections, provided that, in the aggregate, 81 per cent of the Aventis shares tendered were exchanged for Sanofi-Synthélabo shares and 19 per cent of the Aventis shares were exchanged for cash. The offer contained a premium of 15.2 per cent based on the average Aventis share price over the month ended on 21 January 2004.

Under the offered conditions, Aventis's management assessed a merger with Sanofi-Synthélabo as suboptimal. Hence the management and the supervisory board of Aventis rejected this initial offer. Furthermore they started a defence strategy that included investor conferences, advertisement campaigns, legal allegations in France and the USA, proposing poison pills (like limiting voting rights or issuing warrants) to make the takeover less attractive and invited the Swiss-based competitor Novartis to act as a 'white knight' (that is, an alternative (and friendly) bidder viewed as a more desirable partner in a combined company and which agrees to buy a sufficient share portion in order to prevent the unfriendly bidder gaining control). The main events of the takeover battle are outlined in Table 5.2.

Table 5.1 Key figures about Sanofi-Synthélabo and Aventis (as of 31 December 2003)

	Sanofi-Synthélabo	Aventis
Consolidated sales (in EUR million)	8 048	16 791
R&D expenditure (in EUR million)	1 316	2 863
Employees worldwide	33 086	69 170
Corporate headquarters	Paris, France	Strasbourg, France
Legal form	Stock corporation ('société anonyme') pursuant to the French Commercial Code	Stock corporation ('société anonyme') pursuant to the French Commercial Code
Corporate governance structure	One-tiered board structure with a single board of directors ('conseil d'administration')	Two-tiered board structure with a management board ('directoire') and a supervisory board ('conseil de surveillance')
CEO	Jean-François Dehecq	Igor Landau
Stock listings	Paris Stock Exchange, New York Stock Exchange	Paris Stock Exchange, New York Stock Exchange, Frankfurt Stock Exchange
Largest shareholders (share ownership)	Total S.A. (24.4%), L'Oréal (19.5%)	Kuwait Petroleum (13.5%)
Highest share price in 2003 (in EUR)	60.00	54.55
Lowest share price in 2003 (in EUR)	41.50	37.50
Year-end share price 2003 (in EUR)	59.70	52.40

Stock market capitalization (in EUR million)	43 751	42 040
Therapeutic areas	Cardiovascular/thrombosis, central nervous system, internal medicine, oncology	Cardiovascular, diabetes, oncology, human vaccines
Main products (therapeutic area; consolidated sales 2003 in EUR million)	Stilnox®/Ambien®/Myslee® (central nervous system; 1 345) Plavix® (cardiovascular/ thrombosis; 1 325) Eloxatine® (oncology; 824) Aprovel® (cardiovascular/ thrombosis; 683) Fraxiparine® (cardiovascular/thrombosis; 319) Dépakine® (central nervous system; 277) Xatral®/UroXatral® (internal medicine; 222) Solian® (central nervous system; 148) Cordarone® (cardiovascular/ thrombosis; 146) Tildiem® (cardiovascular/ thrombosis; 131)	Allegra®/Telfast® (allergies; 1 736) Lovenox®/Clexane® (cardiovascular/ thrombosis; 1 659) Taxotere® (oncology; 1 362) Delix®/Tritace® (cardiovascular/ hypertension; 1 066) Copaxone® (central nervous system; 617) Amaryl® (diabetes; 596) Lantus® (diabetes; 487) Nasacort® (allergies; 278) Campto® (oncology; 264) Arava® (arthritis; 255)
Late stage R&D projects	29	29
Expected product launches until 2006	3	6

Source: Company information.

Table 5.2   Major events in the takeover battle

---

26 January: Sanofi-Synthélabo announced an unsolicited offer to acquire all of the shares of Aventis through separate, but substantially identical, offers in France, Germany and the United States. The offer documentation in France was submitted to the Autorité des marchés financiers (AMF). Sanofi-Synthélabo's main shareholders, Total and L'Oréal, announced that they supported the merger and would approve the corresponding capital increase. The Aventis management board rejected the hostile offer. The chairman and the vice chairman of the Aventis supervisory board supported the position of the Aventis management board.

28 January: The Aventis supervisory board met and unanimously rejected the initial offer.

29 January: Sanofi-Synthélabo's press campaign was admonished in Germany.

3 February: The AMF declared the initial offer acceptable ('recevable').

12 February: The AMF granted its approval ('visa') of Sanofi-Synthélabo's information memorandum ('note d'information') in respect of the initial offer in France.

13 February: Aventis appealed the AMF's decision ('avis de recevabilité').

17 February: The initial offer commenced in France. The Aventis supervisory board met and unanimously concluded that the initial public offer was not in the best interest of the company, its shareholders and employees. Therefore the Aventis supervisory board unanimously decided to recommend to Aventis shareholders not to tender their shares into the initial offer.

19 February: Aventis filed with the AMF an information memorandum in response to Sanofi-Synthélabo's initial offer documentation in France ('note d'information en réponse').

23 February: Aventis appealed the AMF's grant of approval ('visa') of the information memorandum.

4 March: The AMF granted its approval of Aventis's 'note d'information en réponse'.

5 March: Aventis detailed the rejection of the initial offer.

9 March: The notification of the initial offer was filed with the European anti-trust authority.

12 March: Novartis confirmed in response to a request by the AMF that it explored the feasibility of a combination with Aventis.

15 March: The initial offer commenced in Germany.

16 March: Aventis published a defence brochure 'Say NO to Sanofi's Offer' for shareholders and employees and started to place four-page advertisements in the French, German and other European business media.

19 March: Sanofi-Synthélabo announced the successful completion of the first round of syndication of the EUR 12 billion credit facility put in place for financing the offer on Aventis.

23 March: In response to a second request by the AMF, Novartis confirmed that it had completed its feasibility study on a potential combination with Aventis. Although a combination appeared to be promising, Novartis decided, due to the negative attitude of the French government, to enter into negotiations only if formally invited by the Aventis supervisory board and if the French government assumed a neutral position.

26 March: Aventis made pre-commencement filing with the SEC. In addition to the 'note d'information en réponse', information regarding the litigation in the US against Sanofi-Synthélabo's product Plavix® was communicated, which challenged the validity of its patent, and put on the websites of Aventis and the AMF.

2 April: The Aventis supervisory board unanimously invited Novartis to enter into negotiations about a potential combination and decided on resolutions to be proposed to shareholders at their next general meeting. Among others, a resolution should be proposed to amend the articles of association of Aventis to limit shareholders' voting rights to a maximum of 15% as long as a shareholder obtained less than a 50% shareholding. Furthermore a resolution should be proposed to issue warrants ('bons de souscriptions d'actions') in the event that the hostile takeover were to succeed and a generic version of Plavix® were launched in the US before the end of 2007.

5 April: The notification of the initial offer was filed with the US Federal Trade Commission (FTC). Mr Dehecq sent a letter to Mr Landau which served as formal notice ('mise en demeure') that Aventis desist from denigrating Sanofi-Synthélabo and certain of its products.

8 April: Sanofi-Synthélabo met with Aventis's employee representatives and trade unions.

Table 5.2   continued

---

9 April: The Securities and Exchange Commission (SEC) declared effective the US registration statement relating to the shares of Sanofi-Synthélabo to be issued in the initial US offer.

12 April: The initial offer commenced in the United States.

13 April: Sanofi-Synthélabo and GlaxoSmithKline signed an agreement, conditioned to the successful completion of the offer, about the divestment of Arixtra® and Fraxiparine® and related assets.

15 April: Mr Landau replied to the letter by Mr Dehecq, dated 5 April, and asserted that Aventis had not engaged in a denigrating campaign but was obliged to inform its shareholders about risks associated with the offer.

20 April: Aventis filed legal action in the US against Sanofi-Synthélabo because the public filings and statements made in connection with the unsolicited offer contained omissions and misrepresentations which did not comply with US federal securities laws.

21 April: Aventis communicated clarifications to the AMF regarding the proposed resolution to issue warrants.

22 April: Novartis accepted the offer of the Aventis supervisory board to negotiate the conditions of a potential business combination. In the afternoon Mr Dehecq and Mr Landau met for the first time since the offer was publicly announced to discuss in general terms whether an agreed offer was possible. The discussion was continued during the following days and started to include various representatives and advisers of both companies.

23 April: The AMF published a press release that it deemed the issuance of warrants foreseen by Aventis not to be in compliance with the principles that regulate the due process of public offers.

25 April: Sanofi-Synthélabo and Aventis agreed on an improved offer, a balanced governance structure of the combined company and its name 'Sanofi-Aventis'. The management board and the supervisory board of Aventis recommended that Aventis shareholders tender their shares into the increased offer. The decision of the supervisory board was based on a majority of 13 members, with two opposing votes by employee representatives and an abstention by the representative of Kuwait Petroleum. Aventis decided to withdraw all claims against Sanofi-Synthélabo and the AMF in connection with the initial offer as well as the resolutions to limit shareholders' voting rights and to issue warrants. Novartis announced its

decision to discontinue negotiations with Aventis and not to submit a bid for a combination of Aventis and Novartis.

26 April: Sanofi-Synthélabo announced the friendly improved offer. The European Commission approved the planned acquisition of Aventis by Sanofi-Synthélabo.

7 May: The AMF approved Sanofi-Synthélabo's information memorandum ('note d'information') about the revised offer.

12 May: The Aventis management board set 11 June as the date of the annual general meeting of Aventis's shareholders.

13 May: The Sanofi-Synthélabo board of directors set 23 June as the date for the joint general and extraordinary meeting of Sanofi-Synthélabo's shareholders.

14 May: Aventis submitted its draft response document ('note d'information en réponse') about the improved offer to the AMF.

24 May: The Sanofi-Synthélabo board of directors met and finalized the proposed list of directors. In accordance with the agreement of 25 April, the Sanofi-Synthélabo board of directors was proposed to be composed of J.-F. Dehecq and eight directors each proposed by the board of directors of Sanofi-Synthélabo and the supervisory board of Aventis, respectively.

26 May: Sanofi-Synthélabo announced the successful completion of the first round of syndication of the EUR 16 billion credit facility put in place for financing the increased offer on Aventis. The US offer for Aventis that had previously been scheduled to expire at 28 May was extended to 30 June.

1 June: The AMF announced that it had set 30 June as the expiration date of Sanofi-Synthélabo's revised offer for the ordinary shares of Aventis.

11 June: At their annual general meeting, the Aventis shareholders voted to approve Aventis's 2003 dividend.

14 June: Based on the decided Aventis 2003 dividend, and in accordance with the terms of the revised offer, the terms of the offer for Aventis's shares were adjusted.

21 June: Sanofi-Synthélabo announced the draft structure of a Sanofi-Aventis management committee intended to be established under the authority of J.-F. Dehecq and bringing together all the main functions and operating divisions necessary to ensure swift integration after successful completion of the offer.

Table 5.2   continued

---

22 June: The AMF determined to postpone the closing date of the revised offer to 30 July in order to receive the required approval from the FTC. One day later Sanofi-Synthélabo confirmed that the offers in France, Germany and the USA would expire simultaneously on 30 July.

23 June: The combined general meeting of Sanofi-Synthélabo's shareholders was held.

25 June: Sanofi-Synthélabo signed an agreement with Pfizer regarding the divestment of Aventis's interests in Campto® in response to requests made by the competition authorities, conditioned to the successful completion of the offer.

29 July: The FTC cleared the offer.

30 July: The tender period expired.

12 August: The AMF published the definitive results of the offer. As of 30 July, in aggregate 769 920 773 Aventis ordinary shares representing 95.47% of the share capital and 95.52% of the voting rights of Aventis had been tendered into the French, German and US offer. After giving effect of the offers, on a fully diluted basis, Sanofi-Synthélabo would hold 89.84% of the share capital and 89.88% of the voting rights of Aventis. In concordance with the terms of the offers, a subsequent tender period was scheduled to commence on 13 August and to expire on 6 September.

20 August: The settlement of the revised offers occurred. Sanofi-Synthélabo controlled Aventis with 95.47% of the share capital and changed its name to Sanofi-Aventis.

30 August: The Aventis supervisory board met and its 12 members representing the shareholders resigned. Subsequently, seven new members representing the major shareholder of Sanofi-Aventis were co-opted and elected J.-F. Dehecq as chairman of the Aventis supervisory board. The four supervisory board members representing the employees remained unchanged. The new supervisory board decided to dismiss the Aventis management board members and appointed seven new members and G. Le Fur as new chairman of the Aventis management board.

Note: All data from 2004.

Sources: Company and press information.

As already mentioned, Sanofi-Synthélabo was eventually able to accomplish its plan. A friendly improved offer was launched that significantly increased both the cash exchange and the premium for Aventis shares. More specifically Sanofi-Synthélabo offered five Sanofi-Synthélabo shares and EUR 120 in cash (instead of only EUR 69) in exchange for six Aventis shares. Correspondingly both the all-stock as well as the all-cash elections were modified so that either 1.1739 Sanofi-Synthélabo shares or EUR 68.93 in cash were offered for each Aventis share. Aventis's shareholders could opt for any combination of the elections, provided that, in the aggregate, 71 per cent of the Aventis shares tendered into the offer were exchanged for Sanofi-Synthélabo shares and 29 per cent were exchanged for cash. In August 2004 the combination of the two companies was finalized in law.

MEASUREMENT CONCEPT

Principles of Reasoning

Managerial decisions about change actions, such as implementing specific governance structures or pursuing a merger strategy, are recommended solutions to complex management problems. Since these recommendations are nontrivial assertions, that is, their validity is not obvious without further details and cannot be proved or verified by evidence, they have to be supported by argumentation to gain acceptance.

A line of reasoning or argumentation is comprised of one or more reasons (for the following, see v. Werder 1994, 1999). Each reason, or argument, consists of one or more data propositions and one rule proposition. These propositions do not have to be explicitly articulated if they are evident to the addressee of the argument. Whereas data propositions describe the unique characteristics of a given situation, rule propositions express general interrelations of different phenomena. The arguments' convincing power is in evincing their claim from the data and the rule. Arguments convince by identifying the asserted issue as the mere application of a regularity that factors in because of the specific situation. For example, Sanofi-Synthélabo argued that the merger of the companies should be recommended because it would enhance shareholder value (see Table 5.3, argument A1). This argument is comprised of the propositions that increasing shareholder value is a goal of the change action (criterion *data*), the merger will lead to higher shareholder value (consequence *data*) and an alternative with valuable consequences must be chosen (*rule* of the teleological maxim).

Such a global reason is the first step for supporting an action recommendation and generally brings up a pursued goal (criterion data) for the judgement, describes the relatively high contribution of the recommended alternative to reach that goal (consequence data) and includes the teleological maxim (as an evaluative rule proposition), which states that the most effective of all alternative courses of action must be chosen.

Of course, global reasoning can still coexist with disbelief in the preferability of the claimed action recommendation. Global reasons can therefore be legitimately doubted if they contain propositions that are nontrivial and unprovable. Whereas the relevance of the teleological maxim must not be questioned seriously (at least in a managerial context), objections can be raised about the tolerability of the criterion data and the reliability of the consequence data. In that case, normative arguments must be put forward in a discussion of goals to back the tolerability of the criterion data (that is, increasing shareholder value), or descriptive reasons must be used to support the reliability of the proposed action's contribution to the goal as described by the consequence data (that is, the merger would lead to higher shareholder value). In short, disputable propositions must be backed by further reasoning to increase the soundness of the argument.

The thoroughness of a (managerial) decision preparation or its argumentation rationality is determined by the soundness of the arguments that support the decision. The factors influencing the convincing power of managerial reasoning can be divided into structure determinants and substance determinants. While the structure determinants describe the configuration of an argumentation in a formal perspective, represented by its breadth and depth, the substance determinants address the cognitive quality of the single arguments and relate the quantity of the arguments to the state of accessible knowledge.

Main Levels of Argumentation Rationality

To measure the argumentation rationality of complex managerial decisions more precisely, v. Werder (1994, 1999) developed an ordinal scale of argumentation rationality, elaborating the argumentation theory of Stephen E. Toulmin (1958; Toulmin *et al.* 1979). This scale encompasses four main levels of argumentation rationality and contains a further differentiation of one of these main levels. The main levels of argumentation rationality are the unfounded, the global-founded, the detail-founded and the qualified-founded decision or change action.

An *unfounded change action* has the lowest level of argumentation rationality since management does not support its recommended measure with any reason. *Global-founded change actions* are backed with propositions about the positive consequences of the proposed alternative to realize certain goals. Yet there is no further backing for the global consequence propositions. Why the recommended measure will realize the pursued goals is not explained. If global consequence propositions are not only stated but backed, there are then *detail-founded change actions*. The argumentation rationality of detail-founded actions varies according to the soundness of the detail-reasoning. Consequently the detail-founded level of argumentation rationality can be further differentiated. Among other factors, a detail-founded argumentation can be evaluated with regard to its breadth, depth and pro/contra relation.

An argumentation's *breadth* depends on the number of arguments put forward to discuss a proposition on a higher layer. Since global consequence propositions can be backed by a variety of reasons, a complex argumentation can follow various lines and thereby be more or less *narrow* or *broad*.

The *depth* of an argumentation complex refers to the number of argumentation layers of the reasoning developed. Depth reflects the fact that arguments directly supporting a global consequence proposition can be questionable. Doubts about the reliability or the relevance of arguments thus open another 'round of reasoning', leading to a further layer of the argumentation complex. Since the arguments of this round of reasoning can be doubtful as well, these reasons themselves also have to be backed. Thus, depending on the number of argumentation layers, or of the rounds of reasoning, respectively, argumentations can be more or less *flat* or *deep*.

The *pro/contra relation* of an argumentation provides information about the extent to which known contra-arguments are taken into account (aside from pro-arguments, or arguments supporting the backed proposition). The pro/contra relation is especially important in the context of complex, unstructured management decisions. Such decisions by definition are always risky, so that possible reasons in opposition to the proposition in question should be considered. With respect to its pro/contra relation, an argumentation can be more or less partial or impartial. *Partial argumentations* are biased towards the proposition and take only a few or even no contra-arguments into account. In contrast, *impartial argumentations* include a more balanced ratio of pros and cons.

The fourth and final main level of argumentation rationality, called *qualified-founded change action*, is achieved if the state of the issue-related accessible knowledge has been completely exhausted while preparing the decision. In this case, with regard to the breadth of the argumentation, all aspects deemed relevant for the management problem in question are taken into account. Regarding the depth of the argumentation, the last layer of each line of reasoning contains maximum-dependable arguments, that is, reasons that are true, well-tried or evident-plausible and of which the dependability cannot be raised any further (for details, see v. Werder 1999). Therefore demanding additional arguments is epistemologically justified neither with respect to the breadth nor the depth of the argumentation. A qualified-founded change action is thus the form of decision making with the highest degree of rationality.

EMPLOYING THE CONCEPT

The expedience of the concept can be elucidated by referring to the proposed merger between Sanofi-Synthélabo and Aventis. In order to do this, we identified and structured the arguments put forward by the two companies in order to reason why the initial offer should be accepted or rejected. Our examination draws primarily on those arguments that were articulated in the information notices about the initial offer and its rejection, respectively. These information notices highlight the position of the respective company and include those arguments which corporate authorities view as especially important. Comparisons with other means of communication show that press releases, conference presentations and advertisements do not reveal additional arguments which are not covered by the information notices. Of course, the information memoranda and prospectuses contain, due to their length and legal stipulations, more information. However, appraising the multitude of these arguments cannot be accomplished within this study. Nevertheless we will make reference to these sources in order to assess whether or not the state of the issue-related accessible knowledge is exhausted.

The Reasoning of Sanofi-Synthélabo

The argumentation by Sanofi-Synthélabo of why Aventis's shareholders should accept the offer is shown in Table 5.3. Three global reasons are put forward: Accepting the recommended offer will be advantageous to stock owners because they will benefit from an enhanced firm value (A1) and, in the short run, a premium paid for their Aventis shares (A2). In addition the merger is supposed to be beneficial to patients, who can be served better after the two companies combine (A3). Since these nontrivial rationalizations refer to the future, they cannot be verified by empirical evidence. Rather their validity may be doubted legitimately. Whereas the criteria data (that is, providing benefits to shareholders and serving consumers) appear to be tolerable goals, the reliability of the consequence propositions demands further backing because it is highly uncertain whether or not and under which conditions the claimed consequences become real.

Since further rationalizations are encountered for backing the global reasons, the argumentation mirrors (at least) the main level of a detail-

Table 5.3   Argumentation by Sanofi-Synthélabo, based on the information notice about its offer for Aventis's shares from 26 January 2004

| **Change action:** | **Merger between Sanofi-Synthélabo and Aventis** |
| **Basic claim:** | **Aventis's shareholders should accept the offer by Sanofi-Synthélabo** |

Global reasoning	*Layer of detail-reasoning*		
	1	*2*	*3*	*4*

Because A1: The combination of both companies will enhance shareholder value.

Because A11: The new group will have an enhanced position in major international markets, in particular in the US.

Because A111: Based on pharmaceutical sales, the new group will be ranked 3rd among pharmaceutical companies worldwide.

Because A112: Based on pharmaceutical sales, the new group will be ranked 1st among pharmaceutical companies in Western Europe.

Because A113: Based on pharmaceutical sales, the new group will be ranked 9th among pharmaceutical companies in North America.

Because A114: The new group will have increased financial strength.

Because A115: Sanofi-Synthélabo and Aventis have complimentary strengths.

Because A1151: The combination of the two companies will allow to add the extensive sales and marketing and life-cycle management expertise of Aventis to Sanofi-Synthélabo's recognized R&D expertise and demonstrated capacity to generate sales growth in all major international markets.

Because A11511: Sanofi-Synthélabo will be able to use Aventis's extensive sales force in the US to accelerate the sales growth of

Table 5.3 continued

Global reasoning	Layer of detail-reasoning			
	1	2	3	4

products already on the market and to launch successfully the new products expected to flow from the combined R&D pipeline of the new group.

Because A11512: Aventis's direct presence in the Japanese market will further accelerate international sales growth.

Because A12: The new group will have an increased ability to manage the product development risks inherent in the pharmaceutical industry.

Because A121: The research portfolio of the new group will be more diversified.

Because A1211: The two companies have complimentary product portfolios.

Because A12111: The combined company will have a large portfolio of fast-growing drugs, with nine products having individual annual sales in excess of EUR 500 million in 2003.

Because A12112: The combined company will have significant products in five product categories, which are among the seven highest performing product categories in terms of growth.

Because A12113: The combined company will have a strong position in the area of vaccines.

Because A13: The combination will give the opportunity to realize significant cost savings and other synergies.

Because A131: Sanofi-Synthélabo believes that combining the two companies will generate approximately EUR 1600 million in synergies.

Because A1311: Sanofi-Synthélabo believes that these synergies will be realized from savings in sales and general costs, optimization of R&D expenses and the acceleration of revenue growth of the new group.

Because A1312: Sanofi-Synthélabo believes that 10% of these synergies will be achieved during 2004, with 60% achieved in 2005 and 100% achieved in 2006.

But A1313: Sanofi-Synthélabo estimates that, in total, the realization of these synergies will require non-recurring cash restructuring costs of approximately EUR 2 billion pre-tax during the first two years following completion of the offer.

But A132: Sanofi-Synthélabo can give no assurance that these synergies will in fact be achieved in the amounts or the time frame envisaged.

Because A1321: The amount and nature of the synergies, as well as the timing of their implementation, remain subject to change as Sanofi-Synthélabo obtains additional information regarding Aventis.

But A1322: Sanofi-Synthélabo believes that the amount and timing of the synergies are reasonable and is confident of its ability to realize them.

Table 5.3 continued

Global reasoning	Layer of detail-reasoning		
	1	*2*	*3*	*4*
	Because A14:	Sanofi-Synthélabo will carry out necessary reorganizations in order to facilitate the realization of the merger goals.		
		Because A141:	Sanofi-Synthélabo intends to modify the composition of Aventis's management and supervisory board in order to reflect the shareholder base of the new company.
		Because A142:	Sanofi-Synthélabo intends to propose to Aventis's shareholders the transformation of their company into a 'société anonyme' with a 'conseil d'administration', that is, with a one-tiered board structure.
		Because A143:	Sanofi-Synthélabo will carry out necessary operational restructurings of the new group.
		But A144:	Sanofi-Synthélabo has not determined the legal structure of such operational reorganizations.
			Because A1441:	Sanofi-Synthélabo had only access to publicly available information regarding Aventis.
			But A1442:	Sanofi-Synthélabo will finally determine the legal structure of such operational reorganizations only after a thorough study of Aventis.
	Because A15:	Sanofi-Synthélabo will explain its plans to the bodies representing the employees of Aventis.		
		But A151:	Sanofi-Synthélabo is unable to state its intentions regarding Aventis's workforce in a precise manner.
			Because A1511:	Sanofi-Synthélabo had only access to publicly available information regarding Aventis.

124

But A1512:	Sanofi-Synthélabo may reorganize the functions of R&D, production, marketing and services and combine the existing entities of Sanofi-Synthélabo and Aventis, country by country.
But A1513:	Sanofi-Synthélabo will implement reorganizations only after phases of information, dialogue and consultation with the employees' representative bodies of the affected entities.
But A1514:	Sanofi-Synthélabo will implement and support programmes which take into consideration and respect the concerns of all employees and leave nobody to face an employment question alone.

Because A16: The offer is fully supported by Sanofi-Synthélabo's major shareholders, Total and L'Oréal.

Because A2: The acceptance of the offer will be awarded by a premium.

Because A21: Each Aventis share is valued at EUR 60.43, which is equivalent to a premium of 15.2% based on the average share price over the month ended 21 January 2004.

Because A3: The combination of both companies will allow the new group to better serve patients worldwide.

Because A31: The new group will have enhanced R&D capabilities.

Because A311: The new group will have the third largest R&D budget in the pharmaceutical industry.

Because A3111: The R&D budget of the new group will total over EUR 4 billion in 2002 on a pro forma basis.

Because A312: The new group will have 58 projects in late R&D stages in key therapeutic categories.

Because A32: The new group will have significant opportunities to improve the productivity of the R&D function.

125

Source: Company information.

founded change action. In sum, the detail-reasoning consists of 43 reasons. On the different lines and layers of the argumentation its breadth varies between one and six reasons. After all, it occurred six times that more than two reasons (for instance, A12111, A12112 and A12113) are backing an argument on a higher layer (that is, A1211). With respect to its depth, the argumentation contains four layers of detail-reasoning. However, the deepest layers are only entered by the argumentation lines following global reason A1. Four arguments (A1, A11, A12 and A3) are supported by more than two layers of detail-reasoning. Regarding the pro/contra relation, we classify arguments as cons if they speak against the basic claim about the preferability of the exchange offer. Accordingly the argumentation contains a total of seven contra-arguments (for instance, A1313 or A1321).

The argumentation conspicuously emphasizes the reasoning of A1. This comes as no surprise since it is the shareholders who have to be convinced to accept the offer and to have a lasting interest in the new group. In Table 5.3 some additional explanations of the offered premium (A2) were ignored. These reflect various calculations of the premium that would be yielded dependent on the combination of the cash and the exchange offer as well as on the historical time frame selected for determining which share prices have to be assumed. Finally A3 could have been coded as a sub-goal for enhancing shareholder value because, in the long run, it will be impossible to increase shareholder value if consumer needs cannot be fulfilled satisfactorily. However, Sanofi-Synthélabo presented the improved capability to serve patients unequivocally as a global reason for preferring the merger. Notwithstanding, A31 and A32 also contribute to the convincing power of A1 inasmuch as enhanced and more productive R&D capabilities will strengthen the market position of the combined company (A11).

Exceeding the formal aspects of the argumentation structure and entering a discussion of its content, we signify the materiality of contra-arguments, a few reasons' lack of comprehensibility as well as missing arguments. Some contra-arguments can easily be outweighed (for example, A1313) as they take into account costs which are expected to be caused by the combination of the two companies and, at the same time, to be settled by the gains from the merger. Yet the majority of contra-arguments indicate that Sanofi-Synthélabo can give neither assurance that aspired goals will be reached nor more detailed information because the offer could only be founded on publicly available data about Aventis (see A1441, A1511). This entails risks because the proposed course of action may fail due to hidden perils of the acquired company. However, this lack of knowledge is inherent to hostile bids since they are always deficient in privileged information about the target company. Although it would be highly unlikely that the offer would have been published otherwise, Sanofi-Synthélabo at least assures that its representatives are confident to reach the asserted goals (for instance, A1322). More importantly Sanofi-Synthélabo's representatives commit themselves to carry out thorough analysis before they determine more specific implementation measures (A1442, A1513).

A very few arguments lack significance and comprehensibility. For instance, A1514 asserts that the concerns of all employees will be taken into consideration when the implementation of the merger has to be planned in more detail. But this argument leaves it open to debate as to how these considerations will look. More precise information about planned downsizing activities, which are deemed necessary for realizing the ambitious synergies, is missing. Although these considerations have to be characterized as rather unspecific, they form a commitment for justifying employee-related activities after they were decided. Yet it remains incomprehensible what meanings shall be attached to the assurance that nobody will be left to face an employment question alone (A1514).

Apparently the recommended change action cannot be classified as a qualified-founded one because the dependability of the arguments is still increasable. Regarding A32 as an example, it is possible that the new group will have significant opportunities to improve the productivity of the R&D function (for scientometric evidence, based on patent data, see, for example, Koenig and Mezick 2004). Yet successful biotech firms illustrate that scale does not represent the only determinant of R&D effectiveness. Rather human capital and scientific ingenuity are critical success factors (Lacetera 2001). Further backing is particularly necessary as enhancing productivity may be inhibited due to cultural, organizational or technological misfits between the various R&D units. Whereas the prospectus about the offer contains additional information and adds more details to some reasoning lines, this information cannot lead to a different conclusion about the main level of argumentation rationality the merger proposition captures. Referring to the breadth, some aspects, particularly employee and implementation matters, are left unappreciated even though they are doubtlessly important for making the merger a success. Naturally these omissions and weaknesses become easily apparent in confrontation with the reasoning of Aventis as to why the offer should be rejected.

The Reasoning of Aventis

Aventis's reasoning is depicted in Table 5.4. Aventis recommended rejecting the initial offer because it was not in the best interest of either the shareholders (A1) or the employees of Aventis (A2). Additionally it was mentioned that the merger was not in the interest of the company. We neglected this argument because the interest of the company is assumed to integrate, among other things, shareholder as well as employee interests and there were no further reasons which could not be related just to shareholder or employee interests but needed reference to an overall interest of the company.

In accordance with the reasoning by Sanofi-Synthélabo, Aventis's argumentation centres on A1. This was to be expected since it is, again, the shareholders who are the primary addressees of the reasoning. Approval by the shareholders could be gained, on the one hand, by articulating downsides of the merger which were left unconsidered in the competing reasoning by Sanofi-Synthélabo. On the other hand, the obvious thing to do is to refute the arguments put forward by Sanofi-Synthélabo whenever possible. Therefore similarities (and differences) between the two reasonings are, for large parts, framed by the argumentation of Sanofi-Synthélabo, the convincing power of which Aventis intended to cast doubt upon.

Since the global reasons (that is, A1 and A2) are further backed, Aventis's reasoning reflects (at least) a detail-founded change action, too. The detail-reasoning consists of 43 arguments. The breadth varies between one and four reasons put forward for backing the assertion of a higher layer of reasoning. In eight instances more than two reasons are put forward in order to support an argument on a higher layer (for example, A12). Regarding the depth, the argumentation contains four layers of detail-reasoning following A1. A total of two arguments (that is, A1 and A13) are backed by more than two layers of detail-reasoning. To resume these formal characteristics of the reasoning, overall the similarities with the argumentation of Sanofi-Synthélabo are striking. However, in contrast to the former reasoning by Sanofi-Synthélabo, the argumentation by Aventis does not include any contra-arguments and is thus very partial. Hence, although the reasoning contains some maximum-dependable arguments (for instance, A1312), the reasoning neglects to capture a qualified-founded change action.

In essence, Aventis's shareholders were recommended to reject the offer because they would otherwise sell their shares under value and face potential losses due to significant risks associated with the future development of Sanofi-Synthélabo and its share price. Whereas some of Aventis's objections (for example, A121) could easily be made obsolete by increasing the value of the offer, others (for instance, A1342) are related to the hostility of the tender offer and could thus become superfluous after an agreement between the two companies. In addition, however, some arguments speak against the merger in general (for example, A132 or A13434) and should therefore remain valid even if a collaborative solution to the takeover battle were found. How these pleas were overruled is particularly intriguing against the background that the two companies eventually came to an agreement to form a combined entity. Finally, we briefly investigate how the friendly

Table 5.4 Argumentation by Aventis, based on the press release from 5 March 2004 about its rejection of the offer

Change action:	**Merger between Sanofi-Synthélabo and Aventis**		
Basic claim:	**Aventis's shareholders should reject the offer by Sanofi-Synthélabo**		
Global reasoning	*Layer of detail-reasoning*		
1	*2*	*3*	*4*

Because A1: The combination of both companies is not in the best interest of Aventis's shareholders.

	Because A11:	The offer was opportunistically timed to disadvantage Aventis's shareholders.	
		Because A111:	The offer was filed prior to Aventis announcing its targets for 2004–2007.
		Because A1111:	Aventis expects an acceleration of growth linked to the planned launch of new products as well as further expansion of sales of existing products.
		Because A112:	The offer was filed before the outcome of the legal challenge to Plavix® became clear.
	Because A12:	The offer clearly undervalues Aventis.	
		Because A121:	The offer fails to recognize Aventis's growth potential and is at a discount of 23.4% to the average multiple for the sector.
		Because A122:	The offer does not take into account that Sanofi-Synthélabo is seeking to acquire control and should have to pay a premium to do so.
		Because A1221:	The price offered is 31.5 percentage points below the average premium offered in comparable pharmaceutical transactions.
		Because A1222:	The price offered is 30 percentage points below the average premium offered in hostile takeover bids in France.
		Because A123:	The offer does not reflect the fact that Aventis will contribute the majority of the earnings of the combined company.

Table 5.4   continued

Global reasoning	Layer of detail-reasoning 1	2	3	4
				Because A1231: The exchange ratio is on average 25% lower than the ratio implied by Aventis's earnings contribution.
			Because A124:	Aventis's shareholders would only have 39% of the voting rights of the combined company.
				Because A1241: Sanofi-Synthélabo's shareholder structure includes double voting rights.
	Because A13: The offer has major downside risks.			
		Because A131:	The offer is mainly in Sanofi-Synthélabo shares.	
			Because A1312:	Aventis's shareholders are being asked to exchange their shares for a combination of Sanofi-Synthélabo shares (81%) and cash (19%).
		Because A132:	Sanofi-Synthélabo faces serious product risks.	
			Because A1321:	Patents on Plavix®, which accounted for 30.5% of Sanofi-Synthélabo's developed sales in 2003, are subject to imminent legal challenges in the US and Canada.
			Because A1322:	Ambien®, which represented 12% of Sanofi-Synthélabo's developed sales in 2003, will lose its patent in 2006 and face competition from generic drugs.
			Because A1323:	Eloxatine®, which is Sanofi-Synthélabo's fastest growing product and already represents 8% of its sales, will lose patent in Europe in 2006 and its exclusivity in the US in 2007, increasing the risk of competition from generic drugs.

Because A133: Sanofi-Synthélabo shares could come under pressure when one or both of its major shareholders sell their shares.

Because A1331: Sanofi-Synthélabo's two major shareholders hold 44% of the company.

Because A1332: The agreement of the two major shareholders to hold their shares expires in December 2004.

Because A134: The sales and earnings growth potential of the combined entity is subject to uncertainty.

Because A1341: The sales and earnings growth potential would be impacted by the disposals required by antitrust authorities.

Because A1342: A change of control may have adverse consequences on certain of Aventis's important alliances which are also related to potential future blockbusters.

Because A13421: Exubera® and Actonel® are part of alliance contracts.

Because A1343: The amount and timing of Sanofi-Synthélabo's stated cost synergies are highly uncertain.

Because A13431: Sanofi-Synthélabo has provided few details.

Because A13432: The realization of any synergies will be impacted by the magnitude of restructuring expected in France and Germany, in which restructuring usually takes much longer.

Because A13433: Sales synergies would be limited.

Table 5.4   continued

Global reasoning	Layer of detail-reasoning			
	1	2	3	4
				Because A13434: The significant differences between Aventis and Sanofi-Synthélabo in size and organizational culture could lead to major integration difficulties.
	Because A14: The proposed combination presents limited benefits for Aventis.	Because A141: The combination will not materially alter Aventis's critical mass.	Because A1411: Aventis has a 3.8% global market share against a mere 1.7% for Sanofi-Synthélabo.	
		Because A142: The combination will dilute the proportion of sales in the US and increase the reliance on European markets.	Because A1421: Aventis currently generates 38% of its sales from the US. Because A1422: The combined company would generate only 30% of its sales from the US.	
		Because A143: The combination will not reinforce Aventis's competitive positioning in key therapeutic areas such as vaccines, oncology, diabetes and respiratory.		
Because A2: The combination of both companies is not in the best interest of Aventis's employees.	Because A21: The combination of the two companies would cause major job cuts for Aventis's employees, particularly in France and Germany.	Because A211: Major job cuts are necessary in order to realize the level of synergies Sanofi-Synthélabo has proposed.		
		Because A212: 40% of the combined workforce of some 102 000 employees would be located in France and Germany.		
		Because A213: Sanofi-Synthélabo wishes to benefit from Aventis's global infrastructure.		

Source: Company information.

improved offer and the related agreement address the objections made by Aventis.

Features of the Revised Offer

In response to the concerns raised by Aventis, the friendly improved offer contained both a higher cash component and a higher premium to Aventis's shareholders. The financial elements of the revised offer, to which reference has already been made (see above), were modified to reflect Aventis's value more accurately. Whereas the premium increased significantly (from 15.2 per cent in the initial offer to 31.4 per cent in the revised one, based on the average Aventis share price over the one-month period ending on 21 January 2004), its rise amounting to 16.2 percentage points was evidently not large enough to satisfy the criteria set forth in Aventis's initial reasoning (Table 5.4, A121, A1221, A1222).

Whereas Aventis had a two-tier board structure (see again Table 5.1), the combined company would apply the one-tier structure of Sanofi-Synthélabo. Furthermore, J.-F. Dehecq would remain chairman as well as CEO, although recent amendments of the French Commercial Code do not prescribe a CEO duality anymore if the one-tier governance structure has been chosen but allow for splitting the roles of chairman and CEO in the unitary board structure (LOI no. 2001–420 du 15 mai 2001 relative aux nouvelles régulations économiques, articles 106 and 107, which contain modifications of articles L 225–51–1 and 225–56 of the French Commercial Code). The introduction of the option to separate the roles of chairman and CEO was unambiguously favoured by the French Committee on corporate governance chaired by Mr Vienot (Vienot 1999, p. 3). Whereas business associations stress that each company is free to decide on the basis of its own specific conditions whether to apply or to abandon CEO duality (Association Française des Entreprises Privées and Mouvement des Entreprises de France 2003, p. 6), L'Association Française de la Gestion Financière (AFG) – the French Asset Management Association, representing investment funds and individual portfolio management – strongly recommends separating the functions of chairman and CEO in the interest of shareholders (Hellebuyck 2001, p. 7). This recommendation is in accordance with corporate governance experiences made in other countries and international codes of corporate governance because splitting the two roles establishes a system of checks and balances (Dahya *et al.* 1996). However, the revised offer did not enter into a discussion about the strengths and weaknesses of the different governance models.

The revised offer envisaged arrangements for a more balanced governance structure in order to facilitate the integration between the two companies, the process of which Aventis assumed to be rather difficult (Table 5.4, A13434). More precisely, besides J.-F. Dehecq as chairman and CEO, the Sanofi-Synthélabo board of directors ('conseil d'administration') would be composed of eight directors selected by (the supervisory board of) Aventis and eight directors selected by (the board of directors of) Sanofi-Synthélabo. The vice chairman of the board would be a German Aventis director. In accordance with generally accepted governance recommendations (Vienot 1999, pp. 7–8; Hellebuyck 2001, p. 8; Association Française des Entreprises Privées and Mouvement des Entreprises de France 2003, p. 12), standing board committees would be established to increase the efficiency of the board's work and the handling of complex issues. The combined company would have four board committees, that is, an audit, a remuneration and nominating, a scientific and a newly set up strategic committee. These board committees would consist of an equal number of Aventis and Sanofi-Synthélabo directors. Even more, two of the committees would be chaired by Aventis directors and the remaining two would be chaired by Sanofi-Synthélabo directors. Finally the board of directors would include employee representatives as non-voting members. The supervisory board of Aventis was codetermined as a consequence of the German heritage of the Hoechst AG. Whereas in Germany codetermination on the supervisory board level is mandatory for (larger) stock corporations, in the case of private companies the French corporate governance system does not prescribe but allows workers' representatives on the company's board (Urbain-Parleani 2004). Compared to other continental European countries, labour influence on corporate decision-making is weak in France (Goyer and Hancké 2005, p. 175). Accordingly the voluntarily codetermined supervisory board of Aventis was primarily a concession to the Hoechst employees' representatives in order to gain approval to the merger with Rhône-Poulenc. Aventis's supervisory board was composed of 12 representatives from the shareholders and four representatives from the workforce who had the same rights and responsibilities on the board as the shareholders' representatives. Interestingly Sanofi-Synthélabo offered Aventis to fill half of the board seats of the combined company without making any restrictions that employees' representatives must not be selected. As J.-F. Dehecq admitted later in an interview, it would also have been possible to delegate employees' representatives as fully-fledged members to the board of the new company if Aventis's negotiants had demanded the right to do so (Dehecq 2004).

In addition a management committee ('comité de direction') would be established and include key officers and managers from the combined entity. The committee would be chaired by J.-F. Dehecq and composed initially of equal numbers of Aventis and Sanofi-Synthélabo executives. Finally an integration committee would be formed to oversee the integration of the two companies' operations. The members of this committee would be selected based upon criteria to find out the most suitable candidates for the ongoing operations of the new group.

Whereas this balanced governance structure could contribute to swifter implementation processes, it can by no means guarantee success. For instance, a joint integration committee may, under some circumstances, offer better potentials to identify cultural, organizational and technological misfits between the merging companies. However, the authority of such a committee is unable to make these misfits completely disappear. Moreover it seems to be open to debate whether strict proportion rules for the composition of governance organs and committees are the best solution for providing the appropriate information and facilitating the knowledge flows required to integrate different capabilities and to enhance innovation (see Lacetera 2001). Lessons learned from other mergers include that, on the one hand, proportion rules were given up after the major negotiators had left the new group and some time had elapsed. Then, usually the acquirer's executives prevailed. On the other hand, adherence to proportion rules can be too rigid and inhibit innovation and necessary adaptation inasmuch as personnel selection for leadership positions is based on proportional representation and not on merit.

Finally major risks persisted because they were left unaddressed by the revised offer. Perhaps most importantly, Sanofi-Synthélabo represented to Aventis that its disclosure regarding the Plavix® litigation was true and correct in all material aspects and in general not materially misleading. None the less doubts were still legitimate since Plavix® accounted for approximately one third of Sanofi-Synthélabo's developed sales (Table 5.4, A1321) and the outcome of patent litigation is difficult to predict. Even worse, some objections put forward by Aventis against the merger were entirely discounted without any (disclosed) reasoning (for instance, Table 5.4, A1322 or A13432).

KEY LEARNING FEATURES

Disclosure of information is necessary for accomplishing transparency about the company and its intended measures. Companies have to communicate in order to gain the confidence of their constituencies. This is particularly crucial in the case of takeover battles because the competing companies strive to convince the shareholders whether the proposed tender offer is to be accepted or rejected. Communication is thus an important issue of corporate governance. However, communicating complex decisions is difficult insofar as the solutions to complex management problems (for example, whether or not a merger should be carried out) can neither logically nor empirically be proved to be optimal. Rather assertions about the expected consequences of the recommended solutions have to be supported – more or less thoroughly – by argumentation. Accordingly the preferability of a recommended change action is associated with the thoroughness of the corresponding decision preparation.

Good corporate governance demands that decisions are made on a sound base and are transparent to corporate constituencies. Since decisions can be more or less thoroughly prepared, the question emerges whether or not the reasoning of the 'winner' is different from the reasoning of the 'loser' in a takeover battle. Naturally the bidder emphasizes the advantages of the combined entity whereas the defence of the target company demands highlighting the weaknesses of the proposed merger. None the less differences remain because the respective positions can be backed more or less thoroughly.

In order to assess the thoroughness, or argumentation rationality, of the reasoning inherent to a specific decision preparation, a measurement concept can be applied which includes an ordinal scale with four main levels of argumentation rationality. The determination of the rationality level of a concrete action recommendation (like, for instance, implementing a specific governance measure) is accomplished by examining which cognitive requirements of the scale are still satisfied by the argumentation supporting the recommendation. The lowest level of argumentation rationality is reflected by an unfounded change action, which claims only that a specific action is to be evaluated positively and lacks any reason why the recommended alternative should be chosen (for instance, the merger should be carried out).

The second level is marked by global-founded change actions. In this case, the corresponding recommendations are backed with arguments that contain propositions about the positive consequences of the recommended option for realizing certain goals (for instance, the merger should be carried out because it will enhance shareholder value). If global consequence propositions (that is, shareholder value will be enhanced) are not only stated but also backed themselves in a detail-reasoning, there are then detail-founded change actions (for instance, shareholder value will be enhanced because the merger will give the opportunity to realize cost savings and other synergies). Depending on the soundness of the detail-reasoning, the argumentation rationality of detail-founded change actions varies. Among other factors, a detail-founded argumentation can be assessed with regard to its breadth, depth and pro/contra relation. In any case, detail-founded change actions have in common that their foundation does not fully exhaust the issue-related state of accessible knowledge. Otherwise the level of qualified-founded change actions is achieved. At this point, demanding additional reasons is epistemologically not justified. Consequently a qualified-founded change action anchors the high end of the span of the thoroughness of managerial decision preparation.

On the one hand, both the unfounded and the global-founded change actions are, in the case of complex governance problems, insufficient because the validity of the assertions about the preferability of the recommended measure and the consequences of its implementation are not obvious and can hence be doubted legitimately. On the other hand, to reason change actions is not free but causes costs associated with the decision preparation. Accordingly demanding a qualified-founded change action will frequently be inappropriate due to the resources which have to be invested in order to achieve this highest level of argumentation rationality. Hence detail-founded change actions will prevail. Yet important differences remain with respect to the extent of detail-reasoning because the state of the issue-related knowledge can be exhausted more or less completely.

We elucidated the argumentation rationality of the reasonings by Sanofi-Synthélabo and Aventis about why the initial tender offer should be accepted or rejected, respectively. Both companies were urged to gain approval for their recommended course of action from Aventis's shareholders. Accordingly the representatives of the two companies had to publish arguments in order to convince their addressees. For measuring the argumentation rationality, the arguments by Sanofi-Synthélabo and Aventis related to the initial offer were identified and structured. Both reasonings capture the level of a detail-founded change action. Overall the formal similarities between the two argumentations are striking because the arguments put forward by Aventis are very much framed by Sanofi-Synthélabo's argumentation, the convincing power of which Aventis intended to cast doubt upon. Furthermore it turns out that the reasoning of Aventis is excessively partial because it contains no argument which could support the proposed merger and speak against the recommended rejection of the initial offer.

The developed structures of reasonings not only allow formal assessments, but in addition offer starting-points for a substantial discussion of the recommended change action. More precisely, argumentation lines which should be employed more carefully or aspects which are relevant for the problem in question but neglected in the current argumentation can be revealed. French stock corporations can opt for either a one-tier or a two-tier model of corporate governance. If the unitary board structure is chosen, companies may none the less split the roles of chairman and CEO. Aventis had established a two-tier structure with separated organs for managing the company and for overseeing management. In order to reflect its German heritage, Aventis's supervisory board was (voluntarily) codetermined. The combined company will apply the one-tier governance structure of Sanofi-Synthélabo. Accordingly there will be a unitary board and J.-F. Dehecq will combine the roles of chairman and CEO. Whereas these governance solutions can have tremendous impacts on the further development of the combined company, neither Aventis nor Sanofi-Synthélabo reasonings make reference to this topic.

As was to be expected, Aventis criticized Sanofi-Synthélabo's reasoning because it lacked important information or mis-stated specific facts. In the end, the revised offer replied to some but by no means all of these objections. This is a crucial observation because both Aventis's management and the supervisory board made up their minds to agree with the new offer and, as a consequence, to recommend Aventis's stockowners to tender their shares, even though the board members had vigorously advocated the rejection of the merger and the corresponding reasoning before. If the board members did indeed change their opinions substantially, this phenomenon requires more detailed analyses as to why this happened, and what this implied.

DISCUSSION QUESTIONS

1. What is market control? How can mergers and acquisitions enhance market control?
2. Discuss whether or not there are downsides if corporate governance depends only on market control. Do you assess these downsides to be significant?
3. What is the relation between corporate governance and the thoroughness of managerial decision preparations?
4. Do you think that managerial decisions are more successful when they are more thoroughly prepared? Please back your statement by comparing the costs and benefits of thorough decision preparations.
5. How can the thoroughness of a decision preparation be measured?
6. There are four main levels of argumentation rationality. Which level will be most frequently reached by managerial decision preparations in practice?
7. Is it (a) possible and (b) necessary to further differentiate detail-founded change actions?
8. In France, companies can opt for either a one-tier or a two-tier system of corporate governance. Explain the differences between the two systems and discuss their strengths and weaknesses. Can you imagine specific contingencies which promote either one or the other of the two models?

9. Takeover offers should be thoroughly prepared in order to convince the addressed shareholders. None the less companies can evidently gain approval from the shareholders even when the presented reasoning for the recommended merger is poorly founded. What other factors besides the thoroughness of the decision preparation might explain why shareholders approve a recommended course of action?
10. Develop the argumentation structure of Sanofi-Synthélabo's revised offer for Aventis's shares. Do you think that this argumentation is more convincing than the reasoning for the initial offer as shown in Table 5.3? Why?

REFERENCES

Association Française des Entreprises Privées and Mouvement des Entreprises de France (2003), *The Corporate Governance of Listed Companies: Principles for Corporate Governance Based on Consolidation of the 1995, 1999 and 2002 AFEP and MEDEF's Reports*, Paris: Association Française des Entreprises Privées (AFEP) and Mouvement des Entreprises de France (MEDEF).

Ben-Asher, Dror (2000), 'In need of treatment? Merger control, pharmaceutical innovation, and consumer welfare', *Journal of Legal Medicine*, **21**, 271–349.

Cadbury, Adrian (2002), *Corporate Governance and Chairmanship: A Personal View*, Oxford: Oxford University Press.

Dahya, Jay, A. Alasdair Lonie and David M. Power (1996), 'The case for separating the roles of chairman and CEO: an analysis of stock market and accounting data', *Corporate Governance – An International Review*, **4**, 71–7.

Danzon, Patricia M. (2000), 'The pharmaceutical industry', in Boudewijn Bouckaert and Gerrit De Geert (eds), *The Encyclopedia of Law and Economics*, Cheltenham, UK: Edward Elgar, pp. 1055–91.

Danzon, Patricia M., Andrew Epstein and Sean Nicholson (2004), 'Mergers and acquisitions in the pharmaceutical and biotech industries', Working paper, The Wharton School, University of Pennsylvania.

Dehecq, Jean-François (2004), 'Politiker durften nicht mitreden', *Die Zeit*, **59**(25), 26.

Fox, Merritt B. (1998), 'Required disclosure and corporate governance', in Klaus J. Hopt, Hideki Kanda, Mark J. Roe, Eddy Wymeersch and Stefan Prigge (eds), *Comparative Corporate Governance: The State of the Art and Emerging Research*, Oxford: Clarendon Press, pp. 701–18.

Ghemawat, Pankaj and Fariborz Ghadar (2000), 'The dubious logic of global megamergers', *Harvard Business Review*, **78**(4), 64–72.

Goyer, Michel and Bob Hancké (2005), 'Labour in French corporate governance: the missing link', in Howard Gospel and Andrew Pendleton (eds), *Corporate Governance and Labour Management: An International Perspective*, Oxford: Oxford University Press, pp. 173–96.

Grant, Wyn, William Paterson and Colin Whitston (1988), *Government and the Chemical Industry: A Comparative Study of Britain and West Germany*, Oxford: Clarendon Press.

Gregory, Holly J. and Robert T. Simmelkjaer, II (2002), *Comparative Study of Corporate Governance Codes Relevant to the European Union and Its Member States*, Brussels: Weil, Gotshal & Manges.

Grundei, Jens and Till Talaulicar (2002), 'Company law and corporate governance of start-ups in Germany: legal stipulations, managerial requirements, and modification strategies', *Journal of Management and Governance*, **6**, 1–27.

Hara, Takuji (2003), *Innovation in the Pharmaceutical Industry: The Process of Drug Discovery and Development*, Cheltenham, UK: Edward Elgar.

Hellebuyck, Jean-Pierre (2001), *Recommendations on Corporate Governance*, Paris: L'Association Française de la Gestion Financière.

Jemison, David B. and Sim B. Sitkin (1986), 'Corporate acquisitions: a process perspective', *Academy of Management Review*, **11**, 145–63.

Jensen, Michael C. and Richard S. Ruback (1983), 'The market for corporate control: the scientific evidence', *Journal of Financial Economics*, **11**, 5–50.

Koenig, Michael E.D. and Elizabeth M. Mezick (2004), 'Impact of mergers and acquisitions on research productivity within the pharmaceutical industry', *Scientometrics*, **59**, 157–69.

Lacetera, Nicola (2001), 'Corporate governance and the governance of innovation: the case of pharmaceutical industry', *Journal of Management and Governance*, **5**, 29–59.

Lubatkin, Michael H. and Peter J. Lane (1996), 'Psst ... The merger mavens still have it wrong!', *Academy of Management Executive*, **10**(1), 21–37.

Macey, Jonathan R. (1998), 'Institutional investors and corporate monitoring: a demand-side perspective in a comparative view', in Klaus J. Hopt, Hideki Kanda, Mark J. Roe, Eddy Wymeersch and Stefan Prigge (eds), *Comparative Corporate Governance: The State of the Art and Emerging Research*, Oxford: Clarendon Press, pp. 903–19.

Manne, Henry G. (1965), 'Mergers and the market for corporate control', *Journal of Political Economy*, **73**, 110–20.

Monks, Robert A.G. and Nell Minow (2004), *Corporate Governance*, 3rd edn, Oxford: Blackwell.

Productivity Commission (2001), *International Pharmaceutical Price Differences: Research Report*, Canberra: AusInfo.

Toulmin, Stephen Edelston (1958), *The Uses of Argument*, Cambridge, UK: Cambridge University Press.

Toulmin, Stephen, Richard Rieke and Allan Janik (1979), *An Introduction to Reasoning*, New York: Macmillan.

Urbain-Parleani, Isabelle (2004), 'La participation des salariés aux organes de gestion des sociétés anonymes', in Theodor Baums and Peter Ulmer (eds), *Unternehmens-Mitbestimmung der Arbeitnehmer im Recht der EU-Mitgliedstaaten*, Heidelberg: Verlag Recht und Wirtschaft, pp. 47–62.

Vienot, Marc (1999), *Recommendations of the Committee on Corporate Governance*, Paris: Association Française des Entreprises Privées (AFEP) and Mouvement des Entreprises de France (MEDEF).

Walsh, James P. and James K. Seward (1990), 'On the efficiency of internal and external corporate control mechanisms', *Academy of Management Review*, **15**, 421–58.

v. Werder, Axel (1994), *Unternehmungsführung und Argumentationsrationalität*, Stuttgart: Schäffer-Poeschel.

v. Werder, Axel (1999), 'Argumentation rationality of management decisions', *Organization Science*, **10**, 672–90.
v. Werder, Axel, Dong-Sung Cho and Till Talaulicar (2000), 'Argumentation rationality in the German and Korean automotive industry', *Journal of International and Area Studies*, **7**, 15–58.

PART 2

Corporate governance in Central and
Eastern European countries

6. The Northern Russia Electric Company case: to whom is the Director-General accountable: the company, the board of directors or the controlling shareholder?

James Gillies

INTRODUCTION

Uri Katinov, the General Director of Northern Russia Electric Company (NREC), faces a very difficult problem. He has just heard that a project requiring, at a minimum, a doubling of the available supply of electricity in the region is going ahead and he fears that, if his company cannot increase its output relatively rapidly, a new competitive company will be built that in the long run might put his organization out of business. Although NREC has been doing well, earning a 15 per cent return on equity, it does not have anywhere near the amount in reserves necessary to finance an expansion that would almost double output. Moreover, he is almost certain that the controlling shareholder of the firm will be unwilling to either advance the funds necessary to expand operations or sell more equity to another investor to raise the funds needed to finance growth. Indeed, the regional manager of the controlling shareholder, United Electric Power Transmission System of Russia (UEPTSR) had more or less indicated to him last year that, given the holding company's many areas of activity throughout Russia and the possibility of it making some investments abroad, it would not make any new substantial investment in NREC for several more years. And yet Uri is certain, given the fact that there are great economies of scale in the production of electricity, new investment to expand output would be very profitable and he does not want to see the opportunities presented by an expanding market go to someone else.

THE NEW MARKET CHALLENGE

The Northern Russia Electric Company (NREC) is situated close to the centre of one of the largest bauxite deposits in the world, estimated to be more than 250 million tons. In 2000 SUAL Holdings decided that a new aluminium mill should be built in the area and in the spring of 2002 the head of the regional government, the president of SUAL and the president of a major Canadian engineering company signed a general tripartite agreement to go ahead with the development of the bauxite. The most recent action, precipitating Uri's concern, is the announcement by the bauxite group of a decision to proceed in 2005 with the construction of the mill, which is expected to have the capacity to produce more than a million tonnes of aluminium substance and 500 000 tonnes of pure aluminium a year. It will create thousands of jobs in the area, and there will be a requirement for a great deal more electricity – about twice the current output of Northern Russia Electric during the building stage and three times the amount when the project is completed.

THE NORTHERN RUSSIA ELECTRIC COMPANY

For the past 25 years the Northern Russia Electric Company has been one of the most important wholesale generators of power in northwestern Russia (Figure 6.1). It is fuelled by natural gas and regularly produces about 3000.3 million kilowatts of electric power, which is fed into a federal wholesale electric power grid for distribution via local power companies to consumers. The company employs 1200 people and operates through four divisions: production, distribution, maintenance and repair, and administration. In 2003 NREC had an income from the sale of power of 2.3 billion rubles and profits of slightly more than 135 million rubles before administrative and other costs. Total assets of the company were valued at 1.5 billion rubles, short-term liabilities at 350 million rubles, retained earnings 250 million rubles and shareholders' equity at 900 million rubles and the company has no long-term debt.

At the time of Perestroika, when the government announced that its goal was to have competition in the supply of energy to the wholesale markets, the company was privatized. Very quickly control of NREC was acquired by a major holding company, the United Electrical Power Transmission System of Russia, which in a relatively short period of time, through acquisition of companies such as NREC, gained control over most of the transmission of electricity in northwestern Russia. Although the United Electrical Power Transmission System of Russia is a private company, it operates within

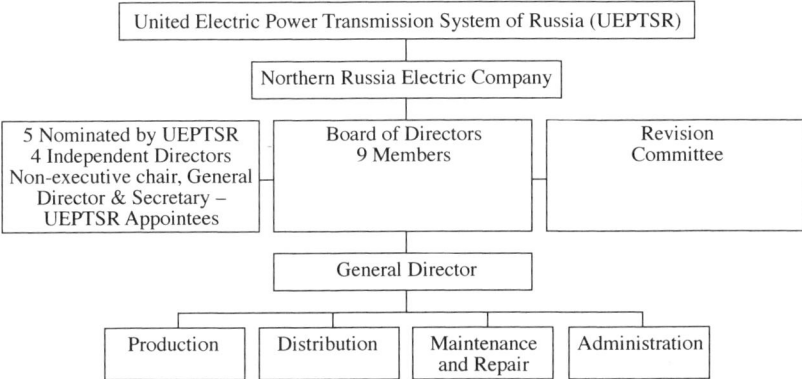

Figure 6.1   *Governance and senior management structure of Northern*
Russia Electric Company

the framework of the national energy policy, the goal of which is to have
competition among wholesalers of electricity. Consequently the mandate
of the parent company and of its subsidiaries is, as a result of general
market reforms in Russia, to become competitive participants in supplying
the wholesale market with electrical energy. By 1996 the United Electrical
Power Transmission System of Russia had, including its original investment,
slightly over 600 million rubles invested in NREC and was to all intents
and purposes the only shareholder.

Over the years the strategy of the parent was to increase the capitalization
of Northern Russia Electric Company by bringing in new equity from
abroad. It was successful in doing so to the extent that in 2003 the total
capitalization of the company had grown to 900 million rubles, with the
great bulk of the new capital coming from three private investment funds
– one domiciled in Great Britain and two in the United States (Figure
6.2). While it remained the controlling shareholder, after the new capital
infusions, the total ownership of the holding company was reduced to a
comfortable 66 per cent. In 1997 trading of NREC shares began on the
Russian Trading System Stock Exchange, but little or no capital was raised
from the offering. The number of transactions was few and the listing simply
created a market value for the shares. It did not lead to a great inflow of
investment by individual Russian citizens.

Uri knew that the rate of return on assets on capital investment met the
hurdle rate of the major shareholder and that all the shareholders were
reasonably content with the progress of the company. However, from various
conversations with representatives of the holding company he also knew that
the majority shareholder, was not only unwilling to invest more in NREC

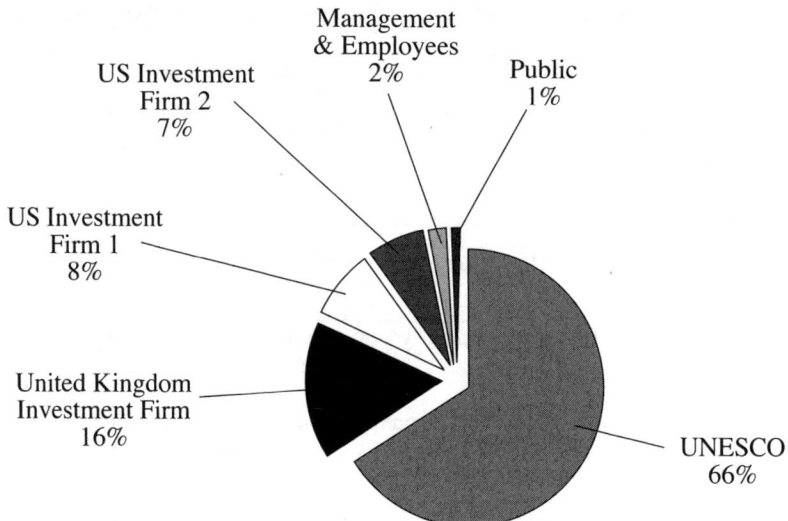

Figure 6.2   Ownership structure of Northern Russia Electric Company

but also had no plans to dilute its percentage of the ownership by selling more of its shares. While he was not privy to the strategies of the parent, he believed it had reduced the percentage of its ownership in the past to acquire foreign exchange to invest in, and gain control of, several manufacturing plants in the United States and Great Britain, from which it could import high-tech equipment for use in its more sophisticated operations.

THE GOVERNANCE OF THE NREC

Uri firmly believed that one of the reasons United Electric Power Transmission Systems had been able to raise capital for NREC from investors outside of Russia was the fact that it had insisted on sound modern corporate governance practices at the subsidiary company. The parent had approved and paid for Uri to attend a two week programme on modern corporate governance practices in England and had encouraged his participation in governance conferences sponsored by organizations such as the OECD and the Institute of Corporate Directors in Moscow. As a result he believed that NREC was probably one of the most advanced companies in Russia in terms of the development of sound corporate governance practices, at least as they were defined by Western standards. The company issued only one class of stock – there are no multiple voting shares – and the shares are traded on the Russian Trading System Stock Exchange (although the amount of activity was slight). A code of best practices that included a commitment was adopted in 1998:

(a) to treat all shareholders the same with respect to dividends and board representation;
(b) to operate in a transparent fashion;
(c) to hold an open annual meeting;
(d) to issue a comprehensive annual report;
(e) to include independent directors on the board; and
(f) to accept that the directors' duties of care and of loyalty were to the company.

THE NREC BOARD

In 2004 the Northern Russia Electric Company has a board of nine members: five from the parent company and four – two from Russia, one from the United States and one from the United Kingdom – from the minority investors (Table 6.1). Eight of the nine directors participate actively in the decision-making activities of the board, one member is the secretary (a nominee of the controlling shareholder who is basically ex officio and does not participate in the decision-making duties or have a vote). Andre Romanov, a nominee of the holding company, serves as a non-executive chair and has a tie-breaking vote if one is necessary. To date there has never been a tie vote.

Table 6.1   Director representation of shareholders of Northern Russia Electric Company

Five directors including Non-executive Chair, General Director, Secretary	UEPTSR
Two independent directors	Jointly elected by minority shareholders on the recommendation of the Association for the Protection of Shareholders and the Institute of Directors, Moscow
One director	United Kingdom investment firm
One director	US investment firm 1 and 2

The board is responsible for the effective management of the company's activities. It considers that within the law and the general parameters determined by the major shareholder, its duties to be :

(a) overseeing and effectively monitoring the company's activities;
(b) controlling the company's activities;
(c) protecting the rights of shareholders;
(d) resolving internal conflicts; and
(e) assuring transparency of the company's operations.

It fulfils these responsibilities by overseeing the activities of the General Director (Uri), a nominee of the controlling shareholder, and with a special committee of the Board – the Revision Committee (Audit Committee) through which it monitors the company's financial activities. It obtains regular reports from the General Director on the planning, staffing, organizing, controlling and directing of all activities. It constantly reviews and assesses its own activities and meets for two days every two months. It considers itself to be an effective board and issues a very informative annual report. It constantly measures itself against the standards established by the Institute of Directors in Moscow and the guidelines of the OECD.

While there was some minor consultation with the board by the major shareholder when Uri was appointed the General Director of the company, the appointment was made by the controlling shareholder. The board concurred in the appointment but did not have the power to veto it.

Uri generally gets along well with the board. He has assessed the individual strengths and weaknesses of the members, their individual reasons for being on the board, their commitment to the company, and their competencies and behavioural characteristics. Of the four (other than himself) from the parent company, two are engineers who have spent their entire working life in power companies. They are skilled in engineering matters but have little understanding about business techniques in general, the role of markets in business and modern corporate governance. Of the other two, one serves as a Non-executive Chair and one serves as Secretary. Both are over 60 years of age, are junior officers of the Electric Power Transmission Systems of Russia, but are not active in its management and have basically been appointed directors of NREC as a reward for long-term service in the parent company. Both, before being employed by the parent company, had political appointments. They worked in various government departments where they learned to be acutely attuned to the wishes of their superiors, and they have brought the same skill to the NREC board.

The two Russian directors representing the minority were selected by all three foreign investors acting in concert. They retained a Russian consulting firm and gave it the assignment of finding Russian candidates who spoke English, who preferably had some experience in the electrical transmission industry and who had considerable knowledge of modern corporate governance practices. The consultant, in turn, canvassed the Association for the Protection of Shareholders and the Professional Institute of Directors in Moscow and came up with eight suitable people. They all were extensively interviewed by a three-man committee of the investors and two were put forth as directors.

Basically Uri has concluded that the director from the United States, while well intended and very fully informed about modern governance practices, is naïve about Russian politics, government, culture and social values. As for the director from the United Kingdom, while he speaks Russian (his wife is a Russian), he has not spent much time in Russia and has no experience with Russian firms.

All four of the directors representing the minority are well aware that they are perceived at large to be, and expected to act as, independent directors. However, they are not naïve and they know that if the major shareholder had objected to their being on the board their appointments would have been vetoed. They know that the method of their appointment was as much to demonstrate to foreign investors that the company is following sound corporate governance principles, as it was to get their advice. But that being said, all four directors representing the minority shareholders are well versed in corporate governance matters and two, as noted above, have had experience working in the administration of power companies. Uri believes that all are committed to good corporate governance when governance is defined in terms of the need for transparency in the activities of the enterprise, the treatment of all shareholders in a fair and equitable manner and the need for careful monitoring of the activities of the management. They have been helpful to Uri in insisting that the company have a business plan, a proper budget, good cash management, a capital spending plan for maintenance of assets and so on. In short, they help Uri, as General Director, and his staff, to run the business efficiently. He believes that, in spite of the fact that they can at any time be removed by the parent, he can talk to them about any differences he may have with the parent company openly and honestly and that the confidentiality of any conversation will be honoured. On balance, Uri is extremely pleased with the process that the three foreign investors and the holding company had agreed upon for picking directors.

The one minor problem that Uri has with the board is that on the whole it is very inward looking, and is overly concerned with details about internal operations almost to the exclusion of dealing with external issues, such as environmental problems, stultifying regulations, and so on. The board leaves such issues to be settled at the parent company level. Inasmuch as such issues usually involve considerable political manoeuvring, the board believes the parent is best equipped to handle such problems, and Uri feels that the board is probably correct in their assessment.

A much greater problem, as far as Uri is concerned, is he feels intuitively that the board lacks any entrepreneurial drive and would not support him in any major initiatives. The American representative is simply too inexperienced to understand Russian markets and the four representatives from the parent automatically oppose anything that might cause the parent concern or that even might appear to be challenging the parent's authority or responsibilities. Indeed, their major aim is not to do anything that might draw the parent's attention to the operations of the Northern Russia Electric Company. While the three other Russian-speaking directors are very aware of their responsibilities as directors representing the interests of the minority shareholder, they have a rather narrow view of the extent of these responsibilities. They don't believe that they should have a major input on long-term strategy matters and are content to maintain the status quo. Their goal is not necessarily to assure the maximum rate of return for the company's owners, but rather to have the company recognized as a model of modern corporate governance in traditional terms.

URI'S DILEMMA

When he was in Moscow a few weeks ago at a meeting of the Institute of Professional Directors, Uri listened to a paper given by a Western-trained consultant, now working on his own, about 'management buy-outs' and the thought flickered through his mind that if he only had the money it would be a wonderful thing if he could acquire control of the company. He remembered that the consultant had talked about ways and means of raising funds for such buy-outs, but they all involved activities about which he knew little. He really did not give the matter much thought because he was aware that the transfer of ownership of many companies through the voucher programme and the 'loans for shares' in the mid-1990s had resulted in a generally negative public feeling about buy-outs and that it was not a practical possibility anyway. He did not even know whether it was legal for a corporate officer to get involved in such things. At the same time he knew that the company could attract foreign capital – it had already done so – and that there might be some way in which he could come up with a scheme:

(a)　to entice the parent to raise more capital for the company; or

(b) perhaps, if the controlling shareholder was not willing to put more capital into NREC, he might be able to develop a plan with the minority shareholders to raise more capital.

If he did so, maybe he could leverage his position in such a manner that he would end up having more direct say in the strategic direction of the company? He knew that the controlling shareholder was not going to take the initiative necessary to grow the company, keep it competitive and take advantage of the great opportunity that was within its grasp. Moreover, he felt that if he didn't do something the company might actually be forced out of business. Perhaps, he thought, I should give the consultant a call and ask him what alternatives he could suggest to raise the capital to implement the growth that the company must have if it is to survive.

But then it occurred to him he did not know what the major shareholder of the company would think if it learned that he was interested in doing something designed to reduce its control. Since the parent company's four appointees (other than himself) on the nine-man board were congenitally opposed to new ideas and change, it was unlikely that he could ever get them to agree to support an approach to the major shareholder by someone to buy control of the company. Moreover, he knew that it was the policy of the government to have competition in the wholesale market for the distribution of electricity, so perhaps the government would support the construction of another plant rather than allow Northern Russia Electric Company to expand, and if a new competitive plant was constructed it could be disastrous. Perhaps it was his obligation to bring the matter to the board?

Uri really did not know what to do. Perhaps he should call the consultant and ask his general advice on the responsibilities of a director-general in such a situation and particularly on whether capital could be raised to bring about a change in control? Or perhaps he should go to the board and discuss with them his concerns about recent developments? Or perhaps he should really say nothing at this stage, since no construction on the aluminium plant had started? Or since major strategic decisions were made by the controlling shareholder, maybe he should arrange to meet the president of the holding company – a man he did not know – in Moscow. But that would mean going behind the back of the board of NREC – a board with which he worked well.

In his heart, Uri knew that he should discuss the issue with the Northern Russia Electric Company board. But he was afraid that they would do nothing. Rumours of major projects abounded and even when a new one had the support of the regional political leaders and an agreement with foreign investors there was always great scepticism that anything would really happen. The board members were basically risk averse and very anti-entrepreneurial. He was almost certain they would simply suggest that there was no need for any decision at this time, that it was not in their mandate to deal with such a large potential change in demand for power in the region, and that they should concentrate on their terms of reference which they had adopted only two years before. Last year he had proposed that the board request a relatively modest capital expenditure for expansion of the plant, but the board decided not to go forward to the parent company with the request, even though a good case could be made for the expenditure. Uri also knew that the board might order him to do nothing about the potential new situation and a great opportunity would be lost. It was a real dilemma. Did he have a responsibility to the board? To the major shareholder? To the company? Or, indeed, to himself to take advantage of an opportunity that the company might not want?

He called his secretary and told her to get Eli Petrov of the Petrov Consulting firm in Moscow on the telephone.

PETROV CONSULTING

Eli Petrov was 35 years old. He was born in Moscow in 1969, the son of a Russian diplomat. When Eli was five his father was posted to the Russian Embassy in Switzerland and Eli was enrolled in a Swiss boarding school. He learned English and French and studied the normal curriculum. When he was 18 he enrolled at Oxford where he studied economics and history, specializing in the modern history of Russia. In 1991, when he was 22 years old he entered the Harvard Business School, graduating in 1993 with an MBA degree. Although he lived outside of Russia for most of his life, he spent every summer in Moscow with his grandparents and, after his father retired from the Foreign Service, with his parents.

A very good student, with an international background, upon graduation he was much sought after by several major consulting firms. He joined one of the more prestigious and after a short internship was assigned to the Moscow office of the company. In 2000 he decided to organize his own firm, specializing in finance and governance problems. He became involved with various organizations associated with corporate governance reform, spoke at their conferences and generally networked with the officers of Russian corporations who attended such meetings. He was not surprised to receive Uri's call and after a brief review of the situation he agreed to meet with him the following week at the Grand Marriott Hotel in Moscow, when Eli would be in the city on business.

THE MEETING

The meeting between Uri and Eli went very well. Uri was impressed with the fact that Eli had a solid grasp of modern corporate governance principles, but at the same time a clear understanding of Russian culture, history, government, politics and corporate development. Quickly they agreed that there were three governance issues and one practical issue involved in the problem. First, thinking, but not certain, that the board would not take any action to deal with the probability that the demand for electricity in the area could double or triple within the next three years, and that it might even instruct him not to discuss the matter with the controlling shareholder, could Uri bypass the board in dealing with the issue? Second, was he fulfilling his responsibilities as the General Director if he did not pursue the issue with the controlling shareholder even if the board did not want him to? Third, was it proper for Uri, in the general interests of the company, to start any discussions with minority shareholders about increasing their investment in the company to the point where their collective ownership surpassed that of the major shareholder without first discussing it with the board and/or the major shareholder? Indeed, would it be legal for him to do so? And fourth, could money be raised for a buy-out of the controlling shareholders interest if the shareholder agreed to sell its position?

Eli believed that they should deal with the fourth issue first for the simple reason that if the financing of a change in control was impossible to arrange, none of the other issues mattered. It was his opinion that arranging financing for the expansion of the plant would not be difficult since it could probably be financed on the basis of contracts with SAUL Holdings for electricity used for the construction and operation of the new aluminium mill. It was left that Eli would make some very informal inquiries, for information purposes only, about the possibilities of the availability of obtaining capital for a major expansion of the plant, with Uri as the major player from the management side, without any disclosures to anyone. He was pleased to do so without a fee, since he would gain substantially if a deal did go forward.

With respect to the other issues, since the major shareholder, the Electric Power Transmission Systems of Russia, would obviously at some point have to be approached about any proposal for a change in ownership, and since Uri was currently in its employ, Eli believed that the major shareholder could well assume that Uri had acted in bad faith in even considering orchestrating a change of control without discussing such a major proposal with it. It certainly could be considered unethical and it might even be against some law for him to do so. He suggested that Uri receive legal advice before he did anything rash.

THE RESOLUTION

Reflecting on the discussion with Eli, Uri felt that he was making 'a mountain out of a mole hill'. He was responsible to the board members and so he decided he should discuss the matter with them. They would have heard, or would hear, about the potential bauxite development anyway and were not stupid – indeed the board members were quite bright – and would have some thoughts about what should be done. The possible development of the aluminium mill was no secret, so why shouldn't he bring to the board a plan involving the major shareholder to deal with the potential market bonanza? If the directors refused to do anything and the company missed a great opportunity, it would not be his fault. On the other hand the directors had always been reluctant to discuss major ideas with the controlling shareholder or to recommend any new activities that might involve some risk. They would postpone doing anything and possibly instruct him not to discuss the matter with the major shareholder. After all it was the duty of the board members representing the shareholders to decide the issues to take to the people who appointed them. And as far as the minority shareholders were concerned, the other board members could speak for them. It would not be his fault if, because of the timidity of the directors, the company lost the biggest contract ever to come to the area. It would be extremely unfortunate if, through the lack of apparent interest on the part of NREC in growing, a major competitor was built in the market place, but no one could blame him. If, on the other hand, he did not get the matter before the controlling shareholder, NREC might fail and his job would disappear. However, if he did go to the major shareholder against the wishes of his board he might be fired.

At the same time he might be misjudging the board. If he did not bring a proposal for dealing with the enormous potential demand for electricity, they might consider him negligent and lose confidence in his judgement. And certainly, if they learned that he was speaking to the major shareholder on some type of change of control scheme without mentioning the potential opportunities to the board, they could very well be outraged. Sometimes he wished that he had not been so keen on having a board and following all the ideas about modern corporate governance.

From all his study of corporate governance, Uri knew that the one thing stressed in all discussions was that the duty of care and duty of loyalty of a director was to the company – not to the board and not to the controlling shareholder. It was also clear in the governance charter the company had adopted almost 10 years earlier that the duties of the directors were to the company. He was convinced that it was in the best interest of the company to expand. What should he do?

TEACHING POINTS

The purpose of this study is to illustrate the problems that (a) minority shareholders and (b) managers have in dealing with a controlling shareholder. While the Northern Russia Electric Company is committed to following the 'best practices' of corporate governance, there is no question that the controlling shareholder – the United Electrical Power Transmission System of Russia – exercises complete control over the company. It nominates five directors of the board and appoints from the group the General Director, as well as the Executive Chair and Secretary of the Board. The strategy of the Northern Russia Electric Company is determined by the controlling shareholder as demonstrated by the fact that it sold some of its shares in the NREC to foreign investors in order to obtain foreign exchange to invest abroad and to acquire suppliers of high-technology equipment. It does not appear to have any plans to invest more capital in NREC.

The controlling shareholder has the right to use its majority position to determine what happens at NREC, but at the same time it is a public company with publicly owned shares, owned largely by three major foreign investors. The board, according to good corporate governance practices, has an obligation, within the law and appropriate social behaviour, to maximize shareholder value for all shareholders. When it attracted capital by selling shares to foreign investment firms, those firms would have the expectation that this would be done and they have the right to expect the board will ensure that actions are taken in the interests of all shareholders, not simply the majority.

The case illustrates the decision process involved when:

1. A corporate officer perceives conflict between duties, under the law and according to good corporate governance, to all shareholders and duties to the company or to the controlling shareholder;
2. A corporate officer wishes to maintain good relationships with the board and the perception of good corporate governance, but does not have faith in the ability of the board to reach the right decision.
3. The board adopts the principles of good corporate governance, including fair treatment for all shareholders, when the interests of the minority shareholders and controlling shareholders diverge.
4. The challenges to directors representing the interests of the minority shareholders.

QUESTIONS FOR DISCUSSION

1. Considering the five 'Duties of the Northern Russia Electric Company' board as outlined in its rules of corporate conduct adopted by the board and as perceived by Uri, what are the arguments for and against him doing each of the following:
   (a) Bypass the board and discuss the possible expansion with the majority shareholder first.
   (b) Discuss the expansion with his own board with the understanding that he would not approach the majority shareholder unless given permission by the board.
   (c) Discuss the possible expansion with his own board, with the understanding that he would in any case approach the majority shareholder with the issue. Uri is not asking the board for permission, but simply their opinion on the expansion issue.
   (d) Begin discussion with the minority shareholders about increasing their level of investment in the company:
      i. Before discussing the matter with either the majority shareholder or with the board so he could present each with his findings.
      ii. After discussing this with the majority shareholder but not with the board.
      iii. After discussing this with the board and then with the majority shareholder.
2. What should the board do in each of the alternative possibilities – a , b, c, or d – that Uri might follow, for example, if he bypasses the board, and so on?
3. What should the independent directors and the directors representing the non-Russian investors do if Uri follows (d)?
4. Should the independent directors when they are informed, or otherwise learn, of the potential profitable situation which is being passed over by NREC because the controlling shareholder does not want to invest more in the company:
   (a) Try to sell their investment back to the controlling shareholder?
   (b) Go around the NREC board to the controlling shareholder and try to convince it to invest more in NREC?
   (c) Try to convince their companies to buy control from the controlling shareholder?
   (d) Do nothing?
5. In your opinion which of the various alternatives should Uri follow?

ACKNOWLEDGEMENTS

The author is indebted to Dmitry Shtykov , General Director of the Institute of Professional Directors in Moscow for providing him with background information regarding the distribution of electric power in Russia. Ms Olga Melitonyan, Manager of the Corporate Governance Centre at the Higher School of Economics and Professor Donald Thompson of the Schulich School of Business also provided important information used in developing this chapter. Without their support it could not have been written. This is a fictional case, and while reflecting some current corporate governance problems in Russia, it is not based on the activities of any actual organization. It has been prepared for teaching purposes and none of the individuals or information in the case is based on any existing or past corporations, boards or individuals, dead or alive.

7. Polish supervisory boards in practice – a few snapshots

Izabela Koładkiewicz

THE SUPERVISORY BOARD IN POLAND – PRINCIPLES OF ITS FUNCTIONING IN THEORY AND PRACTICE

In Poland, the supervisory board plays the role of a basic mechanism within the framework of corporate governance structures established in the company. In a historical context, the institution of the supervisory board as an oversight body was introduced into Polish companies on a broad scale with the signing into law on 13 July 1990 of the Act on State Enterprise Privatization.[1] Over the next few years, the board of supervisors has managed to become an integral component of the internal governance structure of Polish capital companies.

Currently, the character of its responsibilities and its operations are regulated by the provisions of the Commercial Company Code (CCC), which came into force on 1 January 2001. In line with solutions approved within that legal framework, the primary task of the supervisory board is continuous supervision over company operations in all areas of activities. In order to meet its obligations, the board may examine all company documents, demand reports and explanations from the management board and all employees, and audit the state of company assets.[2] Moreover, the appointing and dismissing of members of the management board, evaluation of the management board's annual company reports and monitoring company operating plans all lie within the jurisdiction of the supervisory board. At this point it should be added that in line with approved legal regulations the supervisory board does not have the right to issue orders that are binding on the management board with respect to managing company affairs. Furthermore, the management board may approach the general assembly directly in cases in which it is incapable of procuring the approval of the supervisory board for its charter activities.

The supervisory board is appointed by the general assembly of shareholders by way of majority or group voting (as moved by shareholders representing at least one-fifth of the share capital). The Commercial Company Code also allows other ways of appointing and dismissing members of the supervisory board as defined by the company charter.

The supervisory board should consist of a minimum of three members, with at least five members in the case of a public company, appointed for terms no longer than five years. Pursuant to legal solutions, a member of the supervisory board cannot be a member of the management board, a proxy, a liquidator, a department or division manager nor be employed by the company as a chief accountant, legal adviser or lawyer.

The supervisory board should meet as necessary, but no less than three times over the course of the fiscal year. It meets its responsibilities as a group, but it may delegate its members to undertake defined supervisory actions independently.

As to the method of remuneration for the supervisory board, in line with regulations contained in the Commercial Company Code, a member of the supervisory board may receive remuneration as defined in the charter or resolution of the general assembly of shareholders.

Analysis of the provisions of the Commercial Company Code demonstrate that although it in no way forces action on the part of the supervisory board, it contains no ban on its activity and it most certainly allows for augmentation of supervisory board rights through such documents as the company charter and the bylaws of company bodies. However, observations to date based on studies on the activities of supervisory boards (still too few) show that supervisory board involvement in the life of the company is, as a rule, too small. It is the view of many experts that the supervisory board becomes active only when something is amiss in the company, conflicts make an appearance, economic results deteriorate or the company is threatened with bankruptcy (Rudolf *et al.* 2002, pp. 49–54).

In summary, it should be stated that the practice of supervisory board functioning in companies operating in Poland is extremely varied. Such an observation should not be a cause for surprise because the usefulness and character of involvement of the supervisory board in the company is determined by a very complex set of parameters – ownership structure and owner identity encompassing much more than just the context of whether or not the owner is a corporate entity or individual, including a distinction between domestic and foreign investors.

Moreover, the position occupied by the supervisory board in the continuum defined by the extremes of 'passive stance–active stance' is determined by the size and complexity of the organization. Expectations with respect to the supervisory board will be different in the case of a single company where its size will also be a significant factor and different in the case of a complex economic group, including capital groups characteristic of Polish conditions.[3]

For this reason, as well as due to space constraints, the present study should be treated as something of an illustration of certain trends that presently can be observed in perceiving the supervisory board as well as in the approach of the supervisory boards themselves to the function they fill.[4]

THE ROLE OF THE SUPERVISORY BOARD IN THE LIFE OF COMPANIES OPERATING IN POLAND – A SELECTION OF EXPERIENCES

The Supervisory Board in Cases in which there is No Separation of Ownership and Management

The set of primary functions of the board of directors/supervisory board encompasses monitoring, consulting and services (Zahra and Pearce, 1989). However, stress on their implementation varies depending on the needs of the company. What should be identified among basic factors determining their assigned weight and importance is the level of organizational development, including size, and the character of the ownership structure. For example, due to their rather lucid ownership structure as compared with public companies (ownership concentration as opposed to its dispersion) as well as the frequent, direct involvement of the owner in management in the case of small and medium companies, the interest of the supervisory board in such entities is concentrated on activities linked with performance of the oversight function to a significantly lesser degree. The presence of the owner in the company's internal governance structure means an absence of typical problems derived from the separation of ownership and management (rights stemming from ownership and management responsibility pertain to a single person).

At the same time, the direct involvement of the company owner in management often bears fruit in the supervisory board being assigned the role of a dummy organization or even it not being appointed (under conditions when the law allows this, of course). This last situation occurred in the case of a well-known Polish manufacturer of women's, men's and children's underwear – a leader on the Polish underwear market – that managed to take over almost one-third of the market in less than ten years from its start-up and became one of two significant players on the Polish market amidst a field of minor manufacturers.

The presence of the owner in the company's internal governance structure (a limited liability company),[5] who serves as president of the management board and remains the sole shareholder, is seen as a factor responsible for the absence of a supervisory board. One of the company directors put it this way: 'If the shareholder himself takes part in the process of company management, then there is no need for the functioning of a supervisory board to monitor management board activities.' Moreover, in his view:

> the system as it has developed at this point – the lack of a supervisory board – is absolutely adequate for the way in which the company presently functions. In essence, it is only a matter of setting up control processes and mechanisms and that is why there is no need for the presence of such a body in our company today.

What is even more interesting is that the present solution in this area seems to be sufficiently satisfactory since even the company's entry onto the stock exchange, which is planned for the nearest future, is not bringing in any change: 'If we change forms and become a joint stock company, then the existence of a supervisory board, if nothing else changes, will only be there to satisfy the requirements of the Commercial Company Code.'

Examples of Supervisory Mechanisms Applied in the Absence of a Supervisory Board

Obviously, the absence of a supervisory board does not mean an absence of control over what is happening in this company, which employs over 300 people. The person responsible for direct supervision over the in-house monitoring of the entire organization is its financial director. The financial director is aided in these efforts by the chief accountant, who provides something that may be termed 'direct monitoring', as well as a person employed as an in-house auditor conducting examinations *ex post*.

The basic task of the chief accountant, in addition to overseeing the operations of the accounting department (where the chief accountant is not a participant in operations on a day-to-day basis), is supervision over the execution of company procedures. These procedures have been laid down in a code of procedures, inclusive of detailed information regarding who is responsible for implementation. Reports relating to this aspect of monitoring subsequently are passed on to the financial director. Should any significant infringement occur – one that might potentially expose the company to losses – an appropriate report is delivered directly to the desk of the president of the management board – the company owner.

The in-house auditor, for his part, heads the audit department, which conducts complete, cross-section audits of specified areas and processes as ordered by any of the company's directors, especially the financial director. It is on the basis of accumulated data that post-audit recommendations, inclusive of a list of violations to be eliminated, are directed to the appropriate person. At the same time, the final conclusions from the audit go to the president of the management board. At this point, it should be stressed that the control mechanisms applied in this case combine in-house audits with controlling.

In company practice in the realm of monitoring as characterized above, it is clear that the main role in this area is played by the financial director as well as the company owner, who also heads the management board. At the same time, supervisory mechanisms developed in this area effectively replace a supervisory board.

THE SUPERVISORY BOARD IN LARGE AND COMPLEX ORGANIZATIONS

The importance of the supervisory board grows in the case of more complex companies in which there is a separation of ownership and management. This not only relates to matters of conducting oversight over company activities in all its areas of operation, but experience shows that rather broad and varied expectations are formulated with respect to the supervisory board, putting it in the role of an adviser as well as a provider of services.

This is confirmed by the results of studies conducted on corporate governance in the case of complex economic groups such as the capital groups active in Poland.[6]

Before presenting actual results, it should be added that the structure of the capital group puts the supervisory boards of group subsidiaries in a special position. There, existing conditions make the supervisory board a platform where the interests and expectations of the parent company and of the subsidiary meet. Depending on the level of divergence, what emerges is a rather complicated map of objectives that may result in multiple difficulties within the framework of relations between the parent company and subsidiary. This encumbers the supervisory board of the subsidiary with the requirement to continuously search for a balance between the diverse needs of the two entities. Due to the almost total lack of research in this field, an important aspect of the above-mentioned research project was the identification of key components in the role that should be played by the supervisory board of the subsidiary in the activities of the complex economic entity.[7]

The study included participants from the top management of the subsidiaries making up the X SA Capital Group – active in the construction sector.

Top Management Expectations with Respect to the Supervisory Boards in Subsidiaries – the Case of X SA Capital Group

Based on the statements of the management, a list of factors has been assembled demonstrating aspects prerequisite to the efficient forming of a supervisory structure within the group's framework. Among these, of particular importance are:

1. The functioning of the supervisory board;
2. The behaviour of the parent company as stemming from the position that its majority shareholder occupies (including attention to the interests of the subsidiaries);
3. Supervision and control infrastructure; and
4. The performance of the monitoring system.

The set of opinions forwarded by the investigated subsidiaries point out that one of the most important tasks of the supervisory board, in the view of a significant part of those examined, is the precise defining of the set of criteria for appraising the work of the management board. One of the respondents put it this way:

> An efficient system of owner supervision as implemented by supervisory boards in the subsidiaries should be based on criteria for evaluating management board efficiency that are clear, accurate and identical for all entities making up the group. Financial indicators selected so they take into account financial liquidity to a greater extent than is the case today should be among the criteria.

In their statements relating to the role of supervisory boards in the life of the companies that they manage, representatives of the top management of subsidiaries of the X SA Capital Group pointed to a need for the following:

1. An increase in the activeness of such bodies, especially a more active participation of these boards in developing strategies for subsidiaries as well as the consistent implementation of their tasks.
2. Strict collaboration between company management boards and supervisory boards in performing continuous (over the course of the financial year) supervision and control of company operations.

3. De-formalizing the principles of the functioning of supervisory boards and a lowering of the costs of their operation.
4. A permanent, running system for informing members of the subsidiary's supervisory board about the situation in the company – the forwarding of analytical materials as a part of the reporting cycle (monthly).
5. Directing competent representatives of various specializations to the supervisory boards.
6. Increased involvement of the supervisory boards in building appropriate systems for selecting a company's managerial staff that would take into account the needs of the company, including expectations of help in implementing appropriate instruments motivating and mobilizing the managerial staff to achieve better results.

THE PRACTICE OF POLISH SUPERVISORY BOARDS – A CASE STUDY[8]

The Supervisory Board as a Source of Added Value to the Company – the Example of the Carrier Ltd Shipping and Trading Company

Experience on the functioning of supervisory boards under Polish conditions as accumulated to date is very diverse. There can be no doubt, however, that the usefulness of the supervisory boards and their creating of added value for the company are determined by resources in the form of knowledge and skills as well as networks of social contacts brought in by individual members. Moreover, a well-composed make-up of the supervisory board expressed in the presence of people of appropriate authority and contacts may be particularly useful in relations with organizations from the external environment (e.g. banks).

Thus, in the case of such an approach, it is the selection of appropriate members for the supervisory board that becomes very important. A starting point for the performance of this task should be the conducting of a detailed analysis of what needs supervisory board members – people with appropriate knowledge, experience and a network of connections – should satisfy (Forbes and Milliken, 1999, p. 501).

The Carrier Ltd Shipping and Trading Company (Carrier),[9] owned by ten shareholders, is an example of a company with such a specification under the title of 'Criteria for Selecting Supervisory Board Members'.

Carrier has been operating on the Polish market since 1992. It is primarily concerned with the shipping of bulk cement by rail using special 'cement cars'. The need to break the monopoly of the Bulk Cement Transportation and Forwarding Company was the basis for establishing Carrier. The Bulk

Cement Transportation and Forwarding Company – the only organization offering such services in Poland prior to the appearance of Carrier – often took advantage of its monopolistic position and forced customers to accept unfavourable terms.

Advice and Support – the Main Tasks of the Carrier Supervisory Board as well as a Factor Defining Selection of Its Members

In spite of the fact that Carrier is a relatively small company, its three-man supervisory board plays a very important role. Its importance is defined by not only its supervisory activities, but primarily by its role as a 'support' for the management board in its operations. The supporting role of the supervisory board is mainly seen in its delimiting directions of company operations and in its filling the function of strategic adviser. Moreover, the management board considers the supervisory board an important source of information regarding the market, which facilitates the attracting of new customers. This role of the supervisory board stems from the fact that the market on which Carrier is active is characterized by unique qualities as well as the narrow scope and range of its operations. However, such a market character restricts possibilities for advertising the company in the mass media, something that the company could not afford anyway in light of its lack of appropriate financial resources, and because the only effective way of reaching the customer is direct contact. It is for this reason that a key criterion applied in selecting supervisory board members is the knowledge they hold regarding the market situation and the actors active on that market.

Such knowledge and the broad network of contacts that a Carrier supervisory board member should have are not only intended to simplify the quest for new customers, but are also the basis for predicting changes taking place on the market. Thanks to their network of contacts, the supervisory board members are expected to play an important role in preparing the company so it can operate under continuously changing conditions. Special importance is attached to their ability to catch information that is significant to the functioning of Carrier and subsequently pass that information on to the management board. In light of the specifics of the market on which the company is active, such a role of the supervisory board is considered a key to its stability.

An equally important principle applied in selecting members for the Carrier supervisory board is their possession of practical experience as well as appropriate substantive preparedness. It is for this reason that the supervisory board includes both railroad men and economists. It may be interesting to note that a prerequisite to being appointed to the supervisory board is the holding of shares in the company. This criterion may prove to be a source of potential problems, however. On the one hand, it guarantees company loyalty, which is desirable. On the other hand, however, it significantly narrows the circle of potential board members exclusively to Carrier shareholders, of which there are ten. This may prove to be a 'dead end' at some point, cutting off the influx of new knowledge and skill-related resources.

Due to the fact that the supervisory board of Carrier plays a major role in the process of decision making, a factor determining selection to the supervisory board also encompasses skill in collaborating with the management board. The reasons behind including this criterion are found in earlier events that occurred within the framework of supervisory board–management board relations. Due to significant age differences between the 'young' members of the management board and the 'older' individuals sitting on the supervisory board, there were many conflicts in the past. It was the desire of the supervisory board to dominate the management board as well as problems with mutual communications that were at the root of misunderstandings. Pressure applied by the supervisory board to force through its ideas in the realm of company management as well as efforts at exceeding management board jurisdiction were the source of many unnecessary problems. Having learned their lesson, company shareholders try to have the supervisory board serve as an adviser who, benefiting from seniority, is better able to act with sensitivity and tact, but who primarily provides help instead of becoming a source of conflict. Moreover, in the case of a difference of opinion arising, the supervisory board uses its negotiating skills and strives to achieve a consensus.

As can be seen today, the supervisory board's approach to the management board has undergone a positive evolution. Currently, the supervisory board tries not to act from a position of power, but prefers to play the role of a wise and helpful 'council of elders' that is capable of understanding the situation of the management board. Adopting such a position has led to a regulating of mutual relations and their significant improvement. An important mortar cementing relations is the trust given to members of both bodies.

For its part, the Carrier management board appreciates actions undertaken by the supervisory board. It particularly values the knowledge and support it receives from it. At the same time, in striving to maximize help received, the management board puts great stress on keeping the supervisory board properly informed. The premise behind this is that the more the supervisory board knows about what is currently happening in the company, the better and quicker it can help. An important manifestation of the management board's information-oriented activity is the forwarding of important information about the company to supervisory board members even between supervisory board sessions.

The above characterization of supervisory board–management board relations at Carrier shows that the supervisory board is perceived as an important moving force prerequisite not only to stable development, but also for identifying potential sources of danger in the surrounding world. Due to the high efficiency of information flow, the supervisory board knows exactly what is happening in the company. Simultaneously, that knowledge is supported by the supervisory board members' knowledge regarding the market. This facilitates the effective use of the supervisory board's assets for continuous company development.

The experiences of Carrier confirm the statement that for a supervisory board to generate added value for a company, the process of forming a supervisory board must begin with an analysis of company needs followed by the selection of specific board members on that basis. Unfortunately, current practice in the selection of supervisory board members relevant to company needs shows that this is not an easy matter. Since awareness of the weight of this matter is growing in the world of companies, the problem has also been raised in the Stock Exchange's 'Best Practice in Public Companies 2002' document (http://www.gpw.com.pl/zrodla/gpw/pdf/bestpract.pdf [in Polish]). There, the nineteenth principle states: 'A member of the supervisory board should have an appropriate education, professional experience, and real life experience, represent a high moral standard, and be capable of devoting a sufficient amount of time to allow him to properly perform his functions in the supervisory board.' (More information on 'Best Practice in Public Companies 2002' may be found in Appendix A.)

THE SUPERVISORY BOARD IN A COMPANY WITH THE PARTICIPATION OF THE STATE TREASURY – THE EXAMPLE OF THE AIRPORT COMPANY[10]

Airport Ltd. (Airport) was established in 1994 in reaction to a conflict that occurred at that time between the PPL Polish Airports State Enterprise and a handling company that serviced one of Poland's airports. The founders of the company were two State Treasury companies – LOT Polish Airlines (PLL LOT SA) and PPL. These companies continue to be its main shareholders. Thus, the Airport Company also belongs to the State Treasury.

The scope of services offered by Airport is rather broad. The core of its offer is made up of:

1. the repair, maintenance and overhaul of aircraft and their engines;
2. the sale of solid, liquid and gas fuels, metal ores, and industrial chemicals;
3. trading in industrial machines and equipment as well as aircraft;
4. catering services for external customers;
5. road freight shipping;
6. warehousing and storage of goods in ports;
7. aircraft ground services;
8. passenger services; and
9. janitorial services.

In 2003 Airport employed 45 workers, of which 30 were employed full time while the remainder worked on the basis of job contracts.

The Airport Company's Internal Governance Structure

Airport is operated as a limited liability company. Pursuant to the requirements of the Commercial Company Code, the governance structure of the company consists of the management board, which manages its affairs and represents it, the supervisory board, which oversees company activities, and the assembly of shareholders, which passes resolutions.

The Management Board of the Airport Company

The management board of Airport is made up of two persons. In line with principles assumed in the company, the president of the management board is appointed by PPL, while the vice-president is appointed by LOT.

The management board is appointed and dismissed by the assembly of shareholders, and its term is two years. Its range of responsibilities is defined by the Commercial Company Code, the company charter and the resolutions of the assembly of shareholders.

The management board is obligated to present a report on its activities to the supervisory board at the close of each quarter.

The Supervisory Board of the Airport Company – Selection Process and Tasks

The activities of the Airport Company management board are monitored by a four-man supervisory board. Pursuant to agreements reached among the partners, the chairman of the supervisory board is designated by LOT from among its own board members, while the deputy chairman is designated by the other shareholder, PPL. The remaining two members of the supervisory board represent the companies making up LOT and PPL and are specialists in their fields.

Members of the supervisory board are appointed for a two-year term and their appointment to the supervisory board – if the skills and competencies of members are considered – is determined by the fact that Airport founding capital is derived from the State. Every member of the supervisory board in a company where at least 50 per cent of the capital belongs to the State must have successfully passed an examination for members of supervisory boards in State Treasury companies. The Airport Company is no exception and the members of its supervisory board undergo such examinations. In addition to the above requirements, an important criterion prerequisite for appointment to the Airport supervisory board is good knowledge of the aviation and shipping industries. Additionally, that knowledge must be supported by at least two years of professional experience connected with business activity, finance, commercial law, management or corporate governance.

Moreover, members of the Airport supervisory board are required to have organizational skills and are expected to improve these on a continuous basis.

A significant quality of the supervisory board member selection process in this company is that a board member must be connected with company shareholders (as has already been noted, one supervisory board member is a representative of LOT, the second the PPL, while the remaining two represent companies linked with the main shareholders).

The supervisory board of Airport meets at least once every three months. Moreover, the chairman of the supervisory board has the right to call a session of the supervisory board at any time upon receiving a written request from the management board or a written demand from at least 25 per cent of the supervisory board. At this point it is worth adding that supervisory board members can vote not only in person, but also in writing or by telephone.

The main task of the supervisory board in the case of Airport is moulded by the fact that it is part of a State Treasury company. In line with the main directives in this area, the primary task of the Airport supervisory board is oversight encompassing:

1. growth in operational efficiency, management effectiveness and company value;
2. the rational use of State assets;
3. the preparing and conducting of privatization in an efficient manner; and
4. achieving a transparency in the companies that are owned by the State Treasury that is comparable with the information standards of listed companies.

Action on the Part of the Airport Company's Supervisory Board and Management Board Expectations

The practice to date in the functioning of the Airport supervisory board demonstrates that its activities are significantly broader than what is defined by the provisions of the Commercial Company Code. From the point of view of the management board, what is of particular importance is that the supervisory board encompasses wide-ranging familiarity with the industry in which the company operates. Worth adding is that this knowledge is not only used in the process of developing strategy (i.e. supervisory board formulated strategic targets), but the management board also tries to utilize it in daily practice. However, according to one of the members of the board this, at times, results in absurd situations. As an example he described a situation where a session of the supervisory board was called in which the main topic was the procurement of aircraft steps – something that is not only an 'everyday use' item, but also one whose value is within limits set on the decision-making capacity of the president of the management board (the president may make investment decisions up to an amount that does not exceed one half of the share capital – it is in matters when a planned investment project exceeds this sum that the supervisory board must be consulted). This matter was treated by supervisory board members as being 'inadequate' in terms of supervisory board tasks as well as a source of unnecessary expenses (two supervisory board members must travel several hundred kilometres to attend a session, and travel expenses are covered by the company) and the wasting of their time. It is for this reason that the company bylaws were amended to include a provision to allow the taking of decisions by telephone, electronic means or fax (the above incident was a significant factor in making such an amendment, and was also intended to prevent its repetition in the future).

Company experience shows that the above situation was not something exceptional in its history, however. In practice, the president of Airport consults with the supervisory board prior to every decision, because he maintains that: 'I prefer my actions to be approved by the supervisory board because that means I feel more certain and it also relieves me of a part of the responsibility.'

From the point of view of the president, the supervisory board should primarily serve an advisory and opinion-generating function. Its input is particularly desirable in the process of taking key decisions, including the reviewing of company development plans as well as intended projects. Moreover, the management board is very appreciative of the supervisory board's help in the assessment process of the company's situation prior to the taking of decisions of significance to its functioning, operations, or in monitoring the results or decisions already taken (the monitoring function of the supervisory board).

Presently, among the main expectations of the Airport president with respect to the supervisory board is the procurement of its assistance in building an in-house early warning system mainly intended to monitor the company's economic and financial situation. Its principles should be similar to those in listed companies and its main feature should be transparency.

The above discussion demonstrates that an important aspect of supervisory board–management board relations in the Airport Company is a peculiar dependence of the management board on the supervisory board. The management board needs frequent and regular contact with the supervisory board (in order to facilitate an exchange of information, mainly financial) and expects large quantities of advice from it. Such a stance on the part of the management board does not always gain the appreciation of members of the supervisory board, but there can be no doubt that it has an impact on the level of activity of the supervisory board (for example, in the form of an increased number of sessions over and above what the provisions of the Commercial Company Code require) and forces it to improve its accessibility. It should be stressed, however, that the supervisory board is not directly involved in the management of the company. For its part, the supervisory board sees its role in the life of the company through the perspective of its share in developing strategies for Airport operations, primarily the formulation of strategic targets, followed by its monitoring of the process of their implementation as well as oversight over whether or not plans approved for execution are implemented in line with previously approved principles and guidelines. At the same time, the Airport supervisory board points to the appointment of management board members – the people who will implement the above strategic targets – as being among its key tasks. Also worth noting is the active collaboration between the supervisory board and the company auditor in all audit phases.

The Airport Company and 'Best Practice in Public Companies 2002'

In spite of the fact that the Airport Company is not a listed company and has no obligation to implement 'Best Practice in Public Companies 2002', its actions are consistent with this document in most cases. Thus, in agreement with:

1. Principle 18, the Airport supervisory board prepares an assessment of the company situation on time.
2. Principle 19, members of the supervisory board are selected diligently and meet all required criteria relating to competence.

3. Principle 22, the management board provides the supervisory board with information on all significant activities undertaken in the company on a regular basis.
4. Principle 25, the management board is informed of all supervisory board sessions.
5. Principle 29, the supervisory board agenda is established prior to the session and is never changed without the consent of members.
6. Principle 31, to date there has never been a situation in which the resignation of a supervisory board member made the proper functioning of the supervisory board impossible.

A SUPERVISORY BOARD WITHOUT SENTIMENTS – THE CASE OF AUTOMATIC, A COMPANY LISTED ON THE STOCK EXCHANGE[11]

The Automatic Company (Automatic) was established in 1991 by way of privatization using the state enterprise leasing method.[12] The primary area of its activity is the electromechanical sector. Automatic is the largest manufacturer of industrial automation subassemblies in Poland and occupies sixth place in the world. The European market is the main sales market for its products, but from time to time it also sells its goods in the United States.

Ownership Structure and Management Board Duties

Today, the Automatic Company is a joint stock company listed on the Warsaw Stock Exchange. Financial investors hold the majority of shares; they account for over 30 per cent of shareholders. Moreover, a package of over 12 per cent belongs to a single private individual. The remaining shares are in the hands of minor investors.

The company employs approximately 500 persons (in 2004) and is run by a management board made up of two members. The jurisdiction of each member is precisely defined. The president is responsible for sales, marketing and finance, while the vice-president is concerned with technical and development matters. The persons serving functions in the management board have no capital involvement in the company and have no links with the shareholders.

The Supervisory Board of Automatic Company – Selection Criteria

Pursuant to the Commercial Company Code, the body responsible for continuous supervision over the activities of Automatic in all fields of its endeavours is the supervisory board. The supervisory board consists of five persons. Three members of the supervisory board represent the financial investors (who also employ them as analysts or members of teams managing portfolios). The remaining two supervisory board members are, for their part, the representatives of individual investors.

Company needs determine the frequency of supervisory board sessions; there are usually one or two every two months.

Among the basic criteria influencing the selection of supervisory board members are:

1. familiarity with questions related to company finances; and
2. the capacity to directly represent the interests of selected investors.

Practice to date in the activities of the Automatic supervisory board shows that it is primarily oriented towards performing in line with the provisions of the Commercial Company Code. However, this in no way signifies the taking on of a passive role; in cases in which a need to go beyond the framework of the Code occurs, the Automatic supervisory board takes up that challenge. A recent example of such behaviour is its co-initiation of a change process in the realm of company organization and finance.

The Role of the Supervisory Board in the Life of Automatic Company

In contrast to the supervisory board of the Carrier Company described earlier, the Automatic supervisory board does not involve itself in the day-to-day management of the company. It undertakes no actions on its own initiative that might encroach upon the scope of responsibilities of the management board – viewed as a very competent body. For example, questions tied to the sector in which the company operates are considered an exclusive domain of management board operations – something in which the supervisory board does not involve itself. Of course, if the management board had asked the supervisory board to get involved in this area, then steps would certainly have been taken aimed at lending support to the management board. However, in the view of one of the members of the supervisory board, the existence of such a situation would raise a huge question mark over the matter of the management board's qualifications.

As to matters relating to developing a strategy, the Automatic supervisory board is involved in this task only partially. This is usually expressed through collaboration in preparing the strategy. It only helps in implementation if the management board makes such a request. To date, the management board has demonstrated significant independence in this field. At this point it might be worth adding that the management board's expectations with respect to the supervisory board are, in general, not overly great; in fact, its main desire is 'to be left alone'. However, it is possible to notice new trends in the relations between the management board and supervisory board that a supervisory board member defined as 'a phase in which the management board is getting used to greater involvement on the part of shareholders' representatives in significant company decisions'.[13]

In spite of the decided competence and independence of the management board, there are situations that crop up in a company's life that require the support of the supervisory board. For example, the management board needed the supervisory board when it undertook major organizational changes in the company aimed at creating a capital group. It was then that the supervisory board was asked to involve itself in organizational work relating to the shape of the newly formed grouping.

In characterizing the supervisory board of the Automatic Company, it is necessary to stress the large amount of knowledge in the financial field that is accumulated within it. This knowledge is utilized by the supervisory board both in the process of overseeing the safety of the interests of company shareholders and support for the management board in its operations. In the first case, the supervisory board's skill in defining risk, including the defining of areas as well as methods of safeguarding against it, is extremely useful. The familiarity of the supervisory board members with the objectives of Automatic's shareholders plays a significant role in such actions. In its turn, the management board places great weight on the ability to receive assistance from the supervisory board in solving advanced problems in the realm of finance. The supervisory board's input is especially valuable in defining exchange risk – the company's export is an important component of its operations.

In summarizing the role of the supervisory board in the life of the company, one of its representatives primarily pointed to its large role in serving in an opinion-generating and advisory capacity, describing the effectiveness of the supervisory board in this field as being very high. Another statement by the same person sparks some curiosity as it is maintained that monitoring is primarily the domain of the auditor, where the supervisory board as such does not possess effective mechanisms for oversight.

The Management Board in the Eyes of the Supervisory Board

From the point of view of the supervisory board, the management board is fully competent and knows how to benefit from the knowledge of the supervisory board. In commenting on this matter, it was said that 'someone who is merely an engineer cannot fill a managerial function in any company. Unless, of course, that company is small and it operates out of a garage.'

In concluding, it was stressed that 'if the people serving as members of the management board did not know how to utilize such resources as the knowledge in the supervisory board, then they would cease filling that function'.

As to conflicts or misunderstandings occurring between the management board and the supervisory board, these usually have their roots in questions of jurisdiction. An example is the most recent problem that occurred that was linked with the establishing of jurisdiction in defining the degree of exposure to exchange risk in the case of company liabilities.

The Automatic Company and 'Best Practice in Public Companies 2002'

Because Automatic is a listed company, it is aware of the actions of stock exchange authorities in the year 2002 connected with preparing and subsequently distributing the 'Best Practice in Public Companies 2002' among companies. Aware of the weight of questions linked with corporate governance, the company undertook the development of its own, independent set of best practice procedures that regulate the behaviour of its supervisory board and management board and their members; it also defined the desirable positions of its majority and minority shareholders. To date, the supervisory board has prepared procedures regulating access to information as well as principles for procedures with respect to shareholders in the light of regulations governing public trading.

CONCLUSIONS

Questions relating to the functioning of supervisory boards form a very interesting and complex field of study that remains largely untouched in Poland. The past few years have seen supervisory boards become an integral part of Polish companies, at least in terms of codified regulations. Meeting legal provisions is one matter, however. Another is the problem of activating the supervisory boards in terms of events occurring in the company. Thus, one of the main tasks in this area is the reorienting of supervisory boards from passive meetings and the generating of formalized reports to active involvement in the life of the organizations, without attempts at encroaching on the jurisdiction of the management board, of course.

A factor fostering increased activity on the part of these boards is individual members holding special competencies. Among these, special importance is assigned to practical experience encompassing a familiarity with the company as well as the industry in which it operates. Thus, it is important for shareholders, in selecting their representatives to the board, to be aware of company needs so as to endeavour to meet those needs through careful choice. At this point it should be added that the skills held by members of the board are prerequisite to implementing the board's supervisory function as it is vital to know what is to be overseen and how that can be done. Moreover, these skills define the quality of information flow channels created by the board, and therefore of the performance by the board of its function as a middleman between the shareholders and the management board. There can be no doubt that knowledge facilitates the asking of questions of the management board regarding phenomena and occurrences taking place in the company.

Yet another important aspect relating to the activities of the supervisory board observable in the above presented case studies is the building of a relationship between the supervisory and management boards. The core of these relations, apart from trust, should be an orientation on the part of both institutions to work together as opposed to confrontation. What is interesting is that at present, this perspective seems to evade discussions regarding the supervisory board, which is treated primarily as a 'bogeyman' for the management board. The heated debate seems to forget the simple truth that more is usually achieved through collaboration than battle. This is especially true as the supervisory board is uniquely dependent on the management board, which serves as its basic source of information, the quality of which determines the effectiveness of its actions.

In conclusion it should be added that the examples of supervisory boards in various companies as presented above are mainly meant to illustrate selected questions connected with their activity, summarized below.

SUMMARY/KEY LEARNING POINTS

1. In Poland, the supervisory board is a primary mechanism within the framework of corporate governance structures established in the company.
2. The main task of the supervisory board is continuous supervision over company operations in all areas of its activities. However, the supervisory board does not have the right to issue orders that are binding on the management board with respect to managing company affairs.
3. The practice of supervisory board functioning in companies operating in Poland is extremely varied. The usefulness and character of involvement of the supervisory board in the company is determined by a very complex set of parameters such as:
    (a) Ownership structure (dispersed versus concentrated, including a lack of separation between ownership and management) and owner

identity (manager-owner, strategic investor, financial institutions or State Treasury).

(b) The size and complexity of the organization.

4. In cases when there is no supervisory board (when allowed by legal regulations, which is most often the case when there is no separation of ownership and management usually characteristic of small and medium enterprises) great stress is placed on creating effective in-house control mechanisms in the company.

5. In the case of a complex organization (such as Polish capital groups), the supervisory boards of subsidiaries play the role of a platform where the interests and expectations of the parent company and of the subsidiaries meet. The most important task of the supervisory board of the subsidiary is a continuous search for balance between the varied needs of the two entities.

6. The usefulness of the supervisory board and its creating of added value for the company are determined by knowledge and skills (competencies), professional experience as well as networks of social contacts brought in by individual members. That is why the selection of appropriate members for the supervisory board is very important. A starting point for this process should be the conducting of a detailed analysis of exactly what company needs the supervisory board should satisfy.

7. To a great extent the quality of the supervisory board's work also depends on the character of established relationships with management board. Trust should form the basic foundation of these relations.

8. The supervisory board's involvement in the life of the company is, as a rule, too small in Poland. The problem is that in many cases supervisory boards prefer to keep a passive stance.

QUESTIONS

The discussion questions below cover the key learning points of this chapter.

1. What function does the supervisory board perform in companies operating in Poland?

2. List the criteria that should be considered as prerequisites for selection to a supervisory board.

3. Present the basic factors that influence the efficiency of supervisory board operations. Give examples.

4. Give a critical analysis of factors determining good collaboration between the management and supervisory boards.

5. Critically discuss matters relating to the role of the supervisory board in subsidiaries.
6. Critically discuss the potential for influence on the part of shareholders on the supervisory board. How does this translate into the role played by the supervisory board in the life of the company?

NOTES

1. In line with the ratified wording, each joint stock company established as a result of the commercialization of a state enterprise had a legal obligation to establish a board of supervisors.
2. It is the view of many experts that the supervisory board is too dependent on information from the management board. According to these experts, questions of access by members of the supervisory board to information independently of the management board should be regulated.
3. According to the definition of M. Trocki, a capital group is an economic group established to achieve common economic objectives that is made up of legally independent economic entities in the form of capital companies (limited liability companies or joint stock companies) that are permanently bound through capital links and that are capable of achieving joint objectives as stemming from the type and intensity of bonds making them (Trocki 2004, p. 41). This definition should be expanded with the additional explanation that the parent company has a capital exposure with respect to the subsidiary.
4. NB: In line with their request, the names of companies used in this study have been changed.
5. In the case of limited liability companies, the presence of a board of supervisors is regulated by Article 213 §1 of the Commercial Company Code, which states that 'the company deed *may* establish a board of supervisors or a board of auditors, or both such bodies'.
6. The studies were conducted within the framework of the Committee for Scientific Research (KBN) project entitled 'The Management of Polish Capital Groups in the Face of Challenges Linked with Processes of Integration with the European Union (1999–2001)' [in Polish]. This project was undertaken by a research team made up of G. Gierszewska, J. Solarz, J. Dąbrowski, I. Koładkiewicz, J. Szaban, K. Stobińska and P. Wróbel under the scientific guidance of Prof. B. Wawrzyniak. Results of the project were presented in Dąbrowski *et al.* (2002).
7. Research project entitled 'The Management of Polish Capital Groups in the Face of Challenges Linked with Processes of Integration with the European Union (1999–2001)' – see above.
8. Work by students was used in preparing cases presented in this section. They were developed in line with an interview questionnaire prepared by I. Koładkiewicz within the framework of a lecture series entitled 'Corporate Governance' conducted over the 2003/2004 academic year.
9. This example is based on a study by Ciszewska *et al.* (2003). The name of the company has been changed.
10. This example is based on a study by Kibler *et al.* (2003). The name of the company has been changed.
11. This example is based on a study by Perczak (2004). The name of the company has been changed.
12. Privatization using the leasing method is a form of capital-based privatization where the company is handed over for a fee for use by workers, where the operation is financed through a capital leasing scheme known as leverage.

13. Such contrasting opinions are characteristic of situations in which new shareholders, who have an interest in what is happening with the capital they invested, make their appearance and stimulate an increase in the activity of the supervisory board with respect to overseeing the activities of the management board, which was not used to such a situation when it had acted in a strong management board–weak supervisory board situation.

REFERENCES

Ciszewska, U., A. Minko, M. Turzyńska and K. Wasielczuk (supervisor I. Koładkiewicz) (2003), 'Rada nadzorcza na przykładzie firmy "Przewoźnik" Sp. z o.o.' [The Carrier Ltd. supervisory board, a case study], unpublished material.

Dąbrowski, J., G. Gierszewska, I. Koładkiewicz, J. Solarz, J. Szaban and B. Wawrzyniak (eds) (2002), *Polskie grupy kapitałowe. Perspektywa europejska* [Polish capital groups, the European perspective], Warsaw: Leon Koźmiński Academy of Entrepreneurship and Management Press.

Forbes, D.P. and F.J. Milliken (1999), 'Cognition and corporate governance: understanding board of directors as strategic decision-making groups', *Academy of Management Review*, **24**(3), 489–505.

Kibler, M., K. Oleś, K. Stachyra, K. Szczepańska and A. Wietrzykowska (supervisor I. Koładkiewicz) (2003), 'Cykl życia firmy a z rozwój struktury nadzoru' [The company life cycle and the development of its supervisory structure], a case study, unpublished materials.

Perczak, A. (supervisor I. Koładkiewicz) (2004), 'Nadzór korporacyjny w spółce akcyjnej. Na przykładzie przedsiębiorstwa Automatyk' [Corporate governance in a joint stock company – a case study of the Automatic company], unpublished materials.

Rudolf, S., T. Janusz, D. Stos and P. Urbanek (2002), *Efektywny nadzór korporacyjny* [Effective corporate governance], Warsaw: PWE Polish Economic Press.

Trocki, M. (2004), *Grupy kapitałowe. Tworzenie i funkcjonowanie* [Capital groups. Their creation and functioning], Warsaw: PWN Scientific Publishers.

Zahra, S.A. and J.A. Pearce II (1989), 'Board of directors and corporate financial performance: a review and integrative model', *Journal of Management*, **15**(2), 291–334.

APPENDIX A*

Awareness of the weight of the problem of corporate governance in the Polish corporate world is growing. A manifestation of this is the desire to strive to prevent pathological situations from appearing in this area. An important tool in this battle is the development of a set of best practices

---

* In 2005, companies listed on Warsaw Stock Exchange should follow a new version of best practices entitled 'Best Practice in Public Companies 2005', www.gpw.com.pl/zrodla/gpw/pdf/bestpract.pdf. This document is a revised version of 'Best Practice in Public Companies 2002', and the changes and modifications that have been made are based on the practical experience, opinions and suggestions of market participants, gathered over the last two years, and recent European Commission recommendations in this field.

that tries to show ways of evading conflicts within the framework of corporate relations as well as demonstrating ways to solve any difficulties that might appear.

Since supervisory boards under Polish conditions are a basic component of governance systems and the experience they have accumulated is not free of pitfalls, the creators of best practice principles, in wanting to improve the efficiency of the actions of this body, have also devoted much attention to them.

Below is a presentation of best practice principles applicable in the case of supervisory boards active in joint stock companies listed on the Warsaw Stock Exchange. The principles are an integral part of the 'Best Practice in Public Companies 2002' document and were developed by the Best Practice Committee of the Corporate Governance Forum. The supervisory board and management board of the Warsaw Stock Exchange have accepted this document and approved the concept of implementing the best practices it contains in line with the principle of 'comply or explain' (September 2002).

At the same time, following examination of these principles, the reader will have no problem in identifying the main sources of difficulties that the day-to-day practice of the supervisory boards of Polish companies must face.

BEST PRACTICES IN PUBLIC COMPANIES IN 2002

Best Practices of Supervisory Boards

18. The supervisory board submits to the general meeting an annual concise evaluation of the company's standing. The evaluation should be part of the annual report of the company, made available to all shareholders early enough to allow them to become acquainted with the same before the annual general meeting.
19. A member of the supervisory board should have relevant education, professional and practical experience, be of high morale and be able to devote all time required to properly perform the function on the supervisory board. Candidates for members of the supervisory board should be presented and supported by reasons in sufficient detail to allow an educated choice.
20. (a) At least one-half of members of the supervisory board should be independent members. Independent members of the supervisory board should not have any relations with the company and its shareholders or employees which could have significant impact on the ability of the independent member to make impartial decisions.

(b) Detailed criteria of independence should be laid down in the statutes of the company.

(c) Without consent of at least one independent member of the supervisory board, no resolutions should be adopted on the following issues:
   • Performances of any kind by the company and any entities associated with the company in favour of members of the management board.
   • Consent to the execution by the company or its subsidiary of a key agreement with an entity associated with the company, member of the supervisory board or the management board, and with their associated entities.
   • Appointment of an expert auditor to audit the financial statements of the company.

The above rule may be implemented by the company on a date different than that for the remaining rules of the set, but no later than by the end of 2004.

21. A supervisory board member should, most of all, bear in mind the interests of the company.

22. Members of the supervisory board should take relevant actions in order to receive from the management board regular and complete information on any and all significant issues concerning the company's operations and on the risk related to the carried out business and ways of managing such risk.

23. A supervisory board member should inform the remaining members of the board of any conflict of interest that arises, and should refrain from participating in discussions and from voting on passing a resolution on the issue in which the conflict of interest has arisen.

24. Information on personal, actual and organizational connections of a supervisory board member with a given shareholder, and, in particular, with the majority shareholder, should be available to the public. The company should have a procedure in place for obtaining information from members of the supervisory board and for making it available to the public.

25. Supervisory board meetings, save for issues which directly concern the management board or its members, and, in particular, removal, liability and setting remuneration, should be accessible and open to members of the management board.

26. A supervisory board member should enable the management board to present publicly, and in an appropriate manner, information on the transfer or acquisition of the shares of the company or of its dominant

company or a subsidiary, and of transactions with such companies, provided that such information is relevant for his financial standing.

27. Remuneration of members of the supervisory board should be fair, but should not constitute a significant cost item in the company's business or have material impact on its financial results. The remuneration should be in reasonable relation to the remuneration of members of the management board. The aggregate remuneration of all members of the supervisory board should be disclosed in the annual report.

28. The supervisory board should operate in accordance with its by-laws which should be available to the public.

29. The agenda of a supervisory board meeting should not be amended or supplemented during the meeting which it concerns. This requirement does not apply if all members of the supervisory board are present and agree to the amendment or supplementation of the agenda, and in instances where the adoption of certain activities by the supervisory board is necessary in order to protect the company against damage and in the case of a resolution which concerns the determination whether there exists a conflict of interest between a supervisory board member and the company.

30. A supervisory board member delegated by a group of shareholders to permanently exercise supervision should submit to the supervisory board detailed reports on the performance of his task.

31. A supervisory board member should not resign from his function during a term of office if this could render the functioning of the board impossible, and, in particular, if it could hinder the timely adoption of an important resolution.

PART 3

Corporate governance in South East Asia

8. Corporate governance in Singapore: a case study

Martin J. Conyon

INTRODUCTION

This chapter focuses on corporate governance in Singapore. First, I examine contemporary developments in Singapore, in particular the Code of Corporate Governance that became effective in 2003. Next, I examine the governance structure of Singapore Technologies Engineering (ST Engineering), a prominent large firm listed on the mainboard of the Singapore Exchange (SGX). I then examine the relation between corporate performance and board structure. My aim is to add to the growing literature on international corporate governance by examining the board of directors, executive compensation and ownership structure at this enterprise.[1]

An analysis of corporate governance arrangements in Singapore is warranted for at least two reasons. First, the East Asian financial crisis that commenced in July 1997 represented a large adverse shock to the region. Commentators have speculated that weak corporate governance structures may have been an important factor in the collapse (Lemmon and Lins 2003; Khan 2003). Second, in January 2003 amended listing rules required firms to make certain disclosures in their annual reports in respect of the new Code of Corporate Governance. It seems appropriate, therefore, to examine the implementation of the new Code.

The rest of this chapter is organized as follows. The next section provides an overview of corporate governance in Singapore. The purpose is to provide background information on the salient features of the governance system in Singapore. The newly introduced Code of Corporate Governance (see Corporate Governance Committee 2001) is examined in some detail. This is followed by a case analysis of ST Engineering, which is one of the most valuable and largest enterprises on the mainboard of SGX. By focusing on this firm, important features of the Singapore corporate governance system can be articulated. An analysis of the relation between corporate performance and board structure is then interpreted against more general econometric evidence, after which some closing remarks are made.

CORPORATE GOVERNANCE IN SINGAPORE

Corporate governance refers to the mechanisms by which firms are owned and controlled. The Singapore corporate governance system is fashioned along the lines of the US and UK model, although qualitative differences abound. Chee (2004) explains the salient features of the system: There is a unitary board structure consisting of insiders (executives) and outside (non-executive) members. The mainboard of SGX consists of about 400 firms and so the capital market is somewhat small compared with the USA and the UK. Until recently the amount of publicly available corporate information was lower quality relative to the USA and the UK. The takeover market is also weak compared with the USA and the UK. The ownership of publicly traded firms is highly concentrated and important investors include the government, other corporations, individuals and financial institutions.

The ownership structure of Singapore firms is particularly distinctive since it consists of a large state-owned element as well as the presence of so-called 'pyramids' where a controlling ownership is exercised through at least one other firm (La Porta *et al.* 1999; Claessens *et al.* 2000). The Singapore corporate governance landscape is characterized by the predominance and importance of government-linked corporations (GLCs). The Singapore government invests in corporations (private and public) via three holding companies. These are MND Holdings, Singapore Technologies and Temasek Holdings.[2] Via the use of these investment vehicles the government is the ultimate owner in many firms. Chee contends that

> Towards the end of the 1980s, GLCs comprised 69 percent of total assets and 75 percent of profits of all domestically controlled companies in Singapore. In the 1990s, the government embarked on a privatization program, which resulted in the dispersal of equity of these companies. Still, the government continues to hold majority ownership, through its holding companies (Temasek Holdings, MND Holdings, and Singapore Technologies) in these GLCs. (Chee 2004, p. 314)

The GLCs are consistent with evidence by La Porta *et al.* (1999) who classify ownership structures around the world by ownership type. Specifically, they identify whether firms in a given country are widely held (a variable equal to one if there is no controlling shareholder), State owned (a variable equal to one if the State is the controlling shareholder) and family owned (a variable equal to one if a family is the controlling shareholder). In the case of large firms in Singapore the evidence indicates that 0.30 are family owned, 0.45

are State owned and 0.25 are widely owned (either by individuals, financial or other corporations). The 0.45 figure for State ownership is very high – the figure contrasts markedly to the USA and the UK which takes a value of zero. The pyramid structure of Singapore publicly traded firms is also salient. La Porta *et al.* (1999) define a pyramid variable which is set equal to one where the controlling shareholder exercises control through at least one publicly traded company, and zero otherwise. For Singapore, this variable takes a value of 0.41, indicating pyramid structures are common (for the USA this variable takes a value of zero). Similar evidence for Singapore is presented in Claessens *et al.* (2000). Overall, ownership of Singapore firms is concentrated, there is a large State-owned presence and control is exercised through a pyramid ownership structure.

A consequence of pyramid structures is that they potentially motivate 'tunnelling' activities. Tunnelling is defined as the transfer of assets and/or profits out of firms for the benefit of those who control them (see Johnson *et al.* 2000). La Porta *et al.* (1999) illustrate that pyramids are a common procedure by which controlling shareholders have control rights that exceed their cash flow rights. As Denis and McConnell state:

> In the pyramid structure, one entity owns a controlling interest in a chain of firms in such a way that the controlling shareholder of the firm at the top of the pyramid achieves effective control of all of the subsidiaries down the line, while actually owning an ever smaller portion of each firm. The controlling shareholder can extract value from the firms that are farther down the line by transferring resources of those lower-level companies to the firms that are higher in the pyramid. (2003, p. 25)

In consequence, the presence of pyramid ownership means that power can be exercised by one shareholder block or entity at the expense of some other shareholder. Such private benefits of control are, of course, a matter of corporate governance concern and investigation. For example, such benefits permit those in control to choose who the senior managers will be and who directs the assets of the firm. This appears to be the case as evidenced by Claessens *et al.* (2000) in East Asian countries and also La Porta *et al.* (1999), who find that controlling shareholders are typically participants in management.

The Code of Corporate Governance

An important contemporary development in Singapore is the enactment of a new corporate governance code. The Code of Corporate Governance[3] was issued by the Corporate Governance Committee (CGC) in March 2001. Listed issuers on the Exchange are required to make certain disclosures in respect of the Code pursuant to Rule 710 of the Listing Manual. In particular, rule 710 requires an issuer to:

(1) describe its corporate governance practices with specific reference to the principles of the Code in its annual report. It must disclose any deviation from any guideline of the Code together with an appropriate explanation for such deviation in the annual report; and (2) state in its annual report whether and how it has complied with the section on dealings in securities in the Best Practices Guide.

The new rule has been enacted from January 2003 and applies to publicly traded firms issuing annual reports after that date.

The Code applies to listed companies. There are 452 companies listed on the mainboard of SGX and Table 8.1 illustrates that these companies had a combined market capitalization of S\$427 501 279 000 as at 29 October 2004. ST Engineering, which is analysed in the following section, has a market capitalization of S\$6 042 332 000 representing about 1.41 per cent of the total. The 15 companies identified in Table 8.1 account for about 45 per cent of the market capitalization of SGX.

Table 8.1   Fifteen Singapore mainboard companies by market capitalization

Company	Closing price (S\$)	Market capitalization (S\$000)	% of total
Singapore Telecommunications	2.42	40 209 425	9.41
DBS Group	15.6	23 278 924	5.45
UOB	13.5	21 228 934	4.97
OCBC	13.8	18 310 592	4.28
Jardine Matheson	US\$14.80	14 700 159	3.44
SIA	10.7	13 034 579	3.05
Jardine Strategic	US\$6.90	12 020 934	2.81
Hong Kong Land	US\$2.06	7 865 541	1.84
SPH	4.7	7 365 497	1.72
Keppel Corp	8	6 217 853	1.45
Singapore Tech Engineering	2.09	6 042 332	1.41
Great Eastern	11.7	5 537 356	1.30
City Developments	6.3	5 412 055	1.27
Dairy Farm International	US\$2.40	5 374 767	1.26
Capitaland	1.85	4 667 386	1.09
		191 266 334	*44.75*
Market total		427 501 279	100.00

Source: Singapore Stock Exchange, 29 October data
http://info.sgx.com/webmktstatistics.nsf/0b0324dae84b770948256dad0009440a/
79e9998e9af40d3348256f41003317ba?OpenDocument.

The Corporate Governance Committee defined corporate governance as:

> the processes and structure by which the business and affairs of the company are directed and managed, in order to enhance long term shareholder value through enhancing corporate performance and accountability, whilst taking into account the interests of other stakeholders. Good corporate governance therefore embodies both enterprise (performance) and accountability (conformance). (2001, p. 1)

The statement also reflects one concern raised by some governance theorists that relates to the potential trade-off between conformance and enterprise. The argument is that the costs associated with more disclosure and compliance with the Code may result in bureaucratic firm structures. Such bureaucracies may stifle the enterprise culture within the firm and hence lead to inferior organizational performance. Getting the balance right between accountability and enterprise, therefore, is a major challenge for firms. The Corporate Governance Committee considered three alternative approaches to promoting shareholder value maximization and good corporate governance. First, a prescriptive approach which would require firms to adopt and adhere to specific corporate governance practices; second, a non-prescriptive approach that allows firms to determine their own corporate governance practices; and third, a 'balanced approach that specifies corporate governance best practices but allows companies to depart from these practices subject to appropriate disclosure'. The Committee concluded that 'the balanced approach adopted in markets such as the UK and Canada provide the best approach for improving corporate governance in Singapore'.

The Code of Conduct is split into four areas: Board matters; remuneration matters; accountability and audit; and lastly communication with shareholders. Each area contains a set of principles, and in the full code each principle has a set of guidance notes.[4] There are 15 principles in all. Given the importance of the principles, and the fact that they are clearly articulated, it is worth reproducing them here (the guidance notes can be accessed in the full Code). The principles are:

Board matters

1. Every company should be headed by an effective board to lead and control the company.
2. There should be a strong and independent element on the board, which is able to exercise objective judgement on corporate affairs independently, in particular, from management. No individual or

small group of individuals should be allowed to dominate the board's decision making.

3. There should be a clear division of responsibilities at the top of the company – the working of the board and the executive responsibility of the company's business – which will ensure a balance of power and authority, such that no one individual represents a considerable concentration of power.

4. There should be a formal and transparent process for the appointment of new directors to the board. As a principle of good corporate governance, all directors should be required to submit themselves for re-nomination and re-election at regular intervals.

5. There should be a formal assessment of the effectiveness of the board as a whole and the contribution by each director to the effectiveness of the board.

6. In order to fulfil their responsibilities, board members should be provided with complete, adequate and timely information prior to board meetings and on an on-going basis.

Remuneration matters

7. There should be a formal and transparent procedure for fixing the remuneration packages of individual directors. No director should be involved in deciding his own remuneration.

8. The level of remuneration should be appropriate to attract, retain and motivate the directors needed to run the company successfully but companies should avoid paying more for this purpose. A proportion of the remuneration, especially that of executive directors, should be linked to performance.

9. Each company should provide clear disclosure of its remuneration policy, level and mix of remuneration, and the procedure for setting remuneration, in the company's annual report.

Accountability and audit

10. The board is accountable to the shareholders while the management is accountable to the board.

11. The board should establish an audit committee ('AC') with written terms of reference which clearly set out its authority and duties.

12. The board should ensure that the management maintains a sound system of internal controls to safeguard the shareholders' investments and the company's assets.

13. The company should establish an internal audit function that is independent of the activities it audits.

Communication with shareholders

14. Companies should engage in regular, effective and fair communication with shareholders.
15. Companies should encourage greater shareholder participation at AGMs, and allow shareholders the opportunity to communicate their views on various matters affecting the company.

The principles outlined above are designed to enhance corporate governance, recognizing the agency costs that arise from the separation of ownership and control. The board (and specifically the CEO and inside executive directors) has delegated authority to manage corporate assets on behalf of the shareholders. Since the goals of the two parties may diverge, the board is supremely important in ensuring that insiders promote shareholder interests. The Singapore Code of Conduct recognizes this important function of the board. As Jensen remarks: 'The Board, at the apex of the internal control system, has the final responsibility for the functioning of the firm. Most importantly, it sets the rules of the game for the CEO. The job of the Board is to hire, fire and compensate the CEO and to provide high level council' (1993, p. 862). More specifically, the task of the inside (executive) directors on the unitary board is decision management (i.e. the initiation and implementation of strategic goals of the firm). The task of the outside (non-executive) directors is decision control (i.e. the ratification, monitoring and reward of the decision management function).

The Code of Conduct has some noteworthy features. First, the Code of Conduct recognizes the need for a strong, independent non-executive element on the board of directors to safeguard shareholder interests. Defining an independent director is notoriously a difficult task. The Code states that 'An "independent"[5] director is one who has no relationship with the company, its related companies or its officers that could interfere, or be reasonably perceived to interfere, with the exercise of the director's independent business judgment with a view to the best interests of the company' (The Governance Code, p. 1). The Code continues by providing examples of such relationships. A director would not be deemed independent in the following cases:

a) a director being employed by the company or any of its related companies for the current or any of the past three financial years; b) a director who has an immediate family member who is, or has been in any of the past three financial years, employed by the company or any of its related companies as a senior executive officer whose remuneration is determined by the remuneration committee; c) a director accepting any compensation from the company or any of its related companies other than compensation for Board service for the current or immediate past financial year; or d) a director being a substantial shareholder of or a partner in (with 5 per cent or more stake), or an executive officer of, any for-profit business organisation to which the company made, or from which the company received, significant payments in the current or immediate past financial year. (The Governance Code, pp. 1–2)

Given the importance of family and the predominance of multiple directorships and interlocked boards in Singapore (see Phan *et al.* 2003), it is clearly important to arrive at a satisfactory notion of director independence.

Second, the Code stresses the importance of an appropriate balance of power between decision management (the executive team) and the decision control (the chairman and the non-executive directors). It is important that the Code errs on the side of advocating that the posts of CEO and chairman be split (i.e. that they be held by different people). This is typically the case in the United Kingdom, but is not so in the United States, where the posts are generally held by the same person (see Conyon and Murphy 2000).

Third, the process of appointing a director to the board should be undertaken by a nominating committee. The Code recommends that it should comprise at least three directors, a majority of whom, including the chairman, should be independent. The Code further recommends that the nominating committee should have written terms of reference that describes the responsibilities of its members. The nominating committee should also have the 'responsibility of re-nomination having regard to the director's contribution and performance (e.g. attendance, preparedness, participation and candour) including, if applicable, as an independent director'. It should also deliberate and decide whether or not a director can be defined as 'independent'. It is clear, then, that the nominating committee is designed to perform an important task in the promotion of good board governance. Indeed, Ruigrok *et al.* (2004) study nomination committee effects in a sample of Swiss firms in 2003. They find that firms with nomination committees are more likely to have higher percentages of independent and foreign directors (but not female board members). Generally, they conclude that firms with well constructed nomination committees promote diversity in the boardroom.

Fourth, the Code requires that firms establish a remuneration (or compensation) committee to determine the level and structure of executive compensation. The guidance notes require only that the committee is comprised of a majority of non-executive directors rather than be exclusively non-executive. The members should be independent of management as well as 'free from any business or other relationships, which may materially interfere with the exercise of their independent judgement. This is to minimise the risk of any potential conflict of interest'. The remuneration committee is not required to reveal the identity of individuals who supply it with information, such as compensation consultants. This is consistent with current US governance practice, but not with UK rules. Currently, British regulations require the remuneration report to name any person who provides the committee with advice, or services, as well as the nature of any other services that that person has provided to the company.[6]

The compensation committee, then, is potentially an important device for resolving latent agency costs arising between shareholders and the management of the firm. Bonet and Conyon (2005) review the extant evidence on the effectiveness of the compensation committee. They conclude that empirical research testing the relation between compensation committee structure and executive pay has yielded mixed results. While some papers have found the existence of compensation committees affects the level and structure of executive pay in ways that resolve agency costs and so promote shareholder interests (for example Conyon and Peck 1998), other papers have failed to demonstrate this (for example Daily *et al.* 1998). On balance, they conclude the evidence supports the idea that insider-influenced compensation committees are prone to agency costs and yield outcomes divergent with shareholder interests. Moreover, using a short panel of UK executives from 1998 to 2002, Bonet and Conyon (2005) find evidence that weak governance structures, measured as the presence of insiders on the compensation committee, is positively correlated with executive pay.

The Singapore Code of Corporate Governance also promotes a high level of disclosure relating to the level and structure of executive compensation. However, unlike US and UK disclosure requirements it appears that Singapore firms do not have to give complete information for each named director separately. Instead companies are required to report compensation within specific pay bands. The guidance note indicates that:

> The report should set out the names of directors and at least the top 5 key executives (who are not also directors) earning remuneration which falls within bands of S$250,000. There will be no upper limit. Within each band, there will be a breakdown (in percentage terms) of each director's remuneration earned through base/fixed salary, variable or performance-related income/bonuses, benefits in kind, and stock options granted and other long-term incentives. Companies are however encouraged, as best practice, to fully disclose the remuneration of each individual director. (The Governance Code, p. 7)

Companies could indicate, for example, that a given director earned between S$250 000 and S$500 000, but not say the precise dollar amount. It turns out that in the case of ST Engineering, the case to be examined in the following section, there is full disclosure of compensation and the precise dollar amounts of salary, bonus and so on, earned are revealed.

Finally, the Code addresses the issue of shareholder relations. The Governance Committee indicated it:

> is mindful of the risk that close contact between companies and its shareholders might lead to different shareholders receiving different information. In particular, unpublished price-sensitive information may often be disclosed at analysts' briefings and private conversations with major investors. The Committee therefore subscribes to the view that all investors, whether institutional or retail, should be entitled to the same level of communication and disclosure…. Further, one of the OECD Principles of Corporate Governance states that processes and procedures for general shareholder meetings should allow for equitable treatment of all shareholders. Such an equitable and equal treatment should be extended to the issue of disclosure. (Corporate Governance Committee 2001, p. 7)

However, given the high degree of ownership concentration in Singapore publicly traded firms, as well as the presence of large block holders, the protection of minority block holders may be a very important consideration. However, the Code is largely silent on the asymmetries that might exist between small and large shareholders and their implications. It is also worth recalling that the governance Code was developed from the UK model – but ownership structures between Singapore and the UK are very different. In consequence, one might have expected a more complete treatment of the governance and performance implications of Singapore's pyramid ownership structure.

CORPORATE GOVERNANCE AT ST ENGINEERING

ST Engineering is a holding company that owns a group of engineering firms. ST Engineering is an ideal case study candidate. First, the firm has received many prestigious Singapore corporate governance awards.[7] Second, it is one of the largest firms on the SGX main board, accounting for about 1.5 per cent of the market capitalization. ST Engineering's business activities are divided into four business segments: aerospace, electronics, land systems and marine. Hoovers states that:

> Its aerospace unit maintains, repairs, overhauls commercial and military aircraft like F-16 fighters; its land systems unit upgrades and manufactures military vehicles and weapon systems as well as provides custom design, maintenance,

and repair services. The company's electronics unit designs communications, transportation, simulation, microwave, and industrial electronic products; its marine segment builds and repairs ships; primarily patrol, container and military vessels. (2004, p. 1)

The share price performance of ST Engineering, and that of market, is plotted in Figure 8.1. The data indicate that stock performance has improved since January 2003, the period when the corporate governance code was implemented.

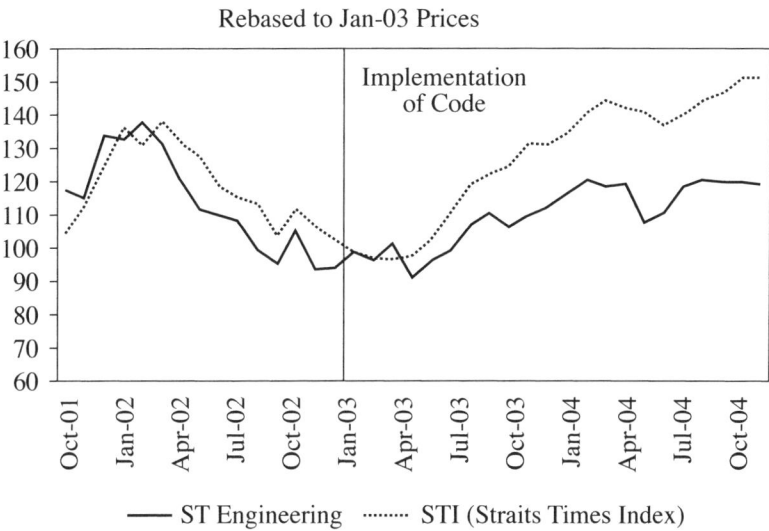

Rebased to Jan-03 Prices

— ST Engineering ⋯⋯ STI (Straits Times Index)

Source: Bloomberg.

Figure 8.1 Stock price performance at ST Engineering

The Board of Directors

The board of directors is a central theme within the corporate governance literature since the size and structure of the board can have important consequence for firm performance. A review of the recent economic literature on boards is provided by Hermalin and Weisbach (2003). Pettigrew (1992), Pettigrew and McNulty (1995) and Huse (2005) provide a managerial perspective on the study of boards of directors. ST Engineering explains how it has adhered to the principles of the Singapore Code of Corporate Governance in Chapter 4 of its 2003 annual report. The focus of the governance report is on how the principles of the Code have been implemented rather than on the specifics of individual guidelines. ST Engineering appears to have a well-developed and mature governance structure that is consistent with the high disclosure and transparency standards of major economies.

The board of directors is made up 12 individuals and one alternate director. The Chairman of Singapore Technologies is Mr Peter Seah, a non-executive director who is independent of company management. He was appointed as non-executive chairman in 2002. The President and CEO of ST Engineering is Tan Pheng Hock. He was appointed director in May 2001. The complete list of board members, and their committee membership, is provided in Table 8.2. One can compare the size of ST Engineering's board with extant studies. Mak and Phan (1999) report the average board size of SES[8] listed companies in 1995 is about eight (with a range from four to fourteen). Mak and Yuanto (2002) and Bradbury *et al.* (2004) report the average size of the board in about 270 Singapore firms in fiscal year 1999/2000 is about seven (with a range from four to fifteen). Williams (2004) reports that the average size of the board in about 390 Singapore firms in fiscal year 2000 is about 7.2. Since board size increases with firm scale, the size of the board at ST Engineering is to be expected.

The size of the corporate board is often a matter of corporate governance concern – specifically, large boards are thought to be less effective than small boards. Hermalin and Weisbach (2003) review the evidence that bigger boards adversely affect company value. If this is the case smaller, leaner boards might be preferred by shareholders. ST Engineering are mindful about the size of their board: 'The board has further determined that it is of an appropriate size to meet the objective of bringing a balance of skills and experience to bear on the deliberations of the various board committees that its directors sit on.' It is noteworthy that Mak and Yuanto (2002) find little relationship between most corporate governance mechanisms and financial performance measured by Tobin's Q in a sample of 550 Singaporean and Malaysian firms in 2000. However, they do find a statistically significant negative relation between Tobin's Q and the log of board size. We later present evidence that is consistent with this. We find that large boards adversely affect firm performance (measured as return on assets) in Singapore.

In accordance with the Singapore code of corporate governance there is a clear division of responsibilities at the top of the company. The posts are held by two separate people. In this respect, the Singapore board is akin to the typical UK board where the posts of CEO and chairperson are held by different people. However, it is different to standard practice in the USA, where the posts of chairman and CEO are generally held by the same person. Conyon and Murphy (2000) present evidence on USA–UK

Table 8.2   Board composition and committee membership at ST Engineering

	Audit Committee	Business Investment and Divestment Committee	Executive Resource & Compensation Committee/ Nominating Committee*	Budget & Finance Committee	Research Development & Technology Committee	Senior Human Resource Committee	Risk Review Committee	Tenders Committee
Board members								
Peter SEAH Lim Huat			C			C		Rolling list of any 3 Board members
TAN Pheng Hock		M		M	M	M	M	
KOH Beng Seng	C							
TAN Guong Ching		C	M	C		M		
MG NG Yat Chung		M				M	M	
Dr TAN Kim Siew								
Prof LUI Pao Chuen					C			
Winston TAN Tien Hin		M			M		C	
Lucien WONG Yuen Kuai	M			M			M	
Dr Philip Nalliah PILLAI			M					
QUEK Poh Huat		M		M				
Venkatachalam	M	M					M	
KRISHNAKUMAR								
BG Bernard TAN Kok Kiang†								
Non-board members								
NG Kee Choe			CM					
CHANG See Hiang							CM	

C: chairman, M: member, CM: co-opted member.
* The members of the Executive Resource & Compensation Committee and the Nominating Committee are the same.
† Alternate director to MG NG Yat Chung.

Source: ST Engineering Annual Report 2003.

199

differences in corporate leadership structure. They illustrate that about 80 per cent of US firms combine the posts of CEO and Chair, whereas about 80 per cent of UK firms separate these positions. Mak and Phan (1999) report that approximately 46 per cent of SES-listed companies separate the posts of CEO and chairman based on a sample of 158 firms in 1995. Clearly, ST Engineering is adopting best practice in this particular governance area.

The ST Engineering board is comprised mainly of non-management members. Of the 12 members, 11 directors are non-executive. The CEO (Tan Pheng Hock) is the insider. Moreover, the company identifies six members that are considered 'independent' directors. 'The board has determined that six of its directors are independent and do not have a material relationship with ST Engg as defined by the Code. These directors are Koh Beng Seng, Venkatachalam Krishnakumar, Tan Guong Ching, Winston Tan, Lucien Wong and Dr Philip Pillai.' Thus, the ratio of non-executive directors on the board is 11/12 (or 92 per cent) and the ratio of independent directors is 6/12 (or 50 per cent). Mak and Phan (1999) report the average proportion of outsiders for SES firms in 1995 is about 57 per cent. Williams (2004) reports the average proportion of independent outsiders on the board, for 390 Singapore firms in 2000, is about 39 per cent. Both the Audit Committee and Remuneration Committee are comprised of independent non-executive members. The history of corporate governance research has stressed the importance of a strong and independent non-executive element on the board in order to safeguard shareholder interests. However, whether firms with a higher fraction of outside directors actually have better corporate performance is an open question. The review of the economic literature on board effectiveness conducted by Hermalin and Weisbach (2003) suggests there is little relation between corporate performance and the proportion of non-executive directors on the board. However, they also conclude that boards with more independent members are better at implementing board functions; for instance, removing CEOs when corporate performance is poor.[9] Phan *et al.* (2003) find some evidence that interlocked boards are correlated positively with accounting performance.

Executive Compensation

The function of the board of directors is to hire, fire and compensate the CEO (Jensen 1993). The level of compensation and the design of the contract are clearly central to aligning shareholder and management interests. There is a voluminous literature on executive compensation which is comprehensively reviewed by Murphy (1999) and Jensen and Murphy (2004). Early research by Jensen and Murphy (1990) identified appropriate ways to measure incentives and stressed the importance of equity-based compensation as a way to motivate senior management. Core *et al.* (2003), in their recent review, specifically focus on the determinants of such equity incentives showing that firm growth opportunities, firm risk, corporate scale and governance are all important factors shaping the pattern of incentives observed within firms. An analysis of compensation and incentives in the context of ST Engineering is therefore clearly warranted.

As an institutional matter compensation decisions are typically deliberated by a sub-committee of the full board who make recommendations to the full board for consideration (Murphy 1999; Jensen and Murphy 2004). At ST Engineering the Executive Resource and Compensation Committee (ERCC) performs this function. All the members of the Remuneration Committee are deemed independent of management and it is important to note that the CEO, Mr Tan, is not a member of this committee. This is in line with best practice corporate governance, since if he were a member a potential conflict of interest might arise. The annual report states that:

> The ERCC has access to professional advice from appropriate external advisers as and when it deems necessary. The ERCC may meet with these external advisers without management being present. All decisions at any meeting of the ERCC shall be decided by a majority of votes of the ERCC members present and voting (the decision of the ERCC shall at all times exclude the vote, approval or recommendation of any member who has a conflict of interest in the subject matter under consideration). (ST Engineering 2003, p. 61)

Such professional external advisers are typically remuneration consultants – experts who advise the committee on the appropriate level and design of the compensation package. As far as is possible to discern, ST Engineering does not reveal who its external advisers are in relation to director compensation. This is not surprising since typically firms do not reveal this information and so ST Engineering is no different to other firms. However, recent US research has been critical of the role of compensation consultants. Bebchuk and Fried (2003, 2004) argue that compensation consultants may facilitate managerial rent extraction. The rent extraction/managerial power model predicts that consultants bring about higher executive pay because of their distorted incentives (for example, the desire to please the CEO or solicit repeat business). In addition, firms with higher pay feel a greater need to get a consultant to help legitimize their compensation levels.

At ST Engineering the Remuneration Committee has the following duties: 'Consider, review and approve and/or vary (if necessary) the entire specific remuneration package and service contract terms for each senior management executive (including salaries, allowances, bonuses, payments, options, benefits in kind, retirement rights, severance packages and service contracts) having regard to the executive remuneration policy for ST

Engg.' And to 'consider and approve termination payments, retirement payments, gratuities, ex gratia payments, severance payments and other similar payments to senior management executives'. The committee met four times in 2003 and:

> The key activities centred on the assessment and development of the management team, target setting, and the determination of their compensation, incentives plan and award. During the year, the senior management team also went through a 360 degree feedback exercise aimed at enhancing awareness of their managerial competencies as perceived by others and this led to a better understanding of their strengths and development areas. Another major area of discussion was that of succession planning for the key positions in the Group. The Committee also reviewed and approved the grant of share options and conditional performance share awards under ST Engg's approved share plans.

The material above describes the institutions of pay setting and their role at ST Engineering. The actual CEO compensation package is made up of salary, bonus, fees and stock options. Table 8.3 contains information from the firm's summary compensation table in 2003. The main individual of interest is the CEO, Mr Tan. The total cash payment received in fiscal year 2003 is S\$1 925 858 of which 41 per cent is made up of a salary, 50 per cent is made up of a bonus and 9 per cent is made up of directors' fees. The disclosure of compensation is consistent with the principles and guidance notes of the Singapore Code of Corporate Governance. In particular, Principle 9 states that 'each company should provide clear disclosure of its remuneration policy, level and mix of remuneration, and the procedure for setting remuneration, in the company's annual report'. The Code requires companies to report compensation levels within specific pay bands. This is what used to be the case in the UK prior to the Cadbury and Greenbury reports. However, the code further states: 'Companies are however encouraged, as best practice, to fully disclose the remuneration of each individual director.' And, indeed, this is precisely what ST Engineering does.

Stock Options

Another important element of CEO compensation is the granting of stock options. Stock options are an important source of compensation as well as providing incentives that align management and shareholder interests (Core *et al.* 2003; Murphy 1999; Jensen and Murphy 2004). Bradbury *et al.* (1999) report on the adoption and structure of executive stock option plans in a sample of 158 Singapore publicly traded firms. They find that only about 50 per cent of these firms actually have such an option plan in place. Moreover, they find that firms where the CEO and executive directors have

Table 8.3 Directors' remuneration at ST Engineering in 2003

	Salary	Bonus	Director's fee	Total	Stock options granted in 2003	Exercise price	Exercise period
Peter SEAH Lim Huat	–	–	60 000‡	60 000	44 500 40 500	1.79 1.86	7.2.2004 to 6.2.2008 12.8.2004 to 11.8.2008
TAN Pheng Hock	785 414	967 944	172 500‡†	1 925 858	200 000 200 000	1.79 1.86	7.2.2004 to 6.2.2013 12.8.2004 to 11.8.2013
KOH Beng Seng**	–	–	16 583	16 583	–	–	–
TAN Guong Ching	–	–	15 000*	15 000	–	–	–
MG NG Yat Chung***	–	–	5 417*	5 417	–	–	–
Dr TAN Kim Siew#	–	–	208*	208	–	–	–
Professor LUI Pao Chuen	–	–	56 500†	56 500	21 500 21 500	1.79 1.86	7.2.2004 to 6.2.2008 12.8.2004 to 11.8.2008
Winston TAN Tien Hin	–	–	116 000†	116 000	56 500 46 500	1.79 1.86	7.2.2004 to 6.2.2008 12.8.2004 to 11.8.2008
Lucien WONG Yuen Kuai	–	–	41 834	41 834	23 500 19 500	1.79 1.86	7.2.2004 to 6.2.2008 12.8.2004 to 11.8.2008
Dr Philip Nalliah PILLAI	–	–	55 000†	55 000	31 000 29 000	1.79 1.86	7.2.2004 to 6.2.2008 12.8.2004 to 11.8.2008
QUEK Poh Huat	–	–	92 000‡†	92 000	35 000 33 000	1.79 1.86	7.2.2004 to 6.2.2008 12.8.2004 to 11.8.2008
Venkatachalam KRISHNAKUMAR							
BG Bernard TAN Kok Kiang *** (Alternate to MG NG Yat Chung)	–	–	–	–	–	–	–
Philip TAN Yuen Fah##	–	–	43 417	43 417	27 500 27 500	1.79 1.86	7.2.2004 to 6.2.2008 12.8.2004 to 11.8.2008
LG LIM Chuan Poh@	–	–	2 500*	2 500	–	–	–

* The salary and bonus amount shown is inclusive of allowances and CPF and performance shares; ** appointed on 15 September 2003; *** appointed on 15 June 2003; # appointed on 15 September 2003; ## resigned on 15 December 2003; @ retired at AGM on 3 April 2003; ‡ fees are payable to Directors' employer company. † Includes fees for directorship in subsidiary/subsidiaries; fees for public sector Directors are payable to government agencies.

Source: Annual Report 2003, pp. 195–7.

a large fraction of ordinary shares are less likely to have such stock option programmes. Similarly, firms with substantial blockholders (share stakes in excess of 5 per cent) are also less likely to have stock option programmes.

It is widely understood (see Murphy 1999; Jensen and Murphy 2004) that employee options issued at the money have economic value even though their intrinsic value, which is the stock price less the exercise price, is zero. The current accounting treatment of stock options in Singapore is similar to the treatment in other jurisdictions such as the United States. Companies are not currently required to recognize the stock options issued as an expense in their profit and loss accounts at the point of grant (see Jensen and Murphy 2004). Companies recognize options as an expense when the employees exercise the options, but for options honoured by the issue of new shares there is no impact on the profit and loss account. If options are effectively 'free' from an accounting perspective, then perverse incentives may arise. For instance, firms may issue more options than is optimal or design option packages that meet favourable regulatory requirements rather than economic considerations of motivating employees.[10] However, in September 2004 the Council on Corporate Disclosure and Governance (CCDG) adopted FRS102 Share Based Payment, which is expected to significantly affect the ways in which companies account for and design stock option programmes.[11] For listed companies the new rules come into effect for accounting periods beginning after January 2005 and the FRS requires companies to recognize share-based payment transactions in its financial statements.

ST Engineering does indeed have a stock option plan for its senior managers. From the summary compensation table (see Table 8.3), the number of options, the exercise price and the maturity term are provided. However, the expected value of the option package is not reported in the table.[12] If one has further information on the volatility of the stock, the dividend yield and risk-free rate, we can use the Black-Scholes formula to provide an approximate expected value of the options. Using this method, the value of a (European) call option paying dividends is:

$$\text{option value} = c = Se^{-qt}N(d_1) - Xe^{-rt}N(d_2),$$

$$\text{where } d_1 = \{\ln(s/x) + (r-q + \sigma^2/2)t\}/\sigma\sqrt{t},$$

$$d_2 = d_1 - \sigma\sqrt{t},$$

where S is the stock price, X is the exercise price, T is the maturity term, r is the risk-free interest rate, q is the dividend yield and σ is the volatility of returns. $N(.)$ is the cumulative probability distribution function for a standardized normal variable and e is Euler's constant. Using data from the summary compensation table, let $S = X = 1.79$, $T = 10$, and suppose for illustrative purposes only that $q = 2$ per cent, $\sigma = 30$ per cent and $r = 2$ per cent. In this case the first tranche of 200 000 options are worth about S$107 000 and the second tranche of 200 000, where $S = X = 1.86$, is worth about S$111 000. Of course, the value of these options will change as the input values change, but the example illustrates the approximate value of the granted options. If the option valuation is approximately correct then the value of the combined 400 000 options is about S$218 000. Suppose we now define 2003 CEO total compensation as cash compensation plus the expected value of the options granted during the fiscal period, so total compensation is equal to approximately $2 143 858 (= S$1 925 858 + S$218 000). This implies that option compensation as a percentage of total compensation is about 10 per cent. This figure is considerably less than is observed in the United States. Murphy (1999) gives evidence illustrating that during the 1990s the use of stock option pay in the United States increased dramatically (see also Jensen and Murphy 2004). For the year 2000 the typical CEO at an S&P 500 firm received approximately 50 per cent of pay in terms of stock options. The USA, however, is different from practices elsewhere in the world regarding the extent of stock option use. Conyon and Murphy (2000) show that share options account for about 12 per cent of CEO pay in the United Kingdom.

Economic analysis predicts that agency costs associated with the separation of firm ownership from control are reduced by managerial equity holdings (Jensen and Murphy 1990). The higher are CEO fractional holdings of equity the lower are agency costs and the more aligned are managerial and shareholder interests (Murphy 1999). At ST Engineering one can estimate that Mr Tan held 73 864 shares (at 31 December 2003). In addition, Mr Tan has 2 012 500 aggregate options outstanding at the end of the financial year under the company's ESOS/ESOP plans. Adding these together and dividing by the number shares outstanding (= 2 886 803 389; see Table 8.4) and expressing as a percentage yields approximately 0.07 per cent. Thus we might suggest that CEO ownership of this company is approximately 1/10 of 1 per cent.[13] One may contrast this ownership figure to other extant research. Mak and Phan (1999) report the average CEO ownership of SES companies is 0.3 per cent using 1995 data. However, it is well known that fractional CEO holdings decline with firm size (for a discussion, see Core *et al.* 2003) and since ST Engineering is large we would expect lower fractional holdings.

An important question is whether CEO financial incentives are at their desired level. Namely, are the observed incentives too low, about right or even too high? There is no easy answer to this question, but one way to

Table 8.4   Shareholder distribution in ST Engineering

Range of shareholdings	No. of shareholders	%	No. of shares	%
1–999	1 721	5.29	550 718	0.02
1 000–10 000	25 474	78.35	108 997 955	3.77
10 001–1 000 000	5 295	16.28	184 927 032	6.41
1 000 001 and above	25	0.08	2 592 327 684	89.80
Total	32 515	100	2 886 803 389	100.00

Source: ST Engineering Annual Report 2003, p. 198.

think about it is to consider the purpose of incentives and stock options. Economic analysis indicates that options etc. are used to resolve agency costs arising between shareholders and managers. However, options are only one corporate governance mechanism. Another might be active monitoring by a large blockholder. Firms with active monitors may need fewer incentives compared to firms where ownership is relatively diffuse. It is the combination of incentives and monitoring that is pertinent, not simply the amount of options.

Ownership Structure

In Table 8.4 the ownership distribution of ST Engineering is presented. There are approximately 32 000 separate shareholders. The distribution is highly skewed since only 25 shareholders (or 0.08 per cent of the total shareholders) hold in excess of 1 000 000 shares. However, these few shareholders together own about 90 per cent of shares in ST Engineering. The ownership distribution therefore is highly concentrated. In Table 8.5 more detail on the ownership structure of ST Engineering is presented. The largest 20 shareholders own approximately 90 per cent of the shares in ST Engineering. One can then calculate the Herfindahl index of concentration (i.e. the sum of squared ownership shares) for this set of 20 shareholders. The figure turns out to be about 0.32 (where the feasible range is 0–1). Once again we conclude that ownership at ST Engineering is concentrated.

The story however is much richer than this because of GLCs in Singapore as well as the presence of pyramid ownership control. This is illustrated in Figure 8.2. The largest shareholder is Singapore Technologies Pte Ltd, whose direct shareholding is approximately 55 per cent. Singapore Technologies is itself a conglomerate that operates in five main business areas. These are engineering, technology, infrastructure and logistics, property, and financial

Table 8.5   Major shareholders in ST Engineering (Top 20)

	Name	Number of shares held	%
1	Singapore Technologies Pte Ltd	1 567 918 719	54.31
2	Raffles Nominees Pte Ltd	348 064 502	12.06
3	DBS Nominees Pte Ltd	306 598 894	10.62
4	Citibank Nominees Singapore Pte Ltd	129 769 044	4.50
5	HSBC (Singapore) Nominees Pte Ltd	81 331 544	2.82
6	United Overseas Bank Nominees Pte Ltd	67 867 630	2.35
7	Oversea-Chinese Bank Nominees Pte Ltd	21 908 984	0.76
8	KI Investments (HK) Limited	13 370 000	0.46
9	UOB Kay Hian Pte Ltd	8 982 525	0.31
10	Morgan Stanley Asia (S'pore)	8 858 342	0.31
11	DB Nominees (S) Pte Ltd	6 472 000	0.22
12	Societe Generale S'pore Branch	4 038 000	0.14
13	The Asia Life Assurance Society Ltd – S'pore Life Fund	3 158 809	0.11
14	Ang Beng Siong @ Hendrik Atmaja	2 706 947	0.09
15	OCBC Securities Private Ltd	2 536 155	0.09
16	Phillip Securities Pte Ltd	2 502 917	0.09
17	Bank of East Asia Nominees Pte Ltd	2 331 505	0.08
18	Singapore Newspaper Services Pte Ltd	2 200 000	0.08
19	Shanwood Development Pte Ltd	2 077 000	0.07
20	G K Goh Stockbrokers Pte Ltd	2 070 460	0.07
		2 584 763 977	*89.54*

services. The pyramid structure is evidenced by the fact that Singapore Technologies in turn is owned by Temasek – a major government-linked corporation (GLC). Temasek's only shareholder is the government and the appointment and reappointment of the board and the CEO is subject to the approval of the elected president of the Republic of Singapore. However, Temasek's shareholder requires it to operate as a commercial entity earning a proper return on investments. Temasek Holdings (Private) Limited has a total share interest of 1 613 707 137 shares representing 55.9 per cent of the total common shares of ST Engineering. The figure illustrates that Temasek owns Singapore Technologies which itself has a total shareholding of 1 599 168 719, representing about 55.4 per cent of the common shares (= 2 886 803 389) in ST Engineering.[14] Also, the pyramid ownership structure is evidenced by the fact that Temasek has ownership of the Keppel Group, which in turn has a 0.47 per cent interest in ST Engineering. Similarly, the right-hand side of the figure illustrates that the

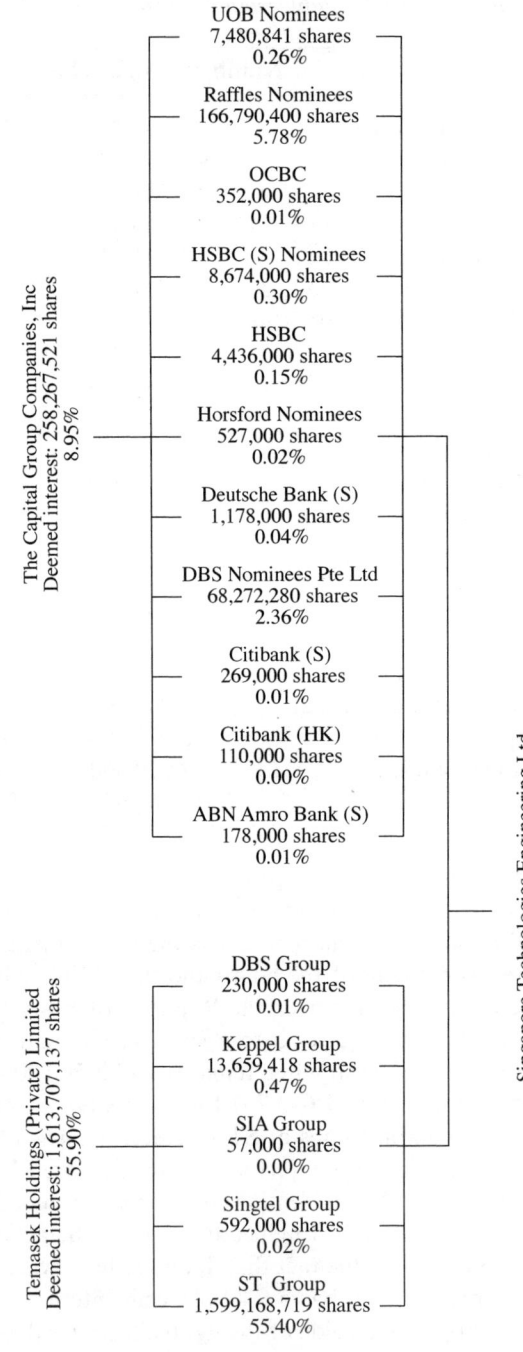

The Capital Group Companies, Inc
Deemed interest: 258,267,521 shares
8.95%

UOB Nominees
7,480,841 shares
0.26%

Raffles Nominees
166,790,400 shares
5.78%

OCBC
352,000 shares
0.01%

HSBC (S) Nominees
8,674,000 shares
0.30%

HSBC
4,436,000 shares
0.15%

Horsford Nominees
527,000 shares
0.02%

Deutsche Bank (S)
1,178,000 shares
0.04%

DBS Nominees Pte Ltd
68,272,280 shares
2.36%

Citibank (S)
269,000 shares
0.01%

Citibank (HK)
110,000 shares
0.00%

ABN Amro Bank (S)
178,000 shares
0.01%

Temasek Holdings (Private) Limited
Deemed interest: 1,613,707,137 shares
55.90%

DBS Group
230,000 shares
0.01%

Keppel Group
13,659,418 shares
0.47%

SIA Group
57,000 shares
0.00%

Singtel Group
592,000 shares
0.02%

ST Group
1,599,168,719 shares
55.40%

Singapore Technologies Engineering Ltd
Number of shares issued: 2,886,803,389

Source: Based on ST Engineering Annual Report (2003, p. 198).

Figure 8.2 Substantial ownership structure in ST Engineering

Capital Group of Companies is the ultimate owner of 8.95 per cent of ST Engineering shares. This occurs via their direct holdings in intermediate companies. For example, this occurs via DBS, HSBC or Raffles nominee holdings in ST Engineering. Of course, such pyramid structures are of great interest to applied governance researchers. As La Porta *et al.* (1999) and Johnson *et al.* (2000) illustrate, and as discussed above, such pyramids may enable ultimate owners to have control rights in excess of cash flow rights or allow the possibility of tunnelling activities to expropriate funds from downstream enterprises.

FIRM PERFORMANCE, BOARD SIZE AND THE FRACTION OF OUTSIDE DIRECTORS

The objective in this section is to complement the single company case study with a statistical regression analysis of the relation between firm performance and elements of board structure. It is important to understand the previous case analysis in the context of more general results. Specifically, we examine the relation between board size, the fraction of outsiders on the board and firm performance. Previous research on this subject has typically been confined to Anglo-Saxon economies (see Hermalin and Weisbach 2003). In contrast, we present new and unique evidence for Singapore and compare the results to those obtained for the United States and the United Kingdom. We find that board size is negatively correlated with firm performance – a result consistent with previous research. Singapore provides a fertile environment for testing board effectiveness. First, along with other Asian economies it experienced a severe financial crisis in 1997. Second, Singapore has adopted Anglo-Saxon style governance rules for the composition of boards.

Corporate finance theorists have previously considered the effects of board structure on corporate performance. These were highlighted in the previous section. Jensen (1993) argues that large boards are less effective compared to small boards. The basic idea is that when boards become too big agency problems become more acute. For example, directors may free-ride on other directors' monitoring, or the board may be 'captured' by the CEO. The extant research, from Anglo-Saxon economies, suggests that large boards are associated with poor corporate performance (e.g. Hermalin and Weisbach 2003; Yermack 1996). Corporate governance theorists also predict that more outside directors on the board increase firm performance. They hypothesize that a greater fraction of outsiders on the board is associated with better monitoring quality. In turn, this ameliorates the agency costs associated with a potentially self-serving management. However, the large empirical literature examining this proposition has yielded mixed and largely inconclusive results (see for instance Bhagat and Black 2002). Indeed, Hermalin and Weisbach conclude: 'Overall, there is little to suggest that board composition has any cross sectional relationship to firm performance' (2003, p. 6). To test the relation between firm performance and board structure we estimate the following simple linear model using ordinary least squares:

$$\pi_i = \alpha + \beta_1 BS_i + \beta_2 OR_i + \beta_3 S_i + \beta_4 MS_i + \gamma_t + \delta_j + \varepsilon_i \qquad (1)$$

where π_i is the ith firm's accounting performance (measured as the firm's return on assets). The model includes board size (BS_i) and the fraction of outsiders on the board (OR_i). The term S_i is a firm size control variable and MS_i is the firm's market share. The γ's are time dummies and δ_j are eight 1-digit SIC industry dummy variables. Finally, ε_i is a stochastic error. Equation (1) is estimated separately for firms in the United Kingdom, the United States and Singapore. We expect $\beta_1 < 0$ and $\beta_2 > 0$. The reported standard errors in the regressions (reported in Table 8.7) are robust to heteroscedasticity.

To test the relation between corporate performance and board structure we use the OSIRIS database supplied by Bureau van Dijk (BVD). It contains financial and management information on globally listed public companies. We selected Singapore, the United Kingdom and the United States. For each economy we selected only currently listed industrial firms (i.e. we excluded banks, insurance companies and so on, whose SIC code is in the range 6000–6999).[15] We have time-varying data on the financial performance of firms. We selected the years 1999–2003 (that is, the period after the Asian financial crisis). We only have a snapshot (that is, cross-section) of data on board structure for each firm. This information pertains to the latest fiscal year for the firm. The cross-section data are then mapped to the time-varying financial data. The dependent variable (π_i) in Equation (1) is the firm's return on assets (BVD data item 31 015). Board size, BS_i, is measured as the sum of outside and inside directors. The outsider ratio, OR_i, is calculated as the number of outside directors on the main board divided by board size. It is assembled using information from the OSIRIS board members and managers database. Firm size, S_i, is measured as the log of firm sales and MS_i is market share calculated as the firm's sales divided by total sales in the industry.

Table 8.6 contains descriptive statistics on the governance variables. Median board size is approximately between 6 and 7 in Singapore, the United States and the United Kingdom. In all countries, outside directors form the majority of the board. Table 8.7 presents the ordinary least squares regression results. Column 1 contains the results for Singapore, column 2 the United States and column 3 Great Britain. The important conclusion from the table is that there is a significantly negative correlation between accounting performance and board size (that is $\beta_1 < 0$), which is consistent with prior research (such as Yermack 1996). Contrary to our expectations, board composition, measured by the proportion of outsiders on the board, has a negative effect on accounting performance for Singapore and Great Britain (that is the sign on Outsiders Board size<0 when we expected $\beta_2 > 0$). However, it is significantly positive for the United States. This result is

Table 8.6   Descriptive statistics

	(1) Singapore	(2) United States	(3) Great Britain
Return on assets	3.39	0.10	3.38
Board size	7.00	7.00	6.00
Proportion of outsiders	0.67	0.75	0.66
Log(firm sales)	11.33	11.16	10.62
Number of unique firms	421	6483	1538

Table 8.7   Regression results

	(1) Singapore	(2) United States	(3) Great Britain
Board size	−0.56	−1.98	−0.44
	$(0.26)^{**}$	$(0.19)^{***}$	$(0.25)^{*}$
Proportion of outsiders	−3.92	20.95	−16.98
	(3.09)	$(3.71)^{***}$	$(4.11)^{***}$
Log(firm sales)	3.60	15.09	7.25
	$(0.89)^{***}$	$(0.38)^{***}$	$(0.45)^{***}$
Market share	−13.58	−304.09	−56.12
	$(6.18)^{**}$	$(121.41)^{**}$	$(14.06)^{***}$
Constant	−33.27	−186.02	−69.01
	$(10.17)^{***}$	$(5.00)^{***}$	$(5.90)^{***}$
Time dummies	Yes	Yes	Yes
Industry dummies	Yes	Yes	Yes
Observations (=firms×years)	1831	30 532	6572
Adjusted *R*-squared	0.04	0.21	0.14

Notes: The dependent variable is the firm's return on assets. Heteroscedastic robust standard errors reported in parentheses. * significant at 10%; ** significant at 5%; *** significant at 1%. Estimation method is ordinary least squares. Pooled cross section and time series data from 1999 to 2003.

consistent with previous findings in the literature (Hermalin and Weisbach 2003) which finds both positive and negative correlations between the fraction of outsiders on the board and firm performance. In non-tabulated results, we estimated Equation (1) using alternative econometric methods. When using robust regression techniques (which control for potential outlier problems in the data) we also established a negative correlation between firm performance and board size. We would recommend further statistical analyses using alternative measures of firm performance (such as the market to book ratio or the firm's profit margin) to establish the robustness of the findings reported here.

KEY LEARNING POINTS AND DISCUSSION QUESTIONS

This chapter has considered recent changes in corporate governance in Singapore and has illustrated these issues using ST Engineering as a case study. The analysis illustrates a number of important learning points. We first established that the historical development of corporate governance in Singapore is unique and based on liberal free-trade flows and the strategic promotion of a strong enterprise by the government (Chee 2004). The governance system resembles the model established in the USA and UK. In particular, there is a unitary board of directors consisting of executive and independent non-executive directors. Singapore, however, is quite different from the USA and the UK in terms of ownership structure. There is significant effective State ownership of firms as well as the presence of other large block holders. Effective ownership operates through a pyramid structure. Second, in January 2003 the new Code of Corporate Governance was enacted. The Code is flexible and promotes a balanced perspective to achieve high standards of corporate governance and corporate performance. The Code is similar in spirit to the models adopted in the United Kingdom and Canada, and sets out a clear set of principles describing appropriate approaches to the governance of enterprises. The Code also contains important guidance notes relating to director independence, accountability and disclosure – especially in respect of executive compensation and internal control systems such as the audit committee.

We then provided an analysis of ST Engineering against this background of continued development in Singapore corporate governance. The level of disclosure and transparency at ST Engineering is very high and is at least on a par with disclosure and transparency in other economies such as the United States and the United Kingdom. We examined the board of directors, the board committees, executive compensation, stock options and ownership structure at this firm. The board is comprised of non-executive directors who are independent of management and the firm clearly identifies which non-executive directors are independent. Board size and composition are comparable to other large firms. Executive compensation is made up a mixture of salary, bonus and equity instruments such as stock options. Option use is not as dramatic as it is in the United States. We documented recent accounting changes which may affect the use and structure of option packages. We documented the ownership structure at ST Engineering illustrating the importance of Temasek, the government investment vehicle. The pyramid ownership structure, common in Singapore, is clearly seen at ST Engineering.

Finally, we illustrated the relation between corporate performance and board structure more generally. We investigated the empirical relation between corporate performance, board size and the fraction of outsiders on the board using data from Singapore, the United Kingdom and the United States. We found that accounting performance was negatively correlated to board size in Singapore, the United Kingdom and the United States. Using single company case analysis combined with more general statistical modelling we hope to have provided some further insights into international corporate governance.

DISCUSSION QUESTIONS

1. What are the distinctive features of corporate governance in Singapore?
2. In what ways is ownership structure in Singapore distinctive? How is this manifested at ST Engineering?
3. What are the main features of the new corporate governance code in Singapore?
4. How effective do you think the corporate governance code will be in enhancing corporate performance?
5. Does ST Engineering comply adequately with the Code of Corporate Governance?
6. How does board size and board composition affect the performance of firms?
7. Are there any improvements that ST Engineering can make to its board structure?
8. How important are stock options in motivating senior management?
9. What recommendations would you make to improve the design of the executive compensation programme at ST Engineering?

ACKNOWLEDGEMENTS

I would like to thank Lerong He, Chris Mallin (the editor), Simon Peck and Mitchell Van der Zahn for discussions and comments during the preparation of this paper. I am especially grateful to Julian Wee Ching Wei for excellent research assistance. This research was funded by the Wharton-SMU Research Center at Singapore Management University. I am grateful to Singapore Management University for their gracious hospitality during my visit there in the Spring of 2005.

NOTES

1. Denis and McConnell (2003) provide a review of important recent contributions to the international corporate governance debate. They focus on board composition and equity ownership issues in individual countries as well as more recent studies that examine how differing legal structures across different countries can affect corporate governance effectiveness. Similarly, see Mallin and Jelic (2000) for a discussion of developments in Central and Eastern Europe.
2. For example see the reports at http://www.temasekholdings.com.sg/ and http://www.st.com.sg/.
3. The Code of Corporate Governance can be accessed at the Singapore Stock Exchange: http://info.sgx.com/weblist.nsf/newDOCNAME/ST_CCGReport?opendocument
4. The Singapore Code appears similar in design to the corporate governance codes enacted in the United Kingdom (see, for example, Hampel 1998). This too contains a set of key principles which is accompanied by a set of guidance notes to issuers.
5. This is cross-defined by the SGX Listing Manual.
6. Specifically, recent UK legislation (HMSO 2002) says that if there is a compensation committee, constituted of the company's directors, then the directors' remuneration report shall '(a) name each director who was a member of the committee at any time when the committee was considering any such matter; (b) name any person who provided to the committee advice, or services, that materially assisted the committee in their consideration of any such matter; (c) in the case of any person named under paragraph (b), who is not a director of the company, state (i) the nature of any other services that that person has provided to the company during the relevant financial year; and (ii) whether that person was appointed by the committee.' Web access at: http://www.legislation.hmso.gov.uk/si/si2002/20021986.htm
7. The company identifies these achievements in its 2003 annual report. The Transparency Excellence Award was presented to ST Engineering by the Securities Investors Association (Singapore) in the Investors' Choice Awards. ST Engineering was highly commended under the Best Investor Relations by a Singapore Company category by IR Magazine in 2003. It was voted as A Leader in Corporate Governance (Singapore) in a survey by The Asset Benchmark Research. The company was also named joint runner up in the Best Managed Boards by the Singapore Institute of Directors, the Business Times, the Singapore Business Federation, the Economic Development Board and the Singapore Exchange (ST Engineering 2003).
8. The Stock Exchange of Singapore (SES) and the Singapore International Monetary Exchange (SIMEX) were merged on 1 December 1999 to form the Singapore Exchange (SGX). SGX was demutualized on 23 November 2000 to become Asia-Pacific's first demutualized and integrated securities and derivatives exchange.

9.   In the case of Singapore, where there is majority ownership by the government or a family, it is possible that these majority owners will take a closer scrutiny of the CEO's performance and directly influence the replacement of the CEO where necessary.
10. There is a global debate about whether and how stock options should be expensed.
11. See the Council on Corporate Disclosure and Governance at http://www.ccdg.gov.sg/frs/index2004.htm.
12. This practice differs from the United States where publicly traded firms report the value of stock options granted during the fiscal year in the definitive proxy statement. The valuation method used is often the Black-Scholes procedure. Firms also provide the intrinsic value of the aggregate stock of options held, split by those that are exercisable and those that cannot be exercised.
13. We have made the simplifying assumption that the ownership of share options can be treated like the ownership of ordinary shares. A more sophisticated analysis would want to cater for the possibility that the options are not exercised.
14. Singapore Technologies group of companies has a direct interest of 1 567 918 719 shares in ST Engineering (as per Table 8.5). However, the ST Engineering annual report (2003, p. 198) indicates that Singapore Technologies group has a further 31 250 000 shares of deemed interest giving a total share interest of 1 599 168 719 (or 55.4 per cent of total shares). The total interest by Singapore Technologies in ST Engineering is recorded in Figure 8.2.
15. We selected only publicly traded firms on the major exchanges. The exchanges in the USA are the New York Stock Exchange, the American Stock Exchange and the Nasdaq National Market. For the UK it is the London Stock Exchange. For Singapore it is the mainboard exchange.

REFERENCES

Bebchuk, L.A. and J. Fried (2003), 'Executive compensation as an agency problem', *Journal of Economic Perspectives*, **17**, 71–92.

Bebchuk, L.A. and J. Fried (2004), *Pay without Performance: The Unfulfilled Promise of Executive Compensation*, Cambridge, MA: Harvard University Press.

Bhagat, S. and B. Black (2002), 'The non-correlation between board independence and long term firm performance', *Journal of Corporation Law*, **27**(2), 231–73.

Bonet, Rocio and Martin J. Conyon (2005), 'Compensation committees and executive compensation: evidence from publicly traded UK firms', in K. Keasey, S. Thompson and M. Wright (eds), *Corporate Governance: Accountability, Enterprise and International Comparisons*, New York: Wiley.

Bradbury, Michael E., Janice C.Y. Ching and Yuen Teen Mak (1999), 'The adoption and structure of executive stock option plans', http://ssrn.com/abstract=161548

Bradbury, Michael E., Yuen Teen Mak and S.M. Tan (2004), 'Board characteristics, audit committee characteristics and abnormal accruals', http://ssrn.com/abstract=535764

Chee Leong Chong (2004), 'Corporate governance in Singapore: issues, options and the impact on firm productivity', in Eduardo T. Gonzalez (ed.), *Impact of Corporate Governance on Productivity: Asian Experience*, Asian Productivity Organization (http://www.apo-tokyo.org).

Claessens, Stijn, Simeon Djankov and Larry H.P. Lang (2000), 'The separation of ownership and control in East Asian Corporations', *Journal of Financial Economics*, **58**, 81–112.

Conyon, Martin J. and Kevin Murphy (2000), 'The prince and the pauper? CEO pay in the United States and United Kingdom', *Economic Journal*, **110**, 640–71.

Conyon, Martin J. and Simon Peck (1998), 'Board control, remuneration committees, and top management compensation', *Academy of Management Journal*, **41**, 146–57.

Core, John, Wayne Guay and David Larcker (2003), 'Executive equity compensation and incentives: a survey', *FRBNY Economic Policy Review*, April, 27–44.

Corporate Governance Committee (2001), *Report of the Committee and Code of Corporate Governance*, Singapore: Corporate Governance Committee.

Daily, C.M., J.L. Johnson, A.E. Ellstrand and D.R. Dalton (1998), 'Compensation committee composition as a determinant of CEO compensation', *Academy of Management Journal*, **41**, 209–20.

Denis, Diane K. and John J. McConnell (2003), 'International corporate governance, European corporate governance network', *Journal of Financial and Quantitative Analysis*, **38**, 1–36.

Hampel, R. (1998), *Committee on Corporate Governance: Final Report*, London: Gee Publishing.

Hermalin, Benjamin and Michael Weisbach (2003), 'Boards of directors as an endogenously determined institution: a survey of the economic literature', *FRBNY Economic Policy Review*, **9**, 7–22.

HMSO (2002), *The Directors' Remuneration Report Regulations 2002*, Statutory Instrument No. 1986, Crown Copyright 2002, London: HMSO.

Hoovers (2004), 'Hoover's online report builder for Singapore Technologies Engineering Ltd', web access November 2004.

Huse, Morten (2005), 'Accountability and creating accountability: a framework for exploring behavioural perspectives of corporate governance', *British Journal of Management*, **16**, S65–S80.

Jensen, Michael C. (1993), 'The modern industrial revolution, exit, and the failure of internal control mechanisms', *Journal of Finance*, **48**, 831–57.

Jensen, Michael C. and Kevin. J. Murphy (1990), 'Performance pay and top management incentives', *Journal of Political Economy*, **98**, 225–64.

Jensen, Michael C. and Kevin J. Murphy (2004), 'Remuneration: where we've been, how we got to here, what are the problems, and how to fix them', Finance Working Paper No. 44/2004, July, European Corporate Governance Research Institute.

Johnson, S., R. La Porta, F. Lopez-de-Silanes and A. Shleifer (2000), 'Tunneling', *American Economic Review*, **90**, 22–7.

Khan, Haider A. (2003), 'Corporate governance in Singapore and Hong Kong: what can other Asian economies learn?' Working paper, University of Denver.

La Porta, R., F. Lopez-de-Silanes and A. Shleifer (1999), 'Corporate ownership around the world', *Journal of Finance*, **54**, 471–517.

Lemmon, Michael L. and Karl V. Lins (2003), 'Ownership structure, corporate governance, and firm value: evidence from the East Asian Financial crisis', *Journal of Finance*, **LVIII**, 1445–68.

Mak, Yuen Teen and Kusnadi Yuanto (2002), 'Size really matters: further evidence on the negative relationship between board size and firm value', NUS Business School working paper, http://ssrn.com/abstract=303505

Mak, Yuen Teen and Phillip Phan (1999), 'Corporate governance in Asia: a comparative perspective', Conference proceedings Seoul, March 1999, Organization for Economic Cooperation and Development Report.

Mallin, Chris and R. Jelic (2000), 'Developments in corporate governance in Central and Eastern Europe', *Corporate Governance: An International Review*, **8**(1), 43–51.

Murphy, Kevin J. (1999), 'Executive compensation', in O. Ashenfelter and D. Card (eds), *Handbook of Labor Economics*, **3**, Amsterdam: North Holland.

Pettigrew, Andrew M. (1992), 'On studying managerial elites', *Strategic Management Journal*, **13**, 163–82.

Pettigrew, Andrew M. and Terry McNulty (1995), 'Power and influence in and around the boardroom', *Human Relations*, **48**, 845–73.

Phan, Phillip, Soo Hoon Lee and Siang Chi Lau (2003), 'The performance impact of interlocking directorates: the case of Singapore', *Journal of Managerial Issues*, **25**, 338–52.

Ruigrok, Winfried, Simon Peck, Sabina Tacheva, Peder Greve and Yan Hu (2004), *Happy Few, Band of Brothers? Determinants and Effects of Board Nomination Committees in Switzerland,* Research Institute for International Management (FIM-HSG), University of St Gallen.

ST Engineering (2003), *Annual Report 2003*, Singapore Technologies Engineering.

Yermack, D. (1996), 'Higher market valuation of companies with a small board of directors', *Journal of Financial Economics*, **40**, 185–211.

Williams, Mitchell (2004), 'Explanatory factors of audit committee composition of Singapore publicly traded firms', Singapore Management University working paper.

9. The rise and fall of China's corporate dragon: Kelon and its old and new owners

Guy S. Liu and Pei Sun

INTRODUCTION

The collapse of corporate empires in contemporary capitalist economies tends to be no less dramatic than the vicissitudes of political empires in history. While the political ones often slipped into a less than envious position through a gradual process, in which the decline could be discerned widely by both outside political observers and ordinary people, the sudden collapse of corporate dinosaurs nowadays can take even the closest, long-term corporate analysts by surprise. Unfortunately, this was the case in the example of Kelon, a domestic household appliance manufacturer that once enjoyed the honour of being cited as a typically successful case study on Chinese firms in international business schools. Entitled *Kelon: China's Corporate Dragon*,[1] the study regarded it as an exemplar of dynamic Chinese firms rising from China's embracing of the market economy during the 1980s and 1990s.[2] The timing of the publication, namely the year 2001, could not have been more embarrassing for both the authors and business school students. Guangdong Kelon Electrical Holdings Co. Ltd shocked investors and equity analysts alike by reporting an unprecedented net loss of RMB 1.5 billion (HK$17 million) in the same year, with appalling scandals of the controlling shareholder's expropriation of company assets.

The rise and fall of Kelon is deeply rooted in its corporate governance system, which was developed when China's economy was under a complex transition that induced block shareholders to play a dual role – of helping on one hand and appropriating on the other – in controlling their publicly-owned corporations. Kelon rose due largely to the support of its largest shareholder – the local government; and it fell on account of asset stripping by the government as the controlling owner. Although Kelon's huge losses were finally covered by the injection of private investment, thanks to a rapid development of private business in China, its sustainability in future still remains uncertain as there is no guarantee that a new private owner will not tunnel assets away from business when weak corporate governance is present. In short, there are profound lessons that we can learn from Kelon's case, in particular, a complicated ownership arrangement that is mixed with a weak legal system in protecting minority investors, and its impact on corporate behaviour and performance.

The rest of the chapter provides a detailed chronicle of Kelon from its emergence and successful growth to its abrupt operating and financial failures, and to the latest development that concerns the takeover by an aggressive entrepreneur – Mr Chujun Gu. It is then followed by intensive discussions on the lessons and policy implications of the case from the perspective of state-of-the-art corporate governance theories.

THE RISE OF KELON (1984–96): A MODEL OF PUBLIC–PRIVATE PARTNERSHIP

By all accounts the successful story of Kelon was a typical result of the boom of China's township and village enterprise (TVE) sector in the 1980s and early 1990s. Unlike the traditional state-owned enterprises (SOEs), TVEs are founded, financed and directly controlled by very low-level governments, i.e. township and villages, who exhibited a tremendous degree of pro-business attitude to support local entrepreneurs. Despite the ambiguous property rights arrangements between township governments and TVE managers, they developed at least in the early stage of business a relatively efficient division of labour, in which managers in the start-ups demonstrated their entrepreneurial talent in China's emerging market economy while the local governments offered a crucial helping hand to make TVEs overcome pervasive market failures and the volatile business environment.[3] The following brief overview of the history of Kelon clearly demonstrates the point.[4]

The predecessor of Kelon was the Guangdong Shunde Pearl River Refrigerator Factory, which was founded in 1984 through collaboration between an entrepreneur and a local township government. The entrepreneur, Guoduan Wang, ran a small factory producing cheap transistor radios for a Hong Kong firm. The government was a state agency of a small town, called Rongqi township, which is under the subordination of Shunde county in Guangdong, China's southern province adjacent to Hong Kong. Both Wang and the township government were keen to explore new business opportunities at the advent of economic liberalization in China. To discover new business opportunities, the township government investigated nationwide which consumer goods were in high demand. Despite the fact that they had neither experience nor technical capability in refrigerator production at that time, Rongqi township government provided the collaboration with both a seed capital of RMB 90 000 (roughly HK$30 000 at the prevailing exchange rate) and the security of a bank loan of RMB 4 million for the construction of the plant. Mr Ning Pan, a vice-head of the township, was assigned as the general manager to work with Wang.[5]

Another essential support from local governments was political. Apart from the collective ownership provided by the township as a political cap to cover private interests in ownership, local governments ranging from the township to the county, municipal and the provincial levels actively lobbied the central government on behalf of Kelon for a production licence in the mid-1980s. This was a time when China's central government intended to implement a consolidating industrial policy in the increasingly fragmented white goods sector. The entry barrier was erected via a licence system, so that Kelon's application was initially rejected by the Ministry of Light Industry because of its low status. However, local governments, especially the provincial one, offered critical help for Kelon to overcome the entry barrier by bargaining intensively with the central government.[6] Eventually, it became the only non-SOE in the list of 42 firms that were granted the manufacturing licence, in spite of a volume limit of 50 000 to Kelon.

The subsequent takeoff of Kelon in the household white goods sector was dramatic, which totally surprised both economic bureaucrats in Beijing and those multinational corporations that had been keen to grab a lion's share of China's domestic market. By 1991, Kelon had already leapfrogged to be the top refrigerator maker in China, producing 480 000 fridges and enjoying 10.3 per cent market share in terms of units sold. Figure 9.1 shows the explosive growth of Kelon's production capacity between 1985 and 1996, the year when it was listed on the Hong Kong stock market. The listing was not until Kelon became a market leader in the refrigerator industry. The political recognition of Kelon's success came from Xiaoping Deng's visit in January 1992, and also Zeming Jiang in 1994. In China these two visits represented a crucial commitment of the central government in support of the enterprise. As a result, Kelon became the first Chinese TVE to be allowed by the central government to float as a firm in Hong Kong.[7]

In terms of corporate governance arrangements, Kelon was also a pioneer in the corporatization experiment. As early as 1992, the firm was transformed to a shareholding company, in which Rongqi township government held 80 per cent of shares via a holding company called Rongqi Township Economic Development Company, and managers and employees were offered the remaining 20 per cent stakes (see Figure 9.2). Thus the newly formed Kelon Electrical Holdings Co. Ltd was the envy of peers in the domestic sector at that time, in which it perfectly combined the high incentives for employees and the high commitment of government support.

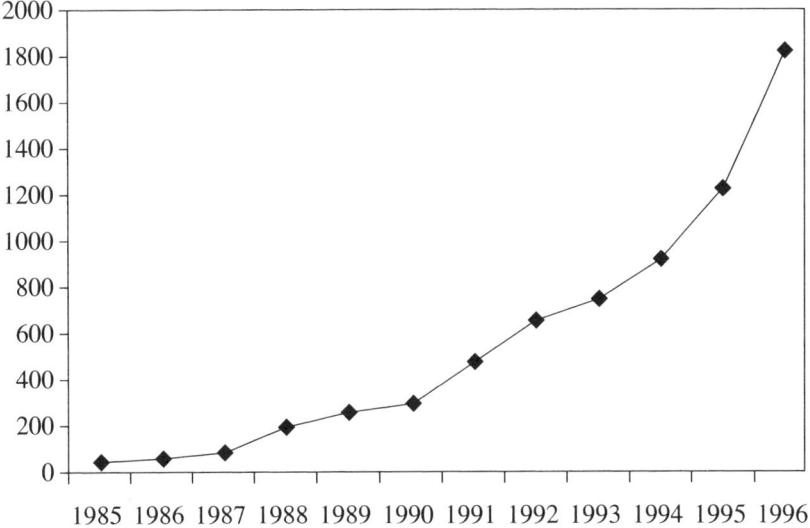

Source: Zhang (2004).

*Figure 9.1   The production volume of refrigerators at Kelon (1985–96,
thousands)*

During the first half of the 1990s, not only did Kelon maintain its top
position in China's highly competitive household appliance sector, but it
also diversified into related segments, including freezers and air conditioners.
Moreover, the significant corporate growth helped the company secure
a nationwide presence in the white goods industry in terms of both
production and distribution network. Kelon's business peaked in 1996,
when it started stock flotation in Hong Kong and the subsequent domestic
listing in Shenzhen in 1999. The sales of shares resulted in a cash injection
of HK$1.44 billion and RMB 1.06 billion by the public investors, while on
the other hand the holding rights of the township government were sharply
diluted to only around 34 per cent (see Figure 9.3).

To sum up, the success of Kelon has been much to do with the synergy
achieved from the joint ownership of government with private entrepreneurs
in a unique market environment that was of high economic growth and
rapid economic reform in China. The beauty of the mixed ownership is,
on the one hand, the 'local government entrepreneurship' effectively offers
administrative support for the firm to grow faster. On the other, private
participation in ownership provides the management with a good incentive
to compete in the market.

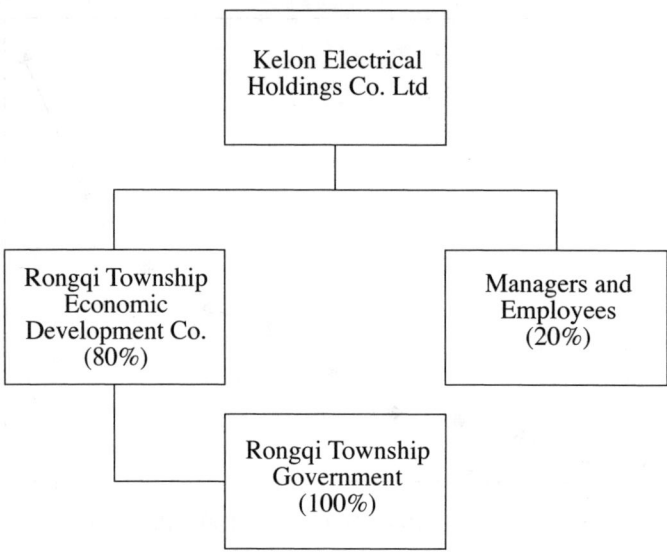

Note: Percentages in the brackets are the fractions of stakes held by respective owners. Rongqi township government was the ultimate controlling shareholder of Kelon Ltd, since the government owned 100% shares of Rongqi Township Economic Development Co., who held the 80% share of Kelon Ltd.

Figure 9.2   The shareholding structure of Kelon (1992–96)

THE SUDDEN COLLAPSE OF KELON IN 2000: HOW GOVERNMENT'S HELPING HAND BECAME AN APPROPRIATING ONE

Representing the successful model of reformed Chinese enterprises, Kelon was once the king of 'red chips'[8] in the Hong Kong equity market. In 1999 Kelon's sales revenues reached an unprecedented level of RMB 5.6 billion (HK$0.7 billion), despite a decline in profit margin over the last few years. It captured the largest market share in the domestic refrigerator sector in the 1990s and had already become one of the largest air-conditioner manufacturers in China. Actually even at the start of the year 2000, the company predicted an annual 11.7 per cent growth in sales and RMB 0.7 billion net income (*Caijing* 2001a). The year-end result could not have been more staggering: Kelon fell into the red for the first time in its history, reporting a huge net loss of RMB 0.83 billion, with a 30.9 per cent sales decline. A further financial loss of more than RMB 1.4 billion followed

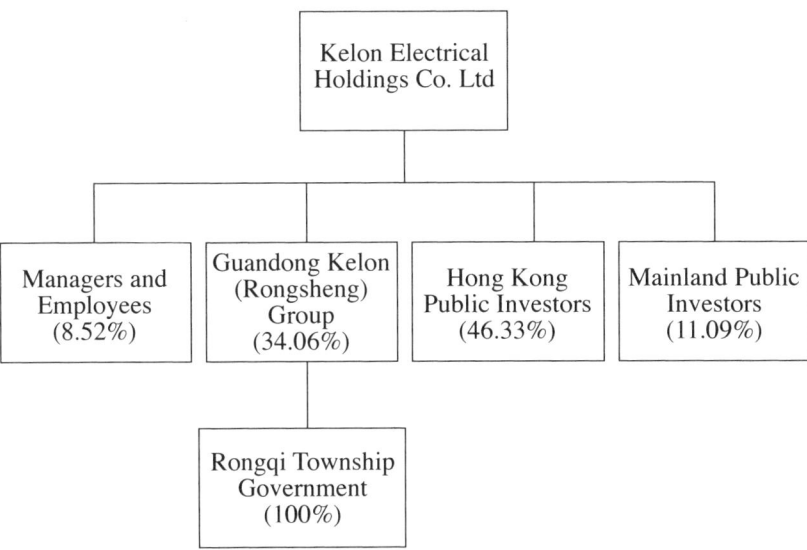

Note: Just before the public listing in Hong Kong, Rongqi Township Government created the Guangdong Kelon (Rongsheng) Group Company (GKG) to take the place of Rongqi Township Economic Development Co. as the intermediate controlling shareholder. Numbers in parentheses are the percentages of shares held by respective entities. Rongqi Township Government was the ultimate shareholder of the Kelon Ltd.

Figure 9.3   *The shareholding structure of Kelon after stock flotation (year-end 1999)*

in 2001, which left Kelon on the verge of collapse. This section presents a corporate governance interpretation of the collapse and traces the abrupt failure to the deteriorating agency problems on the part of the township government during the post-listing period.

The Agency Costs of a Government-controlling Shareholder

It is commonly assumed that government-controlled firms that have gone public should have a significantly improved corporate governance mechanism, as they have rationalized the internal structure such as with the establishment of executive and supervisory boards and are presumably subject to the external discipline of capital markets. Unfortunately, the Chinese experience in the 1990s suggests otherwise. Despite cash windfalls contributed by public investors through initial public offerings (IPOs), listed firms have on average exhibited a significant decline in financial performance over their post-IPO years (for example Wang *et al.* 2004).

Moreover, as suggested by Steinfeld (1998) and Tenev and Zhang (2002), a web of new agency problems can arise in this particular hybrid – 'public' companies controlled by government. How could it be the case? In this section we apply state-of-the-art corporate governance theory to the Kelon case, which can precisely explain why the government's previous helping hand degenerated into an appropriating one under the new institutional environment.

In modern public corporations ownership is diversified to individual stockholders so that those who have secured an absolute control of the company may not hold a vast majority of the total shares outstanding. And it is very likely, according to the corporate control theory developed by Cubbin and Leech (1983), that even a minority shareholder can obtain an effective control of the firm given a rather dispersed distribution of remaining shares. Taking Kelon as a case in point, whereas before the public listing the township government held 80 per cent of cash flow rights over the firm, its ownership stakes sharply reduced to little more than one-third of the total after the flotation (see Table 9.1). Nevertheless, the government maintained a larger shareholding than the 'critical control level' calculated in Table 9.1, which clearly indicates that the government control in Kelon remained incontestable. Therefore, a considerable deviation of cash flow rights from control rights prevents the dilution of the government control post the listing. That is, the government only contributed 34 per cent of cash flows but enjoyed nearly complete control of the company.[9]

In theory, the agency costs associated with such a controlling-minority structure (CMS)[10] involve potentially a severe moral hazard problem on the part of the minority controller, since he or she has the power and incentive to expropriate the company and public investors. Controllers in the CMS internalize only a small fraction of the negative consequences induced by their own opportunistic behaviour, but can appropriate all of the private control benefits arising from entrenchment and some more significant 'tunnelling' activities such as fund diversion and asset stripping (Johnson *et al.* 2000; Cronqvist and Nilsson 2003). And when legal and regulatory constraints on controllers' self-dealing behaviour are largely ineffective, which is the norm rather than an exception in transition economies and emerging markets, the chances are that even a highly supportive controlling shareholder may degrade into a corporate expropriator, as the Kelon case subsequently illustrates.

Regarding government as a specific category of controlling shareholder, the agency problem is exacerbated by an additional dimension of incentive incompatibility between bureaucrats and managers. In comparison with many UK and American companies, where they have the higher

Table 9.1   Kelon's top ten shareholders after Hong Kong and Shenzhen quotation

After Hong Kong but before Shenzhen listing		After Shenzhen listing	
Top ten shareholders	Shares held (%)	Top ten shareholders	Shares held (%)
Guangdong Kelon (Rongsheng) Group	38.31	Guangdong Kelon (Rongsheng) Group	34.06
Standard Chartered Bank	12.31	Standard Chartered Bank	8.63
HSBC Co. Ltd	12.04	HSBC Co. Ltd	7.47
The Chase Manhattan Bank	10.19	Franklin Templeton Group	6.92
Citibank N.A.	6.16	The Chase Manhattan Bank	5.87
Morgan Stanley Dean Witter Hong Kong Securities Ltd	1.87	Citibank N.A.	5.24
The Bank of Bermuda Ltd	0.54	Deutsche Bank AG	2.85
Jardine Fleming Broking Ltd	0.53	Morgan Stanley Dean Witter Hong Kong Securities Ltd	0.74
Deutsche Bank AG	0.5	Jardine Fleming Broking Ltd	0.64
Merrill Lynch Far East Ltd	0.49	Tongyi Securities Investment Fund	0.17
		Taihe Securities Investment Fund	0.17
Critical Control Level	37.32		33.44

Note: The 'Critical Control Level' is defined as a certain shareholding benchmark necessary for the largest investor to gain the effective control of a company under a pre-assigned confidence level. The critical control shares in the table are derived by applying a probabilistic-voting model developed by Cubbin and Leech (1983). To calculate the critical level of shareholdings, the model requires the two pieces of information: shareholding concentration and the probability that a given stockholder would attend the general shareholder meeting. We assume that all the shareholders will attend the meeting for sure.

degree of separation of management and ownership, state-controlled public corporations are not very much different from them in terms of the separation perspective, which explains why they have similar agency problems – managerial discretion and opportunism. Moreover, when government is in control of public companies, another problem in addition to the lack of management accountability is possible expropriation[11] by the large shareholder of state from other minority investors. The large shareholder's expropriation problem is often found in Continental European and Southeast Asian companies with family as the controlling shareholder, where ownership is concentrated with less separation of managers and family owners.[12] In the next two subsections, we present a detailed examination of the two facets of agency problems at Kelon, which we ascribe to Kelon's sudden collapse in 2000.

The Failure in Incentive Alignment of the Management

It has been argued that the long tenure of Mr Pan and Mr Wang, which spanned from 1984 to 2000, is one of the most crucial contributing factors to Kelon's success (Huang 2003). However, it proved that the incentive schemes of the management lagged far behind the fast business growth in the 1990s to align their interests with those of the company as a whole. For instance, the government persistently failed to offer ownership stakes as material incentives to company managers, so that it is not surprising to find out that Kelon's two corporate founders were not rewarded with any share options. They only held a negligible number of shares in the listed firm: as can be seen in Table 9.1 none of the corporate insiders enter the list of the top ten shareholders and the tenth largest shareholder in Table 9.1 only has less than 1 per cent of total stocks.

When management efforts could not be rewarded via formal incentive contracts such as share ownership and stock options, they chose to capture their control rents through value-subtracting activities. A typical abuse of their operational control of the firm was transfer pricing. Various anecdotes from the business press reveal that before the 2000 collapse many managers at Kelon were engaged extensively in related party transactions with firms owned by the relatives and friends of the managers. Although there are large economies of scale in procurement, Kelon usually paid abnormally higher prices for parts procurement, and also large discounts in the distribution network, for the manager-related suppliers or dealers. The upshot of this managerial agency problem can be reflected in the soaring operating expenses during 1996–2000. Following Yafeh and Yosha (2003), we identify selling and administrative expenses as a key measure of activities related to managerial moral hazard. Figure 9.4 then shows the time trend of Kelon's selling and administrative expenses deflated by sales revenues, and we compare the expenses with two competing refrigerator producers, namely Haier Ltd and Meiling Ltd, who are competitors of Kelon in the domestic market. Clearly, Kelon not only underperformed in comparison with its two rivals in this aspect, but also experienced a sharp rise in the post-IPO years.

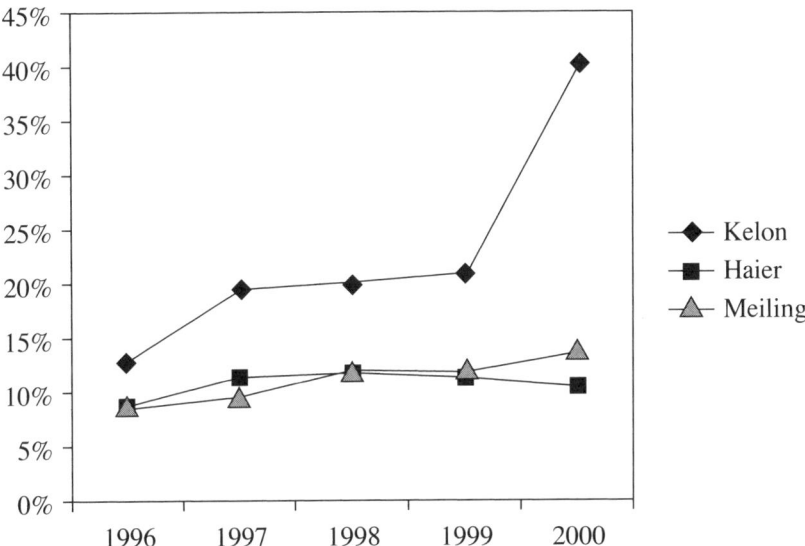

Note: Expenses to sales ratio = selling and administrative expenses/sales revenues.

Source: Calculated from data disclosed in the annual reports of Kelon, Qingdao Haier Co. Ltd, and Hefei Meiling Co. Ltd.

Figure 9.4   Expenses to sales ratios at Kelon and its competitors (1996–2000)

Another dimension of the failure is related to a series of turbulent managerial turnover events triggered by the retirement of corporate veteran Mr Ning Pan in June 1999. It is widely known that in China's politicized business environment senior managers typically maintain intimate patron–client relations with local bureaucrats. Although Mr Guoduan Wang, the former No. 2 figure in the firm, took the positions of board chairman and CEO as expected, rumours abound that internal power struggles were intensified behind the scenes. In March 2000, at the risk of triggering a corporate earthquake, Mr Wang reshuffled the management team by replacing all the vice-CEOs formerly working for Pan with outsiders. This unpopular reshuffle resulted largely in Wang himself being forced to leave the CEO post three months later.[13] Mr Tiefeng Xu, a vice mayor of the Rongqi township with little business experience, became the new CEO, which later proved a typical case of government intervention and a big blow to Kelon's performance.

The Weak Constraint of Monitoring and Asset Tunnelling

Managerial agency cost aside, the distorted incentives provided by the government as the controlling owner to management and the significant transfer of Kelon's cash flows to non-business uses on government projects have proved fundamentally responsible for the failure. It will become clear if we briefly examine the payoff structure of Chinese local governments during the transition. Liu *et al.* (2005) argue that the benefits of local governments owning an industrial firm are composed of three parts:

1. dividends and corporate income tax arising from firm profits;
2. value-added tax (VAT) derived from sales revenues; and
3. the private benefits that can be captured from corporate control, which can span from pecuniary favours to political interests.

Our discussion in the first subsection immediately leads us to predict that the weight the government assigns to the first component of its three benefits would be much smaller than those it puts on the other two. The dilution of income rights rather than the control rights makes the government not care much about dividends it receives from the listed firm; rather, it may capture private control benefits at the expense of long-run profitability. Second, the Chinese tax system was traditionally designed in a way that government revenues rely predominantly on indirect turnover tax (VAT) collected from firm sales, rather than corporate income tax. And this further dampens the government's interest in profitability but misdirects the company to pursue excessive sales growth.[14]

Figures 9.5 and 9.6 perfectly illustrate how the government directed Kelon in the post-IPO years to seek more sales at the expense of profitability. Despite a superficial boost of sales from 1996 to 1999, operating profits experienced an annual 6 per cent decline in the three consecutive years from 1997. Over the same period, a significant deterioration in profitability measured by both ROA and ROE was in evidence, which indicates that the government as the largest owner destroyed the value of the company for its own self-interest. What's more, the sales slump in 2000 and the resultant enormous decline in profits suggest that earning quality in the previous years could be problematic. Specifically, the accounts receivable at Kelon remained considerably large during those years. For instance, more than 20 per cent of sales shown in the 1997 income statement came from the accounts receivable. It is widely believed that during the period Kelon took undue credit sales to boost revenues in an artificial manner (Zhang 2004).

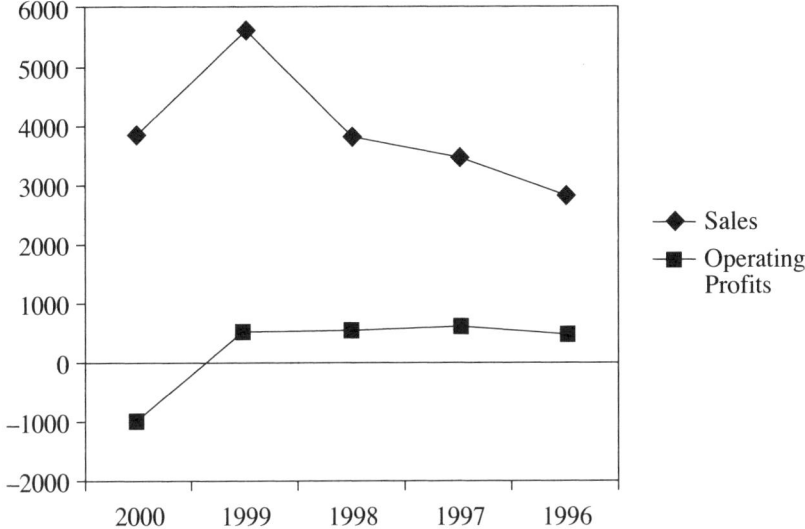

Source: The annual reports of Kelon Electrical Holdings Co. Ltd (1996–2000).

Figure 9.5 *Sales and operating profits at Kelon (1996–2000, RMB million)*

However, the promotion of value destroying sales for more tax revenues by the state owner is not the worst. The worst conduct of the government owner that is finally revealed is that the township government actually acted in a manner that regarded its controlled public corporation as a 'cash cow' and transferred the corporate cash assets, arising from bank borrowings or private invested money, to public uses. The cash asset stripping by the government gave a vital and final impact to the collapse of Kelon. Similar to other corporate scandals around the world, the clue of corporate funds being tunnelled to non-business uses was not obvious to the public in Kelon's quarterly and annual reports, except for the report on deteriorating corporate performance. The cash transfers remained under cover until the

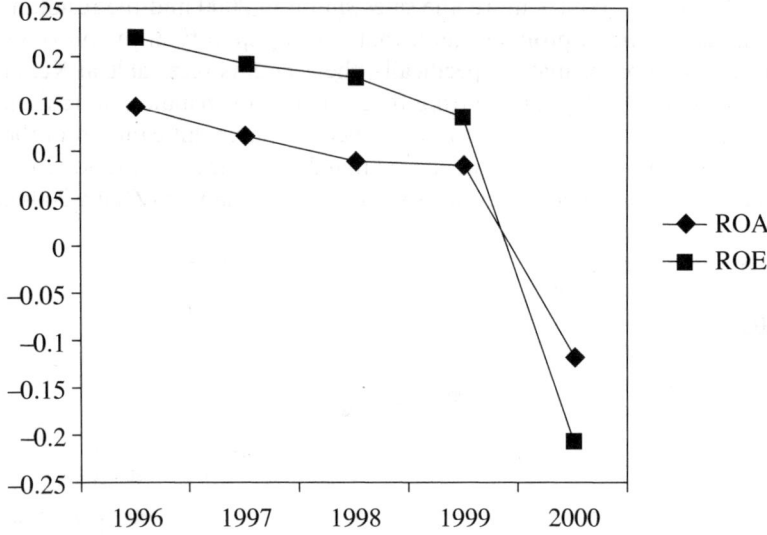

Note: Return on assets (ROA) is defined as net income divided by total assets. Return on equity (ROE) is defined as net income divided by equity capital.

Source: Calculated from data disclosed in the annual reports of Kelon Electrical Holdings Co. Ltd.

Figure 9.6   Profitability at Kelon (1996–2000)

perpetrator was no longer able to disguise them. When Rongqi government realized that the accumulated crisis at Kelon had reached a point that could hardly be settled by its own fiscal capability, it had to decide painfully to give up its controlling stakes to Mr Chujun Gu, a refrigerant-manufacturing entrepreneur, in late 2001. Only then was the financial black hole finally revealed by both the new entrant and the regulatory bodies.

Plainly speaking, Rongqi township government via its controlled Guangdong Kelon (Rongsheng) Group diverted a total of RMB 1.26 billion (HK$0.15 billion) from the listed Kelon Electrical Holdings Co. Ltd through a string of secretive related-party transactions from 1997 to 2001. Table 9.2 organizes the main part of them into three categories and displays them in detail. It is worth noting that such related-party transactions are a two-edged sword. That is to say, on balance the controlling shareholder could either tunnel funds from its listed subsidiary or inject cash into the company for the benefit of all shareholders (Friedman *et al.* 2003). As Table 9.2 shows, in 1997 the holding group in effect contributed more than RMB 100 million net to Kelon. The dynamics, however, was a reversed trend that signified the increasing expropriation of Kelon's funds, especially in 2000 and 2001. Taking the year 2001 as a case in point, it can be seen from Table 9.2 that the government-owned holding company managed to channel more than RMB 1 billion from Kelon in less than 12 months,[15] given the fact that the net assets Kelon possessed in year-end 2000 was RMB 3.96 billion!

Table 9.2   *Major fund diversion between Kelon and Guangdong Kelon (Rongsheng) Group (1997–2001)*

Year	Kelon→ Rongsheng Group	Rongsheng Group →Kelon	Balance (RMB)
	Bank loans and interest payments		
1997	308 373 000	410 299 000	–101 926 000
1998	7 163 622 000	7 106 870 000	56 752 000
1999	4 389 922 000	4 362 194 000	27 728 000
2000	4 599 826 000	4 496 662 000	103 164 000
2001	5 083 814 000	4 378 515 000	705 299 000
	Sub-total		791 017 000
	Loans guarantee		
2001	211 220 000		211 220 000
	Payment transfer		
2001	101 370 000		101 370 000
	Total		1 103 607 000

Notes:
1. Kelon→Rongsheng Group means that the direction of fund diversion is from Kelon to its parent; and Rongsheng Group→Kelon suggests the other way round.
2. Bank Loans and Interest Payments denote the situation in which Kelon and its holding company share their respective lending quota in commercial banks by obtaining loans in the name of each other. That is, the holding company has access to banks loans borrowed by Kelon, and the reverse also holds. Moreover, they pay back the debt and interest with each other. For example, Kelon may have to pay the principal and interest its parent owes to the banks. The annual and accumulated balances of the fund exchange are shown in the 'balance' column.
3. Loans Guarantee suggests the incident that the holding company illicitly asked one of Kelon's subsidiaries to stand guarantee for a bank loan worth RMB 0.21 billion in mid-2001. Since the holding company failed to service this debt afterwards, Kelon had to pay the principal and interest instead.
4. Payment Transfer suggests the incident that the holding company asked Kelon to buy products in 2001 from a joint venture between Kelon and the Sanyo Group (Japan) at a cost of RMB 101.4 million that Kelon paid for in cash.

Source: The annual report of Kelon Electrical Holdings Co. Ltd (2001), and the announcement of Kelon Electrical Co. Ltd on 14 March 2002.

The expropriation of Kelon's assets also is reflected in a particular account in the balance sheet of Chinese public corporations – 'other receivables'. It is a Chinese-style item that incorporates all the miscellaneous receivables other than normal accounts receivable based on credit sales. Cash appropriated by the dominant shareholder is often recorded in 'other receivables', which the firm is supposed to be able to collect from its controller. So it is believed that this account has in practice become a rough proxy to indicate the extent of the large shareholder's tunnelling. Figure 9.7 clearly shows the exponential growth of 'other receivables' during 2000 and 2001, which coincided with the time when the new CEO was appointed directly by the government to replace the former corporate hero, Mr Lin Pan, who created Kelon.

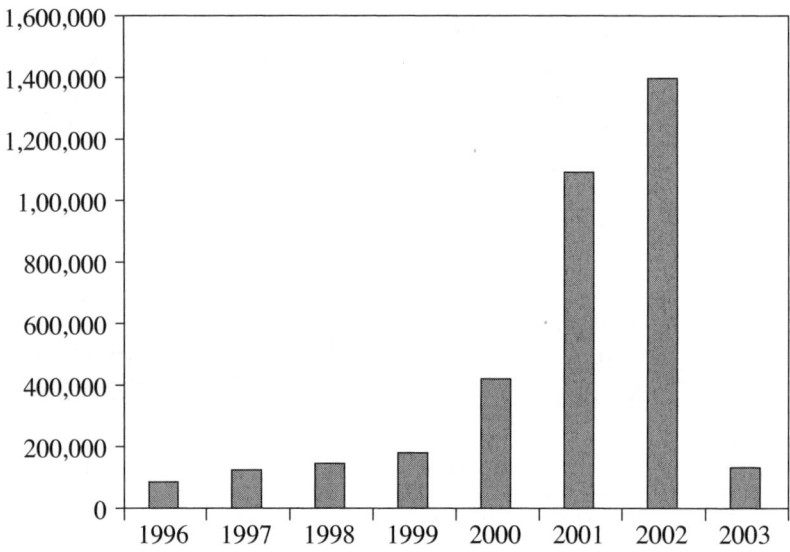

Source: The annual reports of Kelon Electrical Holdings Co. Ltd (1996–2003).

Figure 9.7   The amount of 'other receivables' at Kelon (1996–2003, RMB thousands)

In sum, the vicissitudes of Kelon so far suggest that the government-dominant ownership arrangement of corporate governance was helpful for Kelon's success when the company was small and the business was at an early stage of development. During this period, the government can be a good supporter by providing public resources for facilitating the growth of the business, and this support is essential for business at an infant stage, and therefore the agency problem of both government and government-appointed management could be covered or mitigated by the state's constructive and significant support. When the company becomes bigger, and less dependent on the support of the government, the role of government ownership will become different. This change, in particular, after the stock flotation of the firm, can turn the firm towards a difficult situation where both the moral hazard problem of the government as the controlling owner and the agency problem of the management will become more acute, in which the problems could offset the benefits gained from government ownership. Kelon's story illustrates clearly this argument that the government changed its role from a supporting one to a predatory one at the time when the company built up its value to trade its ownership for public funds. The trade of ownership for finance dilutes cash flow rights, but not the corporate control of the government. Therefore, one pound of private control rents becomes more valuable than one pound of profits gained from efficiency improvement, inducing the government as the largest owner to change its interest from profit seeking to fund stripping.

For Kelon, the government's predatory behaviour towards corporate cash assets was evident. The government seemed to develop a self-destructive strategy for the business, in which this suicidal behaviour is inconsistent with the conventional wisdom of rationality in choosing a chance to survive. One possible explanation is that the short-term opportunism dominated the long-run commitment, which induced the government to take a chance and ended up with what is in Olson's (2000) term called a 'roving bandit', who, even worse than a 'settled bandit', maximizes the amount of extraction without internalizing any damages he/she will have caused simply because of his/her exit option.

Clearly, the discussion above raises an interesting question of how corporate governance can help when the largest shareholder becomes irrational.

THE ARRIVAL OF A PRIVATE OWNER: SAVIOUR OR NEXT EXPROPRIATOR?

The richness of the case is manifest not only in the complicated government–enterprise relationships just elaborated, but in the ownership transfer from government to the private sector and the associated question of whether an effective corporate governance mechanism would necessarily emerge after privatization. In particular, what role has the new private owner played in restructuring Kelon? Can the arrival of the new private owner dispel our misgivings about potential governance failures such as the large shareholder expropriation?

Perhaps few people in the Chinese white goods sector heard of Mr Gu prior to his surprising takeover of Kelon. On 31 October 2001, Kelon announced that its holding company – Guangdong Kelon (Rongsheng) Group – had signed a share transfer agreement with Shunde Greencool Enterprise Development, a 'shell' company then owned by Gu and his father.[16] According to the agreement, the government wholly-owned group released 20.64 per cent out of 34.06 per cent of shares it held[17] to Gu at the price of RMB 2.7 per share, which made Gu the ultimate controller of Kelon[18] (see Figure 9.8). From then on Gu and his business have been in the limelight, since people wondered about the real intention of this new owner and how he could possibly reverse the deteriorated Kelon. Is he a saviour of the troubled company or simply the next expropriator who attempts to extract wealth again from vulnerable minority investors?

Public information reveals that before the takeover Gu's main business was producing his patented Greencool Refrigerants for use in the refrigeration and air-conditioning systems. In mid-2000, he succeeded in merging the commercial distribution and service segment in a company called Greencool Technology Holdings Ltd and got this listed on the Hong Kong Growth Enterprise Market (GEM) which is the counterpart of the US's NASDAQ. In return, more than RMB 500 million of cash was raised for the company through the IPO. Interestingly, the newly floated company sells refrigerants that are supplied exclusively from a connected party called Greencool Refrigerant (China) Co. Ltd (the 'Tianjin Greencool Factory'), Gu's manufacturing centre of refrigerants in China (see Figure 9.8).

In general, people are quite sceptical of Gu's motives for the acquisition and his business capability of revamping Kelon. Against this scepticism, Gu explains that the move from the upstream sector into the downstream white-goods-manufacturing sector is a natural and rational business strategy. The press questions the reliability of accounting numbers in Greencool Technology Holdings, not least because it is virtually a trading firm in that all the goods sold are provided by an unlisted related party whose financial status is not verifiable. A number of anecdotes, through field investigations, point out the inconsistency between sales leapfrogging in the listed firm during 1998–2001 (see Table 9.3) and the dubious financial situation of its Tianjin supplier, suggesting a considerable possibility of earnings manipulation (*Caijing* 2001b, 2002). Moreover, in late 2001 Greencool Technology Holdings gave an enormous amount of advance payment worth nearly RMB 230 million to Tianjin Greencool, which can be identified in the receivables column in Table 9.3. Since the advance payment coincided with Gu's purchase of Kelon's controlling stake, it is widely suspected that Gu channelled funds from his controlled HK-quoted company to finance his acquisition, but to the detriment of Hong Kong

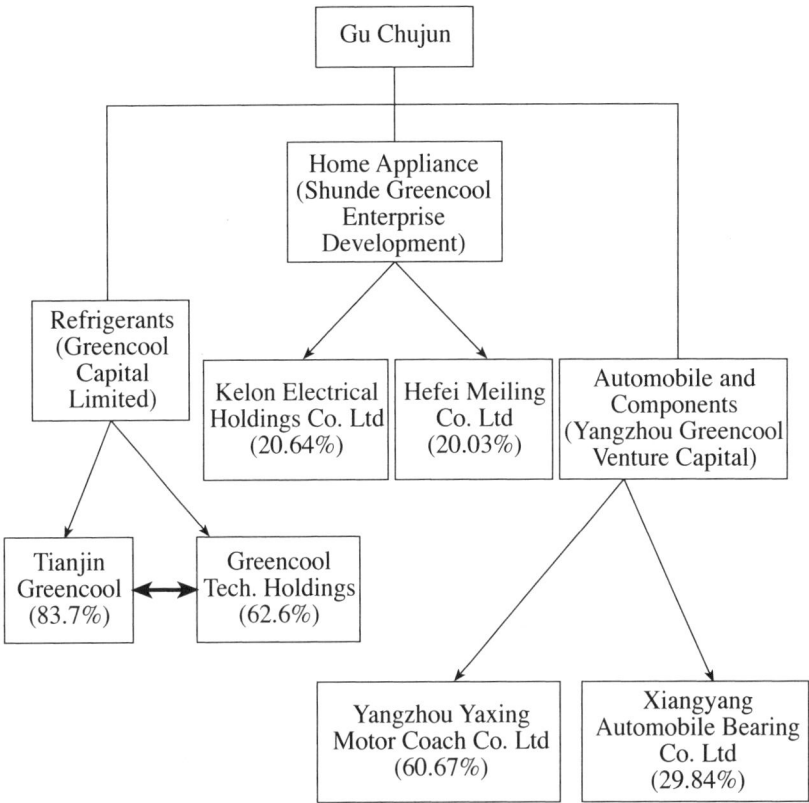

Notes:
The figure depicts the group structure of Gu Chujun's fast expanding businesses as of year 2004, which consists of three sectors: refrigerants, home appliance and automobiles. In the refrigerants sector, Gu uses Greencool Capital Limited, his wholly-owned firm registered in the British Virgin Islands, as the holding company of both Greencool Technology Holdings Co. Ltd, a Hong Kong listed firm, and unlisted 'Tianjin Greencool', the official name of which is Greencool Refrigerant (China) Co. Ltd. Regarding the home appliance industry, Shunde Greencool Enterprise Development Limited (SGE) is the holding company employed by Gu to control two newly acquired downstream listed firms, namely Kelon Electrical Holdings and Hefei Meiling Co. Ltd. Gu and Tianjin Greencool held 60 per cent and 40 per cent of shares in SGE respectively. Besides, Gu enters the sector of automobile and auto components by taking over two listed firms, namely Yangzhou Yaxing Motor Coach and Xiangyang Automobile Bearing. Yangzhou Greencool Venture Capital, wholly owned by Gu and his father, is used as the intermediate control device for the two firms. Numbers in parentheses corresponding with all the downstream companies are the percentage of shares held by Gu's respective holding companies. The arrow between Tianjin Greencool and Greencool Technology denotes their close business link.

Figure 9.8   Gu Chujun's business conglomerate as of year-end 2004

minority investors. And this has eventually invited the censure issued on 31 August 2004 by the listing committee of Hong Kong GEM for the company board in gross negligence of stock exchange regulations (see the document titled 'Exchange's Announcement in relation to GREENCOOL TECH' on website: http://www.hkgem.com/company). A more thought-provoking message that Table 9.3 conveys is a significant decline in turnover and profitability after 2001, which further undermines Gu's credibility on business performance and corporate governance.

Table 9.3   Key financial and accounting data at Greencool Technology Holdings Co. Ltd (1998–2003, RMB thousands)

Year	Sales	EBIT	ROA (%)	ROE (%)	Receivables from related parties	Payables to related parties
1998	113	–6 816	–9.7	–10.0		
1999	92 827	41 300	10.4	10.6	10 701	2 722
2000	363 897	269 217	22.3	23.6	0	31 585
2001	516 330	339 365	22.0	24.3	229 983	6 963
2002	321 420	103 368	5.6	6.2	1 024	17 002
2003	106 834	10 550	0.6	0.6	238	16 658

Notes: EBIT denotes earnings before interest and tax, i.e. operating profits. ROA and ROE are net earnings divided by total assets and equity capital respectively. Receivables and Payables are accounts exclusively due from and to the company's related parties, that is other firms controlled by Gu. The data for 1998 are unaudited.

Source: Annual reports of Greencool Technology Holdings Co. Ltd (1998–2003).

Nevertheless, it would be wrong, at least in respect of the Kelon case, to perceive Gu's entry as totally negative. In effect, it is Gu who, under his presiding over the board, unveils the disguised financial scandal that shows the government's tunnelling of the assets (see Table 9.2). After he signed the initial agreement with Rongqi government, Gu and his team undertook a comprehensive audit of Kelon between December 2001 and March 2002. Of course Gu acted out of his own interest as he found that he had overpaid the target without prior knowledge of such large-scale asset stripping. Hence he subsequently revised the terms of agreement with Rongqi government, in which the price was lowered to RMB 1.7 per share and the total amount was changed from RMB 560 million to 348 million.

Kelon in Gu's ownership control, at least up to now, seems to continue the bright side of the story. A U-turn of key financial indicators before and after the acquisition is evident in Figures 9.9 and 9.10. Sales have maintained a steady growth, reaching an unprecedented level of more than 6 billion in 2003. In contrast to sales, the profitability is less impressive, but at least helps the firm recover from the haemorrhage. Intensive cost-cutting measures adopted by Gu are reported to have contributed to the recovery, which can be reflected in the trend of expenses to sales ratio shown in Figure 9.11. Concretely speaking, the ratio has fallen to the 1999 level due to the reportedly effective streamlining of procurement and distribution networks (*Xin Caifu* 2002; *Xin Caijing* 2004). On the dark side, sceptics such as Professor Larry Lang, a corporate finance expert at the Chinese University of Hong Kong, argue that the positive effect of Gu's entry is overestimated, since he intentionally reported an abnormally large loss in year 2001 via earnings management techniques including the exaggeration of expenses.[19] In so doing, it would make the profitability figures look relatively more attractive in subsequent years. Hence, Gu still needs more time to prove his business and management competence as profitability indicators at Kelon have yet to get back to the 1999 level (see Figures 9.9 and 9.10).

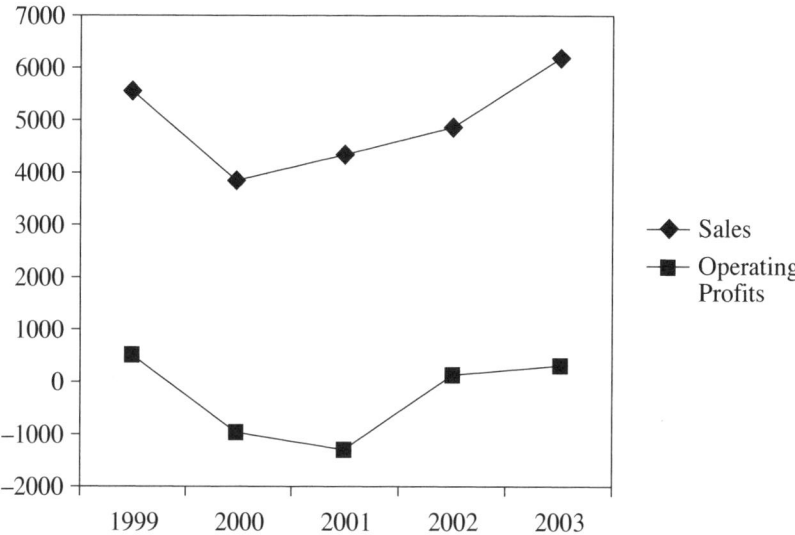

Source: The annual reports of Kelon Electrical Holdings Co. Ltd (1999–2003).

Figure 9.9   Sales and operating profits at Kelon (1999–2003, RMB million)

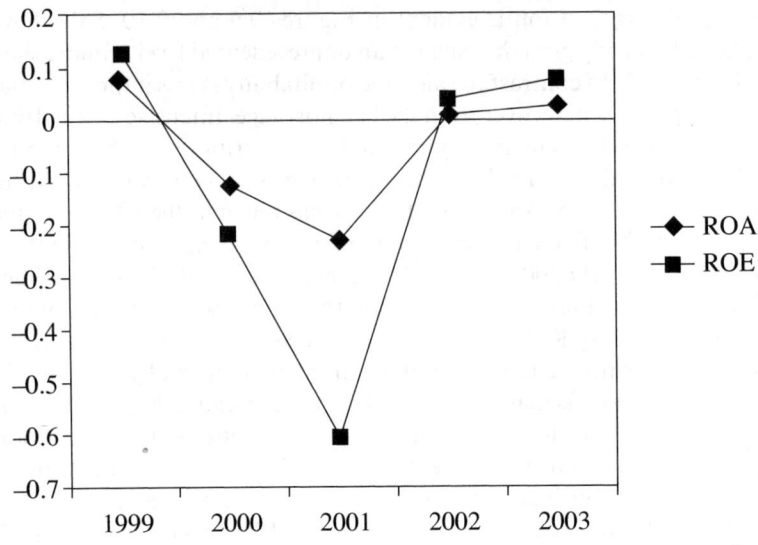

Source: Calculated from data disclosed in the annual reports of Kelon Electrical Holdings
Co. Ltd.

Figure 9.10   *Profitability at Kelon (1999–2003)*

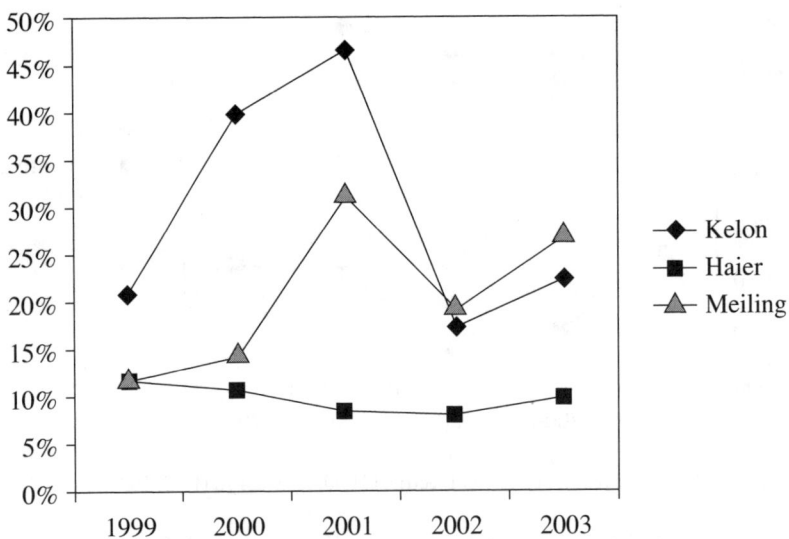

Figure 9.11   *Expenses to sales ratios in Kelon and its competitors
                  (1999–2003)*

Another key concern is about the role Gu will play as the new controlling shareholder. Could it be possible that Gu will fail to resist temptation and become the next expropriator of Kelon through asset stripping and fund diversion? A glance at the disclosure of the 'other receivables' account in 2002 and 2003 endorses the feeling that Gu has so far refrained from tunnelling Kelon[20] (see Figure 9.7). However, it is still rumoured that considerable cash flows generated in Kelon's sale of refrigerators and air conditioners are a potentially important source of finance for Gu's takeovers in 2003 and 2004.[21] Shown in Figure 9.8, Gu acquired another key domestic refrigerator maker – Hefei Meiling – from its ultimate controller Hefei city government in mid-2003. Several months later, he made a further bold move to enter the highly competitive automobile industry by buying controlling stakes in Yaxing Motor Coach and Xiangyang Automobile Bearing from their respective local governments. More interestingly, each of the three targets has surprisingly similar characteristics to Kelon: while they have sound production capacity and substantial market shares in their respective domestic industries, they all suffered from the severe agency problem of moral-hazard-prone government and managers. Government predators and managerial moral hazard are so prevalent in these listed companies as to result in poor financial performance. A space limit prevents us from detailing each of the acquisitions, but the fascinating Kelon story we elaborated tends to have been repeated in these firms to a significant degree.

FURTHER DISCUSSION AND CONCLUDING REMARKS

[T]he process of transition in general and privatization in particular demonstrates an old lesson of market economies – incentives matter; but it also demonstrates a key lesson that was lost on many of the so-called reformers: only under highly idealized situations do incentives result in efficient outcomes; misdirected incentives can provide incentives for asset stripping rather than wealth creation. In many of the countries in transition, that is precisely what happened. (Stiglitz 2001)

The case of Kelon, we believe, supplies one of most perfect illustrations of the profound corporate governance lessons for us. Our discussion of the case finds that Kelon has experienced two plunders: one from the largest shareholder's irregularity in using company assets and another from management's moral hazard of taking related party transactions to such a significant extent as to transfer investors' assets. In the West, a conventional wisdom is that an ownership-concentrated company is concerned more about the controlling shareholder's expropriation, an ownership-dispersed company is concerned more about the moral hazard of the inside management's control. Thus, which concern is dominant for a firm depends on its ownership structure. In China, Kelon enriched the wisdom: the dominance of a governance problem is not really relevant to the ownership structure. Kelon has a relatively concentrated ownership, but it suffered, first, the predatory action of the controlling owner, and second, the moral hazard of the inside management's control.

The lost control of a government as the controlling shareholder over the management's conduct was a result of: the incompetence of the government in business management; the separation of cash rights and control rights; and the mis-specified incentives for the government to run a firm, since a performance appraisal for a government is on the basis of the economic development of the whole region rather than a firm. These three points explain why an ownership-concentrated firm with state control can result in two contradictory problems appearing at the same time for the same company: large shareholder's expropriation and inside management's control.

Although Kelon showed a failure in setting up effective governance to prevent the firm from asset stripping by the largest shareholder and the management, we believe that a private controlling shareholder could not have guaranteed such prevention. Effective corporate governance to prevent asset stripping from related parties must come from an arrangement that is on the basis of both a contextual analysis of corporate dynamics in close relation to the unique institutional environment and the careful selection of independent directors on the board.

Government ownership of control is like a two-edged sword. Government ownership can help the firm to success, but it can also bring the firm to collapse. This is the typical lesson of Kelon. The company rose from the effective shield of local government at the very lower administrative tier so that the usual symptoms associated with large fossilized SOEs were minimized, while the government's help was provided for strengthening the firm's capability to compete in the market where competition is incomplete, regulations are poor and the judicial system is inefficient.

When Kelon became big and transformed itself to a public-traded company, the improvement of corporate governance did not match the corporate ownership changes from highly concentrated state ownership to a diluted one. The gradual deviation of local government interests from company's profitability resulted largely from the separation of cash rights and control rights: diluting substantially cash rights from 80 per cent to 30 per cent, but the control rights still remained intact. On account of the pursuit of fast local GDP growth which requires a lot of investment to support, the corporate cash assets arising from the IPO inevitably became government-controlled capital that could be channelled for public uses to support local economic development and also for financing some high-risk projects that promoted short-term sales to boost a rise in tax revenues but at the expense of long-run profitability of the firm. Meanwhile, the government decreasing its interest in profits created an opportunity for the management to raise costs via related party transactions. The management's moral hazard was further worsened since poorly designed incentive contracts were introduced for the company directors. This resulted finally in entrepreneurship giving way to predatory action.

The entry of Mr Gu after the abrupt failure of Kelon seems a mixed blessing. On the one hand, he has had initial success in turning the troubled Kelon into a fairly profitable business; on the other, it is still a vital concern that Gu, a controlling shareholder, similar to the previous owner of Rongqi government, could one day be lured to substitute rent-seeking for profit-making. Indeed, being a private owner alone does not mean immunity from the generic agency problems deeply seated in the system, which is also evidenced by a recent glaring collapse of D'Long Ltd, China's largest private business group (*Far Eastern Economic Review* 2004).

The preceding account of the case clearly implies that the agency problem of an expropriating blockholder is endogenous to the institutional environment characterized by a weak legal system and poor regulatory protection of investors (La Porta *et al.* 2000). Given the few efficacious internal organizational constraints on the blockholder's self-dealing behaviours (Holderness and Sheehan 2000), the reform of the legal and government regulatory system to better monitor and punish the large shareholder's opportunism definitely should be on the top agenda of corporate governance reform. Both statutory provisions[22] and legal enforcement must be put in place to deter those potential corporate expropriators. Needless to say, this is a difficult task and a painful institution-building process for a transitional and developing economy, not least because on many occasions the predatory offender is the government itself. However, unless there are significant improvements in corporate governance, Chinese public companies will repeat the experience of Kelon, regardless of whether the government or private sector[23] is a controlling owner.

Investor protection aside, China's regulatory bodies should endeavour to redress the current short-termist ethos prevalent in large Chinese shareholders. Worse than the similar charge on the part of Anglo-American corporate managers, who allegedly pursue short-term stock market valuation at the expense of long-run competitiveness (for example Porter 1992), Chinese controlling shareholders seem to maximize the funds that they can tunnel from the listed firm before their eventual exit! To prevent such egregious opportunism, the Chinese reform of corporate governance should be advanced in two dimensions. One is to improve the legal environment.

That is to say, it needs appropriate regulations to ensure that no one can get away with their prior value-destroying behaviours even after they retreat from business. Another is to improve the board for more independence from its large shareholders. This requires the board to consist of more independent directors for ensuring the effective monitoring of the decision process. Furthermore, new private shareholders should be asked to hold their newly acquired stakes for a minimum of several years, which may reorient their incentive structure towards long-term wealth creation.

QUESTIONS FOR DISCUSSION

1. In 1999, the retirement of corporate veteran Mr Ning Pan, who had been the general director of Kelon since 1984, marked a turning point of Kelon from its successful rise to a fall in business. Does this suggest that a corporate hero is more important than corporate governance in influencing the fate of a company, in particular, a Chinese company?
2. Government ownership is like a two-edged sword, in that it can be helpful for business, but also it can be predatory. In the case of Kelon, how did the government as the largest shareholder behave in controlling the business? Does the case of Kelon imply that government ownership is always bad for business?
3. Which of the following problems was dominant in attributing to the fall of Kelon:

    (a) government ownership and its predatory behaviour;
    (b) managerial moral-hazard;
    (c) the weaker constraint of corporate governance on the largest shareholder;
    (d) failure in selecting a capable CEO to replace Mr Pan; and
    (e) all of the four above?
    Discuss.

NOTES

1. Huang, Yasheng and David Lane (2001), Harvard Business School Case Study No. 702–039 (March 22).
2. In the late 1990s Kelon was lauded to the skies by the business media as well. For example, it was ranked in the top 20 of the world's 300 best small companies by *Forbes*. For more details, see Huang (2003, p. 185, note 47).
3. For a rigorous presentation of the argument on TVE success, see Li (1996) and Tian (2000).

4. The factual details of Kelon in the section are primarily based on Huang (2003, Chapter 4), Bruton *et al.* (2000) and various Chinese sources.
5. Since township leaders are in the lower bottom of the bureaucratic hierarchy in China, their interests are better aligned with the local community and they show more entrepreneurial spirit than those in higher bureaucratic ladders. For more discussion on this, see Huang (2003, pp. 149–50).
6. One of the key measures taken was to make Kelon artificially affiliated to (*guakao*) the Machinery Building Bureau of Guangdong province, so that it would look like a provincial-level SOE. Such arrangements were quite common during the early years of transition, and were called 'wearing red caps' in Chinese. For an elaboration of the reasons why local governments are highly motivated to support their firms, see Liu *et al.* (2005).
7. The listing process of Chinese enterprises is highly regulated by the central government in the sense that it has the complete authority to determine which firm can be listed on international or domestic equity markets for financing. Of course SOEs constitute the bulk of the firms selected by the centre.
8. The term denotes mainland firms quoted on the Hong Kong market.
9. It can also be evidenced by the board structure of Kelon: a majority of the directors are company insiders and only one position is filled by a representative of foreign institutional investors.
10. The term is borrowed from Bebchuk *et al.* (2000).
11. It is verified by La Porta *et al.* (1999) and Claessens *et al.* (2000).
12. It seems that reputational constraints on controlling families alone fall short of preventing tunnelling activities. The blatant fraud and embezzlement conducted by the founding family at Parmalat, Europe's largest dairy-products group, are a highly publicized case in point (e.g. *Business Week* 2004; *Economist* 2004).
13. Wang remained the board chairman until June 2001, when Xu formally took the chairmanship as well. But he disappeared from the public scene after he resigned the CEO position in June 2000, and was reportedly enthusiastic about tourism.
14. Local tax revenues are crucial for local governments to create more jobs and initiate public projects that can promote local GDP growth in the short run.
15. The corporate board in Kelon was restructured in November 2001, when representatives of the township government left the board as a result of a control transfer agreement signed in October. Gu Chujun and his associates henceforth dominated the board.
16. It was founded in October 2001, so it seems obvious it was formed for ease of the planned acquisition. There was a minor change in the ownership structure of the holding company later on; see the note in Figure 9.8 for details.
17. Rongqi Township shortly sold the remaining shares to several local companies in 2002 for a complete exit.
18. Negotiated block transfers, rather than the Anglo-American style tender offers, are the norm in the Chinese equity market. For institutional backgrounds of the phenomenon, see Liu and Sun (2005).
19. Otherwise it would be very hard to understand how the expenses to sales ratio could be reported as high as 46.5 per cent in 2001, which was previously unheard of in the white goods sector (see Figure 9.11).
20. The extremely high level in 2002 is mainly related to the funds tunnelled by the previous government shareholder in 2000 and 2001, which are recorded as amounts due from the township government. When they are written off in 2003, the account drops to a fairly small amount.
21. Another speculation is that Gu obtained bank loans in the name of Kelon and used them to take over his other targets.
22. For example, corporate and securities law reform and the adoption of best-practice corporate governance codes.
23. China Securities Regulatory Commission (CSRC) releases the fact that at the end of 2002, 676 out of 1175 listed firms in China were engaged in the appropriation of funds by the large shareholders, the amount of which totalled RMB 96.7 billion.

REFERENCES

Bebchuk, Lucian Arye, Reinier Kraakman and George G. Triantis (2000), 'Stock pyramids, cross-ownership, and dual class equity', in Randall K. Morck (ed.) *Concentrated Corporate Ownership*, Chicago: The University of Chicago Press, pp. 295–315.

Bruton, Garry D., Hailin Lan and Yuan Lu (2000), 'China's township and village enterprises: Kelon's competitive edge', *Academy of Management Executive*, **14**, 19–29.

Business Week (2004), 'How Parmalat went sour', 12 January.

Caijing [Finance] (2001a), 'Kelong Shuailuo [The decline of Kelon]', 5 February.

Caijing [Finance] (2001b), 'Xitan Gelinke'er [Scrutinizing Greencool]', 5 December.

Caijing [Finance] (2002), 'Tianjin Gelinke'er Tanmi [The secret of Tianjin Greencool]', 20 July.

Claessens, Stijn, Simeon Djankov and H.P. Larry Lang (2000), 'The separation of ownership and control in East Asian corporations', *Journal of Financial Economics*, **58**, 81–112.

Cronqvist, Henrik and Mattias Nilsson (2003), 'Agency costs of controlling minority shareholders', *Journal of Financial & Quantitative Analysis*, **38**, 695–719.

Cubbin, John and Dennis Leech (1983), 'The effect of shareholding dispersion on the degree of control in British companies: theory and measurement', *The Economic Journal*, **93**, 351–69.

Economist (2004), 'Parma splat', 17 January.

Far Eastern Economic Review (2004), 'Entrepreneurship gets a bad name', 2 September.

Friedman, Eric, Simon Johnson and Todd Mitton (2003), 'Propping and tunnelling', *Journal of Comparative Economics*, **31**, 732–50.

Holderness, Clifford G. and Dennis P. Sheehan (2000), 'Constraints on large-block shareholders', in Randall K. Morck (ed.), *Concentrated Corporate Ownership*, Chicago: The University of Chicago Press, pp. 139–68.

Huang, Yasheng (2003), *Selling China: Foreign Direct Investment During the Reform Era*, Cambridge: Cambridge University Press.

Johnson, Simon, Rafael La Porta, Florencio Lopez-de-Silanes and Andrei Shleifer (2000), 'Tunnelling', *American Economic Review, Papers and Proceedings*, **90**, 22–7.

La Porta, Rafael, Florencio Lopez-de-Silanes and Andrei Shleifer (1999), 'Corporate ownership around the world', *Journal of Finance*, **54**, 471–518.

La Porta, Rafael, Florencio Lopez-de-Silanes, Andrei Shleifer and Robert Vishny (2000), 'Investor protection and corporate governance', *Journal of Financial Economics*, **58**, 3–27.

Li, David D. (1996), 'Ambiguous property rights in transition economies', *Journal of Comparative Economics*, **3**, 1–19.

Liu, Guy and Pei Sun (2005), 'Ownership and control of Chinese public corporations: a state-dominated corporate governance system', in Kevin Keasey, Steve Thompson and Mike Wright (eds), *Corporate Governance: Accountability, Enterprise and International Comparisons*, New York: John Wiley & Sons, pp. 389–414.

Liu, Guy S., Pei Sun and Wing Thye Woo (2005), 'Chinese-style privatization: motives and constraints', in Stephen Green and Guy S. Liu (eds), *Exit the Dragon?*

Privatization and State Ownership in China, Oxford: Blackwell Publishing, pp. 51–84.

Olson, Mancur (2000), *Power and Prosperity: Outgrowing Communist and Capitalist Dictatorships*, New York: Basic Books.

Porter, Michael E. (1992), 'Capital disadvantage: American's failing capital investment system', *Harvard Business Review*, **70**(5), 65–82.

Steinfeld, Edward S. (1998), *Forging Reform in China: The Fate of State-owned Industry*, Cambridge: Cambridge University Press.

Stiglitz, Joseph E. (2001), 'Quis custodiet ipsos custodes? Corporate governance failure in the transition', in Joseph E. Stiglitz and Pierre-Alain Muet (eds), *Governance, Equity and Global Markets, the Annual Bank Conference on Development Economics, Europe*, New York: Oxford University Press, pp. 51–84

Tenev, Stoyan and Chunlin Zhang (2002), *Corporate Governance and Enterprise Reform in China: Building the Institutions of Modern Markets*, Washington DC: World Bank and the International Finance Corporation.

Tian, Guoqiang (2000), 'Property rights and the nature of Chinese collective enterprises', *Journal of Comparative Economics*, **28**, 247–68.

Wang, Xiaozu, Lixin Colin Xu and Tian Zhu (2004), 'State-owned enterprises going public: the case of China', *Economics of Transition*, **12**, 467–87.

Xin Caifu [*New Fortune*] (2002), 'Kelong Niukui [Losses eliminated in Kelon]', December.

Xin Caijing [*New Finance*] (2004), 'Gu Chujun: Ziben Zhizou (Gu Chujin: made from capital)', March.

Yafeh, Yishay and Oved Yosha (2003), 'Large shareholders and banks: who monitors and how?', *Economic Journal*, **113**, 128–46.

Zhang, Wenkui (2004), 'Kelong Ershi Nian Fazhan Jingyan Yu Zhongguo Qiye Gaige Lujing [The twenty years development experience of Kelon and the path of Chinese enterprise reform]', Unpublished research report, State Council Development Research Centre, People's Republic of China.

10. Will the Japanese corporate governance system survive? Challenges of Toyota and Sony

Megumi Suto and Motomi Hashimoto

INTRODUCTION

For the ten years since the end of 1989 after the Bubble burst, the 'missing ten years', Japanese companies were exposed to prolonged economic depression and financial distress, and there was a sort of a vacuum in corporate governance mechanisms due to the retreat of the main bank system and the erosion of tight business relations supported by cross-shareholdings. A comprehensive reform plan of the Japanese financial system, known as 'Financial Big Bang', started in 1996, calling for revitalization of the capital market, liberalization in various financial businesses including asset management and banking, strengthening of a sound banking system and increasing transparency of the capital market, aiming to promote a free and fair system competitive with global standards.

Since the end of the 1990s, shareholders' activism gradually emerged among institutional investors. Some public pension funds and several leading corporate pensions have become increasingly sensitive about the execution of voting rights from a viewpoint of fiduciary responsibility. A rapidly ageing society pressed the institutional investors towards improvement in investment performance of the pension funds and such pressures will likely further accelerate shareholders' activism.

In these changing corporate circumstances, the general view on corporate governance that decision-making of companies should be left to professional managers was questioned and a new view to seek independent external monitoring has been gradually but broadly spread in Japan. Some of the big companies began to adopt the US-type internal control system characterized by committees and outside directors, but others still have the Japanese-type system, which is more insider-oriented. There emerged fierce discussion about the superiority of the US system to the Japanese system.

The purpose of this chapter is to overview the recent evolution of the Japanese corporate governance system, throwing light on two gigantic Japanese companies, Toyota and Sony. Both of them have reputations in the global market as excellent companies, but there is a sharp contrast between them on internal control style as well as corporate management policy. Sony introduced the US type of control in the late 1960s on listing on the board of the New York Stock Exchange, while Toyota still maintains the Japanese style stubbornly.

This chapter is organized as follows. First there is a discussion on changes in the circumstances surrounding the Japanese companies since the 1990s and the governance issues they were confronted with. Case studies of the two giants are then presented. Finally there is a summary and discussion of the evolution or degeneration of the Japanese type of governance system in adapting to globalization of corporate activities and enhancing the need of outside stakeholders for transparency and accountability.

CHANGING SURROUNDINGS OF CORPORATE GOVERNANCE IN JAPAN

Features of the Stylized Japanese System

The corporate governance system is widely defined as a system to control or monitor management by solving the conflicts of interests between stakeholders, including corporate managers, shareholders, creditors, employees, trading partners, regional communities and so on. Among the stakeholders, shareholders who bear business risks as suppliers of capital have the strongest incentives to actively monitor the managers. Creditors also desire to monitor corporate managers as lenders but only to avert default risk during maturity. Among shareholders, there could be conflicts of interest due to information gaps. Therefore, ownership structure and relations between insiders and outsiders are important factors to determine corporate control.

Japanese and German systems are characterized as 'relationship-based systems' compared with the 'market-based systems' of the USA and the UK. The Japanese system is conventionally characterized as a relationship-based system with three features: weak external control due to the immature capital market, strong internal disciplining underpinned by co-operation between managers and employees based on lifetime employment and career concerns, and internalization of outside stakeholders such as banks and business partners based on cross-shareholdings and corporate affiliations (keiretsu).

In the conventional view of the stylized Japanese system, relationships are an effective means of reducing agency costs and moderating conflict of interests between insiders and outsiders in a long-term viewpoint so that managers can concentrate on execution of strategy and are prevented from short-term disturbances by outsiders. In the Japanese system, commercial banks behave as long-term suppliers of funds because relationship-lending with cross-shareholding mitigates asymmetric information problems between lenders and owners and reduces duplication of monitoring costs on both sides.

Regarding internal control in a typical Japanese company, members of the board of directors and auditors are internally appointed, and some outside directors are conventionally sent from keiretsu companies and the main bank. The board of directors not only makes decisions on execution of strategy but also monitors the management, whilst corporate auditors are in turn required to monitor the board. Both directors and corporate auditors are appointed at the general meeting of shareholders. Thus, formally there is a double-checking system for the management by both the board and the shareholders in the conventional Japanese corporate system. Actually, this control system does not necessarily function. It has been pointed out that the president usually has a casting vote over the decision-making of both nomination and remuneration of directors and corporate auditors, as the general meeting of shareholders does not work to check the decision-making of both the president and the board under cross-shareholding.

On the other hand, it is likely that lifetime employment with inside promotion works well to discipline management by peer-pressure from employees and the control from the bottom is reflected on decision-making at the board level. But it is difficult to check how this internal control system functions for outsiders, as the decision-making process in the board is opaque and the responsibility of the members is obscure in an insider system. Such opaqueness and obscurity is sometimes recognized as the cause for inefficiency and weakness of the Japanese companies in terms of risk management.

In this stylized Japanese system, the 'main bank' plays a key role to monitor the management of borrowing companies as lender-owner, being complementary to the internal control system. There are a large number of empirical studies examining the effectiveness of the main bank system in corporate governance, but the results are not uniform.[1]

Growing Shareholder Activism

Since the mid-1990s, the ownership structure of the listed companies in Japan has been changing dramatically. Between March 1995 and March

2004, ownership of foreign investors increased from 10.5 per cent to 21.8 per cent and that of institutional investors increased from 26 per cent to 28.6 per cent, while ownership of banks and business companies decreased from 15.1 per cent to 5.9 per cent and from 27.2 per cent to 21.8 per cent each (Annual Reports of Tokyo Stock Exchange). The conspicuous change suggests that Japan's capital market came to a new stage to enable market disciplining in listed companies.

In an ageing society, corporate pension funds and their trustee bodies (external managers including trust banks, life insurance companies and investment advisory companies) began to shift from silent shareholders towards active shareholders from the beginning of 2000.[2] At the annual general meetings of shareholders gathered in June 2003, the Pension Fund Association (PFA) began to exercise voting rights of TSE listed companies which the PFA had invested in themselves in accordance with their own voting proxy guidelines. It was a landmark time for shareholder activism in Japan. The institutional investors are expected to exercise their rights as shareholders for the sake of their customers and intermediated ownership must play an important role in the future.[3]

Revision of Commercial Law for a Market-oriented Corporate System

Deregulation of capital markets in the Big Bang framework is clearly intended to shift the Japanese corporate system towards a more shareholder-oriented one. Japan's Commercial Law has been revised almost ten times since the beginning of the 1990s, revolving around the rights of shareholders, the board of directors and the board of corporate auditors, respectively.

The 2001 revision of Commercial Law is especially noteworthy. It aims at strengthening the monitoring of corporate auditors on two fronts: more rigorous qualification and greater authority (Hashimoto 2002). Corporations which hold more than 500 million yen as stated capital or more than 20 billion yen as liability have to have a board of corporate auditors in which outside corporate auditors must comprise more than half. The revision in the spring of 2002 introduced a new internal governance system patterned after the US-style board of directors, named 'company with three board committees' (Iinkaitou-setti Gaisha), accompanied by an audit committee, remuneration committee and nomination committee, each of which is obliged to comprise at least half outside directors. This revised law permits the companies to choose either the existing system of the new board of auditors or the committee within the board system.

The revision of the Commercial Law in 2001 also lifted the ban on treasury stock (shares repurchased and held by the issuing corporation), introducing a new stock option system and expanding the scope of stock types. All of these measures were aimed at encouraging management to consider their strategy to increase shareholders' value.

A CASE STUDY OF TOYOTA

Corporate Strategy and Business Performance: An Overview

Toyota has accelerated growth successfully since the late 1980s, continuing to strengthen full-line motor manufacturing with global diversification of the production and sales base. However it has been rather moderate in diversification of businesses other than motor manufacturing. In 2000 Toyota established a financial services company, aiming at foreign exchange risk management, global consolidation of financial settlements related to manufacturing within the group and rationalization of motor credit business in local markets. Toyota also entered into housing in 2003 and has gradually extended the business since then. But basically it has elaborated the strategy to explore automobile manufacturing for global markets. More than 90 per cent of its sales come from automobiles with about 60 per cent dependent on the overseas market (Table 10.1).

Table 10.1   Sales of Toyota by sections and by region (consolidated base)

Fiscal year	Total sales (¥billion)	By section (%)		By region (%)			
		Automobile	Others	Japan	North America	Europe	Others
1997	11 678	90.4	9.6	43.0	34.4	–	–
1998	12 749	87.7	12.3	39.4	38.2	9.9	12.5
1999	12 880	87.5	12.5	42.7	37.1	9.1	11.1
2000	13 424	88.9	11.1	42.9	37.1	7.9	12.1
2001	15 106	91.7	8.3	44.3	37.0	10.2	8.5
2002	16 054	92.1	7.9	40.5	39.0	9.9	10.6

Source: Original data are from annual financial reports.

The current corporate organization of Toyota started from merging manufacturing with sales in 1982. It made inroads into the US market in 1984, establishing a joint venture with GM. Toyota developed its overseas business strategy in earnest in the late 1990s, making inroads to Europe and Asia and listed on both the New York Stock Exchange and the London Stock Exchange in 1999. As of 2003, Toyota has 168 sales bases in 26 countries. It is still enthusiastic to pursue a global development strategy while keeping the Japanese-style corporate system.

Ownership Structure and Business Relationship

The ownership structure has been changed significantly in the 1990s (Table 10.2). Until the mid-1990s, Toyota's ownership structure was highly concentrated on financial institutions and business companies. Financial institutions had more than 60 per cent of the shares and non-financial business companies had more than 20 per cent. On the other hand, the personal sector and foreigners held only a small part, 7–8 per cent and less than 5 per cent respectively.

From the mid-1990s Toyota started to resolve cross-shareholdings so that the ownership structure has been significantly dispersed since then. In 2003 the shareholdings by financial institutions were reduced to less than 50 per cent and those of business companies were less than 20 per cent, while shareholdings of both personal sector and foreigners increased to more than twice their previous level (Table 10.2).

Table 10.2   Ownership structure of Toyota

Fiscal year	Financial institutions (%)	Business companies (%)	Foreign investors (%)	Personal sector (%)
1990	63.6	23.0	2.4	9.8
1995	60.9	22.2	7.9	7.9
2000	61.2	18.0	12.6	7.7
2001	56.1	17.9	16.6	10.1
2002	54.2	18.4	15.8	15.5
2003	49.8	18.3	20.6	18.9

Source: Original data are from annual financial reports.

In 2003 the largest shareholder was Nippon Master Trust, which held 8.6 per cent. Among the top ten shareholders, three asset management companies held more than 20 per cent. On the other hand, five financial intermediaries (three banks and two life insurance companies) held about 16 per cent. Only one company in the Toyota group was included in the top ten shareholders and its share was less than 6 per cent. Thus, the shareholdings of Toyota are well diversified among outsiders, some of which are prominent asset management companies independent from business relations.

Internal Control System

Toyota stuck to the Japanese type of governance system with a board of auditors when the 2002 revised Commercial Law was implemented. However, it is not what it used to be. Figure 10.1 compares the old and new internal control systems of Toyota. The old Toyota governance was composed of a large board with 58 inside directors and the board of corporate auditors composed of three insiders and three outsiders. Twelve top members including chairman, two vice-chairmen, president and eight vice-presidents were responsible for all functions of management including direction, monitoring and execution. The other 46 members were charged with the execution of the business.

At the general meeting of the shareholders in June 2003, Toyota decided to reform the governance structure to a new model by reducing the number of directors from 58 to 27,[4] instead, introducing a new position of executive-directors named 'Senmu' for the top 14 business lines, aiming to enhance efficiency of the management by keeping the linkage between executing and monitoring in the board. At the same time the board of corporate auditors was extended from six to seven, including four outside auditors in order to secure independency of the board of auditors. Tenure of both directors and executive directors is one year, which is the same as that of the 'company with three committees' newly introduced by the 2002 revised Commercial Law. There are no outside directors on the board of Toyota, which adopted its own board system different from the US model.

Policies for Shareholders

Since June 1996, soon after the lifting of the ban on acquisition of own shares for redemption by the revision of Commercial Law in June 1996, Toyota has continued to redeem its own stocks in the market in resolution of cross-shareholdings so as to increase its dividend for shareholders. Actually the annual dividend per share has increased continuously since 1997. Between 1997 and 2004, the dividend per share paid to shareholders increased from ¥19 to ¥45. Being listed on the NYSE in 1999 as a turning point, Toyota has reinforced its disclosure policy and communication with institutional investors simultaneously.

As mentioned above, Toyota reformed its internal control system in 2003, aiming at strengthening the monitoring of corporate auditors as well as speedy decision-making of managers. At the same time, Toyota began to make more efforts for accountability, by increasing investor relations (IR) activities and active disclosure. In 2004 Toyota decided to change the date when the general shareholders' meeting is held, in response to a proposal

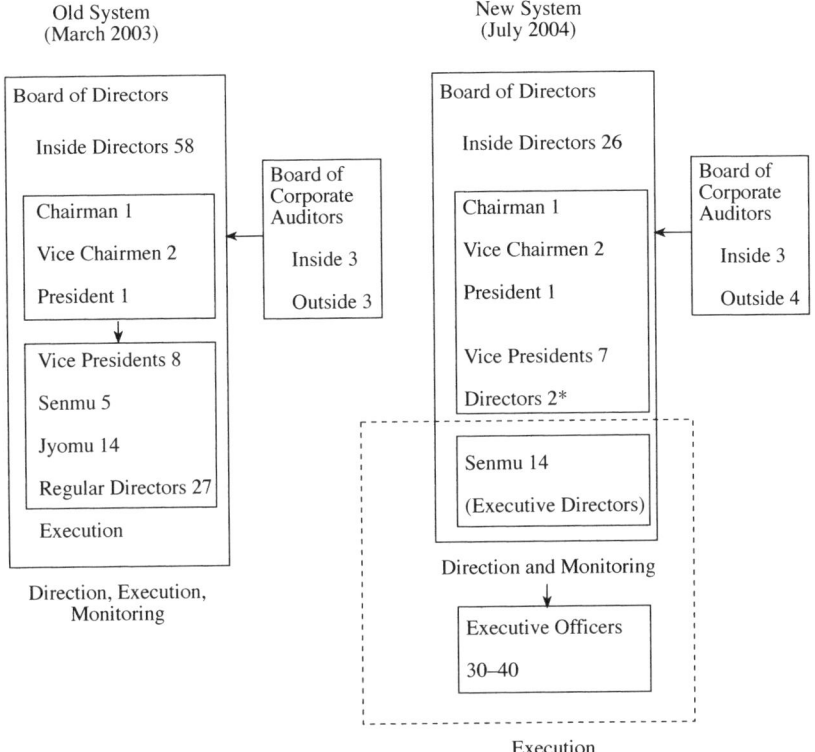

Old System
(March 2003)

New System
(July 2004)

Note: * An honourable director is included.

Source: Annual report, 2003 fiscal year.

Figure 10.1   Internal governance system of Toyota

of shareholders to change from the concentration of the meetings of many other companies on a few days in June after the annual financial reports have been disclosed.

In spite of these efforts for raising dividends and the information supply for general shareholders, Toyota's management has been criticized for not being satisfactorily transparent by not only overseas institutional investors but also domestic investors. The Pension Fund Association, which is a large domestic institutional investor, negatively assessed Toyota's internal control system with its relatively large board of directors without outsiders (from a viewpoint of shareholders' benefit). Toyota was not included in the PFA Corporate Governance Fund organized in July 2004. While Toyota's way is likely broadly accepted, the PFA's corporate governance standards cause questions to be raised in the asset management industry.

Policy for Employees and Other Stakeholders

Toyota traditionally has been concerned with stakeholders' benefits, especially those of employees and the community. With regard to the policy for employees, Toyota continues a seniority system with career concerns aiming at co-operation and co-ordination in the organization based on trust between managers and employees. 'Team-work' and 'peer pressures' among employees is another feature of Toyota's governance system. Toyota considers that human resource is the core of the corporate system, therefore enhancing motivation of employees for self-cultivation is the aim of on-the-job-training and accumulation of experiences in the organization (Inoue 2003, p. 201).

Creation of employment in the region and cooperation with the community, as well as employee welfare, have been its social responsibilities. In April 2002, Toyota professed the 'Toyota Way' of management based on four principles: customers first, improvement on the job and challenge, respects for human resource and growth with harmonization of society.

Toyota invests a lot in training its employees, following its philosophy of management that the human resource is the core of competition (Okuda 2004, p. 10). It has also kept its way of management in the globalization of the business, sharing the dignity of its philosophy with people in different countries (Honma 2003, p. 56).

How Should the Evolution of Toyota's System be Assessed?

Why has Toyota been successful in the fierce global competition in spite of questions on its internal control? We can find three factors to note in its mode of corporate governance.

First, Toyota has resolved cross-share holding speedily since the 1990s, so as to adapt to the changing financial system towards a more market-oriented one. The conventional shareholding structure of Toyota used to be more biased to financial institutions than the market average, but its ownership is rather well diversified. Second, on the other hand, it sees it as important to secure independence of management from intervention or disturbances from outsiders for the sake of technical superiority in motor manufacturing in global competition. It adheres to internal discipline based on long-term employment and career concerns in the organization, but it explains more about its internal control system to the outside world than ever before. Third, the 'Toyota Way' of social responsibility for community and employees has been broadly accepted in overseas countries and regions.

In sum, the new Toyota governance system aims to conduct management efficiently with information sharing between executives and directors, harmonizing with market mechanisms by enhancing independency of corporate auditors and reinforcing accountability through disclosure and IR activities for outside stakeholders. However, the board of directors and executive officers, who are promoted internally, is a weak mechanism to discipline the top managers unless there is outside disciplining to complement the internal control. Toyota has been activating communication with outside stakeholders, but its corporate governance is still interpreted as a closed system by investors.

Toyota's governance system needs to satisfy shareholders and investors by continuing efforts of the top managers for more accountability and social responsibility, whilst also growing through fierce competition in the global product markets.

A CASE STUDY OF SONY

Corporate Strategy and Business Performance: An Overview

Sony is an outstanding Japanese electronics manufacturing company which has modelled itself on the US-style governance system since the 1970s. It was listed on the board of New York Stock Exchange in 1970 and swiftly shifted to a company with three board committees in June 2003 soon after the revision of Commercial Law in 2002.

Sony has been targeting global development of electronics since 1960 when it settled Sony Corporation of America in the USA. At the end of the 1970s, it moved towards more diversification of business areas by using the brand name acquired in electronics manufacturing strategically. It entered into life insurance business in 1979 and expanded its software business, triggered by the acquisition of CBS Record Inc. in 1988. During the 1990s Sony succeeded in diversification of its products as well as diversification of regional markets. In 2003 electronics manufacturing occupied 62 per cent of its total sales, while 27 per cent came from software and 7 per cent from financial services. At the same time, it sought to extend markets to regions other than the USA and Japan. Approximately 70 per cent of its products were sold in overseas markets, including 28.3 per cent in the USA, 23.6 per cent in the EU and 18.5 per cent in other markets (Table 10.3).

In the process of diversification of both products and regional markets, Sony has flexibly and frequently restructured its organization for corporate

Table 10.3   Sales of Sony by sections and by region (consolidated base)

Fiscal year	Total sales (¥billion)	By section (%)		By region (%)			
		Electronics	Others	Japan	USA	Europe	Others
1997	6761	64.8	35.2	27.3	31.1	23.2	18.4
1998	6804	64.1	35.9	28.1	31.8	24.5	15.6
1999	6687	65.7	34.3	31.7	30.3	22.0	16.0
2000	7315	68.4	31.6	32.8	29.8	20.2	17.2
2001	7578	69.8	30.2	29.7	32.5	21.2	16.6
2002	7474	65.3	34.7	28.0	32.2	22.3	17.5
2003	7496	62.0	38.0	29.6	28.3	23.6	18.5

Source: Original data are from annual financial reports.

control. In 1994, it decomposed and slimmed the internal organization by introducing a 'Company System', aimed at swifter decision-making in reflecting changes in and requests from markets. Then, 27 business lines were consolidated into eight companies in the corporation and the R&D section was centralized in the Research Center so as to enhance scale economies.

In 1996 the companies were adversely increased from eight to ten, but the controlling power of both the Headquarter and CEO was strengthened by newly organizing the executive board. Simultaneously the R&D strategy was changed from concentration to divergence by additionally establishing five corporate laboratories. In 1999, a more flexible 'network company system' was introduced by reconsolidation of the 100 per cent owned by the headquarters. In 2001, Sony strengthened the functions of the headquarters by establishing a management platform with global hubs. Thus, Sony repeated a restructuring of its organization frequently in the process of executing the dynamic global development strategy.

Ownership Structure and Business Relationship

It is interesting that ownership structure of Sony used to be, before the 1990s, more concentrated in financial institutions and business companies than Toyota and other typical Japanese companies. Even in 1990, financial institutions occupied more than 40 per cent and business companies about 15 per cent of the ownership (Table 10.4).

The ownership structure has been changed rapidly since then. Between 1990 and 2003, the shareholdings of financial institutions and business corporations decreased from 50 per cent to 25.6 per cent in total. On the other hand, the shareholdings of the personal sector increased from 22.4 per cent to 33.8 per cent and those of foreigners increased from 18.8 per cent to 39.6 per cent. Major shareholders are replaced completely by foreign and domestic institutional investors and diversified from 2000 onward. Actually, the top five shareholders were domestic and overseas asset management companies whose shares amounted to only 26.9 per cent in total as of March 2003 according to the annual report.

Table 10.4   Ownership structure of Sony

Fiscal year	Financial institutions (%)	Business companies (%)	Foreign investors (%)	Personal sector (%)
1990	41.2	15.1	18.8	22.4
1995	32.1	11.4	33.3	20.6
2000	29.4	6.0	39.7	23.1
2001	28.3	5.2	38.8	27.1
2002	27.1	5.6	35.9	30.1
2003	20.8	4.8	39.6	33.8

Source: Original data are from annual financial reports.

Evolution of the Internal Control System

Sony changed its corporate organization frequently while extending its business frontiers and exploiting challenging new markets. Its governance system was flexibly transformed in the 1990s in step with its global corporate strategy development and it was likely patterned after the form of US system.

Sony is the first Japanese company which introduced the post of 'executive officer' in 1996, in order to separate monitoring from execution of management. Further, the next year it shrank the scale of the board from 38 to 10, but increased outside directors from two to three. Before this reform, Sony's internal control was just a stylized Japanese system with a relatively big board. The number of board members was 38, and 35 were actually internally promoted from employees.[5] Sony promptly shifted to a 'company with three board committees' system in 2003, soon after the revision of the Commercial Law in 2002.

Then it limited the number of the board of directors to 10–20, including outside directors, but it defined that five or more of the board members should hold the post of executive officer at the same time. This is because complete separation of the board from execution would harm the efficiency of monitoring rather than improve it (Suenaga and Fujikawa 2004, p. 104). As of July 2004, the board of directors is composed of nine inside members and eight outside members. Increasing the number of outside directors from three to eight is astonishing in Japan, but insiders still lead the board. Additionally, eight of the nine inside directors hold the post of executive officer and they are in the majority of 15 executive officers who are responsible for execution of business (Figure 10.2).

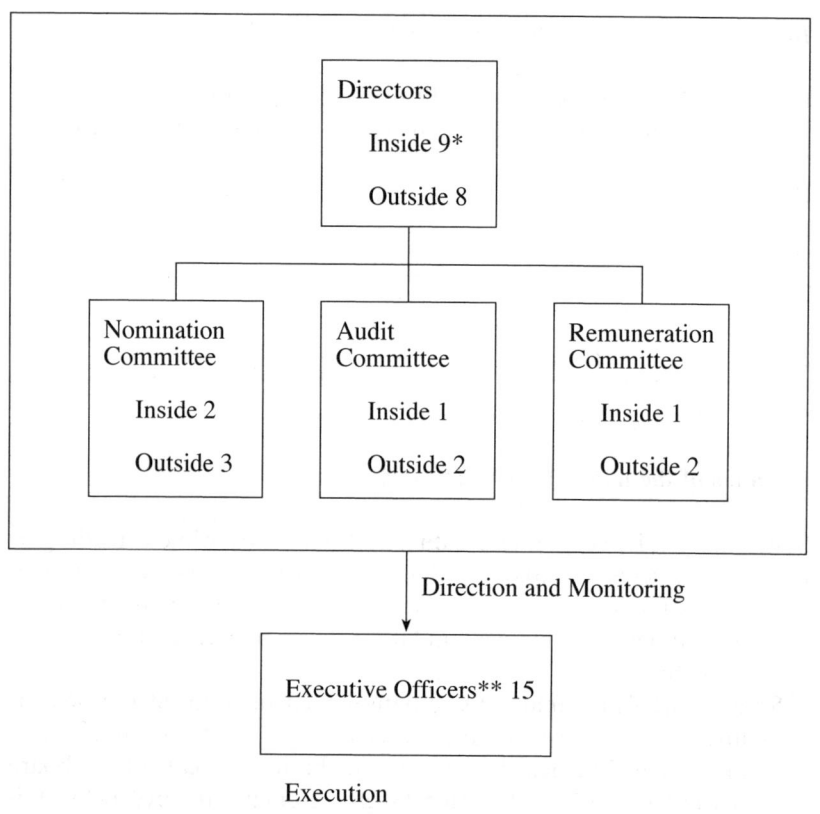

Notes:
*   8 of 9 inside directors concurrently hold the position of executive officers.
**   Executive officers are chiefs of companies and sections in the corporate organization.

Source: Annual report, 2003 fiscal year.

Figure 10.2   Internal governance system of Sony (July 2004)

For all that, the chairman of the board of directors is an outside director, completely separated from the CEO. The chairman of each committee is also elected from outside directors so as to secure independence from management. Sony has been a front runner in reforming the governance system towards the US standards in terms of separation of monitoring from management, but enhancing efficiency in management by keeping ties between directors and executive officers to avert information asymmetry between them. Thus, Sony's internal control should be seen as its own mixture of the US style and the Japanese system.

Policies for Shareholders and Other Stakeholders

Sony was explicitly concerned with a shareholders-first policy in the early stages before the 1990s, which was exceptional among the Japanese companies. Since the 1990s, Sony intended to be in the forefront of IR activities,[6] and encouraged dispersed ownership by stock splits, considered fair proceedings of the general shareholders meeting, and so on.[7] On the other hand, the dividend per share has remained at ¥25 since 1995. Sony has been concerned with high growth strategy but not the distribution of profits, which is a good contrast with Toyota.

Regarding its policy for employees, Sony aims to enhance employee motivation with incentive compensation directly related to performance level. Sony announced its policy to promote incentive compensation in 1997 and adopted stock options in 1999 promptly after they were permitted by the revision of the Commercial Law. In step with this compensation reform, the scale of employment was reduced so as to increase productivity of human resources. Consequently, the turnover rate of employees is higher than Toyota, which maintains a long-term employment and seniority system so as to foster the ability of employees. However, it is noteworthy that Sony still continues an internal career path from employees to managers, which is a feature of the conventional Japanese corporate system. As of July 2004, seven inside directors (five of them hold the post of executive officer) had worked for Sony for about 30 years or more. At this point, also, Sony's system is neither that of the typical US company nor the Japanese one.

Regarding its policy for outside stakeholders other than investors, Sony is also highly rated as an outstanding company for its activities to fulfil corporate social responsibilities. In January 2005, reliable questionnaire research on corporate social responsibility of the major Japanese companies conducted by Nikkei Newspaper Company was published.[8] According to the survey results, Sony gained the highest total score as well as the highest score in transparency, compliance and social contribution. Incidentally, Toyota gained the fifth highest total score, but not so conspicuous at individual item levels. This fact is evidence to reveal Sony's efforts for responding to emerging broad needs from society as well as markets.

How Should the Evolution of Sony's Governance System be Assessed?

The success of Sony's challenging corporate strategy to be a front-runner in the global market depends on how well the headquarters can co-ordinate the independent decision-making of diversified business units and control the corporate organization as a whole. Its governance system has been shifting towards an outsider system, in response to increasing foreign investors who have a much louder voice than domestic investors. Sony's IR activities have been highly assessed both internationally and domestically, but its internal control has still not satisfied international investors.

At the shareholders' meeting in June 2004, Institutional Shareholder Services (ISS) voted against a proposal for nomination of a director, who had been the top manager of a financial institution that had had a long relationship with Sony, because his independence from the management was questioned. At the same time, ISS supported a proposal for disclosure of the remuneration of individual managers. Sony has been reluctant to disclose remuneration of individual managers, as have other typical Japanese companies, although the total amount of remuneration has already been disclosed.[9] From the viewpoint of international investors, these facts could show that Sony shares the same sort of governance problems as other Japanese companies in terms of insufficient transparency.

Sony's own problem in governance might be from a different viewpoint. The corporate performance of Sony has been deteriorating and becoming more unstable since the mid-1990s when it changed towards diversification of its business from manufacturing. Although Sony has frequently reformed its governance system to enhance transparency and accountability in the process of challenging business development, it does not seem to have succeeded in harmonizing its internal control system with its complicated corporate organization and challenging strategy development.

Table 10.5 compares corporate performance between Toyota and Sony in terms of return on equity (ROE), return on total assets (ROA) and earnings per share (EPS). On all these proxies, Sony has lower returns and higher volatility than Toyota. We should be careful when comparing the performance of these two giant companies because their products and corporate strategies are different. Nevertheless, we can see differences between them in terms of harmonization of corporate control with corporate strategy.

WILL THE JAPANESE CORPORATE GOVERNANCE SYSTEM SURVIVE?

Both Toyota and Sony are leading Japanese companies which have survived fierce global competition for a long time. Regarding external control or

Table 10.5   Performance of Toyota and Sony for 1985–2003

| Fiscal year | Toyota | | | Sony | | |
	ROE (%)	ROA (%)	EPS (¥)	ROE (%)	ROA (%)	EPS (¥)
1985	12.6	14.8	97	12.8	19.4	144
1986	8.8	10.8	73	7.0	5.2	82
1987	9.8	11.7	87	5.8	4.4	70
1988	9.9	9.9	95	9.3	7.7	117
1989	11.1	10.7	119	8.8	6.7	141
1990	9.8	8.1	116	8.1	5.8	157
1991	5.1	4.6	64	8.0	2.8	161
1992	3.7	3.4	47	2.5	1.9	49
1993	2.6	2.5	34	1.1	2.3	21
1994	3.6	3.6	35	−25.1	−5.2	−392
1995	5.0	3.9	69	5.0	2.9	73
1996	7.0	5.9	102	10.6	5.7	182
1997	7.8	6.2	119	13.6	7.4	273
1998	5.8	5.4	95	9.8	5.7	218
1999	6.3	5.1	109	6.1	4.0	134
2000	6.8	5.7	128	0.8	3.6	18
2001	8.5	5.9	171	0.7	1.1	17
2002	12.8	6.9	274	5.0	3.0	125
2003	14.9	8.2	349	3.8	1.6	96
Average	8.0	7.0	114.9	4.9	4.5	88.6
Std. Dev.	3.4	3.3	77.9	8.2	4.6	134.9

Note: Toyota's fiscal year is from July to June before 1994 and from April to March since 1994. Figures of 1994 are adjusted. Sony's fiscal year is from September to October before 1987 and from April to March since 1987.

Source: Original data are from annual financial reports.

market discipline, both of them are confronted with severe screening by consumers in the global product markets. Since the end of 1990s after the bubble economy burst, they have been exposed to severe evaluation in the capital markets by domestic as well as overseas investors. Further, they have been confronted with increasingly diversified demands for corporate social responsibility both in the product markets and the capital market.

Regarding internal control, these two companies' systems make a good contrast. Toyota has consistently produced profits since the 1950s, maintaining a typical Japanese management style and internal discipline featured by on-the-job training, teamwork, co-ordination between manager and employees, internal career path and lifetime employment, and coexistence with communities. But its corporate governance system has evolved toward harmonization of efficiency in the internal organization with increasing accountability of its management and governance for outside stakeholders.

On the other hand, Sony has reformed its corporate organization and internal control system so as to match them with the radical development of its global business strategy. Regarding corporate governance, it has always targeted the US standard of openness in corporate governance, parting from the conventional Japanese type of closed corporate system. But in the long-run, Sony has been seeking its own style by a mixture of the two rather than convergence to the US style, considering both openness of internal control and efficiency of management. An internal career path to link managers and employees seems to be a device for Sony to strengthen control of the headquarters and CEO to organize and manage such a complex entity, although it does not look fully successful since the mid-1990s.

Corporate governance systems are so closely connected with the philosophy of corporate management, the stage of corporate development and markets they face that there is no uniform style for every company. We definitely believe that accountability and transparency for outside stakeholders are much more important than the particular form or style of governance in assessing its effectiveness. Toyota and Sony chose different internal control styles in the process of governance reform, while both have made efforts to slim down the board size and to increase communication with shareholders and outside stakeholders, aimed at evolving their systems toward being more transparent and more accountable to outsiders.

Notwithstanding, many institutional investors still question Toyota's internal control from a viewpoint of openness and independence of monitoring, though it has kept extraordinarily high business performance. On the other hand, investors are not satisfied with Sony's corporate governance as well as its business performance, though its governance looks more open and more transparent than that of Toyota. Both Toyota and Sony have to respond to requests from markets as well as social stakeholders.

Toyota's governance system is not the conventional Japanese style anymore, but Sony also does not completely depart from the Japanese system. Both of them have been evolving, but outside shareholders and investors request more explanation and information to monitor them from outside. If the Japanese system is characterized as an internal control system of disciplining both managers and employees, based on career concerns in the organization and harmonizing the incentives so as to enhance motivation and ability of human resources in a long run, it can survive. But the system should be sufficiently understood by outside stakeholders, especially shareholders.

Efficiency of governance of public companies depends on combination of internal and external controls.

LESSONS AND DISCUSSIONS

What are the lessons we learn from the experiences of Toyota and Sony? There are sharp contrasts in their governance styles. Toyota sticks to a combination of a board of corporate auditors and a board of insider directors as its internal control system. On the other hand, Sony adopts a US style of a board of directors with committees dominated by outsiders. They have different types of incentive policies: Toyota puts an emphasis on long-term incentives from a viewpoint of cultivation of human resources in the corporate organization, but Sony actively uses incentive mechanism to enhance motivation to challenge new business creation. Regarding return to shareholders, Toyota distributes growing profits directly to shareholders by the dividend policy, while Sony pays more attention to increasing its stock price.

These differences between their corporate governance styles are partly related to differences between their corporate strategies. Toyota aims at a stable growth and coexistence with communities based on manufacturing, whilst Sony likely aims at a high growth by exploitation of new business across borders and across product fields. For Toyota, a priority matter is to tackle how well it can explain to outside stakeholders its philosophy of cultivation of human resources and maintaining employment in the regions. For Sony, the problem to be solved is likely how swiftly it can shift towards more flexible corporate organization in step with its high growth strategy by developing new product fields. These differences in corporate strategies between the two companies are reflected in incentive policies for stakeholders and governance structures.

Regardless of these differences, we find several features common to their governance systems. First, both of them are exposed to global competition in the product markets in which they participate and are also under increased monitoring by international institutional investors in the capital market. Second, both of them consider that information sharing between executive officers and directors is the key for effective internal governance. Third, both of them recognize that the career path is an important factor for efficient information-sharing to link execution and monitoring of management. Finally, both of them see sensitivity to social responsibilities as critical for public corporations as members of society.

A conclusion from these two case studies of Japanese business giants that have survived global competition is that market discipline is an indispensable governance mechanism, although the internal governance styles are not uniform depending on the aims of corporate strategy, the time perspective of the management, the industry and so on. In addition, the features common to Toyota and Sony give us a clue to solving the problems for efficient internal governance with harmonization of outside stakeholders by escaping from conflict of interests. However, Sony's slow down in growth since the end of the 1990s gives us an interesting lesson that the harmonization of corporate strategy with corporate organization is a necessary premise for the efficient internal control system.

Thus, the corporate governance system of the Japanese companies has evolved significantly since the 1990s, but it is not simply a convergence towards the Western style. Rather it might be seen as a divergence or search for new models of corporate governance in the global competition. Future development of Japanese corporations in general would depend on how they succeed in designing governance systems to enhance transparency of management, to secure independence of the monitoring function and to fulfil accountability in response to demands from stakeholders.

Based on the lessons from the Japanese cases, we suggest two discussion questions related to evolution of corporate governance in general. One is on relations between internal control and external control and another is on the structure of internal control.

First, can insider-oriented internal control be harmonized with market-based external governance? Toyota's governance system is featured as a strong internal control system dominated by insiders as ever, but it strengthens communication with shareholders and investors, solving cross-share holdings and parting from a relationship-based or a bank-oriented external governance system. Thus, we should discuss not only substitution but also complementarity between internal control and external control and possible harmonization between them. Combination of internal control and external control can differ by industry and by growth stage of the corporation and it is also deeply related to corporate circumstances, such as development of institutional investment and capital market regulation on corporations.

Second, how can they create effective information linkages between directors and executive officers not only to enhance transparency but also to increase efficiency of management in the internal control system? Information sharing between a board of directors and executives is a key to strengthening internal disciplining. Both Toyota and Sony allow some inside directors to hold the position of executive officer so as to secure information sharing between them from a viewpoint of efficiency of management. Is it undesirable from a transparency viewpoint and should it be definitely rejected? Otherwise, how can they secure transparency of management for outsiders? Further, how can they be responsible for accountability about their way of information sharing?

Many Japanese companies including Sony have introduced the US-type internal control system dominated by outside directors. However, it is questioned whether outside directors can function well in disciplining the management as representatives for shareholders. Even in US and UK corporations, independency of outside directors and their ability to understand and to monitor execution of the business are generally questionable. Training of directors is an issue to tackle, but it does not seem enough. We should discuss about information-sharing between directors and executives in internal organization as well as independency of monitoring by directors.

NOTES

1. Hoshi *et al.* (1990) found Japanese companies with main banks were more successful than those independent from them. Hoshi *et al.* (1991) and Prowse (1992) had evidence to support the notion that the main bank system mitigated agency problems. On the other hand, Weinstein and Yafeh (1998) found firms with a main bank show significantly lower profit rate and lower growth rate than independent firms. It means that the corporate borrowers paid high costs to their main banks even if the main bank system functioned. Horiuchi and Hanazaki (2004a, 2004b) insisted that monitoring by banks was not effective even in the high economic growth era of the 1970s, but that fierce competition in product markets disciplined the corporate management.
2. Omura *et al.* (2002) conducted questionnaire research on consciousness and attitude of corporate pension funds and their trustee bodies for shareholders activism, for which return rates were about 67 per cent and 64 per cent respectively. According to the research in December 2001, more than 60 per cent of respondents answered that they should execute voting rights at the shareholders' meeting.
3. Kitamura *et al.* (2004) focus on the changing roles of institutional investors and the securities market for corporate governance in Japan since the 1990s.
4. The number was reduced to 26 in 2004.
5. Teramoto and Sakai (2002, pp. 185–213) elaborate the corporate reorganization process of Sony.
6. Sony was awarded several international prizes for excellent IR since 1996.
7. In June 2004, Sony nominated a female director at first, responding to a shareholders' proposition to request a female member in the board.
8. The research was conducted for the period between October and December 2004 by sending a questionnaire to 2171 companies including those listed on Tokyo Stock Exchange. The effective responses were given from 847 companies and the return rate was 39 per cent. The questions were on five items: transparency of management strategies/corporate organization, compliance, social contribution (communication with stakeholders), policies for employees, and policies for consumers and trading partners (*Source*: Nihon Keizai Shimbun 17 January 2005).
9. It is well known that the average remuneration of corporate managers in Japan is much lower than international standards, because wide differences in compensation between employees and managers are not only unacceptable socially but also inappropriate for the lifetime employment system in a Japanese company.

REFERENCES

Hashimoto, M. (2002), 'Commercial code revisions: promoting the evolution of Japanese companies', NRI Papers No. 48, Nomura Research Institute.

Honma, H. (2003), 'The Toyota way and training of managerial human resource', *Management Trend*, **8**(3), 52–63, Tokyo: Institute of Corporate Management (in Japanese).

Horiuchi, A. and M. Hanazaki (2004a), 'Can the financial restraint theory explain the postwar experience of Japan's financial system?' in P.H. Fan, M. Hanazaki and J. Teranishi (eds), *Designing Financial Systems in East Asia and Japan*, New York: Routledge Curzon, Chapter 1, pp. 19–46.

Horiuchi, A. and M. Hanazaki (2004b), 'Governance structure of the Japanese companies – ownership structure, main banks, market competition', Working Paper Series, **24**(1), Research Institute of Capital Formation, Development Bank of Japan (in Japanese).

Hoshi, T., A. Kashyap and D. Scharfstein (1990), 'The role of banks in reducing the costs of financial distress in Japan', *Journal of Financial Economics*, **27**, 67–88.

Hoshi, T., A. Kashyap and D. Scharfstein (1991), 'Corporate structure, liquidity and investment: evidence from Japanese industrial group', *Quarterly Journal of Economics*, **106**, 33–60.

Inoue, Kiichi (2003), 'A review on Toyota's corporate governance', *Financial Review*, **68**(December), 194–202, Policy Research Institute, Ministry of Finance (in Japanese).

Kitamura, Y., M. Suto and J. Teranishi (2004), 'Reflections on the new financial systems in Japan: participation costs, wealth distribution and security market-based intermediation', in P.H. Fan, M. Hanazaki and J. Teranishi (eds), *Designing Financial Systems in East Asia and Japan*, New York: Routledge Curzon, Chapter 14, pp. 334–84.

Okuda, Hiroshi (2004), 'A speech on the vitalization of the Japan capital market', *Capital Market Monthly*, **227**(7), 4–17, Tokyo: Capital Market Research Institute (in Japanese).

Omura, K., M. Suto and M. Masuko (2002), 'Corporate governance of Japanese institutional investors', PRI Discussion Paper Series 02A-28, Japan: Policy Research Institute, Ministry of Finance.

Prowse, S.D. (1992), 'The structure of corporate ownership in Japan', *Journal of Finance*, **47**, 1121–40.

Suenaga, T. and N. Fujikawa (2004), 'Some problems on recent corporate governance reform in Japan: research and analysis on case studies, especially on internal control system', Working Paper Series, **24**(5), Research Institute of Capital Formation, Development Bank of Japan (in Japanese).

Teramoto, G. and T. Sakai (2002), *Corporate Governance of Japanese Companies*, Seisansei-shuppan, Tokyo (in Japanese).

Weinstein, D.E. and Y. Yafeh (1998), 'On the cost of a bank-centered financial system: evidence from the changing main bank relations in Japan', *Journal of Finance*, **53**, 635–72.

PART 4

Corporate governance: additional dimensions

11. v-NET: a case of family-owned conglomerates

Melsa Ararat, Burcu Sener and Esin Taboglu

Bulent Kaya, the Chief Executive Officer of v-NET Bilisim A.S. ('v-NET' or the 'Company'), was not the person Emel knew any more. He had put on weight, consumed more alcohol than ever, often came home early and spent most of his time watching football games on TV. Emel did not quite understand what was wrong with her husband and made jokes about Bulent losing his 'Mojo'. Yes, v-NET, the company he co-founded with the Vakur family, recently had not been doing very well and their foreign partner was causing some problems, but after all, Bulent was offered a shareholding in v-TEK, the new venture of Vakur Holding A.S. ('Vakur Holding'), and his job was secure. He was a respected professional and was elected to the board of the highly acclaimed Turkish Informatics Foundation for the 2003 term.

Emel, hoping that it would help, invited Bulent's best friend Celal to visit them. Celal, Bulent's classmate from Eindhoven University, flew from Amsterdam for the weekend. Bulent gradually opened up during dinner.

Most of the core team members in v-NET that he had personally selected had been transferred to v-TEK despite his objections, all the investment plans which were already approved by the board of directors of the company and had received the blessing of Vakur Holding's Investment Committee had been suspended and the largest contract the company signed last year with a major retail chain had to be subcontracted to v-TEK due to resourcing problems.

He admitted regretfully that Vakur Holding was cannibalizing v-NET and that he had no choice but to be a part of the plan if he were to keep his position as a trusted member of the Vakurs' extended family.

It had all started after the arrival of Ali Osman Vakur, the grandson of the founding Haci Sinan Vakur, right after getting his MBA from Bilgi University.

INTRODUCTION

v-NET is an Istanbul-based software development and IT services company, established in 1990 as a small inter-group service firm to support Vakur Holding and its group companies ('Vakur Group' or the 'Group'). Vakur Holding was always proud of deploying state of the art information technology for the effective management of Group companies. In private conversations, Vakur family members admitted that they owed it primarily to Bulent's relentless efforts as well as his technical and soft skills: 'Bulent understood the business needs of Vakur Holding and the enabling power of cutting edge technology, but more important he was a trusted friend of the family'. v-NET has managed the business applications and data bases of the Group companies and designed the companies' websites, while providing software development and support services. The first Vakur company was established in the 1950s in Antep, where Bulent was born, by Haci Sinan Vakur in order to trade rubber. During the1980s, when Turkey started to liberalize its economy, the Group became one of the leading industrial giants in Turkey. Vakur Group's development followed the same path as most other successful family-owned enterprises in Turkey. The family used their competence in managing their relationships with government and bureaucrats that they had developed during the 1950s and 1960s, when the Turkish state sponsored private sector development through subsidized loans and government contracts. Family-owned enterprises rapidly expanded and diversified during the 1980s and 1990s. Most conglomerates established a holding company, which owned and controlled a diversified portfolio of businesses. In most cases the group structure included both industrial and financial sector companies. In 2003, the Vakur Group was composed of Vakur Holding AS and 19 other companies, one of which was v-Bank. Vakur Holding held an absolute majority stake in all companies through pyramidal structures as well as holding the class of shares with board nomination rights in all companies. Some of the companies in Vakur Group were publicly listed on the Istanbul Stock Exchange and others were solely financed by the family. Public companies within the Holding structure financed their operations mainly through loans from v-Bank and retained earnings.

EVENTS

v-NET had performed its operations solely for the purposes of serving Vakur Group companies until 1999, when Bulent convinced Vakur Holding to offer software products and IT services to third parties to acquire a market share for the Company. He also anticipated that this would strengthen v-NET's negotiating power with Vakur Group companies and decrease v-NET's dependency on Vakur Holding. Although there were both domestic and internationally recognized and reputable IT companies in the market, v-NET's experience in supporting and enabling Vakur Group companies provided for a great advantage and the company's market share had increased considerably by the end of the year 2000. The company had established a good reputation in a noticeably short period through the hard and diligent work of Bulent and all the other employees. The trademark, v-NET, was included in the *IT Magazine* (Turkey's annual market report) and was listed among the top-five well-known IT trademarks in Turkey for the year 2000. They were awarded several, albeit small, government contracts, thanks to the efforts of Vakur Holding's Ankara office, anchoring v-NET in the state organization for substantial projects planned for the coming years. The Company also continued performing its ongoing business duties for the Vakur Group companies. Although Bulent's intention was to strengthen the Company's negotiating powers with Vakur Group companies, services provided to Vakur Group companies were at a cost approximately 20 per cent lower than the prices applicable to v-Net's third-party customers. Group companies were perceived as 'family' by the Company.

In late 2000, Bulent managed to convince Vakur Holding's management, composed mostly of Vakur family members, to offer 15 per cent of v-NET's shares to the public on the Istanbul Stock Exchange. The board of directors of Vakur Holding was composed of nine members – Ahmet Vakur, Zeynep Vakur Vekil, Ayse Vakur Ulusoy, Kemal Ulusoy, Aysen Vakur, Hasan Narin, Hakan Kanat, Kenan Onat and Reha Muhtar. Ahmet, Zeynep, Ayse and Aysen are children of Haci Sinan Vakur, whereas the remaining members are professionals who had worked for Vakur Group companies for a minimum period of 15 years. At the board meeting held for the public offering of v-NET shares, Bulent led a thorough presentation of the legal, financial and other business aspects of going public. He explained that although v-NET revenues had increased considerably due to improved rates within Vakur Group and v-NET's preferred vendor status, the Company's penetration into the rest of the market was not satisfactory. Most companies who competed with Vakur Group companies in the same sectors did not feel at ease discussing their business needs with v-NET, given the extensive consulting required to implement the business solutions which v-NET marketed. Although Bulent never understood the paranoia about so-called 'trade secrets', he thought that the only way to reduce v-NET's dependence on Vakur Group was to offer off-the-shelf software products, which would not require a heavy involvement of v-NET consultants for implementation. In his presentation he therefore also focused on this new idea, and projects including the development of JAVA-based mobile software tools: mainly technologically advanced personal agenda, telecommunication and leisure tools, which will be designed for hand-held personal computers. The project required employing ten new software developers and allocating most of the v-NET team to this project. The Vakur Holding board adopted this public offering, aimed at meeting the new project's financing needs. The Company successfully went public in June 2001 through issuing new shares offered to investors in domestic and global markets. The shares have become highly attractive to Istanbul Stock Exchange and New York Stock Exchange investors since then.

The ownership structure is provided in Table 11.1 to indicate the latest information on the Company's share ledger.

Table 11.1   v-NET ownership structure

Shareholder	Class of shares	%
Vakur Holding	A	51
Ahmet Vakur	B	10
Mehmet Vekil	B	10
Selda Uyanik Vakur	B	10
Public	C	19
Total		100

Since Turkish law does not allow the bestowal of special rights and privileges to shareholders in person but requires the formation of different classes of shares in that respect, v-NET's shares were divided into three classes, with certain rights described in the Articles of Association of the Company. In line with the respective provisions of the Articles of Association, Class A shares were allowed to nominate four members to the board of directors of the Company, whereas Class B shares were allowed to nominate three members and Class C shares were allowed to nominate two members to the board of directors. There were no other rights or privileges granted to the respective classes of shares.

Bulent was very happy with the developments. He was given the freedom to move in the direction he thought was best for the Company and himself, provided that Vakur Group companies were happy and the bottom line did not suffer too much. These events overlapped with the arrival of their baby boy Vural, after 10 years of marriage. Emel referred to these days as the happiest but the hardest working days for Bulent.

Following the public offering of v-NET shares, the company took a giant step forward by using the proceeds obtained to develop 'v-easy', a new, highly innovative product for the mobile communications industry, in 2002. The company's efforts and developments attracted Sorytel Inc. (a US software company specialized in JAVA-based mobile systems) to make an investment in v-NET. Sorytel is a small but innovative software company, established by Ian Sory, which has been developing software for personal computers and mobile phones.

The initial intention of Sorytel was to enter into a technical assistance agreement with v-NET whereby Sorytel would provide the basis for v-NET's deployment of Sorytel's technology in return for a royalty amount. However, because such technical assistance agreements were subject to strict scrutiny from the Turkish Treasury, the parties agreed to change the structure of the partnership and enter into negotiations aimed at forming an equity-based partnership. Finally, during the negotiations between the parties, they decided that the acquisition of a certain percentage of v-NET shares would be the most straightforward option and would serve the interests of both parties. Due to the difficulties in predicting the growth of the new business, Sorytel opted to own a relatively low percentage of shares, continue receiving royalties, while retaining an option to acquire more shares at an agreed fixed price against any royalty payments due to them, should v-NET default in royalty payments. Such a deal would justify the asking price of the Vakur family for block sale of their shares. v-NET's objective was to retain the technical assistance services at lower cost and use the foreign participation to raise their profile and hence increase the share value. The sale of shares would also free some cash for the Vakur family. The members of the Vakur family transferred only 4.8 per cent of shares to Sorytel, keeping the foreign investor below the 5 per cent minority shareholding level, set under the Capital Markets Law. Sorytel paid US$4.8 million to those Vakur family members selling shares – a price established via Price & Young, one of the leading audit companies in Turkey, using the DCF method. Sorytel was exempted from mandatory offer obligations under Capital Markets legislation, as the minimum threshold of 25 per cent was not exceeded. Sorytel obtained 4.8 per cent of v-NET shares and was registered as a shareholder in the Company's share ledger on 13 March 2003. Upon transfer of shares to Sorytel, the shareholding structure of v-NET was as displayed in Table 11.2.

As per the share purchase and shareholders agreement executed between Sorytel and the Vakur family, and in line with the respective amendments made in the Articles of Association, Sorytel, as the Class D shareholder, was entitled to nominate one member to the Company's board of directors, while decreasing the number of nominees by Class B shareholders.

Following the share transfer, v-NET's ordinary general assembly was held on 13 April 2003. The announcement was made by the Company's board

Table 11.2   Shareholding structure of v-NET after Sorytel transfer

Shareholder	Class of shares	%
Vakur Holding	A	51
Ahmet Vakur	B	8.4
Mehmet Vekil	B	8.4
Selda Uyanik Vakur	B	8.4
Sorytel	D	4.8
Public	C	19
Total		100

of directors in line with the principles of the Turkish Commercial Code, the Capital Markets Law and relevant disclosure legislation. The meeting adjourned without any major discussions. Since the board members' term had not elapsed, the election of board members was not included in the general assembly's agenda, except for the resignation of an existing board member and the election of a new Director nominated by Sorytel as per the share purchase and shareholders agreement. Sorytel, being a shareholder for almost one month and trusting Bulent as the Chief Executive Officer, did not raise any objections or request any change to the meeting's agenda. They were assured that any important matters would always be discussed at the 'Executive Committee', of which Bulent was the Chairman, before the Company's board of directors would 'approve' it; board meetings were short and sweet, members had many more important businesses to attend to and they would always approve the resolutions suggested by the Executive Committee 'as long as Bulent and Ahmet reached an agreement'. Although Ian Sory was elected as the Director, he was not included in the Executive Committee. He was glad that he 'insisted on a long list of major decisions for which Sorytel had the veto power at the board of directors' level'.

The Company's mutually agreed restructuring plan, implemented subsequent to Sorytel's participation, included the reorganization of departments and of the duties and obligations of personnel and executives, to align the structure of the Company with the intended strategy; to focus on new products and markets and increase the Research and Development budget. Technically, the projects developed by v-NET were improved through use of Sorytel know-how and products. The royalty agreement between Sorytel and v-NET provided the basis for v-NET's deployment of Sorytel's technology at a substantial discount and also granted v-NET the right to transfer all or some of its rights (including the right to use the know-how and products) under the agreement, subject to the prior written consent of Sorytel. In such a case, royalty fees would be adjusted (increased) to reflect the new users. Failure to inform Sorytel about new users would result in the termination of the royalty agreement and a high liquidation penalty payable by v-NET upon the termination of the agreement by Sorytel with cause.

CONFLICTS

The restructuring led to improvements in staff morale and the successful completion of three new projects. The Company began receiving new orders on a weekly basis and accordingly Company growth became inevitable. New personnel were hired to support the core technical team consisting of 15 designers, analysts and software developers. Bulent, however, started to experience increased interference from Vakur Holding in the form of 'suggestions' in recruitment. He did not object to recruiting a few family acquaintances from Antep, but Recep Uyanik, the son-in-law of Ahmet Vakur, was difficult to accept. He was 'recommended' by Vakur Holding's Human Resources Director for the position of sales and marketing manager. Recep was capable and talented, but he had no experience in sales and marketing and his English was not very good. He was very proud of his Galatasaray High School background, a highly reputable French high school, and his perfect command of French. Bulent had to accept the cost of training Recep and recruited a deputy with good spoken English. As Recep settled in his position, Bulent observed a radical increase in entertaining costs. Recep loved wining and dining and believed that the best deals would be struck over a good bottle of wine.

Meanwhile, Ali Osman Vakur, the grandson of Haci Sinan Vakur, and who had completed his MBA in Bilgi University following his university degree in computer engineering, decided to share his ideas with Bulent for creating a new IT company with operations which could overlap those of v-NET. Although he expected resistance from Bulent, he believed that a considerable shareholding in the new company would entice the Chief Executive Officer. He knew that without Bulent's blessing he would have difficulty in convincing the family. Bulent, on the other hand, faced a dilemma; Ali Osman was the only male offspring of Ahmet Vakur and it would not be wise to become enemies with him. After all, he had no shares in v-NET and did not enjoy his fair share of v-NET's success, despite the fact that he always considered v-NET as his own. He was in a very difficult position. After numerous meetings between Ali Osman Vakur and Bulent, Bulent reluctantly accepted the proposal and Ali Osman decided to inform the Vakur family of their plans. Those Vakur family members with a shareholding in v-NET were very happy with the proposed new company's feasibility study and believed that v-NET's institutional investor shareholders and Sorytel should be kept out of the new company. They were uncomfortable with the extended public disclosure rules imposed by the Capital Markets Board and frequently discussed the merits of delisting to avoid such public disclosure. All decisions relating to the establishment of v-TECH were resolved at Vakur Holding level to eliminate the possible objections by Sorytel and also to eliminate extensive disclosure requirements.

In line with an agreement reached between Bulent and the Vakur family, a new company, v-TEK, was established in June 2003. Shareholders of v-TEK consisted of Vakur family members overlapping with v-NET shareholders and Bulent. v-TEK started its operations in late September 2003 upon the transfer of nine members of the core team from v-NET. The business of v-TEK included development of JAVA-based mobile phone software, for which they had a royalty agreement with v-NET to deploy Sorytel's technology. Although v-TEK did not directly compete with v-NET's product line, the transfer of software developers impacted v-NET's outstanding projects and the company became less competitive and reputable in the market. In the meantime, v-NET also granted v-TEK rights to deploy Sorytel's know-how as provided for by the royalty agreement, but without obtaining prior consent and leaving the royalty payable to Sorytel unchanged. Furthermore, v-NET's largest contracted project was subcontracted to v-TEK alongside the transfer of the core team, since v-NET was unable to complete the project. Bulent saw v-NET being cannibalized in front of his eyes, but he was looking forward to dividends from v-TEK. Meanwhile arguments between Recep Uyanik and the technical team in v-NET started to affect team performance and two designers resigned.

In the meantime, v-NET, short of operational capital due to deprived revenues, entered into a loan agreement with v-BANK (the bank owned by Vakur family) to finance its ongoing projects and operations. Although Bulent did not actually believe that loan was the premium financing option for the company, they were unable to say 'No' to v-BANK's senior management, consisting of three elderly members of the Vakur family. The loan included an interest rate considerably higher than the market rate. Following the turmoil, all resolutions resolved by v-NET's board of directors were passed through collecting board members' signatures without a meeting being held. The Secretary of the Company prepared the draft minutes and sent them to the board members, other than the Sorytel representative in v-NET's board of directors, for their signatures. The Company Secretary prepared draft minutes and distributed them to the board for signing, with the exception of Ian Sory – Sorytel's board representative. As the Turkish Commercial Code specifies that board resolutions adopted without holding a meeting should be passed unanimously, the Secretary, acting upon instructions from the Vakur family through Bulent, drafted the resolutions as if they were passed unanimously during a meeting where Ian Sory was absent.

Sorytel meanwhile was trading in the Company's shares listed in the Istanbul Stock Exchange and from time to time its shareholding in the Company exceeded the 5 per cent minority shareholding level.

Sorytel monitored the Company closely in the market and by early 2004 realized that the Company's business did not indicate any evidence of progress despite Sorytel's ongoing business and know-how support. They also discovered the foundation of v-TEK by the Vakur family together with Bulent and decided to take actions necessary to resolve the issue and improve the Company's business.

LEGAL BATTLE

On 3 February 2004 Sorytel applied to the Company's board of directors in writing, requesting information regarding the financial status and actual relationships with Vakur Group companies. On 8 March 2004 they received a letter politely stating that the shareholders are only entitled to use their rights to obtain such information at the Company's general assemblies and they would therefore not be provided with the information requested.

Sorytel then sent another letter on 10 March 2004 to v-NET's board of directors, requesting that the board convene an extraordinary general assembly of shareholders, exercising its minority rights granted under the Turkish Commercial Code and Capital Markets legislation. On 15 March 2004 the Company sent a written notice to Sorytel, indicating that their shares had to be deposited with a bank in order to demand a general assembly meeting. On 19 March 2004 Sorytel submitted a letter from Citibank where its Class D shares (non-tradable shares) representing 4.8 per cent of the Company's share capital were deposited and a letter from the Central Settlement and Custody Bank (Takasbank) confirming its ownership of Class C shares (shares trading on the Istanbul Stock Exchange) representing 3 per cent of shares. v-NET rejected this request, via a written notification dated 22 March 2004, stating that the number of shares deposited with Citibank was insufficient to call a general assembly and that since the letter from Takasbank dated 17 March 2004 was not up-to-date, the Company could not ascertain Sorytel's shareholding ratio.

On 13 April 2004 v-NET's board of directors scheduled an ordinary general assembly to discuss the preceding year's financials, to be held on 10 May 2004 at v-NET's headquarters. Sorytel requested that a review of intra-group companies' transactions be included in the agenda; the company's board of directors, however, disregarded this request. While these debates were continuing, the company's shares were going down in both national and international markets due to the exit of institutional shareholders.

At the ordinary general assembly of shareholders on 10 May 2004, Sorytel was holding approximately 8.2 per cent of the issued share capital of the company according to the meeting minutes. During the meeting Sorytel's representative insisted on the inclusion of an agenda item on intra-group companies' transactions. The government representative, however, opposed this request on the grounds that the proposal did not comply with the relevant provisions of the Turkish Commercial Code – that is no new items may be included in the agenda of a general assembly if all shareholders are not present during such a meeting. While the shareholders were discussing the balance sheet, the Sorytel representative stated that they had not had adequate time to inspect the balance sheet and demanded that related discussions should be delayed for a month under the Turkish Commercial Code. The Sorytel representative furthermore requested the appointment of a special auditor to review the 2003 financials, in accordance with the Turkish Commercial Code. The postponement request was approved by the general assembly and the meeting was rescheduled for 10 June 2004. The request to appoint a special auditor, however, was declined.

Sorytel issued a press bulletin stating that they had requested postponement of the general assembly under article 377 of the Turkish Commercial Code since they were unable to obtain information about the Company's financial status, transactions with the Vakur Holding companies and the reasons for v-NET's declining business position.

Meanwhile, Sorytel's lawyers applied to the competent court, requesting the appointment of a special auditor for the general assembly on 10 June 2004 and the addition of a new agenda item for the removal of the current members of the board of directors. The Company, as the defendant in this case, stated in its plea that new items may not be included in such a second meeting and the plaintiff should have applied to the statutory auditors in this respect prior to its recourse to the court. They also stated that under article 348 of the Turkish Commercial Code the minority shareholders should have held their shares for a minimum period of six months to be able to request the appointment of a special auditor. The court ruled that Sorytel had to apply to the statutory auditors of the Company before submitting the case before the court and that no new items may be included in the agenda of the second meeting.

The general assembly of shareholders was held on 10 June 2004. Sorytel restated its objections regarding balance sheet discussions and their request to appoint a special auditor. The government representative in the general assembly required verification of ownership of shares six months prior to the general assembly and since Sorytel was unable to submit proof thereof, their objections and claims were not even discussed. The balance sheet was approved despite the minority's objections and new board members nominated by Vakur family were elected.

By late 2004 Sorytel had resorted to the Capital Markets Board, stating that v-NET had been engaged in transactions to the detriment of the Company and indirectly the minority shareholders. They further requested that the financial tables and audit reports for v-NET, v-TEK, Vakur Holding and v-BANK for the years of 2001, 2002 and 2003 be subject to a special audit. Sorytel also suggested that the intra-group transactions should be inspected thoroughly, as there was evidence of thin capitalization, which is prohibited under article 15 of the Capital Markets Law.

Meanwhile Ali Osman Vakur was appointed as Chairman of the board of v-TEK and Recep Uyanik resigned from v-NET to assume the role of v-TEK's sales manager.

'WHOSE SIDE ARE YOU ON?'

Emel knew from Bulent that the Vakurs were not worried about the developments; the core team that took care of Vakur Holding's business was hired into Vakur Holding; all the computer systems were leased by Vakur Holding and had never been transferred to v-NET; and the public did not care much about the exploitation of 'foreigners'. On the other hand, Bulent witnessed the cannibalization of his 'first child', but could not stop the developments. He kept avoiding talking to Ian Sory because of embarrassment. He said to Emel that 'he would probably never feel excited about a new venture again'.

LEGAL FRAMEWORK

Minority Shareholding Rights

Under Turkish law, minority shareholders have certain rights, including the right to request the board of directors call an extraordinary meeting of shareholders, to request that a matter be included on the agenda of both ordinary and extraordinary shareholders meetings, to request the appointment of special auditors and to require the company to take actions against directors who have violated the legislation, the articles of association of the company or who have otherwise failed to perform their duties.

Intra-group Transactions

Under article 15 of the Capital Market Law, 'in the case of transactions with another enterprise or individual with whom there is a direct or indirect management, administrative, supervisory, or ownership relationship, publicly held joint stock corporations shall not impair their profits and/or assets by engaging in deceitful transactions such as by applying a price, fee or value clearly inconsistent with similar transactions with unrelated third parties'.

Non-competition rules under the Turkish Commercial Code
Article 334 – No director may, without having obtained the permission of the general meeting, carry on with the company, in his own name or on behalf of a third person, directly or indirectly, a commercial transaction included in the object of the company. Otherwise the company may claim that the transaction made is null and void. The same right does not exist for the other party.
Article 335 – No director may, without the permission of the general meeting, carry on for his own acccount or for account of third persons commercial transactions of the kind of those included in the object of the company nor enter into, in the capacity of an unlimited liability partner, any partnership engaging in similar commercial transactions. The company may, at its discretion, claim damages from the director who has infringed these provisions or, in lieu of damages, consider the transaction as having been made on behalf of the company and demand the attribution to the company of profits resulting from such contracts.

BOARD NOMINATIONS

Under Turkish commercial law, board members can only be nominated by shareholders and only at the general assembly. This can be problematic if none of the shareholders were to hold majority of voting rights, however this has rarely been an issue given the fact that most companies have a controlling shareholder owning more than 50 per cent of the voting rights, or they hold certain classes of shares with nomination rights. In cases where there is more than one major shareholder as in the case of v-NET, shareholder agreements oblige the major shareholders to vote on the directors nominated by the shareholders owning shares with nomination rights.

KEY LEARNING FEATURES AND MAIN ISSUES

Although the v-NET case is purely hypothetical, all the events included in the case have been based on real examples. The v-NET case is written using the most typical events to describe the corporate governance framework in Turkey characterized by concentrated family ownership and weak institutional framework.

Family-owned firms account for the majority of the companies in every economy; however most family-owned and controlled firms in developed countries are privately held (probably with the exception of Canada). Although 'family influence' is reported to be significant also in Sweden, Norway and the USA, direct control of public firms by owner-managers is a unique feature of emerging markets. Family firms dominate the stock listings in most emerging markets (excluding the countries in transition). Furthermore family ownership and business groups frequently overlap as in Korea, India, Indonesia, Philippines and so on. Arguments about benefits of family ownership of private firms in developed countries focus on altruism, incentive alignment and lower agency costs, whereas concentrated family ownership of public companies in emerging markets are associated with 'private benefits of control', 'tunnelling' and 'expropriation' through transfer pricing, 'pet projects', 'income shuffling' and so on.

There are arguments that concentrated ownership is a response to weak shareholder rights and weak institutional framework in developing countries. Studies on corporate governance issues of business groups in emerging markets are limited. Business groups may also be a response to inefficient markets as a means of diversification by formation of an internal market structure and an organizational structure to deploy the resources and competencies/social capital of successful enterprises. Nevertheless empirical evidence suggests that firms that belong to family-owned business groups in Turkey are not efficient, their performance is worse and they are valued at a discount. Investors pressure for more disclosure, increased professionalism in the boards and in senior management and less interference from owners.

The Capital Markets Board of Turkey issued the 'Corporate Governance Guidelines' in July 2003 as a recommended code of conduct. Listed companies are obliged to report their compliance with it in their annual reports on a 'comply or explain' basis. The guidelines caused heated debates, especially regarding the inclusion of 'independent' members in the boards. The criteria for independence included 'independence from controlling shareholders'.

Students are suggested to read the references to develop an understanding of the institutional framework in emerging markets before discussing the case in class.

The case attempts to demonstrate the following types of conflicts of interest within the context of concentrated family ownership:

1. Controlling shareholder versus minority shareholders.
2. Controlling shareholder versus the company.
3. Controlling shareholder versus the management.
4. Family interests versus company's interests.
5. Personal interests versus company's interests.

The case also tries to raise the following main points in relation to the conflicts of interests listed above:

1. Importance of protection of shareholders rights and judicial efficiency in attracting foreign investors.
2. Importance of a 'functioning board' and the 'fiduciary duties' of the board members.
3. Importance of aligning the interests of the CEO with the interests of the company.
4. Importance of culture in leadership behaviour.
5. Importance of consolidated reporting.

DISCUSSION QUESTIONS

1. What main principles of corporate governance if implemented would have avoided the collapse of v-NET?
2. If you were a board member in v-NET, how you would handle Sorytel's request for information about intra-group transactions?
3. If you were an investor, what would be your criteria for making investment decisions to invest in v-TEK?
4. If you were an independent board member in Vakur Holding, what information would you want to know about the proposed investment in v-TEK?
5. If you were Bulent, how would you react to becoming a shareholder in v-TEK, while holding the position of Chief Executive Officer in v-NET?
6. If you were Bulent, how would you handle the whole situation without taking personal risks, considering that Turkey has a high unemployment rate and that the managerial labour market is underdeveloped?

REFERENCES

Ararat, M. and M. Ugur (2003), 'Corporate governance in Turkey: an overview and some policy recommendations', *Corporate Governance*, **3**(1), 58–75.

Black, B. (2001), 'The legal and institutional preconditions for strong securities markets', *UCLA Law Review*, **48**, 781–858.

Capital Markets Board of Turkey (2003), 'Corporate governance guidelines', available at http://www.spk.gov.tr

Johnson, S., R. La Porta, F. Lopez de Silanes and A. Schleifer (2000), 'Tunnelling', *American Economic Review*, **XC**, 22–7.

Khanna, T. and K. Palepu (1999), 'Emerging market business groups, foreign investors and corporate governance', working paper, available at http://www.nber.org/papers/w6955

Klapper, L.F. and I. Love (2002), 'Corporate governance, investor protection and performance in emerging markets', World Bank Policy Research Working Paper No. 2818, Washington, DC.

La Porta, R., F. Lopez-de Silanes, A. Schleifer and R. Vishny (1999), 'Corporate ownership around the world', *Journal of Finance*, **54**, 471–517.

Oman, C. (2001), 'Corporate governance and national development', OECD Development Center, Technical Paper 180, available at http://www.oecd.org/dev/publication

Yurtoglu, B. (2000), 'Ownership, control and performance of Turkish listed firms', *Empirica*, **27**, 193–222.

12. The structure and governance of Eskom – a case study[*]

Reuel J. Khoza and Mohamed Adam

INTRODUCTION

Eskom Holdings Limited (Eskom) is the national power company in South Africa and is currently amongst the largest electricity companies in the world. It is a 100 per cent state-owned enterprise that existed as a statutory juristic body (that is, an entity that existed by virtue of an Act of Parliament, the Eskom Act No. 40 of 1987) and was converted into a company in 2002. This chapter traces the developments through the conversion process. It suggests that the structuring of state-owned enterprises within a company law framework has distinct advantages.

BACKGROUND

The story of Eskom (Morgan 1994; Conradie and Messerschmidt 2000 – the history is summarized from this publication) starts with the origins of electricity in Africa. The supply of electricity in South Africa started with mining being the catalyst for development – both the discovery of the rich diamond fields in Kimberley in 1866 and the discovery of gold in what was then the province of Transvaal in 1886.

Energy for mining activities was initially produced from steam engines, but a scarcity of firewood and the costs of transporting wood over long distances soon prompted the search for alternatives. The rich mineral deposits provided an alternative in the form of coal and in 1894 a company called Simmer and Jack Mines was granted a concession by government to supply power for its own use and that of five adjacent mines.

What is significant is that the initial generation of power (in May 1897) was a private sector initiative, with government reserving the right

---

[*] This chapter is an extract from *The Power of Governance: Enhancing the Performance of State-owned Enterprises*, R.J. Khoza and M. Adam, 2005, South Africa: Eskom. ©Eskom.

to purchase the enterprise after 15 years. The modest levels of electricity output could not meet the demand and the idea of establishing a large central power station took hold. Professor George Forbes, the designer of the alternators installed at the Niagara Falls Hydroelectric Power Station, visited southern Africa and was impressed by the enormous potential of the Mosioatunya ('the smoke that thunders') – more commonly known as the Victoria Falls. The Victoria Falls Power Company (VFP) was formed in 1906 and grew rapidly with the involvement of the mining companies (Conradie and Messerschmidt 2000).

Establishing the Industry

By the start of the twentieth century there were four categories of electricity suppliers in South Africa (local government, privately owned electricity companies, privately owned mining companies and the railways), but still demand outstripped supply. The Power Companies Commission in the Transvaal found that the establishment of larger power stations would be feasible, provided this was done with government involvement. In 1910 the Transvaal Power Act was passed, providing for government supervision of large power companies and establishing an advisory board – the Power Undertaking Board – to license public power undertakings.

The foundations of the industry were set. The private utilities would be bulk suppliers of electricity while the local authorities would have exclusive rights of supply within their respective areas, essentially for lighting and public transport. The Victoria Falls Power Company quickly consolidated its position as the largest bulk supplier, but the electricity supply industry was still fragmented.

Government had a different view: that a commission should be established to build and operate power undertakings and unify the electricity supply. Despite opposition from the Victoria Falls Power Company and the Chamber of Mines, both fearing the establishment of a state utility, the Electricity Act of 1922 was passed, creating the Electricity Supply Commission (Escom) with a mandate to establish or acquire undertakings to ensure the efficient supply of electricity. The act also established the Electricity Control Board as the first regulator of the industry.

In terms of its mandate, Escom was to operate at neither a profit nor a loss. The Electricity Act effectively put an end to the private generation of power and established the state utility as a monopoly generator of electricity. The Victoria Falls Power Company was taken over by Escom in 1945 in terms of expropriation provisions in the Electricity Act of 1922. Almost 30 years later, in 1972, Escom established the Central Generating Undertaking, which allowed the power stations to be operated as an integrated system.

The Impact of Apartheid

During the 1970s a number of political developments in apartheid South Africa led to the establishment of electricity undertakings in the so-called self-governing territories – also known as 'homelands' – that were created for the millions of Africans who were denied access to the urban areas reserved for whites. In the 1980s apartheid's grand plan saw the passage of legislation that created separate local government authorities for the different race groups. These political developments had a significant impact on the electricity supply industry. They resulted in inefficiency and fragmentation, with more than 400 municipalities, self-governing territories, provincial administrations and regional councils supplying electricity. Black communities (the majority of South Africans) were largely denied access to electricity, whilst the rest of the country, including the white minority and the industrial sector, was well looked after.

The 1980s saw Escom continuing its infrastructural expansion, accompanied by hefty price increases. This led to growing dissatisfaction with the way in which Escom was being run, and in 1984 the De Villiers Commission of Inquiry recommended that Escom operate on business lines with an improved approach to governance. Specifically, it recommended that:

1. A two-tier controlling structure should be established with a board of directors made up of stakeholders overseeing the business, and a management board responsible for running the business.
2. The principle of operating neither at a profit or a loss should be discarded in favour of a sound assets and income structure.

Restructuring and Democracy

The late 1980s saw major structural changes in the electricity utility, which led to a significant impact on South Africa's development. Following the passage of the Eskom Act No. 40 of 1987 and a separate Electricity Act No. 41 of 1987 (with the name of the utility being changed from Escom, the acronym, to Eskom), Eskom embarked upon a phase of rapid commercialization.

The 'new' Eskom contributed more effectively to the development of South Africa. It took over the supply of electricity in certain black local authorities and, during the late 1980s, embarked on a mass electrification programme on a national scale. This became one of the key contributions by Eskom to the upliftment of the people of South Africa.

South Africa's political liberation in 1994 ushered in a new era for Eskom and a new Chairman, Reuel Khoza, was appointed to lead the transformation of the utility. Under his leadership Eskom has prospered and the face of Eskom has become more representative of the people of South Africa. In 2002, with the new democratic government firmly in charge, Eskom was converted into a company in terms of the Eskom Conversion Act No. 13 of 2001, under the leadership of the then Minister of Public Enterprises, Jeff T. Radebe. Its two-tier governance model was replaced with a single board in terms of current practices of good corporate governance.

Today Eskom Holdings Ltd[1] is among the largest electricity companies in the world – ninth largest in terms of sales and eleventh in terms of generation capacity (Datamonitor in Eskom 2003, 145). Figure 12.1 and Tables 12.1 and 12.2 highlight the key operating characteristics of Eskom *vis-à-vis* its competitors in the world market. Since 1991, it has electrified

Table 12.1   *International comparisons by capacity and sales – major electricity utilities in the world rated by sales*

Company	Country	Sales (TWh)	Rating by sales
RAO-UES	Russia	617.4	1
EDF	France	525.2	2
E.On	Germany	343.3	3
TEPCO	Japan	281.9	4
KEPCO	South Korea	278.5	5
RWE Energie AG	Germany	241.1	6
AEP	USA	200.0	7
Enel	Italy	194.3	8
Eskom	South Africa	188.0	9
Vattenfall	Sweden	175.0	10
Tennessee Valley Authority (TVA)	USA	160.1	11
Hydro-Québec	Canada	157.9	12
Southern Company	USA	151.9	13
Kansai Electric Power Co.	Japan	141.8	14
Endesa	Spain	133.1	15
TXU	USA	127.0	16
Ontario Power Generation	Canada	125.3	17
Exelon	USA	123.6	18
Corp Chubu Electric Power Co.	Japan	120.9	19
Entergy Corporation	North America	111.5	20

Source: Data Monitor UK 2003 figures.

1. Customer numbers have been revised to take account of the removal of disconnected customers and homes that no longer exist as a result of floods and other reasons.
2. The GWh sold growth from 2002 to 2003 increased by 4.8% if internal usage is excluded.
3. Prepayments included under Residential.
4. General price increase with effect from 1 January 2003 equals 8.43%

World industrial electricity prices from a representative utility in each country

Sales by category

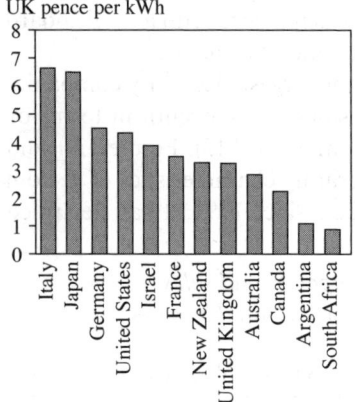

UK pence per kWh

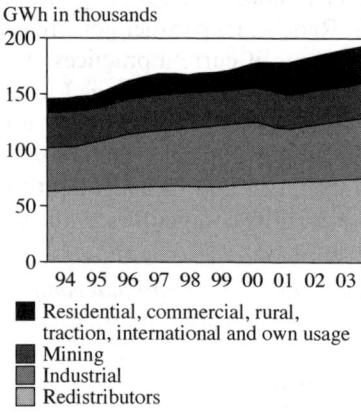

GWh in thousands

Residential, commercial, rural, traction, international and own usage
Mining
Industrial
Redistributors

Price per kWh*, including local taxes but excluding recoverable VAT, from a representative utility in each country for a typical 2.5 MW, 40% load factor supply as at 1 January 2003. Relative purchasing power of the respective currencies is not reflected in these values.

*Converted using 31 December 2002 exchange rates, to UK pence per kilowatt-hour.
Source: Extract from © Electricity Association Services Limited, International Electricity Prices – Issue 30, in Eskom Annual Report 2003.

Figure 12.1   World industrial electricity prices and sales by category

approximately three million homes, and has demonstrated superior performance both technically and financially. In 1997, Eskom was the recipient of the Corporate Governance Award and in 2001 Eskom was recognized by the *Financial Times* as the Global Power Company of the Year. Locally, the company's performance has also won approval. In 2004, Eskom was voted South Africa's most admired brand and won the Grand Prix award for the company that has done the most to uplift the lives of South Africans.[2] Table 12.3 details the comprehensive range of performance indicators that Eskom strives to meet, encompassing different areas of its business and of relevance to various stakeholder groups.

In keeping with Eskom's strategic intent to be 'the pre-eminent African energy and related services business, of global stature', it has expanded its activities into the African continent.

Table 12.2   Major electricity utilities in the world – rated by generation capacity

Company	Country	Generation capacity (MW)	Rating by capacity
RAO-UES	Russia	155 600	1
EDF	France	121 135	2
Tepco Electric Power Co.	Japan	60 337	3
KEPCO	South Korea	53 801	4
E.On	Germany	53 534	5
Enel	Italy	45 300	6
AES	USA	44 323	7
RWE Energie AG	Germany	44 067	8
Exelon Corp	USA	43 000	9
Endesa Group	Spain	39 941	10
Eskom	South Africa	39 810	11
AEP	USA	38 354	12
Hydro-Quebec	Canada	37 944	13
Southern Company	USA	36 351	14
Kansai Electric Power	Japan	35 434	15
Tennessee Valley Authority (TVA)	USA	31 517	16
Electrobrás	Brazil	31 232	17
Vattenfall	Sweden	31 000	18
Entergy Corporation	North America	30 000	19
Chubu Electric Power Co.	Japan	28 975	20

Source: Data Monitor UK, 2003 figures.

RESTRUCTURING ESKOM

In South Africa, numerous major state-owned enterprises have been restructured as companies. This initiative began some time ago when Telkom, the national telecommunications entity, was established as Telkom SA Ltd[3] in 1991. Telkom SA Ltd is perhaps the most advanced in terms of restructuring. A strategic equity partner was introduced in 1997 and an initial public offering of Telkom SA Ltd shares was made in 2003. In the same year, Telkom was also listed on the New York Stock Exchange and the JSE Securities Exchange. Denel (Pty) Ltd[4] was incorporated as a private company, manufacturing arms, in 1992 and the South African Transport

Table 12.3   Eskom high-level performance

Objectives	Key performance indicators	Targets	Performance results
1. Economic	Improve the management of resources through:		
Maintaining long-term financial viability	Profit after interest before fair value adjustment, Rm	R5004m	Exceeded – R5311m (2002: R4858m)
	Profit after taxation, Rm	R3521m	Not achieved – R3226m (2002: R3185m)
	Debt-equity ratio (including long-term provisions)	0.54	Exceeded – 0.35 (2002: 0.52)
	Historic cost return on total assets, %	11.20%	Not achieved – 10.58% (2002: 11.92%)
	Sales growth, GWh%	1.9%	Exceeded – 4.8% (2002: 3.5%)
	Gradually increasing, predictable and stable average electricity prices over the long-term	Real annual price increase above CPI	Not achieved – 2.5% price increase (2003: 8.43%)
	Risk management policies and processes in place, applied and effective	Positive finding	In place
	Maintaining effective financial discipline, governance and accountability	Positive finding	In place
Economic, efficient and effective usage of resources	Productivity improvement for the year, %	1.4%	Exceeded – 2.5% (2002: 1.6%)
	Human resources sustainability index, %	80%	Exceeded – 91.8% (2002: 89.8%)
	Management of HIV/AIDS	HIV/AIDS response strategies implemented	Ongoing

Focusing on customer satisfaction	Customer service index, %	80%	Exceeded – 82.63%
Maintaining excellent technical performance	Operational sustainability index, %	80%	Exceeded – 89.62% (2002: 88.18%)
Improving safety performance	Disabling injury incidence rate, less than target	<0.40	Exceeded – 0.37 (2002: 0.45)
	Work-related fatalities, number	Striving for 0 or less than previous year	Actual – 5 (2002: 11)
	Public electrical contact fatalities, number	Striving for 0 or less than previous year	Actual – 20 (2002: 24)

2. Socio-economic

Demonstrate exemplary corporate citizenship and harmony with society through:

Continued focus on affirmative action and actively promoting women and disability equity	Black management, professional supervisory staff at 31 December, %	>54.6%	Exceeded – 56.3% (2002: 54.6%)
	Women management, professional and supervisory staff at 31 December, %	>24.0%	Exceeded – 27.8% (2002: 24.5%)
	People with disabilities, %	>0.5%	Exceeded – 1.4% (2002: 0.16%)
	Procurement expenditure and supply of services, both capital and operating: Black economic empowerment, Rm	>R5045m (Calculated as a percentage of discretionary expenditure.)	Exceeded – R6861m (2002: R4891m)
	Women empowerment, Rm	R311m	Exceeded – R517m (2002: R197m)

Table 12.3 continued

Objectives	Key performance indicators	Targets	Performance results
Electrification as implementation agent for government	Homes electrified during 2003, number	Agreed government target – 164 107	Exceeded – 175 396 (2002: 211 628)
	Capital expenditure on electrification (subject to government funding), Rm	R560m	Exceeded – R586m (2002: R546m)
Supplying free basic electricity in terms of government policy, taking into account the sustainability of the business	Customers supplied with free basic electricity, number	No target approved	Formal roll out has commenced
Supporting socio-economic development	Expenditure on Eskom Development Foundation, other corporate social investments and rural development commitment, Rm	Minimum of R115m	Spent R158.6m including other initiatives
Support for New Partnership for Economic Development (NEPAD)	Expenditure on projects to encourage electricity development in Africa, Rm	To be calculated when project prioritization and scheduling are finalized	Dedicated NEPAD team established and operationalized
3. Sustainable environment			
Manage Eskom's impact on the environment	Reported legal contraventions counted in the operational sustainability index, number	0	Not achieved – 2 (2002: 3)
	All divisions to be ISO 14001 compliant	Positive assessment	Achieved compliance

4. Future business model

Demonstrate progress towards achieving Eskom's intended business model through:

Diversification of markets, products and services	Eskom Enterprises non-Eskom revenue as a percentage of total sales, %	49.0%	Not achieved as focus was on core business – 36.0% (2002: 43.0%)
	Market-related, risk-adjusted return on new investments as approved per investment, %	Rate of return per individual project	No new equity investments made in 2003
	Investment towards achievement of new business aspiration, Rm	R1739m	No new equity investments made in 2003
	Revenue during 2003 generated from new business since 2001, Rm	R3400m (2000 rand value)	Not achieved – 2003: R1200m 2002: R1200m 2001: R700m
Restructure Eskom to support the strategic intent and align with government policy	Implement government's Electricity Supply Industry/Electricity Distribution Industry restructuring policies and execute plans within Eskom's control	Achievement	Eskom participated and contributed appropriately
	Implement internal restructuring milestones and plans towards Eskom's strategic intent	Achievement of dates	Revised business model was developed and approved by the Board in October 2003 for implementation from January 2004

293

Source: Eskom Annual Report 2003.

Services was incorporated as a public company, Transnet Ltd, in 2000. More recently, in 2004, the South African Broadcasting Corporation, the public broadcaster that existed as a statutory entity, was converted into a public company, SABC Ltd. There are numerous examples of this approach.

Until 30 June 2002, Eskom existed as a juristic body in terms of the Eskom Act No. 40 of 1987. Eskom had a two-tier governance structure comprising the Electricity Council and a management board. The roles of both the Electricity Council and management board were prescribed in the Electricity Act. The planning and overall supervision was the role of the Electricity Council, while the management board was responsible for the day-to-day management of Eskom.

Created by statute, Eskom's mandate and powers were set out in the Eskom Act and it was not subject to the Companies Act. Although government was recognized as the owner of Eskom and this was clarified by legislation in terms of the Eskom Amendment Act No. 126 of 1998, there was no shareholder as there is in company law.

Eskom was converted into a company with effect from 1 July 2002 in terms of the Eskom Conversion Act No. 13 of 2001. As a result:

- The two-tier structure of governance ceased to exist and was replaced by a single board of directors.
- Subject to certain exceptions, Eskom is now subject to the Companies Act of South Africa.
- The Eskom Act was repealed and Eskom's mandate and powers are set out in its constitutive documents (memorandum and articles of association).
- The South African government became the sole shareholder of Eskom.

There were three main drivers that led to the conversion of Eskom into a company. First, it was necessary to locate Eskom's governance in terms of a framework that was better understood internationally. This point is well illustrated by the following example. If Eskom continued to exist in terms of the Eskom Act, there was no provision for the declaration of dividends to government. In the event that government required a dividend from Eskom, this would have to be paid over in terms of some directive or as a donation to government. Clearly, such a payment would have had negative implications in terms of the market perception and could have impacted on Eskom's credit rating as well as the integrity of the loan covenants set out in its loan agreements. However, if Eskom were to make a payment or declare a dividend as a company in terms of the Companies Act, the safeguards of the regulatory framework of company law would apply and therefore Eskom would be obliged to comply with requirements of solvency or liquidity (Companies Act 61 of 1973, Government of the Republic of South Africa 1973, Section 90(2)). In addition, investors would understand the nature of the payment from Eskom to government and as a dividend such a payment would not be cause for concern.

Second, the role and responsibilities of the Electricity Council had to be clarified. Electricity Council members and members of the management board conducted themselves as 'directors' and in all cases benchmarked their conduct against a standard that is no less than the fiduciary duties imposed on directors in terms of company law. Nevertheless, they were appointed from a stakeholder group and, strictly speaking, their duties and accountabilities could be open to interpretation. The appointment of a board of directors in terms of the Companies Act clarifies these responsibilities and removes any uncertainties that may have existed in this regard.

Third, it was necessary to level the playing field by removing the special status of Eskom that existed by virtue of the Eskom Act. The framework for the governance of Eskom was made consistent with governance of all companies (subject to the provisions of the Public Finance Management Act No. 1 of 1999).

Upon the conversion of Eskom, the Minister of Public Enterprises at the time, Jeff Radebe, stated that: 'The strategic challenge for the government, through its restructuring programme, will be to enhance Eskom's capacity in a strategic manner towards our goals of growth and a better life for our people.'[5]

Certain stakeholders, however, were sceptical about the minister's intentions and expressed concerns regarding the conversion of Eskom. Organized labour, in particular, saw the conversion as a precursor to privatization and was concerned that national social and development objectives would therefore be compromised. Government responded by explaining its objectives and assuring all stakeholders that it would be the sole shareholder of Eskom upon its incorporation. Specific provisions were inserted in the Eskom Conversion Act No. 13 of 2001 to address Eskom's developmental role. Unfortunately, organized labour was not appeased and the passage of the Eskom Conversion Act was met with public protests by the labour movement. Government persevered and the conversion was finalized. Figure 12.2 highlights the group structure.

The Conversion Mechanism

Eskom had the advantage that it already existed as a separate entity and for this reason its conversion into a company was a relatively simple matter. Instead of establishing a new entity and then transferring all of Eskom's

Figure 12.2　Eskom group structure

assets and liabilities into the new entity, the legal status of Eskom was changed by legislation that 'deemed' the existing Eskom to be a company established in terms of the Companies Act. The rights and obligations of third parties were preserved since the Eskom Conversion Act provided that they continued to exist. The Eskom Conversion Act also specified that any reference to Eskom in any register or contract would be regarded as a reference to Eskom Limited. Because Eskom was a taxpayer, specific provisions were necessary to ensure that upon the conversion into a company the tax treatment would not be prejudicial to Eskom. These provisions also specified how the tax value of assets for tax purposes was to be determined.

Government was identified as the sole shareholder of Eskom, and Eskom duly registered its memorandum and articles of association.

With regard to Eskom's social and developmental role, the Eskom Conversion Act was specific in that it provided that:

> When entering into the Shareholder compact[6] as well as in determining the articles of association, the Minister must take into account the following:
> (a)　The developmental role of Eskom Holdings Limited; and
> (b)　The promotion of universal access to, and the provision of, affordable electricity, taking into account the cost of electricity, financial sustainability and the competitiveness of Eskom.[7]

There was great pressure by labour on the Department of Public Enterprises to insert further provisions in the Eskom Conversion Act regarding Eskom's developmental role or to remove the qualifications set out in the bill. The first draft of such a clause placed an onerous burden on Eskom to ensure universal access to electricity and its affordable provision. Without qualification, this was clearly not practical as the obligation would not be sustainable. It would ultimately lead to the financial deterioration of Eskom, which would become a burden on the economy. Fortunately good sense prevailed and the compromise is what appears in the current legislation.

Concerns relating to government's role and influence regarding the future direction of Eskom were also addressed. In essence, the relationship has been couched in terms of the company law framework and is therefore a relationship between shareholder and the company. Consequently the shareholder has specific rights and is also required to approve certain initiatives by the board. However, taking into account government as a unique shareholder, the shareholder performance agreement (the shareholder compact) was developed to assist in this regard. The provisions of the Public Finance Management Act No. 1 of 1999 also provide for certain reporting requirements which adequately address these concerns.

The 'deeming' route that was taken to convert Eskom into a company was extremely cost effective, since the due diligence was not as extensive as it might otherwise have been. Unfortunately, this approach may not be applicable in all cases. Where government activities are still housed in government departments, the establishment of such activities in separate state-owned enterprises cannot be achieved through the deeming route.

One of the key challenges of the entire process was to convert Eskom without prejudicing the day-to-day operations of the business. As with any transformation process, there were certain risks that had to be managed well. Furthermore, it was essential that the conversion did not result in a breach of any of Eskom's contractual obligations. Certain contracts required the consent of the other party if any rights were to be transferred by Eskom, and the deeming route solved this problem for all contracts subject to South African law. However, where contracts were subject to the laws of other countries – and this related mainly to the Eskom borrowings – a legal opinion had to be obtained in each country to ascertain whether the legislative conversion would trigger the obligation to obtain consent. Fortunately, after a number of legal opinions were obtained from various European, English and American lawyers, we could breathe a sigh of relief as in most cases the need for consent was not necessary, resulting in a saving of costs, time and resources.

Another significant risk that had to be managed was the possibility that the timing of the conversion could result in a governance vacuum. When the conversion became effective, the new board had to be in place at the same time that the term of the Electricity Council expired. The delegation of authority from the Electricity Council had to remain in place until replaced by a new delegation. The challenge was daunting. It required meticulous planning, uncompromising precision and unprecedented coordination with the Department of Public Enterprises.

The solution to most of these issues relied on a close working relationship with the Department of Public Enterprises. On reflection, attention to the seemingly small issues of detail carried the day. The first of these issues was the development of a mechanism that allowed the minister to determine the effective date of conversion, although the legislation had already become law. This allowed him absolute control over the timing and he could then ensure that the board members were identified first. Once the board members had been determined, the minister then decided on 1 July 2002 as the effective date. The memorandum and articles of association had to be registered on that day and were submitted for registration in advance, as soon as the names of the directors had been provided and after they had signed the necessary paperwork.

Eskom became a company on 1 July 2002 and the new board was in place, with synchronized precision, on that date.

Anticipating that members would not be available for a board meeting on the date of incorporation, or if available, may not be in a position to make a decision on the delegation of powers, a provision was inserted in the articles of association. It provided that any delegation that existed prior to the conversion would continue until revised by the board. In hindsight, this simple provision assisted greatly in avoiding any vacuum in governance and, of course, made it unnecessary to call a board meeting on short notice – a daunting challenge at the best of times. However, without authority being delegated to management, the likelihood of the business grinding to a halt could not be underestimated.

BOARD OF DIRECTORS

The many codes and guidelines on corporate governance around the world emphasize the need for a balanced and independent board. Certain initiatives taken by the South African government in pursuing these objectives at Eskom are instructive. In particular, the move to a single-tier structure, a clear process for appointment of directors and the appointment of international directors has been useful in establishing an effective board.

Board Structure

There are mainly two options for the structure of the board: a unitary board or one-tier governance structure, and a two-tier governance structure. The two-tier model usually comprises a supervisory board and a separate management board (sometimes called an advisory board and an executive board). The role of the supervisory board is exactly that – to supervise and take responsibility for strategic planning. The management board is charged with the responsibility of managing the company on a day-to-day basis. Eskom was an example of the two-tier model prior to its conversion into a company. Two-tier models are also common in Germany and the Netherlands, where they are required by law. In some parts of the world the two-tier model has been used as the preferred model in the public sector.

Those who argue in favour of the two-tier structure cite a number of advantages in support of this model (Corporate Strategy Board 1998):

- They suggest that the two-tier model provides a clear division of responsibility on the basis that non-executive directors are not acting as both monitors and implementers of strategic decisions.
- The focus of the supervisory board is on monitoring and greater independence is ensured through a separation of powers. Furthermore, the supervisory board can play a mediating role between the shareholder and management.
- The supervisory board usually has stakeholder representation and this is one of the main advantages cited for the two-tier structure: stakeholders such as employees can be included in the decision-making process.

However, there is another perspective. Contrary to what is held up as an advantage of the two-tier model, the division of roles is not as clear as is suggested above. In practice, it is not easy to understand the nature of the supervisory and management roles or where the boundaries between these two roles should be drawn. In particular, it is not clear who is to be regarded as a director of the company in terms of the law. More importantly, the role of the director may be obscured because it is not clear to whom the director is accountable. Does a director owe his/her fiduciary duty to the company as is the norm in company law, or to the stakeholder constituency whom s/he represents? Accountability is therefore diluted in the two-tier model. In fact, the experience in China shows that independence and effective oversight over executives is in any event not necessarily achieved in a two-tier model (Dahya *et al.* 2003).

Our preference is thus for a unitary board in which the respective roles of the board and management are clarified by the board (and management) as a deliberate exercise of effective leadership. Our preference is based on the fact that there is no clear division of roles that automatically flows from the two-tier board. Given, however, that the two-tier model does have a number of advantages, how can these be realized in a unitary board?

Good corporate governance places an emphasis on three factors: the appointment of non-executive directors to boards, stakeholder inclusivity and the triple bottom line. If these principles of good corporate governance are applied, the single-tier model can in fact achieve the advantages associated with the two-tier model. In particular, the appointment of non-executive directors can strengthen the independence of the board in a single-tier system, as is recommended in the guidelines of various corporate governance codes. The concerns of stakeholders can be addressed by a board that is enjoined to be responsible to stakeholders and to pursue the objectives of the triple bottom line. The absence of 'stakeholder representatives' on the board would then not be a shortcoming.

In a single-tier model, these benefits can be achieved without the disadvantage of the governance uncertainties that accompany the two-tier model.

The lack of clarity associated with the two-tier governing structure far outweighs any advantages that it may have, especially in the light of the fact that all those advantages can be achieved just as effectively in a single-tier model. It is not surprising that certain governance codes, including the Principles for Corporate Governance in the Commonwealth (Commonwealth Association for Corporate Governance 1999), as well as the King Report 2002 (King Committee on Corporate Governance 2002), recommend a one-tier governance structure. Two-tier boards are only common in countries where they are required by law. Where there is a choice, the single-tier model tends to be the preferred option (Corporate Strategy Board 1998). The OECD *Principles of Corporate Governance* (OECD 2004, 58) provide guidelines that are applicable to both models.

The preferred model is a one-tier structure, with a competent, balanced and independent board that is subject to the ordinary fiduciary duties and the duties of reasonable care and skill, as contemplated in company law.

The two-tier model, however, has benefits in certain circumstances.

The Value of a Two-tier Corporate Structure at Times of Transition

Frans Baleni, a senior member of the National Union of Mineworkers (NUM), was appointed to the Eskom Electricity Council as a representative of organized labour in terms of the Eskom Act No. 40 of 1987, and continues to serve as a director of Eskom since its conversion into a company. He argues that during the early 1990s the two-tier model was appropriate and relevant to Eskom at the start of the process of transformation that led up to democratic elections in South Africa. This was about a decade before Eskom was restructured as a commercial company.

At that time, state-owned enterprises, like other areas of government, wanted to involve various stakeholders that were previously not included in the decision-making processes because of apartheid. There was an urgent need to bring representatives of organized labour, previously disadvantaged individuals (blacks, women and people with disabilities) and representatives of black business into the mainstream of the economy. Eskom achieved this quite easily through the two-tier model. This was because the representatives of these stakeholders had no option in the initial period but to act in the best interests of their respective constituencies in order to rectify the inequities of the previous system of apartheid.

For example, the membership of the National Union of Mineworkers consisted mainly of black employees who were excluded from certain benefits and opportunities through the apartheid system. A large part of the country (in essence black communities) did not have electricity. It would have been unreasonable to expect a representative of the National Union of Mineworkers who was appointed to the Electricity Council to act in the best interests of Eskom if s/he felt that such interests were in conflict with the rights of workers or the communities that did not have electricity.

However, acting on this basis would have been contrary to company law and for this reason the particular status of Eskom as a statutory body and the existence of a two-tier governance structure comprising stakeholders was useful.

So at that time it was not practical to expect directors to act jointly in the best interests of Eskom at all times. There were vested interests at stake and the two-tier model of governance provided council members with the opportunity to resolve these issues without exposing themselves to legal liability. Once South Africa's new democratic government was in place, the two-tier system was no longer useful; it had served its purpose. In democratic South Africa today, a single balanced board is likely to be more effective than a two-tier structure in achieving the goals of Eskom, or any state-owned enterprise for that matter, provided that its approach to governance is based on the triple bottom line and stakeholder inclusivity.

The disadvantage of the 'stakeholder board' model is that the utilization of the best business skills may in certain circumstances be compromised in order to ensure broad stakeholder representation.

Board Size

There is no magical number that can be regarded as the right size for a board, but increasingly there is a tendency towards smaller rather than larger boards.

Eskom has a board of 15 members and it has worked well so far. Fifteen should be regarded as an absolute maximum, as any board that is larger than that may become too cumbersome to manage. Deliberations may become too lengthy and directors may not be able to participate effectively in discussions. With numbers larger than 15, the board could become dysfunctional.

The Eskom structure together with the relevant board committees is set out in Figure 12.3.

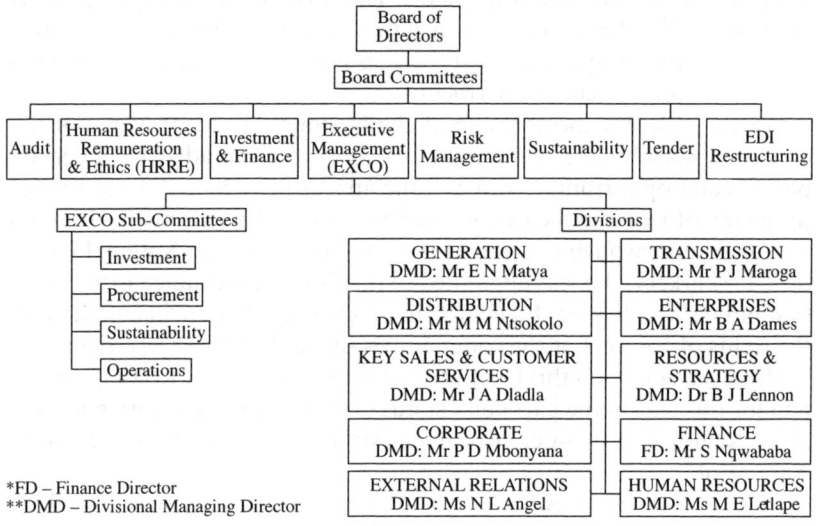

Figure 12.3   Governance structure of Eskom Holdings Ltd

Process

The position of a director of a state-owned enterprise may not in itself be financially rewarding in terms of remuneration. However, some of these positions are very powerful and lead to the incumbent being able to influence significant strategic issues. In addition, it could allow access to influence over the procurement processes of large state-owned enterprises and therefore the awarding of significant contracts. It is therefore not surprising that such board appointments are viewed with suspicion where they are made in the absence of an appropriate process. An appropriate process is necessary not only to ensure transparency so that all stakeholders have confidence in the appointees, but also serves to protect the interests of government by ensuring that the most competent people are appointed to key positions.

The process of locating suitable talent should also include input by the existing board of the state-owned enterprise. It is interesting to note that the South African Department of Public Enterprises guidelines are silent on this important point. However, when one looks at the private sector, directors are appointed by the shareholder(s) on the recommendation of the board. The process for state-owned enterprises should be consistent with this approach as it does reflect best practice in this area. The reasons for this are obvious: the existing board members, particularly the chairperson, are in the best position to determine any weaknesses or shortcomings that may exist on the board. In addition, the board will have a fair idea as to what skills are required and which board members should be removed.

In South Africa, the Department of Public Enterprises is responsible for governance processes relating to state-owned enterprises. Although it is directly responsible as shareholder for only six state-owned enterprises, it formulates policy and provides guidance on issues of governance to all state-owned enterprises. While the department could be regarded as the custodian of the process of appointing board members in the sense of setting the policy framework, the appointments are made by the ministers that are accountable for particular state-owned enterprises.

In Eskom's case, the memorandum and articles of association are explicit regarding board appointments. They clearly set out the process to be followed and outline the role of the board and the minister. In the case of appointments to Eskom's main board, the minister is required to make the appointments in consultation with the board. In respect of appointments to boards of Eskom's main subsidiaries, the Eskom board is empowered to make such appointments after consultation with the minister. The memorandum and articles of association also set out how the process of consultation should occur. In essence, they require the party that is obliged to consult to provide the other party with a list of names and for that party to indicate a preference.

International Directors

With the advent of globalization and the mobility of skills, companies are no longer confined to looking for talent at home. The opportunity to bring diverse skills into the state-owned enterprise arises when appointing their boards. 'The ability to see through the eyes of individuals from a different cultural background is a critical strength' (Gow 2003) and this is a good reason to consider appointing international directors. Nevertheless, relatively few companies have foreign directors on their boards, even though company revenues are increasingly being sourced in the international arena: 48 per cent of the Fortune Global 50 companies have no foreign directors on their main boards despite 57 per cent earning 20–80 per cent of their revenues internationally (Gow 2003).

Although the case for international directors is strengthened when a company operates outside its home market, this is not the only reason for their appointment. Even where a state-owned enterprise only operates locally, it can benefit from the experience of an international director who is involved in the same sector, especially when that experience may have a direct bearing on company strategy.

Government recognized the benefit of appointing international directors to boards of state-owned enterprises and there are now two international directors on Eskom's board. The new board has been in place since July 2002 and already the benefits are evident. The international board members have brought different perspectives to bear on board meetings. At times it is because of their experiences at home, but in some cases it is due to their questioning of issues that local directors tend to take for granted. The international directors are removed from local politics. This is of great benefit and ensures that the board of the state-owned enterprise is truly independent.

The Benefits of Appointing International Directors (Based on an Interview with Dr Brian Count (Director: Eskom Holdings Ltd))

The importance of appointing a diverse board should not be underestimated. The diversity should not be confined to any particular aspect, but should be achieved in general – for example, with regard to skills, expertise, experience and different perspectives that are needed for effective decision-making.

It may not be necessary to appoint international directors for their skills in areas where local skills and expertise are available. However, state-owned enterprises tend to operate in a monopoly environment and appointing an international director with experience in the particular industry may be beneficial. The board will benefit from having available at board discussions the opportunity to benchmark and compare certain initiatives of the state-owned enterprise against similar activities in another country, where such activities may be carried out in a competitive environment. What is helpful in this regard is the international industry perspective and to the extent that this perspective can be provided by a national with appropriate experience, this should be adequate.

One of the unavoidable consequences of leading and managing a state-owned enterprise is that it can never operate without some form of government influence and direction. It is in this context that an international director may be useful in providing the board with greater independence of decision-making. International directors are not influenced by the political environment to the same extent that local directors would be. They are therefore in a better position to challenge the usual way of doing things – they may not know the government stance on a particular matter and will therefore be able to evaluate a decision without any preconceived notions of what should or should not be done.

If the appointment of international directors is considered, there should be a minimum of two such directors. A single international director may be a lone voice without the necessary influence on the board and, more importantly, would bring experiences related mainly to his home country and the ability to compare such experience with developments in other parts of the world is essential.

CONCLUSIONS

For the reasons discussed above, the preferred structure for a state-owned enterprise that is required to operate as a business in a competitive context is that of a separate company registered in terms of company law, supported by the appointment of a credible, competent and independent board. This policy choice, however, must be exercised in the context of the legislative and policy framework in each country. National considerations may require a different approach. To the extent that a different option is necessary for an organizational structure, alternatives must be explored to ensure that good corporate governance prevails in the model adopted. The structure of an organization is a means to an end and not the end itself, and this applies as much to state-owned enterprises as to any other organization.

KEY POINTS

1. A company structure is to be preferred for state-owned enterprises and it has various benefits including being better suited to operating in a competitive environment, and access to a wider pool of finance.
2. The process of converting into, or establishing, a company should be as simple and cost-effective as possible.
3. The governance structure should be premised around a governance model that is both understood and in keeping with best practice generally.
4. The board is one of the most important governance structures and should comprise individuals who are competent, ethical and add value to the business. The significant contribution to be made by independent directors cannot be underestimated.
5. Stakeholders should be involved in the restructuring process and considered in the future strategy and operating decisions of the company.

DISCUSSION QUESTIONS

1. What challenges arise when a state-owned enterprise is restructured?
2. Why is the corporate governance structure so important?
3. What are the potential advantages/disadvantages of appointing international directors?
4. What wider stakeholder and societal interests did Eskom need to take into account?
5. What considerations helped to determine whether Eskom should have a unitary board structure or a dual board structure?

NOTES

1. The sole shareholder is still the Republic of South Africa.
2. The Markinor Sunday Times Top Brands survey is an annual assessment in which the brand reputation of companies is independently measured. Each survey contains an analysis of the comparative ranking of the brand against other companies. The measures include weighted awareness, trust and confidence in the brand, loyalty to the brand and an overall brand relationship score. These measures are also analysed by key demographics such as urban versus rural, age, gender, race and province. The study contains an analysis of the brands' year-on-year movement.
3. 'Limited' (Ltd) denotes a public company that can issue shares to the public in terms of South African law.
4. 'Proprietary Limited' ((Pty) Ltd) denotes a private company which cannot offer shares to the public in terms of South African law.
5. Statement in Parliament by the Minister of Public Enterprises, Jeff Radebe, on 20 June 2001 on the occasion of tabling the Bill before the National Council of Provinces for adoption.
6. The 'shareholder compact' is the term used in Eskom to describe the shareholder performance agreement.
7. Some corporate material has been obtained from the Eskom website and 2003 Annual Report. (www.Eskom.co.za;Annual Report 2003, Eskom Corporate Communications,2003.)

REFERENCES

All online references were accessed between August and October 2004.

Commonwealth Association for Corporate Governance (1999), 'Principles for corporate governance in the Commonwealth', http://www.cacg-inc.com/documents/Guidelines-november-1999-corporate-governance-principles.doc

Conradie, S.R. and L.J.M. Messerschmidt (2000), *A Symphony of Power* Chris van Rensburg Publications, Johannesburg.

Corporate Strategy Board (1998), 'A comparison of unitary and two-tier boards of directors', unpublished primary research report prepared for Eskom, Johannesburg.

Dahya, J., Y. Karbhari, Z.J. Xiao and M. Yang (2003), 'The usefulness of the supervisory board report in China', *Corporate Governance: An International Review*, 11(4), 308–21.

Eskom (2003), *Annual Report 2003*, Johannesburg: Eskom Corporate Communication and Business in Africa Group Limited. http://www.eskom.co.za/about/ Annual%20Report%202003/index.html

Government of the Republic of South Africa (1973), Companies Act No. 61 of 1973, Government of the Republic of South Africa, Pretoria.

Gow, R. (2003), 'There is a new issue in the corporate governance debate: should company boards be international?', *Executive Briefing Series*, vol. 1, July, Gow & Partners, New York.

King Committee on Corporate Governance (2002), *King Report on Corporate Governance for South Africa – 2002* (King Report 2002), Johannesburg: Institute of Directors in Southern Africa.

Morgan, K.J. (1994), 'The changing nature of the South African electricity supply industry', unpublished.

OECD (2004), *OECD Principles of Corporate Governance*, http://www.oecd.org/ dataoecd/32/18/31557724.pdf, accessed 27 August 2004.

Index

accountability 48, 49, 100
  in dual board systems 299
Accounting Oversight Board 15, 16
acquisitions and mergers *see* mergers
  and acquisitions
agency costs of government-
  controlling shareholder 223–6
Airport Company
  background 169–70
  best practice 173–4
  management board 170, 172–3
  supervisory board 170–73
  see also Poland
Aldama Report 84–5
annual general meetings 48
apartheid 286, 300–301
argumentation 117–18
  pro/contra relation 119
argumentation rationality 106, 136–7
  detail-founded change actions 118,
    119, 136–7
  global-founded change actions
    118–19, 136, 137
  qualified-founded change actions
    118, 119–20, 137
  unfounded change actions 118, 137
Arthur Andersen 13, 14
asset stripping 189, 229–33, 240, 281
Association of British Insurers (ABI)
  37, 50
audit committees 15, 47, 48, 85
auditor rotation 73
auditors
  conflicts of interest 99
  corporate 249
  external 73, 77
  independence of 73
  providing non-auditing services 15
  regulation of 15, 16
  statutory 57, 71–2, 73
Australia, oil exploration 12–13

Automatic Company
  background 174
  best practice 177
  management board 174, 176–7
  ownership structure 174
  supervisory board 174–7
  see also Poland
Aventis 104, 108, 109
  argumentation 129–32, 137–8
  board structure 133
  key figures (31 Dec 2003) 110–11
  reasoning 127–33
  see also Sanofi-Synthélabo and
    Aventis
awards 82, 288

bad practice 70
BBC *Money Programme,* reactions to
  Shell affair 27
best practice 47–9, 78, 83
  CEO/chair separation of roles 47,
    68, 97, 133
  communication with shareholders 48
  foundations of 47
  institutional investors' role in 49
  monitoring senior management 58
  see also Codes of Best Practice;
    disclosure; transparency
Best Practice in Public Companies
  (2002) 169, 173–4, 177, 182–4
Big Bang framework 246, 249
blockholders 58, 241
blue-chip companies 58
board structures 298–300
  China 242
  effect on corporate performance
    209–12
  France 108–9
  Germany 299
  Italy 57
  Japan 248

Netherlands 17, 299
Poland 160
Singapore 191–2, 193–4
South Africa 298
Spain 84
stakeholder model 300–301
UK 17
see also dual board systems; unitary
    board systems
boards of directors 57
  regulation to control actions of 14
  size, importance of 198
boards of statutory auditors 57, 71–2,
    73
Boynton, Judith 23, 26, 27
BP 31, 32, 33–4, 35
bribery 10
Brinded, Malcolm 25

Cadbury Code 16, 84
Cadbury Report 16, 47
CalPERS 14, 24
Cambridge Energy Research
    Associates 34
Canada, oil reserves 33
Carrier
  background 166–7
  management board 168
  supervisory board 167–9
  see also Poland
cash asset stripping *see* asset stripping
CEOs
  compensation 200–201, 202–6
  financial incentives 202–6
chair/CEO, separation of roles 47, 68,
    97, 133
change actions 117–20
China
  blockholders in dual role 219
  board structures 242
  corporate reform 241–2
  development of corporate
      governance 218, 220, 241
  market environment 221
  other receivables 232
  publicly-owned corporations 218
  tax system 228–9
  township and village enterprise
      (TVE) sector 219, 220
  transitional period 218

weak legal environment 219, 241–2
  see also Kelon
CMS (controlling-minority structure)
    224
code of conduct, Turkey 281
Code of Corporate Governance,
    Singapore 189–96, 202
  accountability and audit 192–3
  board matters 191–2, 193–4
  communication with shareholders
      193
  disclosure 195
  remuneration matters 192, 194–6
Codes of Best Practice
  Aldama Report 84–5
  Best Practice in Public Companies
      (2002) 169, 173–4, 177, 182–4
  Cadbury Report (1992) 16, 47
  Olivencia Report 84
  Preda Code (1999, 2002) 57, 66, 68,
      74–5, 76
codes of practice 16–17, 300
Combined Code (2003) 16–17, 47–8,
    52
Commercial Company Code (CCC)
    160–61, 170, 172
Commercial Law, Japan, revision of
    249–50
Committee on the Financial Aspects
    of Corporate Governance 47
  see also Cadbury Report
communications
  central issue of corporate
      governance 105–6, 135–6
  managers to shareholders 48, 107
Company Act, Italy 57
company law reform, US 13–16
Company Law, Spain 85
compensation, executive 200–201,
    202–6
comply or explain rule 84, 281
confidence of stakeholders,
    maintaining 49, 105, 302
confidential information 74–5
conflicts of interest 15, 247, 248
conglomerates, family-owned, case
    study *see* v-NET
CONSOB (2002) 72, 75
contra-arguments 126
control mechanisms 105

control premiums 60–61
controlling-minority structure (CMS)
    224
controlling shareholders
    government as 223–6
    problems with 157
Coopman, Frank 26–7
corporate governance
    central and Eastern Europe *see*
        Poland; Russia
    definition 104–5, 247
    in developing countries 241, 281
    Europe *see* France; Germany; Italy;
        Netherlands; Spain; UK
    South Africa *see* South Africa
    South East Asia *see* China; Japan;
        Singapore
    Turkey *see* Turkey
corporate governance codes 16–17, 55
    Principles for Corporate Governance
        in the Commonwealth 300
Corporate Governance Committee
    (CGC) 189, 191
corporate governance systems
    dual board 2, 17, 57, 108, 298–9,
        300–301
    market-based 247
    relationship-based 247
    stakeholder model 300–301
    unitary board 2, 57, 298–300
corporate performance in relation to
    board structure 209–12
corporate scandals 7, 13–14, 47, 48,
    218
corporate social responsibility 52–3,
    261
cross-shareholdings 84, 247, 248, 254
crude oil prices 34

data propositions 117
Davis Polk and Wordwell investigation
    25, 30
Davis Polk Report 25, 30–31
De Villiers Commission of Inquiry 286
decentralization 24
deregulation of capital markets, Japan
    249–50
detail-founded change actions 118,
    119, 136–7
    see also argumentation rationality

developing countries, corporate
    governance 241, 281
directors
    independent 191, 193, 240
    international 303–5
    non-executive 47–8, 66, 299–300
disclosure 74–5, 189–90, 195, 202
    importance of 49
    necessity for 105, 135
Dow Jones Global Index 82
Draghi Reform (1998) 57, 71–2, 73
dual board systems 2, 17, 57, 108, 298–9
    accountability in 299
    benefits of 300–301
    lack of clarity in 300
    see also unitary board systems
dual class shares 84
dual listings 15
Dutch Stock Exchange 17

East Asian financial crisis 187, 246
electricity utilities
    international comparisons by
        capacity and sales 287
    rated by generation capacity 289
    see also Eskom
electricity, world prices and sales 288
employment for life 247, 248
Enron 13
environmental issues 13, 50, 52–3
Eskom
    apartheid, and impact of 286,
        300–301
    awards 288
    background 284–9
    board of directors 298–9, 300–303,
        304
    conversion into company 294–8
    development of South Africa, role
        in 286–7
    Electricity Council 294, 295, 297,
        300–301
    governance structure 294–6, 302
    government's role in 296–7
    international electricity utilities,
        comparison with 287, 289
    performance 290–93
    restructuring 289–98
    stakeholders' concerns 295
    see also South Africa

Eskom Act 294–5, 300
estimating reserves 22–4
ethical issues 50
Europe, corporate governance *see
    individual countries*
executive compensation 194–6,
    200–201, 202–6
external auditor rotation 73
external auditors 73, 77
Exxon Mobil 24, 33, 34–5

family-owned enterprises 270, 281–2
financial analysts 15
Financial Big Bang 246, 249
financial crisis, East Asia 187, 246
Financial Reporting Council 16
financial scandals 47, 48
Financial Services Authority (FSA)
    28–9, 54
Financial Times, reporting on Shell 36
forecasting oil reserves 24, 36
Form 6k filing 15
France
    board structures 108–9
    Commercial Code 108, 133
    decision-making, labour influence
        on 134
    see also Sanofi-Synthélabo and
        Aventis
FTSE e-TX Index 82

gas reserves 7
Germany 109, 134, 247
GLCs *see* government-linked
    corporations
global-founded change actions 118–19,
    136, 137
    see also argumentation rationality
Global Reporting Initiative (GRI) 99
globalization 303
golden shares 61, 87, 99
good practice 49, 55, 70
    see also best practice
governance codes *see* codes of practice
government
    as controlling shareholder 223–6
    local benefits from owning industrial
        company 228
    ownership of control 240
government-linked corporations
    (GLCs) 188–9, 207

Greencool Technology Holdings Co.
    Ltd 234–6
    see also Kelon
Guangdong Kelon Electrical Holdings
    Co. Ltd *see* Kelon

Hong Kong Stock Market 220, 222
hostile takeover bids 104, 126
    see also Sanofi-Synthélabo and
        Aventis

Ibex-35 Index 82, 86, 93, 97, 98, 99
independent directors 240
independent regulators
    Accounting Oversight Board 15, 16
    Financial Reporting Council 16
Indra
    adjusted stock market returns 89, 90
    Annual Corporate Governance
        Report 83, 99
    auditors, external 99
    awards 82
    best practice 97, 99–100
    blockholders 93–4, 95–7
    board of directors 95–7, 98
    board of directors' committees 97–8,
        99
    CEO/chairman separation of roles
        97
    corporate responsibility 99–100
    dividends, evolution of 91–2
    efficiency 88–9, 96
    employment, evolution of 89–91
    General Shareholders' Meeting 98–9
    golden share 99
    governance structure 93–100
    history of 86–93
    Ibex-35 Index companies,
        comparison with 93, 97, 98, 99
    leverage, evolution of 91
    ownership structure 93–4
    performance 92, 95
    privatization 82–3, 87–93
    profile 82–3
    profitability 87–8, 96
    remuneration 98
    restructuring 87, 88
    shares 82, 93–5, 94–5
    stakeholders, commitment to 99
    transparency 99
    see also Spain

Indra Sistemas, SA *see* Indra
insider-dominated systems 57, 240
institutional investors 48, 49–50, 249
  see also shareholders
institutional ownership, UK 49–50
Institutional Shareholders' Committee
  (ISC) (2002) 50
insurance companies 49
integrity, Shell report on 10–11
internal control systems 48, 246
  in Japan 248, 261–2
  US-type 246–7
international directors 303–305
International Energy Agency 35
Investor Relations 82
investors, individual 49
Italian Stock Exchange 58, 75
Italy 57–8, 76
  accountability and monitoring 65
  best practice 58
  board structures 57
  Company Act (2004) 57
  external auditors 73
  institutional investors 58
  regulations 57
  slates system 66, 77
  see also Draghi Reform (1998);
    Preda Code (1999, 2002);
    Telecom Italia

Jacobs, Aad 20, 39
Japan 247–50, 260–63
  Big Bang framework 246, 249
  board structure 248
  Commercial Law, revision of 249–50
  comparison between Sony and
    Toyota 260–63
  corporate auditors 249
  deregulation of capital markets
    249–50
  employment for life 247, 248
  financial system reform 246, 249
  internal control 246–8, 261–2
  shareholder activism 248–9
  transparency 260
  see also Sony; Toyota

keiretsu companies 247, 248
Kelon
  asset tunnelling 218, 228–33, 236, 240

background 218–21
collapse of 226–33
government as controlling owner
  228–33, 240–41
internal power struggles 227–8
management incentive schemes,
  failure of 226–8
managerial agency problems 226–7
performance 221, 227, 238
sales and operating profits 229–30,
  237–8
shareholding structure 222, 223, 225
takeover by private owner 233–9, 241
see also China

legislative reforms, Spain 85
listing requirements, New York Stock
  Exchange 15–16
local government, benefits of owning
  industrial firm 228
London Stock Exchange 17, 36, 39
Lukoil 35

M&As *see* mergers and acquisitions
Madrid Stock Exchange General
  Index 86
management boards
  financial incentives 202–6, 226–7,
    241
  role of 299
managerial decisions about change
  actions 117–18
  measurement of argumentation
    rationality of 118–20
market abuse 29
market-based systems 247, 249–50
market control mechanisms 104
measurement concept 117–20
mergers and acquisitions 32, 104,
  107–8, 117, 135
Middle East oil fields 35
minority shareholders *see*
  shareholders, minority
mobility of skills 303

National Association of Pension
  Funds (NAPF) (1999) 50
Netherlands 17, 30, 299
New Combined Code 16–17, 20
  see also Codes of Practice

New York Stock Exchange (NYSE) 30, 58, 66
    listing requirements 15
New York Times 23
Nigeria 11, 12, 23, 36
nomination committees 47
non-executive directors 47–8, 66, 299–300
Norsk Hydro 24
North Sea gas fields 24
North Sea oil fields 35
Northern Russia Electric Company (NREC)
    background 146–8
    best practices code 149
    board of directors 149–52
    controlling shareholder, power of 146–8, 150, 153, 155, 156
    General Director, responsibilities 145, 150, 151–4, 155–7
    governance practices 148–9, 156–7
    governance structure 147
    ownership structure 147, 148
    privatization 146–7
    senior management structure 147
    shareholders 147, 149, 155, 156
    shares, trading of 147
NYSE *see* New York Stock Exchange

Office of National Statistics (2005) 49
oil companies
    calculation of reserves 24, 33–4
    exploration and production 31–2, 35
oil crisis 11
oil exploration 31, 32, 34–5
oil production, Russia 35
oil reserves 31
    calculation of 33–4
    declining 34–5
    forecasting 24, 36
    overbookings 26
    proven 7, 26, 33
Olivencia Code 84, 95, 97
Olivencia Report 84
Olivetti 60–61, 62
one-tier governance structures *see* unitary board systems
Ormen Lange gas field 23, 24
other receivables 232
Oxburgh, Lord 25, 30–31, 38

Parmalat case 58, 70
pension funds 14, 24, 27, 49, 50, 249
Perestroika 146
Persian Gulf 34
pharmaceutical industry 107–8
Poland
    Act on State Enterprise Privatization 160
    best practice 169, 173–4, 177
    legal framework 160–61
    management boards 160–61
    supervisory boards *see* Polish supervisory boards
    supervisory mechanisms in absence of supervisory board 163–4
    see also Airport Company; Automatic Company; Carrier; Polish supervisory boards
Polish supervisory boards 160–66, 177–9
    absence of, supervisory mechanisms applied 163–4
    best practice 182–4
    and management board relationship 176–7, 178
    practice of, a case study 166–77
    role of 160, 178
    as source of added value to the company 166–9
    in subsidiaries, top management expectations 165–6
    where company is listed on the Stock Exchange 174–7
    where there is no ownership/ management separation 162–3
    where there is ownership/ management separation 164–6
    where there is participation of the State Treasury 169–74
popular capitalism 86
Preda Code (1999, 2002) 57, 66, 68, 74–5, 76
Premier Farnall 52
privatization
    and efficiency 91–2
    and employment 89
    importance of corporate governance in 92–3
    and leverage 91
    in Spain 82–3, 85–6

proven oil reserves
definition 7, 26
estimating 33
see also oil reserves
pyramidal structures 60, 61, 83–4,
188–9, 196

qualified-founded change actions 118,
119–20, 137
see also argumentation rationality

re-statements of accounts 14
reasoning, principles of 117–18
see also argumentation rationality
regulations, reviews of 13–17
regulators, independent
Accounting Oversight Board 15, 16
Financial Reporting Council 16
relationship-based systems 247, 248
remuneration 194–6, 302
remuneration committees 47, 48
Rongqi Township Economic
Development Company 220
see also Kelon
Royal Dutch Petroleum 39
board committees 19
boards of directors 17
merger and unification with Shell
Transport and Trading 38–9
as part of Royal Dutch/Shell group
17–18, 36–7
shares 7
supervisory board 20
see also Shell; Shell Transport and
Trading
Royal Dutch/Shell group *see* Shell
rule propositions 117
Russia
competition among electricity
wholesalers 146–7
oil reserves 35
Russian Trading System Stock
Exchange 147

Sanofi-Synthélabo 104, 108, 109
argumentation 117–18, 121–5, 137–8
board of directors 134
key figures (31 Dec 2003) 110–11
reasoning of 120–27
see also France; Sanofi-Synthélabo
and Aventis

Sanofi-Synthélabo and Aventis
argumentation by Aventis 129–32
argumentation by Sanofi-Synthélabo
117–18, 121–5, 137–8
background 104, 107–9
key figures (31 Dec 2003) 110–11
reasoning of Aventis 127–33
reasoning of Sanofi-Synthélabo
117–18, 120–27, 137–8
revised offer 133–5
takeover battle 104, 112–17
Sarbanes-Oxley Act 14–16, 30, 58
scandals 7, 13–14, 47, 48, 218
Securities and Exchange Commission
(SEC) 16, 23, 25, 37
investigation into Shell 27, 28–9,
31, 33
investigation into Shell, criticism
of 33
rules on booking reserves 24, 26,
33, 34
self-regulation 16
see also codes of practice
separation of CEO and chair 47, 68,
97, 133
shareholder activism 246, 248–9
Shareholder Voting Working Group
(SVWG) 50
shareholders 58
controlling 58, 61
minority 58, 61, 66, 71, 226, 279–80
relationship with board 48
rights of 98–9, 279–80
trust in managers 107
see also institutional investors
shares, voting 50
Shell
Annual Report (2001) 9
Annual Report and Accounts (2003)
29–30
in Australia 12–13
background 8–9, 17
booking of reserves 37
business principles 9–11
CEO/chairman separation 29
Committee of Managing Directors
(CMD) 25–7, 31
complexity of organizational
structure 31
corporate governance 17–21, 29–30

corporate social responsibility 9–11
credit rating 40
Davis Polk and Wordwell
    investigation 25–7, 30
decentralized management 23, 24
dual boards, unification 30, 38, 40
dual company structure 33, 36–40
employee morale 33, 36, 41–2
fines 28–9
Group Audit Committee (GAC) 20,
    25, 30
institutional investors 21–2, 31, 37,
    40
investigation by SEC 22, 37
investigation, internal 25–7, 29, 30
legal action against 28–9
merger and unification 38–9
misbooking of reserves 40
in Nigeria 11, 12, 23, 36
non-executive directors 29
profits 8–9, 34
proven reserves 12, 21–2, 23, 33–4, 40
recovery, difficulties for 35–6
remuneration 25, 28
reputation 8, 32–3
reserves, estimating 22–4, 27, 29,
    30–31
reserves, finding new 31, 33, 34–6
Reserves Replacement Ratio (RRR)
    26
scandal, response to 29–30
share prices 21, 34, 37, 40
shareholders 36, 39, 40
whistleblowing 10–11, 26–7
see also Royal Dutch Petroleum;
    Shell Transport and Trading
Shell Transport and Trading
board of directors 19–20
chairman 11–12, 17, 21
corporate governance arrangements
    review 20–21
merger and unification with Royal
    Dutch Petroleum 38–9
as part of Royal Dutch/Shell group
    36
shares 7, 28
see also Royal Dutch Petroleum;
    Shell
Singapore
accountability and audit 192–3

board structure 191–2, 193–4
CEO/chair separation of roles 194
Code of Corporate Governance
    189–96
Corporate Governance Committee
    (CGC) 189, 191
financial incentives 202–6
government-linked corporations
    (GLCs) 188
ownership structures 188–9, 196
pyramidal structures 196
remuneration 192, 194–6
shareholders 193–6
stock options 202–6
transparency 192
unitary board structures 188
see also ST Engineering
Singapore Stock Exchange 188, 189–90
skills, mobility of 303
slates system 66, 77
social responsibility 52–3, 261
socially responsible investment (SRI)
    50, 261
SOEs *see* State-owned enterprises
solvency rules 54
Sony
accountability 260
board of directors 257–9
Company System 256
comparison with Toyota 260–64
corporate strategy 255–6
disclosure 260
governance system, assessment of
    evolution 260
internal control system 247, 257–9,
    260, 262
ownership structure 256–7
performance 255–6, 260, 261
restructuring 255–6
shareholders 257, 259, 260
stakeholders, policies for 259
transparency 260
Sorytel 273–5, 276–9
see also v-NET
South Africa
apartheid, and impact of 286,
    300–301
board structure 300–301, 303–5
Companies Act 294–5

Department of Public Enterprises
297–8, 302–3
remuneration 302
State-owned enterprises (SOEs) 289,
294, 300, 302–4
during transition period 300–301
see also Eskom
Spain 83–6
Annual Corporate Governance
Report 99
board structure 84
Codes of Best Practice 83, 84, 97, 99
deregulation in financial sector 85
economic restructuring 85
institutional setting 83–5
Law of Reform of the Financial
System 85
legislative reforms 85
privatization process 85–6
State-owned enterprises (SOEs) 87
Supervisory Agency 84, 85
supervisory boards 85
Transparency Law 85
see also Indra
Spanish Stock Exchange 82
Spanish Stock Market 82, 85, 86
ST Engineering
background 196–7
board of directors 197–200
disclosure 198, 202
ownership structure 206–9
pyramidal structure 206–9
remuneration 201–6
shareholder distribution 206–7
stock options 203–4
transparency 198
see also Singapore
stakeholder board model 300–301
stakeholders 302
Standard Life 49, 51–4
board structure 52–3
corporate governance structure 52–3
demutualization 53–4
group funds under management 51
social responsibility 52–3
see also UK
State-owned enterprises (SOEs) 219
governance processes 302–3
international directors, benefits of
appointing 303–5

remuneration 302
in South Africa 284, 289, 294,
300–301, 302–3
in Spain, privatization of 85–6, 87
structuring of, within a company law
framework 284
Statement of Investment Principles 50
Statoil 24
Statute for a Societas Europaea (SE)
108
statutory auditors 57
statutory juristic bodies 284
stock markets 49, 54
popular capitalism in 86
stock options 202–6
subsidiaries, supervisory boards in
165–6
supervisory boards 298–9
supervisory boards, Poland 160–62,
177–9
absence of, supervisory mechanisms
applied 163–4
best practice 182–4
and management board relationship
176–7, 178
practice of, a case study 166–77
role of 160, 178
as source of added value to the
company 166–9
in subsidiaries, top management
expectations 165–6
where the company is listed on the
Stock Exchange 174–7
where there is no ownership/
management separation 162–3
where there is ownership/
management separation 164–6
where there is participation of the
State Treasury 169–74

Tabaksblat Committee Code 17, 30
takeover battles 106–7, 135
see also Sanofi-Synthélabo and
Aventis
Telecom Italia
auditors, external 69, 73
background and profile 59–61, 62
board of directors 62–3, 64–8
board of directors' committees 67,
68–71

board of statutory auditors 69–70, 71–3, 77
boards structure 63–73
chairman, role of 66–8
confidential information, handling 74–5
control structure 61–4
corporate governance structure 77
disclosure committee 75, 77
equity 62
holding companies, reduction of 76–7
insider dealing, code of conduct for 76
institutional investors 61, 76
mergers 61, 76–7
and Olivetti 60–61, 62
ownership structure 61–3
privatization, major events since 62
related parties, transactions with 74
remuneration committee 70–71
shareholders 60, 61, 76, 77
shares 61, 62
see also Italy
tiger economies 3
Total 36
township and village enterprise (TVE) sector 219–20
Toyota
board of corporate auditors 252
board of directors 252
comparison with Sony 260–64
corporate strategy 247, 250–51
employees, policies for 254
governance system, assessment of evolution 254–5
internal control system 252, 253, 261–2
ownership structure 251
performance 250–51
shareholders, policies for 252–4
Toyota Way 254
transfer pricing 226–7
transition, value of dual board system at times of 300–301
transparency 49, 105, 135, 262, 302
in Japan 260
in Spain 85, 99
Transparency Law, Spain 85

tunnelling of assets 189, 229–33, 240, 281
Turkey
Capital Markets Board 279, 281
Commercial Code 276–7, 278, 280
Corporate Governance Guidelines 281
family-owned enterprises 270, 272
see also v-NET
legal framework 272, 279–80
minority shareholders' rights 279–80
two-tier governance structures *see* dual board systems

UK
auditors, regulation of 16
best practice 47–9
board structure 17
Combined Code (2003) 16–17, 47–8, 52
development of corporate governance 55
equity 49
institutional ownership 49–50
Office of National Statistics (2005) 49
voting shares system 50, 54
see also Shell; Standard Life
unfounded change actions 118, 137
see also argumentation rationality
unitary board systems 2, 57, 298–300
see also dual board systems
US
Accounting Oversight Board 16
company law reforms 13–16
corporate governance, style of 246–7, 249, 262
Securities and Exchange Commission (SEC) 16, 23, 25, 26

v-NET 269–83
background 269–75
board of directors 273–4, 276–8, 279
conflicts 275–7
ownership structure 271–2
restructuring 274–5
shareholders 274, 275–6, 278–9
shares 271, 272, 273, 278
and Sorytel 273–5, 276–9
and v-TEK 269, 276, 279

Vakur Holding, interference from 275
v-TEK 269, 276, 279
  see also v-NET
Vakur Holding 269, 271, 275, 278, 279
  see also v-NET
Veer, Jeroen van der 19, 25, 38
Vijver, Walter van de 19, 22, 23, 31
  correspondence with Philip Watts 25–7
voluntary corporate codes
  Aldama Report 84–5
  Best Practice in Public Companies (2002) 169, 173–4, 177, 182–4
  Cadbury Report (1992) 16, 47
  Olivencia Report 84
  Preda Code (1999, 2002) 57, 66, 68, 74–5, 76

voting rights 84, 98–9, 246, 280
voting shares system 50, 54

Warsaw Stock Exchange 182
Watts, Sir Philip 11–12, 13, 17–18, 22, 23
  correspondence with Walter van de Vijver 25–7
weak institutional framework in developing countries 281–2
website-base shareholder information 82, 85
Winter Report 84
WorldCom 13–14

X SA Capital Group 165–6

Yukos 35